Private Equity in Action

Case Studies from Developed and Emerging Markets

Claudia Zeisberger
Michael Prahl
Bowen White

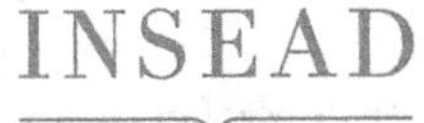

The Business School for the World®

WILEY

This edition first published 2017

Registered office
John Wiley & Sons Ltd, The Atrium, Southern Gate, Chichester, West Sussex, PO19 8SQ, United Kingdom

For details of our global editorial offices, for customer services and for information about how to apply for permission to reuse the copyright material in this book please see our website at www.wiley.com.

Library of Congress Cataloging-in-Publication Data

Names: Zeisberger, Claudia, author. | Prahl, Michael, author. | White, Bowen, author.
Title: Private equity in action : case studies from developed and emerging markets / Claudia Zeisberger, Michael Prahl, Bowen White.
Description: Hoboken : Wiley, 2017. | Includes bibliographical references and index. |
Identifiers: LCCN 2017013990 (print) | LCCN 2017029759 (ebook) | ISBN 9781119328001 (pdf) | ISBN 9781119327998 (epub) | ISBN 9781119328025 (paperback) | ISBN 9781119328001 (ebk) | ISBN 9781119327998 (ebk)
Subjects: LCSH: Venture capital–Case studies. | BISAC: BUSINESS & ECONOMICS / Finance.
Classification: LCC HG4751 (ebook) | LCC HG4751 .Z425 2017 (print) | DDC 332/.04154–dc23
LC record available at https://lccn.loc.gov/2017013990

A catalogue record for this book is available from the British Library.

ISBN 978-1-119-32802-5 (hardback) ISBN 978-1-119-32800-1 (ebk)
ISBN 978-1-119-32799-8 (ebk)

10 9 8 7 6 5 4 3 2 1

Cover design: Wiley
Cover image: Skyline image: © Leontura/iStockphoto; World Map image: © pop_jop/iStockphoto

Set in 10/12pt Helvetica LT Std by Aptara, New Delhi, India

CONTENTS

PREFACE

Private equity (PE) certainly has no shortage of critics, having been referred to as "capitalism on steroids," its general partners (GPs) or fund managers called "locusts" and their preferred deal cycle as a "quick-flip." Attention is generated when the media portray PE as a fast way to multiply invested capital by reducing jobs and overleveraging companies. It is time to clear the air, remove soundbite biases and set perceptions straight by showing how the industry frequently removes inefficiencies and turns underperforming companies into healthier, more dynamic ones or supports fast-growing enterprises with capital and expertise, while taking measured risks other financial players are ill-equipped to pursue.

The sheer complexity of PE deal making often obscures the mechanisms of success from casual observers and the theoretical concepts alone rarely do justice to the reality of investing in private companies. A clear understanding of the PE model is long overdue and this book provides detailed case studies to give senior executives and professionals a ringside seat to the day-to-day challenges tackled by partners in PE and venture funds, in both developed and emerging markets.

Private Equity in Action is the practical companion to *Mastering Private Equity—Transformation via Venture Capital, Minority Investments & Buyouts*, a rigorous textbook providing the theoretical foundations that the case studies bring to life. While this case book can very well be read on a standalone basis, newcomers to the world of PE will certainly benefit from working with both books in parallel and taking advantage of their synergies.

This case book offers a selection of rich, real-life case studies that demonstrate the application of core PE concepts by providing a unique behind-the-scenes look into the investment practices of PE and VC funds. It helps students and executives comprehend the complex processes associated with investing in private companies, from start-ups to mature businesses, and understand the inner workings of the PE model. While academic concepts build the necessary foundation, practical application and execution of these concepts are the critical link that leads to a successful learning outcome.

This book provides a wealth of opportunities for the reader to put oneself into the shoes of leading PE investors and face a range of actual managerial challenges. With a focus on the all-important executional element that is at the core of successful PE investing, it helps to explain how theoretical concepts translate into investment success. After all, the competitive advantage of PE investors arises from the diligent application of global best practices in their portfolio companies—and a lot of hard work.

All case studies have been written in conjunction with leading PE and VC firms, their senior partners, or with advisors who work closely with the industry; they provide insights into real issues faced and tell real war stories about actual (yet at times anonymized) investments. Each case explains how the actions taken by the PE investors contributed to the transformation of companies in practice with examples covering investment situations not only in the established US and European markets, but also in the emerging (or already emerged) growth markets of Asia, Africa and Central Europe.

Section Overview

The first section of the book focuses on the classic "GP–LP" fund model and shows how the relationship between institutional investors and PE fund managers is changing. The cases then move on to share examples from venture capital, growth equity (or minority) investments and leveraged buyouts in various settings (Sections II–IV).

Turnaround situations and distressed investments certainly test the mettle of PE investors—be they majority or minority owners. Dealing with short-term cash constraints, allegations of fraud and disgruntled creditors or (at times public) stakeholders certainly shows whether the operational partners in a PE fund can live up to expectations (Section V).

Given their positive demographic profiles and access to new customers, emerging markets are becoming attractive target destinations for PE. However, investing in these economies comes with additional risks related to the lack of legal certainty, governance frameworks and consistently applied best practices in deal making and execution (Section VI).

INSEAD Context

All cases in this book have been subject to the rigors of classroom debate and continue to be taught in INSEAD's MBA, EMBA and executive education programs, as well as in other top business schools; some have won prestigious case awards. They add color to the theoretical foundations laid in the text book, provide context, clarify theoretical concepts and give the reader a chance to step into the shoes of PE and VC professionals, as they deal with issues from fundraising to deal execution and effecting operational change to exiting their investments.

The selection of cases in this first volume leverages INSEAD and its faculty's international reach, network and connections, especially with professionals in the up-and-coming emerging markets. The settings of the case studies cover PE investing in:

- Early-stage companies and VC in India
- SMEs in the Middle East
- Buyouts in the US and Europe
- Turnaround situations in both Europe and emerging markets
- Food and beverage in Vietnam
- Real estate in Australia
- Agriculture in Africa
- Optimizing a European pension fund's PE portfolio
- Setting up a new sovereign wealth fund in eastern Europe

SECTION I
GP–LP Relationships

One of the competitive advantages we have is we have a large balance sheet, and economies of scale allow us to build big internal teams. We also have very long term time periods, so we never have to sell an asset unless it's at our choosing. We don't need the liquidity. Why aren't we looking for opportunities to invest higher up the capital stack and take advantage of that?

—**Gordon J. Fyfe,** CEO and Chief Investment Officer, British Columbia Investment Management Corp. (bcIMC) and INSEAD Alumnus

CASE

1 BERONI GROUP

MANAGING GP–LP RELATIONSHIPS

SYNOPSIS

This case follows Jack Draper, Managing Director of the Beroni Group, a private equity family of funds, as he manages his growing business and tries to satisfy his investor base. It deals with the issues arising in private equity firms once multiple funds have been raised from various limited partners and are being managed by a related set of general partners. Beroni has just closed its third fund successfully and has started to explore investment opportunities as the financial crisis of 2008–2009 reaches its apex and changes some of the fundamental assumptions for its investor base.

The case is set in a difficult economic environment, which raises some very interesting investment possibilities as well as problems. Jack strives to manage two competing groups of investors seeking exposure to these possibilities, as well as the cash flow problem at one of his leading investors.

The case highlights the different motivations of existing investors: some of them invested in both Funds II and III, others in only one or the other. As Jack starts to address the issue of the composition of the advisory committee (AC), queries regarding overlapping staff resources for both funds and pressure for a reduction in management fees, he is faced with a potentially critical issue: one of his investors is in serious financial distress and has asked to be given preferential treatment to avoid default.

PEDAGOGICAL OBJECTIVE OF THE CASE

The case explains the importance of a professional relationship between investors and managers in a private equity fund and discusses possible solutions that managers can offer to investors facing financial difficulties.

It sets the scene to critically debate investor demands and expectations with regard to the time managers allocate to individual funds and their overall commitment to managing a family of funds.

SUGGESTED ASSIGNMENT QUESTIONS

1. How should Jack handle the allocation of deal flow between the different funds that have overlapping mandates, and/or between one of his current funds and an eventual successor fund? Should allocations be fixed or discretionary? In addition, regarding the impending deal, which AC should he approach first, and with what sort of proposal, to minimize potential tension among the various investors.
2. How should he deal with downward pressure on his management fees as more assets come under management, since some costs (e.g., rental costs, back office

staff) are fairly steady regardless of how much capital is under management? How could he rebut investor demands to lower management fees?

3. Since the senior Beroni principals serve on the deal teams and investment committees of more than one fund, how could he help his investors feel comfortable that the principals (and staff) would allocate their time appropriately between the respective funds?
4. How could he help his investors be comfortable with the prospect of *de facto* cross-liability—that is, if one of his funds were to run into difficulty, how could he "ring fence" other unrelated funds to ensure there were no negative financial or time effects on the managers?
5. How could Jack balance the needs and requests of EUBank, one of his oldest and largest investors, with the legitimate expectation of other investors in BAF II and BAF III that EUBank not be shown any favoritism, and that a portion of EUBank's interest be forfeited and distributed to them? Would he be faced with a flood of defaults and withdrawal requests if he were to treat EUBank gently? What fiduciary duty did he have to the nondefaulting investors in BAF II and BAF III that have managed their finances more prudently than EUBank? Would the managers risk breaching the investment fund agreements to implement EUBank's proposal?

ADDITIONAL RESOURCES

To make the most of this case study, we suggest the following additional sources to provide context and background information:

- In particular, we recommend the following chapters from *Mastering Private Equity—Transformation via Venture Capital, Minority Investments & Buyouts*
  - Chapter 1 Private Equity Essentials
  - Chapter 16 Fund Formation
  - Chapter 17 Fundraising
  - Chapter 19 Performance Reporting
- You may also refer to the book website for further material: www.masteringprivateequity.com.

Beroni Group:

Managing GP-LP Relationships

03/2015-5594

This case was written by Greg Blackwood, Senior Research Associate, in close co-operation with Andrew M. Ostrognai, Partner at Debevoise & Plimpton LLP in Hong Kong, and under the supervision of Claudia Zeisberger, Senior Affiliate Professor of Decision Sciences and Entrepreneurship and Family Enterprise at INSEAD, with revisions by Rob Johnson, Visiting Professor at IESE Business School. It is intended to be used as a basis for class discussion rather than to illustrate either effective or ineffective handling of an administrative situation.

Additional material about INSEAD case studies (e.g., videos, spreadsheets, links) can be accessed at cases.insead.edu.

Introduction

Jack Draper had just completed the initial close of his third private equity fund for the Beroni Group, a family of funds based in Hong Kong and investing across Asia. As Managing Director, Jack had been with the group for nine years since its founding in 2000, and with his two partners had successfully steered the Beroni Asia Fund (BAF I) to a successful conclusion, creating the opportunity to establish follow-on funds in the same mould. BAF II was approaching the end of its investment period, after which remaining capital could only be invested in follow-on investments. BAF III had received US$500 million in commitments from its limited partners (LPs) by late summer 2008, before the fundraising environment for private equity funds became difficult. Notwithstanding these difficult conditions, Jack was able to get to a first closing, and expected to raise an additional US$300 million by the final close. He took pride in their ability to hit fundraising targets despite the difficult fundraising environment. It was typical of what he and the other principals who managed the fund on a day-to-day basis had achieved over the years.

With success, however, had come some unexpected issues. While managing each fund in isolation required essentially the same skills and processes, he was discovering that managing a group of funds required careful strategic (and sometimes political) manoeuvring. Just the day before, he had received final information about a proposed deal that he planned to present to the investment committee the following week. BAF II still had US$135 million in remaining capital that could be deployed (and another year left on the investment period), and BAF III's funds were now available. The seller in the proposed deal was in deep distress and the investment committee felt that the pricing on the deal was exceptionally attractive – it was likely to be one of the most successful deals ever sourced by the Beroni Group. But there were a number of other complications:

- Some LPs had invested in both BAF II and BAF III, while others had invested in one but not the other. LPs sometimes co-invested directly in companies with the fund in which they had invested.
- Each fund had its own advisory committee (AC), and the make-up of each AC was a reflection of LP participation. Hence there was not identical membership across the ACs.
- General partner (GP) resources were sometimes thinly spread across multiple funds since the same team managed all three funds.
- LPs participating in multiple funds were making noises about a reduction in management fees for the latest fund, since many of the costs associated with managing it were essentially fixed (rent, salaries, etc.). In difficult economic times, LPs were looking for any way to cut their costs.
- Finally, in any co-investment situation, the approval of the relevant ACs would be necessary in order to execute.

Jack knew he would end up doing the deal one way or another – he just needed to resolve some of these issues first in order to avoid creating future problems with the LPs.

Another problem facing Jack was that EUBank, one of the Beroni Group's earliest and largest investors, was (as with many financial institutions) having cash flow problems of its own, and was unable to fund its capital commitments to BAF II and BAF III.

As is common in the private equity industry, the limited partnership agreements for BAF II and BAF III had extremely severe penalties for a defaulting limited partner, including forfeiture of half of its interest in the fund. EUBank had proposed to the Beroni Group that it be allowed to suspend making any further capital contributions to BAF II, that its capital commitment to BAF III be reduced from US$120 million to US$60 million, and that none of its interest in either BAF II or BAF III be forfeited. The GP of BAF II had some discretion over enforcement of the forfeiture provision, but there was no mechanism in the limited partnership agreement for BAF III to reduce capital commitments in this way. Nonetheless, in light of the long and otherwise happy history of EUBank and the Beroni Group (and in the hope that EUBank would recover and be a large investor in BAF IV when it was raised), Beroni Group wanted to be as accommodating as possible.

Group History

Jack and his partners had founded Beroni in 2000, closing BAF I with US$250 million contributed by three LPs (see Appendix A). Over the following four years, Beroni successfully deployed all of the capital and went on to exit all portfolio companies in a relatively short six-year timeframe from closing, achieving a remarkable 42% IRR over the period. Shortly after fully investing BAF I's assets, and with a few credible exits under their belts, the Beroni GPs successfully closed BAF II in 2004 at US$350 million. All of the original LPs participated to some extent, and a further two LPs came on board (see Appendix B).

The firm had been less able to deploy BAF II's capital due to a dearth of quality deals, with only approximately US$215 million invested as of the initial close of BAF III. The deals in which the company had invested, however, had again generated spectacular returns, estimated to be around 30% IRR (including unrealised gains) – which in turn had further attracted LPs to BAF III. Prior to the meltdown of the financial industry in late 2008, LPs committed US$500 million to BAF III at the first closing. Even though the fundraising environment had become exceptionally difficult, Jack and his partners believed they could secure an additional US$300 million in further commitments by the final close of the fund (see Appendix C), largely because a number of liquid and savvy LPs believed that there were historically good buying opportunities in the market.

Key Issues

Jack now found himself with two active funds and several issues to manage:

- Disparate LPs

  Because one of the LPs participating in BAF II had elected not to participate in BAF III, and because a number of first-time LPs had subscribed to BAF III, the LP structures of the two funds were significantly different. Jack knew the LP that had opted out of BAF III (Gulf Developments, a sovereign wealth fund with considerable assets and influence which he could not afford to upset) wanted BAF II to fully invest its remaining assets before BAF III began to deploy its capital (particularly because they believed that asset values were now at an all-time low), and would therefore vehemently oppose any investment by BAF III before that time. On the other hand, the BAF III LPs were eagerly looking forward to their first deal in this attractively repriced market, so if a very attractive opportunity went to BAF II in preference to BAF III, Jack risked upsetting his new partners.

- Differing AC compositions

  Because the investor that had not subscribed to BAF III was on the advisory committee of BAF II but not on the AC of BAF III, and because some of the first-time LPs were on the AC of BAF III but not BAF II, Jack had different ACs to manage. Complicating matters was the fact that for the upcoming deal, Jack would have to engineer approval from both committees in order to receive the go-ahead on a co-investment – and this would generate tension depending on which LPs participated in each AC.

- Overlapping human capital

  Like many families of funds, Beroni employed the same staff across all three funds. The same senior staff, investment managers and associates that had executed deals for BAF I and who were currently working on BAF II would also manage BAF III; the synergies of information and experience were obvious, and utilising his staff in this way allowed Jack to generate higher management fees per headcount. Of course, each fund's LPs preferred staff to be 100% focused on their fund to the exclusion of the other, whether it was BAF II or BAF III.

- Reduction in management fees

  Because some of the LPs had invested in all three funds, they felt that Jack should reduce Beroni's management fees in some way to reflect the fact that the group as a whole was able to utilise the same staff to manage each successive fund. In addition, because each successive fund required neither additional office space nor additional administrative staff, the LPs felt certain that costs could be cut – providing additional justification for a reduction in management fees. Moreover, because of the difficult economic context, a number of LPs felt that the Beroni Group should "tighten its belt" and pass some of the cost savings along to LPs.

- EUBank default

  Beroni was faced with an imminent default by one of its largest and oldest investors, which would not only create cash flow problems for BAF II and BAF III (and might even jeopardise the ability of these funds to consummate the investment they were currently considering), but would also create some embarrassment for EUBank and for the Beroni Group. EUBank had put a proposal on the table that would mitigate some of these problems (and yet not leave EUBank in a good position), but accepting the proposal would not only anger other non-defaulting LPs (since they would not receive the forfeited interest to which they had a legitimate claim), but also create a moral hazard should other LPs try to extract a similar deal from the fund GPs. Also, it was not clear whether granting EUBank's requests would violate the GPs' fiduciary duty or even breach the limited partner agreements themselves.

Appendix A
Table of LPs (BAF I)

LP Entity	Amount Invested (US$ million)	Advisory Committee Seat (Yes/No)
Gulf Developments	100	Yes
EUBank	80	Yes
La Famiglia Inc.	70	Yes

Appendix B
Table of LPs (BAF II)

LP Entity	Amount Invested (US$ million)	Advisory Committee Seat (Yes/No)
Gulf Developments	120	Yes
EUBank	70	Yes
La Famiglia Inc.	40	Yes
Pensions-R-Us	70	No
StateFund	50	Yes

Appendix C
Table of LPs (BAF III)

LP Entity	Amount Invested (US$ million)	Advisory Committee Seat (Yes/No)
EUBank	120	Yes
La Famiglia Inc.	30	Yes
Pensions-R-Us	100	No
StateFund	80	Yes
New LP 1	90	No
New LP 2	80	Yes
*New LP 3	75	No
*New LP 4	75	Yes
*New LP 5	75	No
*New LP 6	75	No

*Denotes anticipated funding as of the final close of the fund.

Source: Fictitious data

CASE 2 GOING DIRECT
THE CASE OF TEACHERS' PRIVATE CAPITAL

SYNOPSIS

This case traces the evolution of the private equity investment platform at the Ontario Teachers' Pension Plan ("Teachers"), the largest single-profession pension plan in Canada. Unlike the typical pension fund at the time, Teachers forged a pioneering approach to investing by making a concerted push towards direct investing in private equity, well before disintermediation became popular among limited partners (LPs). The case follows Jim Leech, CEO of Teachers and formerly head of Teachers Private Capital (TPC), the private equity arm of the pension plan. It traces the multiyear journey during which Teachers' worked to develop in house the competence and culture required to move beyond fund investments into direct deals. The case discusses the advantages and limitations of the direct investing model, contrasts it with other approaches to investing in private equity, and raises important issues for institutional investors pursuing strong risk-adjusted returns.

PEDAGOGICAL OBJECTIVE OF THE CASE

The case requires readers to have a basic understanding of the private equity investment model and familiarity with the typical relationship between general partners and LPs. The purpose of the case is to introduce readers to the different avenues available to LPs when deploying capital into private equity, from investing purely in funds and co-investing in deals alongside funds with varying degrees of influence to investing directly in deals, be it for a minority or controlling stake.

In particular, the case delves into the attractiveness of the direct investing model for LPs, offering insights into the internal capability, governance framework and organizational culture that LPs need to build to implement such a model successfully and benefit from its inherent cost savings. The case also discusses the challenges of sustaining and scaling up any direct investment capability, and, more broadly, the challenges that arise when managing a comprehensive private equity program.

SUGGESTED ASSIGNMENT QUESTIONS

1. Discuss the attractions and challenges of the direct investing model for LPs. What characteristics of the Ontario Teachers' Pension Plan have enabled it to build its private equity platform?
2. Why did Teachers' Private Capital pursue the buyout of Bell Canada Enterprises? What lessons were learned in the process?
3. How would you assess the success of Teachers' Private Capital? To support your arguments, calculate Teachers' Private Capital's information ratio and comment on its contribution to the pension plan's overall risk-adjusted returns during different periods. What lessons can other large investors take away from the development of Teachers' program?

ADDITIONAL RESOURCES

To make the most of this case study, we suggest the following additional sources to provide context and background information:

- In particular, we recommend the following chapters from *Mastering Private Equity—Transformation via Venture Capital, Minority Investments & Buyouts*
  - Chapter 1 Private Equity Essentials
  - Chapter 6 Deal Sourcing & Due Diligence
  - Chapter 18 LP Portfolio Management
  - Chapter 21 LP Direct Investment
- Case website for faculty and lecturers: http://cases.insead.edu/going-direct
- You may also refer to the book website for further material: www.masteringprivateequity.com

Going Direct

The Case of Teachers' Private Capital

03/2015-5993

This case was written by Deepa Ramanathan, INSEAD MBA class of December 2012, under the supervision of Michael Prahl, Executive Director, INSEAD Global Private Equity Initiative, and Claudia Zeisberger, Senior Affiliate Professor of Decision Sciences and Entrepreneurship and Family Enterprise at INSEAD. It is intended to be used as a basis for class discussion rather than to illustrate either effective or ineffective handling of an administrative situation.

Funding for this case study was provided by INSEAD's Global Private Equity Initiative (GPEI). The research was partially funded by the INSEAD Alumni Fund (IAF).

Additional material about INSEAD case studies (e.g., videos, spreadsheets, links) can be accessed at cases.insead.edu.

Introduction

As the first snow fell outside his twelfth floor office in the north end of Toronto, Jim Leech, CEO of Ontario Teachers' Pension Plan, contemplated the recent settlement that Teachers' (as the pension plan was known) had reached with Bell Canada Enterprises (BCE). The year was 2012 and the settlement pertained to the leveraged buyout (LBO) of BCE, a transaction that would have been the largest LBO in history. Recalling the transaction that had catapulted Teachers' into the limelight, he marvelled at how Teachers', which belonged to a class of investors known to be very conservative, ended up leading a consortium of investors in the C$52 billion buyout of the telecom giant. Jim mulled over the long and eventful path that Teachers' had traced from first venturing into direct investing in private equity, subsequently emerging as a respected partner and a formidable rival to established private equity funds.

Background

With C$129.5 billion in assets at the end of 2012, the Ontario Teachers' Pension Plan is the largest single-profession pension plan in Canada, investing and administering the pensions of 303,000 active and retired teachers in the province of Ontario. An independent authority on pension fund benchmarking, CEM Benchmarking Inc., ranked Teachers' number one in terms of 10-year returns and 'value add' above benchmark among all peer pension funds in the world for the 10-year period to the end of 2011. The fund had recorded a 10% average annualised rate of return (Exhibit 2.1) and C$60.5 billion in cumulative value added (with compounding) above benchmarks since 1990.

The pension plan for Ontario teachers was originally created in 1917. For the next 73 years it was run by the Ontario government and funds were invested in the debt of government agencies. In 1990, the government privatised the plan by creating an independent, jointly-sponsored pension plan, the Ontario Teachers' Pension Plan Board, with the authority to invest all assets, administer the pension plan, and pay members (or surviving relatives) the benefits promised. The privatised plan was co-sponsored by the Government of Ontario and the Ontario Teachers' Federation (OTF), an umbrella organisation for four teachers' unions. The two co-sponsors appointed four independent members each to the board of directors and an independent chair was chosen jointly. The board members oversaw the pension fund's management team, which carried out the actual work of investing and administering plan assets and paying out benefits. By law, board members were bound to act in the best interests of plan members and their beneficiaries. Teachers' also advised the plan sponsors about its funding status, which was determined annually by an independent actuary hired by the plan.

Teachers' is a defined benefit pension plan, that is, the sponsors are responsible for paying out a pre-defined level of retirement benefits based on factors such as length of employment, salary history, projected lifespan of retirees, etc. What this means in practice is that if the net assets of the pension plan are not sufficient to meet the present value of the liabilities (i.e., the benefits promised to retirees), the sponsors are required to make extra contributions and/or reduce future benefits to bridge the funding deficit. On the flipside, plan sponsors can also make use of funding surpluses, i.e., the excess of net assets over liabilities to reduce the contribution rate of active teachers or increase members' benefits (See Exhibit 2.2, pension fund terminology).

As sole plan sponsor from 1917 until privatisation in 1990, the Ontario government was responsible for all funding deficits and entitled to all funding surpluses. Under the jointly-sponsored framework, the Ontario Teachers' Federation became a co-sponsor, making it responsible for half of any surplus or deficit. Strong investment returns in the early 1990s gradually transformed Teachers' funding status from a deficit of C$3.6 billion in 1990 to consistent funding surpluses in the late 1990s. As a result, teachers in the plan enjoyed low contribution rates and improved benefits during the second half of the 1990s. However, by the 2000s, falling interest rates, a declining ratio of working teachers to retirees (from 10:1 in 1970 to 1.4:1 in 2012) and longer life expectancy leading to an increase in the expected number of years on pension from 20 to 31 years, combined to turn the surplus into a persistent funding deficit. This led to an increase in the contribution rate required from teachers and the government and reductions in the future benefits to be paid to retirees. With these changes the pension fund was able to meet its regulatory obligation of showing a fully-funded plan at least once every three years.

Investment Objectives and Asset Policy Mix

Teachers' 2011 Annual Report stated:

> *"Our investment strategies are designed to earn strong returns that support stable contribution rates and pension sustainability and help meet the plan's long-term funding needs. Our approach is to manage funding and investment risk together. Taking plan demographics and future pension obligations into account, we aim to earn the best return possible at an appropriate level of risk. The need for investment returns must be balanced with strong risk management practices."*

In practice this translated to a target real rate of return of 4.5% per annum for the fund over the long term, an objective which had remained unchanged since the creation of the fund as an independent entity. However, the gradual change in the demographics of the plan had resulted in lower risk tolerance and restrictions on illiquidity, accompanied by an increased emphasis on the cost of implementing investment programmes. At the same time, the changing economic landscape – from the high interest rate environment of the 1980s to the moderation of the 1990s to the asset bubbles of the 2000s and the post-global financial crisis world of today – meant that the means of achieving the targeted rate of return had to be regularly reviewed and revised accordingly. This was reflected in the fund's strategic asset allocation or 'asset policy mix', as Teachers' refers to it.

The plan's investment managers performed an ongoing balancing act between the need to fund promised benefits and the need to control the risk of a loss that would have to be covered by increasing contribution rates and/or reducing benefits for future service. This focus on the ultimate risk facing the plan – funding risk – meant that Teachers' took a holistic view of risk, including market risk, credit risk and liquidity risk facing its assets and liabilities, to determine its asset mix. Teachers' used a proprietary asset-liability model that incorporated long-term historical data and the current economic outlook along with decisions to be made by the plan sponsors on contribution and benefits levels. Using this model, together with management experience and judgment, Teachers' established a weighting for each asset class that reflects its long-term risk and return trade-offs in relation to those of other asset classes. The fund used risk budgeting to allocate risk rather than capital, across asset classes, with the risk budget reviewed by board members annually.

Until 1990, the pension plan invested solely in non-marketable Government of Ontario debentures. Following the creation of Teachers', the asset policy mix of the plan (Exhibit 2.3) changed to allow investment into equities, both public and private, Canadian and foreign as well as income-producing real estate. Teachers' also began investing in absolute return strategies, hedge funds, money market securities and a wider range of bonds, all of which it classified as fixed income. To achieve its investment objectives, Teachers' decided on a strategic asset allocation of two-thirds equities and one-third fixed income in 1990. Initially Teachers' used derivatives to gain exposure to equities, a highly unconventional move for a pension fund. Over five years the fund gradually reduced its holdings of Ontario government securities, increased investment in equities, and reached its target allocation. To allow the investment team to take advantage of tactical opportunities, actual asset allocation was allowed to vary in a 5% band around the strategic asset allocation targets.

Over the years, Teachers' expanded its universe of investments to include commodities, real estate, infrastructure and timber. Along with real return bonds, these assets were then grouped together in a category that Teachers' labelled 'Inflation-sensitive investments'. Starting at 7% in 1996, the target allocation to Inflation-sensitive investments climbed steadily to nearly a third of the portfolio by the early 2000s, and almost half (45%) in 2009. In parallel, in view of the increasing volatility in equity markets and the diminishing risk tolerance of the pension plan given its maturing profile, the target allocation to equities was cut back from two thirds of the portfolio to 40%.

Phase 1: The Origins of Teachers' Private Capital

As a division within the Equities Investment team, Teachers' Private Capital invested in private companies; directly, either on its own or co-investing with partners, and indirectly through private equity and venture capital funds managed by third parties. At the end of 2011, TPC's portfolio of direct investments, co-investments and private equity funds totalled C$12.2 billion. Since inception, this had generated a net-of-fees internal rate of return (IRR) of 19.3%, validating the conviction of Teachers' initial management team which had envisioned investments in private companies and alternative assets to be part of its portfolio from the start.

The original executive team was led by Claude Lamoureux, who joined the fund as President and CEO in 1990, after a 25-year career in financial services in Canada and the United States. Robert Bertram, a former Treasurer of Alberta Government Telephones, was hired as Senior Vice President of the newly established Investments division the same year. Under their combined leadership, Teachers' aimed to build up a C$2 billion private equity portfolio within ten years. Investing in private companies was deemed attractive as the plan had long-term liabilities and could therefore afford to earn the illiquidity premium associated with private equity. However there were few private equity firms in Canada in the early 1990s, so the plan took the unusual step of investing directly in Canadian companies, often in partnership with third-party investors. The first private placements were made in 1991: C$100 million of growth capital was committed to seven privately-owned Canadian companies. Three of these were direct investments: Commcorp Financial Services Inc., a leading national equipment financing and leasing company; Strong Equipment Corporation, a national distributor of construction and related equipment; and White Rose Crafts and Nursery Sales Limited, a retailer of lawn, garden and craft supplies across Ontario. The remaining four investments were made through limited partnerships (LPs) and merchant bankers specialised in the media industry.

Teachers' decision to pursue both direct and indirect investments was driven by the desire to accelerate the pace and efficiency of building up a private equity platform for the fund. Teachers' targeted mature operating companies with a proven track record, strong management and significant management ownership for direct investments, providing them with either development capital or recapitalisation funds to reduce debt. At the same time, it formed alliances with established merchant banks, brokerage houses and a limited number of established private equity funds to invest in their funds and also co-invest alongside them in larger transactions. This channel allowed Teachers' to cast its net wider into markets it was not yet prepared to tackle independently (e.g. the United States and Europe), to tap into specialist expertise (e.g. Providence Equity Partners for telecom sector investments, another fund focused on oil and gas investments in the Canadian province of Alberta), or to access segments of the private equity market that TPC could not invest in cost-effectively on its own (e.g. investments less than C$50 million in Canadian private companies). However, the path Teachers' had chosen was not easy – while it tried to establish itself as an equal to private equity fund managers, often it was not taken seriously by investment banks and established general partners of private equity funds.

Teachers' approach to investing was in marked contrast to that of other large institutional investors (Exhibit 2.4). For instance, the Canada Pension Plan Investment Board (CPPIB) had all its assets invested in government bonds as recently as 1998.[1] CPPIB began a private equity investing programme in 2001, choosing to rely solely on external fund managers. It was only in 2006 that it launched a multi-year transformation to build internal capabilities in making direct investments in private equity. Other large institutional investors, such as the endowment fund of Yale University, saw private equity as an integral part of their investment allocation, yet only performed fund manager selection internally while outsourcing the investment process entirely to the selected fund managers. At the other end of the spectrum, investors such as Norway's Government Pension Fund Global (GPFG) had strong convictions about transparency and performance assessment relative to a benchmark that led to a total avoidance of private equity. Instead it pursued a low-cost beta-only approach, with strict index-linked investments in market-traded equity and fixed income instruments and very limited active management.[2] Occupying the middle of the spectrum of institutional approaches to private equity were investors such as the Government of Singapore Investment Corporation (GIC) that made fund investments as well as direct investments in private equity, but typically limited to minority equity stakes.

By 2000, Teachers' had developed expertise in all facets of merchant banking and held over 100 investments in the consumer products, communications, industrial products, entertainment & media, financial services, retail, and energy industries. Teachers' invested directly in Canadian firms, which represented 40% of the merchant banking portfolio. In the United States and Europe it invested both directly and indirectly as a limited partner. The merchant banking portfolio included C$329 million of venture capital invested in Canada and the US, principally in life sciences and information technology.

Teachers' had become one of the largest sources of private capital in Canada and, with an annual rate of return of 23% from private capital investments since inception, one of the most respected. Typical equity cheques were C$25-500 million, with a sweet

1. Nicole Mordant, "Canada's big pension funds reach for the top", *Reuters* News, April 18, 2007 (Factiva).
2. David Chambers, Elroy Dimson and Antti Ilmanen, "The Norway Model", 19 September 2011, http://www.tilburguniversity.edu/about-tilburg-university/schools/economics-and-management/news/seminars/finance/2011/Dimson.pdf.

spot in the C$75-100 million range. In 2001, Teachers' total direct investment portfolio including co-investments stood at C$1.9 billion and fund investments at C$1.1 billion, with 18 investment professionals managing the overall TPC portfolio.

Jim Leech: Tasked with Taking Teachers' Global

With a nascent platform in place to make (minority) investments in private companies, Teachers' Private Capital was looking for someone with a solid track record in building businesses to expand its direct investing model further into controlling investments and into new markets. With an honours degree in Mathematics and Physics from the Royal Military College of Canada and an MBA from Queen's University, Jim Leech had built a career leading large public companies in the financial services, and real estate and energy industries, as well as smaller technology start-ups. Most notably, he had served as the President and CEO of Unicorp Canada Corporation, one of Canada's first merchant banks, and Union Energy Inc., then one of the largest integrated energy and pipeline companies in North America.

When Claude Lamoureux and Bob Bertram approached Jim in 2001 to head the Private Capital division, he had just completed the sale of a successful technology venture and was poised for a quiet retirement overseas with his wife. But the vision and the ambition they conveyed were compelling. Teachers' had long been known for the way it fearlessly embraced innovation and risk: it was the first pension plan to buy 100% of a real estate development company, the first to use derivatives to achieve its targeted asset mix, and the first to invest in commodities. This willingness to take well-considered risks appealed to Jim's way of thinking. He put his retirement on hold and accepted the opportunity. Soon he would be leading Teachers' to "venture into galaxies where pension funds feared to tread."[3]

Under his leadership, the total amount invested in direct and co-investments increased almost fourfold from C$3.3 billion in 1990–2001 to C$11.5 billion in 2001–2011. As a result, OTTP became one of the earliest pension funds anywhere in the world to make a concerted push into direct investment in private equity. It pioneered the disintermediation approach that gradually gained wider adoption among institutional investors.

Phase 2: Growing Ambition

Following Jim's arrival at Teachers', the minimum equity commitment for direct investments was gradually raised to C$100 and then C$200 million, with the ideal size being C$300-400 million. In 2004, the merchant banking division was renamed Teachers Private Capital (TPC). The rebranding was prompted by the desire to emphasise the association with Teachers', which had a good reputation in capital markets and derivatives, and at the same time downplay the association with pension funds, which Wall Street derided as "dumb money".

Jim reorganised the team, creating regionally focused teams, and also initiated exposure to Asia. He separated the Direct Investments team from a dedicated Fund and Co-Investments team to manage relationships with general partners (GPs). Unlike

3. Karen Mazurkewich, "Teachers' next test; Jim Leech has a big task dealing with the pension plan's $12.7B deficit", *Financial Post/National Post*, August 28, 2008 (Factiva).

many funds which bought a portion of a GP's investment in a company after the GP had already made the investment, Teachers' participated alongside GPs with its own direct investment team in all major steps of the investment process, conducting due diligence, negotiating on deal structure and valuation, and closing the transaction. For this reason, Teachers' preferred to refer to its Co-Investments as "Co-Sponsoring."

Jim re-engineered processes and approvals, brought in senior people and expanded the TPC team significantly. Although the team grew in scale and scope, he continued to remain involved in larger transactions. Based on the early success of TPC's private equity investing, Teachers' also started to invest directly in infrastructure and timber, marking yet another first in the industry. Investing in these assets which produced stable long-term cash flows linked to inflation involved many of the same investment processes required for direct investing that Teachers was by then well versed in. As these asset classes grew in size, they were eventually spun off into a separate division which managed C$10.8 billion in assets by 2011.

It was in 2005 that Teachers' Private Capital's US$450 million purchase of Alliance Laundry Holdings, North America's leading manufacturer of commercial laundry equipment, had first made Wall Street sit up and take notice of TPC as a serious private equity investor. The fact that TPC beat established American fund managers such as Kohlberg Kravis Roberts & Co. (KKR) to buy the asset from Bain Capital sent a clear message to those who until then did not believe in Teachers' commitment to or capability in the asset class. By 2005–07, TPC was looking at cheques of C$1 billion, and opportunistically considered transactions as large as C$4 billion in conjunction with other investors. Simultaneously, as the international diversification that Jim was tasked with bore fruit, the portion of Teachers' private equity portfolio invested in Canada fell from 40% a few years earlier to 32% by 2006.

A star performer during this period was the Yellow Pages telephone directories business. Acquired by Teachers' and KKR in November 2002, Yellow Pages sold units to the public through an income trust less than a year later, netting a 146% IRR for the two investors. On the surface it appeared to be at odds with Teachers' professed long-term investment horizon, but not when one considers that while KKR had exited its stake in Yellow Pages by 2004, Teachers' remained invested in the company for several years longer.[4] This illustrated a crucial point that differentiated Teachers' from the likes of KKR: unlike PE funds that were evaluated mainly on their past IRR track record when they attempted to raise a new fund, Teachers' needed to focus on generating cash rather than percentage returns. As Jim Leech put it, "You can't pay pensions with IRRs – you need cash."

Maple Leaf Sports and Entertainment (MLSE), owner of prominent professional sports teams, venues and television networks in Canada, was a case in point. Teachers' held its investment in MLSE for nearly 18 years before finally selling it. While the fivefold return implied a moderate IRR of about 16% p.a. due to the lengthy holding period (during which additional investments had taken place at various points), the sale proceeds of C$1.3 billion were substantial when compared with the C$4.7 billion in benefits the pension plan had paid out during the year it announced the sale.

4. Immediately after the Yellow Pages Group converted itself to a public income trust, Teachers' reduced its stake in Yellow Pages from 30% to 20.8% while KKR reduced its holding from 60% to 41.7% and BCE, the other remaining shareholder, reduced its share from 10% to 7%. In December 2003, KKR further reduced its stake to 19.4%, eventually exiting Yellow Pages entirely by June 2004.

Teachers' was an active and vocal shareholder in public equities, vigorously advocating good governance by speaking out, talking privately with management and directors of public companies, and voting against management proposals that it judged as being against the interest of shareholders. As a large investor with substantial share ownership in individual public companies, it was in a position to practice what it termed "relationship investing": encouraging company managers to increase shareholder value by practicing good corporate governance, setting strategic priorities, and meeting long-term performance criteria. Spurred on by superior results from in-house management rather than external fund managers, Teachers' increased the proportion of actively managed assets in-house in public and private equities. In 2002, it formed the Canadian Coalition for Good Governance in partnership with other institutional investors to promote good corporate governance practices in Canadian public companies.

Teachers' campaigns for better corporate governance extended to participating in shareholder class action suits in some cases. For example, at Nortel, once the second largest telecom equipment manufacturer in the world, alleged accounting wrongdoing cast suspicion on bonus payments made to the then CEO. To bring governance issues to the fore, Teachers' participated in a class action lawsuit with other shareholders in the U.S. courts, culminating in Nortel agreeing to settle the case for $2.4 billion. Nortel never recovered from the accounting scandal and eventually filed for bankruptcy. In a classic case of journalistic hyperbole, Teachers' activism was described as "a governance jihad that gutted the company".[5]

The fund's practice of active management also extended to its investment in private companies such as Maple Leaf Foods, one of the earliest instances where its investment (C$150 million) was accompanied by a change in the management team as well as the business plan of the company.

Annual returns from the TPC portfolio ranged from 27% to over 40% between 2003 and 2007, substantially surpassing benchmark returns. TPC's prominence as a source of private capital continued to grow. At the 2007 Private Equity International Awards it was named 'Best Buyout Firm in Canada', 'Best Limited Partner' and one of the top 20 private equity firms in the world in terms of total capital deployed over the past five years.

In parallel with the steady increase in in-house active management, Teachers' worked to educate its stakeholders on the need for competitive remuneration to ensure continued value creation through active management. While the lack of fundraising pressure at Teachers' certainly meant more job security for staff at TPC than at a private equity fund, attracting the right financial and operational expertise from the private sector and from private equity into Teachers' quasi-public sector environment required that compensation for investment professionals be competitive. Advised by an independent consultant, Teachers' developed an incentive system that linked compensation to long-term outperformance over benchmarks. The system, which applied to all investment staff, paid out bonuses only if managers did better than their benchmark over a four-year period, while also taking into account the overall performance of Teachers' investments. Payouts could still be substantial: in 2004, 2% of four-year value added over the benchmark, amounting to C$52million, was set aside for long-term incentive payments to staff.

5. Terence Corcoran, "Teachers' arrogant role at Nortel, BCE", *Financial Post/National Post*, December 12, 2008 (Factiva).

Although investment professionals at Teachers' and other Canadian pension funds were among the highest paid in the world,[6] their total investment management costs were among the lowest because they avoided significant fees (paid to external managers) by managing a large portion of assets in house. The typical PE fund charged 1.5-2% in annual management fees and retained 20% of profits in the form of performance fees (carried interest), sometimes even on a deal by deal basis. Given these fees, a 20% gross return achieved by an externally managed fund would (in a typical fee structure) result in a net-of-fees return around 6% lower for investors in the fund. Another advantage from having developed internal capabilities in PE was the flexibility it bestowed: while PE funds required investors to commit capital upfront and then make that capital available when required to fund investments, Teachers' could vary the pace of its direct investments if and when it made sense to do so.

One spectacular success for TPC was the sale in 2007 of Samsonite Corp. for a total of US$1.7 billion in cash, a fivefold increase on its investment. The world-famous luggage maker was on the brink of bankruptcy when Teachers', in partnership with Ares Corporate Opportunities Fund and Bain Capital, had acquired and recapitalised the company in 2003. Under the direction of a new management team, Samsonite was repositioned globally as a stylish, high-quality brand, enabling a headline exit for investors such as TPC.

Partly fuelled by confidence from the success of earlier investments and partly by the ample availability of financing from competing investment banks, TPC set its sights on increasingly large investments. As a Reuters article[7] put it, "Once largely shepherds of low-risk investments", pension funds such as Teachers' were now "invading the boardrooms of some of North America's biggest corporations and have become leading dealmakers in the public and private equity markets." Nothing could illustrate this better than the case of Bell Canada Enterprises (BCE) which, with a market capitalisation of C$25.3 billion, was the most widely held public company in Canada and the parent company of Bell Canada, the country's largest phone company.

Phase 3: The Peak – Leading the World's Largest LBO

Teachers' interest in BCE dated back to 1990 when it began investing in equities. The 1-2% stake it held in BCE (Exhibit 2.5) was one of its largest ever equity positions because BCE was a prominent constituent of the TSX index. BCE had originally been a leader in mobile, but hampered by a lack of focus, it lost ground to two newcomers. Shares in BCE returned 7.1%, including dividends on an annualised basis over a four-year period (2002–2006), while those of its domestic peers Rogers Communications and Telus Corp returned 48.1% and 35.5% respectively over the same period.[8]

6. Jody MacIntosh and Tom Scheibelhut, "How Large Pension Funds Organize Themselves: Findings from a Unique 19-Fund Survey", *Rotman International Journal of Pension Management*, Volume 5 Issue 1 Spring 2012 (http://www.cembenchmarking.com/Files/Documents/How_Large_Pension_Funds_Organize_Themselves.pdf).
7. *Reuters News*, April 18, 2007.
8. Bloomberg Data. Returns calculated assuming dividends are reinvested in the respective security, for the period from 31 Dec 2002 to 31 Dec 2006.

BCE appeared to be clearly undermanaged both by Canadian standards and compared to global benchmarks in the sector. Teachers' had been active in expressing its views to management and had increased its stake in the company to 5% by the end of 2006, steadily gaining influence on BCE's board, but not enough to drive change. Frustrated with BCE, the Public Equities team turned to TPC to see if it was interested in initiating a take-private or a conversion of BCE to an income trust in order to unlock value. Since the team at TPC knew BCE quite well from having purchased two of its divisions – Yellow Pages and CTV Bell Globe Media – in earlier transactions and a recent unsuccessful bid for its satellite business, TPC agreed. Responsibility for BCE was transferred to TPC in 2006, overseen by a team led by Glen Silvestri, who would later become head of investments in Telecom, Media and Technology (TMT) and Energy within TPC. As a response to growing shareholder discontent, the management of BCE began considering various options to breathe life into its lacklustre performance: a large share buyback, a debt repurchase, a blockbuster acquisition or converting itself into an income trust. It decided to convert itself to an income trust.

Income trusts had been growing in popularity with Canadian investors at that time due to the tax advantages they possessed. However, the spurt in income trust conversions led the Ministry of Finance to fear significant erosion in the country's corporate tax base. Shortly after BCE disclosed its intention to convert, government legislation was revised in a way that removed the advantages of conversion, as a result of which BCE was forced to cancel its plans. Exposed and rudderless, with no other value-creation strategy on hand, it went 'back to the drawing board' in late 2006 to consider all of its options, at the urging of external advisors and interested investors. Having recently sold a satellite communications subsidiary for C$3.25 billion, BCE was cash rich but bereft of imminent investment opportunities for that cash, and thus began to attract serious interest from private equity funds including KKR and Providence Equity Partners Inc. This prompted Teachers', which had long been contemplating options for its stake in the company, to throw its hat into the ring.

In early April 2007, a few days after Jim Leech and Jonathan Nelson, CEO of Providence Equity Partners, had met with BCE CEO Michael Sabia, Jim informed BCE that Teachers' planned to file a 13D notice with the U.S. SEC. The implication was loud and clear: the status of Teachers' investment in BCE was changing from passive to active. Realising that a buyout was becoming unavoidable, the board of BCE decided to embrace what it could no longer avoid and decided to extract the best possible deal for its shareholders. It created an official auction process and invited bids from interested buyers, with a June 26 deadline for the submission of bids.

The sheer size of a likely deal meant that Teachers' could not act alone. Teachers' had already decided to partner with Providence and Madison Dearborn Partners, LLC – funds that it knew and respected for their telecom sector expertise from earlier investments.[9] Meanwhile, KKR partnered with CPPIB, and Cerberus Capital Management LP headed another consortium of investors, who all put in competing bids for BCE.

9. OTPP invested in four different buyout funds managed by Providence Equity Partners (1999, 2001, 2005 and 2007). OTPP also made several investments in the Telecom, Media and Technology (TMT) sector alongside Providence Equity Partners such as the purchase of Kabel Deutschland, Germany's largest cable operator, and investments in Grupo Corporativo Ono, Spain's largest alternative provider of communications, broadband internet and pay TV and Idea Cellular, one of India's largest cellular companies.

On June 30, BCE announced that Teachers' and its partners had won the competitive auction: they valued BCE at C$51.7 billion, including C$16.9 billion of debt, preferred equity and minority interest.[10] Teachers' offer of C$42.75 a share represented a 42% premium to the price at which BCE's stock had traded on the day before the potential sale was first reported in March 2007. The valuation meant that Teachers' was poised to enter the history books for leading the largest LBO ever, even bigger than the US$43.2 billion buyout offer for Texas power producer TXU Corp by KKR and TPG earlier that year.

The transaction structure envisaged C$34 billion in debt to be provided by a consortium of banks – Toronto Dominion Bank, Royal Bank of Scotland (RBS), Deutsche Bank and Citibank, implying a 5x Debt/EBITDA multiple and 7.6x EV/EBITDA multiple.[11] The team at TPC working on the transaction envisioned a better governance framework and a turnaround plan for BCE to be executed by a new CEO, George Cope (at that time, BCE's President and Chief Operating Officer). George would be promoted internally, while Michael Sabia would step down once the buyout was completed.

In order to ensure that the new business plan would be executed and to comply with the restriction on foreign ownership of Canadian telecom companies, the deal was structured to give Teachers' a 52% stake in BCE, with Providence taking up 32%, Madison Dearborn 9%, and other Canadian investors the remaining 7%. A 5% option pool was provisioned for management conditional on meeting performance targets. The transaction terms included a break-fee of C$800 million payable by BCE and a reverse break-fee of C$1 billion payable by Teachers' consortium (which ultimately would be significant).

Challenges Emerge to the Largest LBO in History

The first of the challenges facing the deal was the sheer number of regulatory approvals and the length of time it would take to obtain them. BCE navigated these hurdles successfully, securing anti-trust clearance from the U.S. Federal Communications Commission (August 2007) and the Canadian Competition Bureau (September 2007), as well as approval for the transfer of broadcasting licenses from the Canadian Radio-Television and Telecommunications Commission (CRTC) (March 2008) and Industry Canada (April 2008).

While the deal was securing the requisite regulatory blessing, other trouble brewed. Owners of bonds issued by BCE were not pleased with the deal: post-LBO the credit rating on bonds they held would be downgraded to junk due to their subordination to the new and substantial amount of debt being taken on by BCE. Two groups of bondholders, including powerful institutions such as Manulife Financial Corporation, challenged the proposed transaction in court in September 2007, arguing that it favoured shareholders at the expense of bondholders.[12] The legal wrangle dragged BCE into a nine-month-long journey through the Canadian courts, with the challenge being initially dismissed by the Quebec Superior Court, only to be appealed in the Quebec Court of Appeal, and ultimately settled in the Supreme Court of Canada in favour of shareholders.

10. Chris Fournier and Frederic Tomesco, "Fund buys the biggest Canadian phone firm", *Bloomberg News/ International Herald Tribune*, July 2, 2007 (Factiva).

11. Based on 2006 financial data from Bloomberg.

12. Robert Gibbens, "Bondholders have reason to celebrate", *Montreal Gazette*, December 12, 2008 (Factiva).

During the year that it took for the country's legal system to affirm that the directors of BCE were indeed right to act in the interest of common shareholders as long as they fulfilled their contractual obligations to bondholders, bigger external challenges to the deal began to surface. The sub-prime mortgage crisis which began to roil markets in the later part of 2007 unfolded into a full-fledged global financial crisis (GFC) by the middle of 2008, forcing Citibank and RBS to accept bailout funds from the US and UK governments respectively. This raised doubts about whether the deal would proceed, given the significantly weakened position of bank balance sheets and the precipitous drop in credit markets which made the banks wince at the terms on which they had agreed to finance the buyout.

After a prolonged silence, the lenders attempted to renegotiate these terms, although they were contractually bound to abide by them. On June 24 2008, Jim and Jonathan Nelson met with the board of BCE after discussions with the deal's biggest lender, Citibank. Jim delivered an ultimatum: if BCE did not agree to terms including C$2 billion less in debt financing, higher interest rates on the debt, suspension of the dividend, appointment of George Cope as CEO to begin implementing the new business plan immediately, and a six-month delay in closing, the deal would be off. The Teachers' consortium agreed to an increased reverse break-fee of C$1.2 billion. BCE could have taken the banks to court for breaching an agreement they had committed to the previous year, but rather than pursue a court battle which would scuttle the deal, it agreed to the revised terms proposed by the consortium on behalf of the banks, allowing the deal to move ahead, albeit slower than it wished.

While bankers dithered and BCE shareholders waited on tenterhooks for their payout, the media speculated feverishly about the fate of the deal. As the agreed closing date (December 11, 2008) drew nearer, it seemed the transaction would finally succeed despite all the challenges it had faced. But it was not to be. The transaction agreement required that an independent auditor determine the solvency of BCE based on the fair saleable value of assets. This clause had been requested specifically by BCE as a way to satisfy existing bondholders that the deal would go through only if the serviceability of existing debt remained unaffected. In late November 2008, less than two weeks before the closing date, KPMG, the appointed auditor, declared that a post-takeover BCE with C$32 billion in debt would not meet the requirements of the solvency test. This effectively sounded the death knell for the transaction: a few minutes after midnight on December 11, Teachers' and its partners issued a statement announcing the termination of the deal, citing the failure to satisfy the solvency test.

The solvency test was viewed by some as a convenient excuse for the buyout group and the bankers to terminate a deal that had been applauded in the heyday of LBOs but suddenly looked questionable against the backdrop of the credit crisis. The overhang in the market for high-yield leveraged loans was about US$360 billion, and BCE debt would have accounted for nearly 10% of that. Little wonder, then, that the banks were glad to be let off the hook. Teachers' and its partners had been prepared to close the deal, having already wired the funds required.

BCE was not pleased with the outcome. The company lodged a claim in the Superior Court of Quebec for the reverse break-fee of C$1.2 billion – which was finally settled only in October 2012, in the form of non-cash benefits related to the acquisition of Canadian data centre operator Q9 Networks by the original buyout consortium in partnership with BCE.[13] In the immediate aftermath of the aborted buyout, the company took advantage of the steep drop in its share price (Exhibit 2.6) and repurchased 40 million shares, thereby partially appeasing shareholders by returning some cash to them. Having cut its 2007 dividend of C$1.46 per share to half that amount in 2008, BCE reinstated and enlarged the dividend payout to C$1.58 per share in 2009.

Although the LBO was not completed, the active involvement of Teachers "made the company a more focused competitor than it was before the takeover effort began."[14] Many of the changes at BCE, including the elimination of redundant layers of management, a rebranding exercise, as well as a deal with Telus to share the cost of building a 3G network, were prompted by the involvement of Teachers. Under the leadership of George Cope, who was elevated to CEO before the deal was consummated, BCE went on to execute the business plan that Teachers helped develop, eventually exceeding the long-term EBITDA projections in that plan. But in 2009 the future appeared far less optimistic.

With privatisation off the table, responsibility for BCE moved back to the Public Equities team, which decided to sell all 55 million shares of BCE it had originally acquired at about C$30 a share.[15] Teachers' sold its holding at prices ranging from C$23-25, eventually exiting the position by May 2009.

There were a number of questions for Teachers' when it contemplated the BCE saga. Markets showed how the availability of financing could evaporate unexpectedly, leaving mega-LBOs in the lurch. The BCE transaction, had it been completed, would have led to an enormous concentration of the TPC portfolio in the TMT sector. The capital required from TPC to complete the BCE buyout was about C$3.5 billion. TPC had expected to reduce the position immediately after closing by selling about C$1 billion of the deal to other Canadian institutions, including CPPIB, but the remaining commitment would still have represented a significant proportion of the entire TPC portfolio at the end of 2007.[16]

The opportunity cost of pursuing such enormous, all-absorbing deals was not insignificant. At the peak, the six people in charge of Canada at TPC were dedicated to the deal between March and June 2007. Teachers' leveraged itself through its partners (Providence had five or six of its own people in BCE), but with increasing media scrutiny and the numerous challenges to the deal, the pension fund's human resources had been increasingly stretched.

Phase 4: Post-GFC Era

In the thick of the BCE buyout, Jim Leech was promoted to lead Teachers' as President and CEO of the pension plan in December 2007. At the helm of TPC, he now had direct responsibility for nearly C$20 billion of assets (C$9 billion in direct and indirect

13. Q9 Networks Press Release, "Investor Group Completes Acquisition of Q9 Networks", October 17, 2012 (http://www.q9.com/pr158.html).

14. Ross Marowits, "BCE takeover dead, court fight looms over $1.2B termination fee", *The Canadian Press*, December 11, 2008 (Factiva).

15. Dow Jones Newswires, "Ontario Teachers Seen As Big Seller of BCE Stock", May 22, 2009 (Factiva).

16. The total equity commitment from the consortium was to be about C$7.7 billion, depending on the final amount of debt financing.

private equity and C$10 billion in infrastructure) and 40% of risk taken by the fund. He was also on the board of the fund's real estate investment arm, which was set up as a separate company, and thus oversaw another C$20 billion of assets and 30% of risk.

Jim had no doubt impressed the board with the sustained results achieved by private capital investments. In an interview given at that time, his former boss Claude Lamoureux had described him has a "great communicator" with great leadership skills. The media and his staff seemed to agree. A newspaper article referred to him as "the right man for a job that requires some salesmanship and a deft hand managing relationships", while former employees described him as someone who was tough but who could connect with people and was articulate, honest and likeable. Following the promotion, although Jim was tasked with much broader responsibilities, he remained involved in the BCE transaction given existing relationships and the high profile nature of the deal.

Jim Leech's ascendance to the top job at Teachers' came at a time of significant change for the firm. Claude Lamoureux and Robert Bertram, who had led the firm since its establishment as an independent organisation in 1990, were both leaving within a 12-month period. Jim had to ensure an atmosphere of stability even as he pursued an organizational restructuring and turned his focus to talent development. Simultaneously, he had to tackle the issue of the recurring funding deficits that the fund now faced – a dramatic reversal from the late 1990s. The political challenge of gaining support for unpopular measures like increasing contribution rates from active teachers and cutting benefits to be paid to future retirees also lay ahead for the new CEO.

Under the leadership of Erol Uzumeri, who took the reins of TPC from Jim Leech in December 2007, TPC spent several months reorganising itself into industry teams to develop in-depth sector expertise and identify opportunities before they came to the market rather than pursuing targets opportunistically. Along with opening an office in London to better pursue opportunities in Europe, TPC decided to focus on four main sectors: telecom/media, consumer products, diversified industries (chemicals and materials) and financial services and identify attractive segments for investment within those sectors. The group consciously decided to steer clear of mining, metals, oil and gas (although these made up a significant part of the Canadian economy) because it would have had to build a new team to tap into those areas proactively.

While the credit crisis left many economic casualties around the world, TPC's portfolio held up well, with only one of its direct investments resulting in loss of equity. As it did for many other investors, risk management became even more central to Teachers' investment process after the GFC, but risk tolerance did not diminish at TPC, except for the decision to avoid mega-deals like BCE. In 2010, Erol left Teachers' to start his own fund and was replaced by Jane Rowe (who heads the private capital group at the time of writing).

While equities on the whole declined from 60% to 44% of Teachers' portfolio between 2001 and 2011, private equity as a percentage of equities tripled from 8% to 24% over the same period.[17] Canadian investments shrank to 17% of TPC, reflecting the growing internationalisation of the private investments portfolio. In 2012, Teachers' announced its intention to increase exposure to India and Latin America, whereas

17. The reduced allocation to equities was in large part due to a conscious change in the asset mix policy given the volatility of stocks and the fund's lower risk tolerance due to ongoing funding issues.

its earlier investments outside North America and Europe were dominated by small allocations to China, Japan, Korea and Africa. Teachers' made its first fund investment into India through Kedaara Capital Advisors in 2012. The UK, Benelux, Germany and Scandinavia were also identified as priority regions for future investments. In November 2012, Teachers' declared that it would open an office in Hong Kong to manage its activities in the Asia Pacific region, further attesting to its increasing geographical diversification.

The fund continued to emphasise a strong governance model and having the right talent to carry on its direct investing model. In the aftermath of the GFC, Teachers' introduced certain changes to its bonus plan, which had become progressively more complex over time. To bring a renewed focus to cost, all profits used to evaluate performance were measured after cost, including internal overhead costs, which were fully allocated among various teams. The compensation structure continued to include a claw-back feature such that the accumulated bonus pool would diminish in years of underperformance. As Jim constantly reminded his staff, TPC was not a PE fund with a pension plan attached, but a PE entity within a pension fund.

Jim attributed a good part of Teachers' success with direct investments to having a well-informed board that consists of investment professionals rather than politicians or bureaucrats, as is often the case with state-run pension funds and institutions. Having a board that clearly understood the risk of private investments and stayed the course, without getting cold feet when faced with the occasional failure, was essential to realising the illiquidity premium that is the reward of the patient investor. At the same time, making the distinction between management and oversight was crucial. Edward Medland, the Chairman of the board of Teachers' remarked in his 1996 letter to plan members that, "The pension board is not interested in, nor is it staffed for, managing companies in which it invests."

While TPC had built up operational expertise internally by creating a portfolio management group in 2008 to apply best practices in operations and governance consistently across portfolio companies, it strove to limit itself to being a good overseer (rather than a manager) of assets. Teachers' also prided itself on being nimble, an adjective rarely associated with pension funds. When presented with a co-investment opportunity by a GP, few large LPs could respond with the speed and agility demonstrated by Teachers'.

Evaluating the Success of Teachers' Approach: Issues for Teachers', Pension Funds and Other LPs

As Exhibit 2.7 illustrates, on an absolute basis TPC has generated a net-of-fees IRR of 19.3% since inception. On an annual basis, TPC posted positive returns in 14 out of the 17 most recent years for which data is available (1995 to 2011). In relative terms, TPC's returns have surpassed those of its benchmark in 15 of the last 17 years. TPC measures itself against a custom benchmark defined as the returns produced by the relevant public equity markets plus an additional spread, which varies from one market to another.

TPC's IRR since inception is nearly double that of the total pension plan (10%), clearly demonstrating its contribution to the plan's performance over the last two decades.

Teachers' largest active risk budgets are found in private equity, public equities and real estate because of the historic way these assets have outperformed their respective benchmarks. The continuing importance of private equity in Teachers' portfolio stems from its ability to generate higher risk-adjusted returns than those produced on average from other asset classes (Exhibit 2.8).

An analysis of the sources of return within TPC (Exhibit 2.9) indicates that from inception until 2000, while the direct portfolio was being built up, fund investments (IRR 34.3%) outperformed direct and co-investments (IRR 20.9%). However, from 2000 to 2006 this trend was reversed as annualised returns produced by fund investments dropped significantly to 13.8%, while the annualised returns from direct and co-investments improved to 31.6%. The performance of direct investing was partly driven by the superior economics of direct and co-investing, partly by the increased experience of the team, and partly by generally supportive market conditions for private equity. The fact that some of the outperformance is due to co-investment opportunities which would not have come about without the relevant investments in funds is, however, not reflected in these numbers. The returns from fund investments and direct and co-investments have been lower overall and the difference between them less pronounced in recent years (from 2006 to 2011). Yet from inception to 2011, returns from direct investments have been clearly superior to those from fund investments. In 2009 and 2010, TPC rationalized its fund investments into core and non-core holdings.

With fund investments, TPC's record in selecting fund managers who outperform the market appears mixed. According to data from Preqin, 25 of 47 funds TPC invested in underperformed their respective benchmarks (Exhibit 2.10).[18] While it may raise questions about Teachers' manager selection skills, as mentioned it does not consider the fact that many fund investments give TPC access to attractive co-investment opportunities, a fact which is taken into consideration internally when evaluating the performance of external managers. In addition, though direct and co-investments have delivered strong returns, there is a limit to how far the fund can enlarge its portfolio in this area due to the resource-intensive nature of direct deals compared to investing in funds.

The Way Ahead

TPC was inducted in 2011 into The Private Equity Hall of Fame – nominated by the editors of *Dow Jones Private Equity Analyst* – "for exemplary and enduring contributions to venture capital, buyout and related private equity disciplines". The same year, Jim received the "CEO Award of Excellence in Public Relations" from the Canadian Public Relations Society. However, the flood of institutional money into the private equity industry – total assets under management worldwide stood at a record US$3.2 trillion in 2012, up 4% on the previous year[19] – and the resulting competition raised significant questions for Jim and his team, as well as the board, in terms of future expected returns from private equity, the split between internal and external management, and the allocation to private equity within the overall asset mix.

18. 10 funds in top quartile, 9 in second quartile, 13 in third quartile and 12 in bottom quartile.

19. Paul Hodkinson, "Rise and Rise of Private Equity Assets", *Private Equity News*, February 4, 2013 (http://www.penews.com/magazine/news/content/4071712174/40872/).

From small beginnings, Teachers' has come a long way with its direct investing platform, with nearly C$15 billion invested in direct and co-investments in private equity since inception. Teachers' approach resonates with a wide array of institutional investors, especially pension plans, many of which face looming funding gaps, as a means to achieve the risk-adjusted returns they seek. However, Teachers' journey in building internal expertise has been a gradual one, occurring over more than a decade as it steadily shifted from co-investing alongside GPs to independently pursuing direct deals, before finally leading large-scale buyouts. Along the way it has placed a heavy emphasis on creating the right culture and a suitable governance framework to execute its plans.

Going forward, how can Teachers' Private Capital continue its track record of outperformance in an environment of increased competition among investors? From an organisational perspective, how can Teachers' maintain its culture of prudential risk-taking while avoiding undue risk to the assets of the pension plan? Given potential limitations to the scale on which it pursues disintermediation, should Teachers' refocus on fund investments and take advantage of the improving economics of private equity funds to further the expansion of its private equity portfolio? Alternatively, should it consider hiring external managers to invest tailored segregated mandates, rather than be just one of many investors in a pooled fund over which it has little control or bargaining power? Teachers' is a complete newcomer in some of the emerging markets it seeks to diversify into. In such markets it needs to develop relationships with the right external managers to prepare for the day when those markets garner much more significance on the global investment map.

Jim pondered these issues as he considered the organization's future trajectory.

Exhibit 2.1

Snapshot of Ontario Teachers' Pension Plan: Total Fund Size and Annual Returns

	Net Assets				
Year	**Size C$ bn**	**Annual return**	**Benchmark return**	**IRR since 1990**	**Benchmark IRR since 1990**
1990	20.1	5.6%	n.a.	5.6%	n.a.
1991	24.7	19.6%	n.a.	12.4%	18.1%
1992	27.8	8.9%	n.a.	11.2%	n.a.
1993	33.7	21.7%	20.5%	13.8%	7.6%
1994	34.5	1.7%	–0.3%	12.7%	n.a.
1995	40.1	16.9%	17.2%	12.2%	8.3%
1996	47.4	19.0%	18.1%	13.1%	9.7%
1997	54.5	15.6%	15.6%	13.4%	10.4%
1998	59.1	9.9%	11.9%	13.0%	n.a.
1999	68.3	17.4%	17.6%	13.4%	11.2%
2000	73.1	9.3%	5.3%	13.1%	10.7%
2001	69.5	–2.3%	–5.3%	11.7%	9.3%
2002	66.2	–2.0%	–4.8%	10.6%	8.1%
2003	75.7	18.0%	13.5%	11.1%	8.5%
2004	84.3	14.7%	10.6%	11.3%	8.6%
2005	96.1	17.2%	12.7%	11.7%	8.9%
2006	106.0	13.2%	9.4%	11.8%	8.9%
2007	108.5	4.5%	2.3%	11.4%	8.5%
2008	87.4	–18.0%	–9.6%	9.6%	7.5%
2009	96.4	13.0%	8.8%	9.7%	7.6%
2010	107.5	14.3%	9.8%	10.0%	7.7%
2011	117.1	11.2%	9.8%	10.0%	7.8%

IRR since 1990 and Benchmark IRR since 1990 are annualised internal rates of return

Source: Ontario Teachers' Pension Plan Annual Reports from 1990 to 2011

Exhibit 2.2
Glossary of Pension Fund Terms

Active Member	A member who is making contributions to the Plan.
Assets	Assets include the value of everything the Plan owns: equities, bonds, real estate, infrastructure investments, etc., plus the Present Value of Future Contributions.
Contributions	Required remittance to accrue credit based on a specified percent of an employee's pensionable salary. Employers are responsible for remitting contributions monthly.
Defined Benefit Plan	The teachers' pension plan is a defined benefit pension plan. Members' pensions are determined by their years of service credit and the average of their best five school-year salaries, not by the return on investments.
Defined Contribution Plan	A pension plan in which each member's pension is determined by the return on the investment of his or her contributions. The individual member bears all of the risk on his or her investment returns and consequently on his or her pension benefit.
Funding Deficit (also called Deficiency or Shortfall)	If the Plan's liabilities are greater than its assets, then the Plan has a deficit or shortfall.
Funding Surplus	A surplus exists when the Plan's assets exceed its liabilities.
Liabilities	Liabilities include the value of everything the Plan owes: the Present Value of Future Benefits and any other financial obligations such as payroll, outstanding debts, etc.
Member	A person who is eligible to contribute and has service in the plan. Members include those who are receiving benefits and those who are making contributions.
Ontario Teachers' Federation (OTF)	An association representing all teachers in Ontario and one of the plan sponsors.
Pensioner	A member who has retired and is receiving a monthly pension.
Pensions	Regular periodic payments to a member or their survivor who has met the eligibility requirements under the plan.
Plan Sponsors	The plan is co-sponsored by the Ontario Teachers' Federation and the Ministry of Education.
Teachers' Pension Act (TPA)	The Ontario legislation governing the pension plan for teachers.

Source: Ontario Teachers' Federation website (http://www.otffeo.on.ca/english/pensions/glossary.pdf)

Exhibit 2.3
Evolution of Asset Policy Mix

Year	Equities	Inflation-sensitive	Fixed Income
1991	65%	0%	35%
1995	65%	0%	35%
1996	69%	7%	24%
1999	65%	15%	20%
2000	60%	22%	18%
2002	50%	30%	20%
2004	45%	32%	23%
2006	45%	33%	22%
2009	40%	45%	15%
2010	Increased	Redefined	Redefined

Equities include public and private equities. Until 1995, real estate investments were treated as a part of Equities.

Inflation-sensitive investments include Commodities, Real Estate, Infrastructure, Timber and Real return Bonds.

Fixed Income includes Absolute Return Strategies, Hedge Funds, Bonds and Money Market securities.

Source: Ontario Teachers' Pension Plan Annual Reports from 1990 to 2011

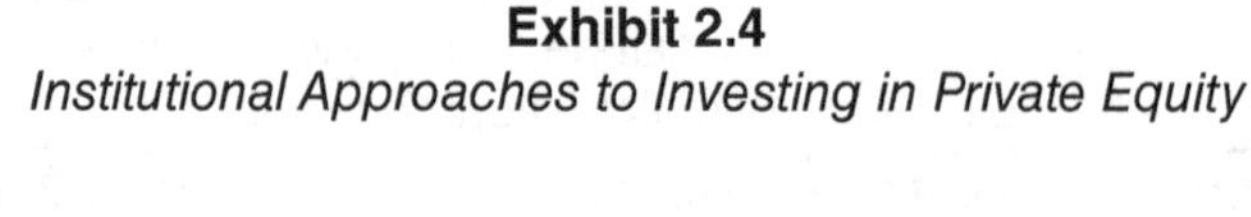

Exhibit 2.4
Institutional Approaches to Investing in Private Equity

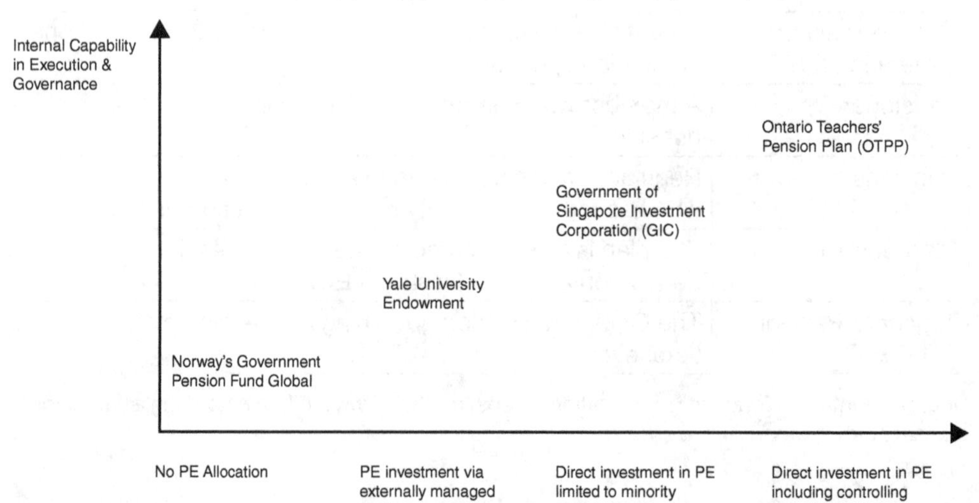

Source: Author

Exhibit 2.5
OTPP's Ownership of BCE Inc.

Year-end	No. of shares (mn)	Value C$ (mn)	Equity Stake
1990	0.6	24.6	0.1%
1991	3.5	164.5	0.6%
1992	3.2	132.8	0.6%
1993	7.9	366.9	1.4%
1994	11.0	494.8	1.9%
1995	10.3	487.0	1.8%
1999	11.2	1,472.6	1.9%
2003	10.4	305.0	1.2%
2004	11.1	324.2	1.3%
2005	44.9	1,266.5	5.3%
2006	42.8	1,357.5	5.3%
2007	50.8	2,032.9	6.3%
2008	50.8	1,295.2	6.3%
2009	–	–	–

Sources: Ontario Teachers' Pension Plan Annual Reports from 1990 to 2011 and Bloomberg data

Exhibit 2.6
Stock Price Chart of BCE

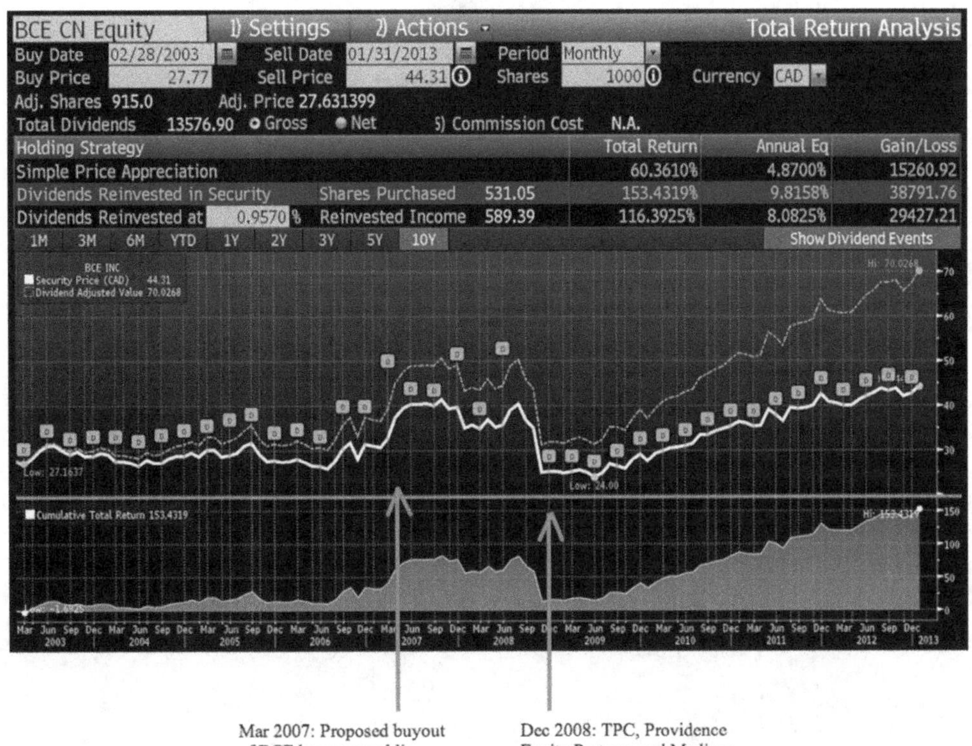

Source: Bloomberg

Exhibit 2.7

Teachers' Private Capital: Portfolio Size and Annual Returns.

	TEACHERS' PRIVATE CAPITAL				
Year	Size C$ bn	% of Net Assets	% of Equities	Annual return	Benchmark return
1990					
1991	0.1	0%	2%	n.a.	n.a.
1992	0.1	1%	2%	n.a.	n.a.
1993	0.2	1%	2%	34.5%	n.a.
1994	0.4	1%	2%	n.a.	n.a.
1995	0.7	2%	3%	21.5%	16.5%
1996	1.0	2%	3%	38.4%	30.3%
1997	1.7	3%	4%	52.9%	17.0%
1998	2.3	4%	5%	12.3%	0.4%
1999	3.1	5%	7%	28.3%	33.7%
2000	3.9	5%	9%	21.8%	7.3%
2001	3.4	5%	8%	1.2%	-12.5%
2002	3.3	5%	10%	-0.2%	-12.2%
2003	4.2	6%	12%	40.5%	27.6%
2004	4.3	5%	11%	27.6%	14.5%
2005	6.0	6%	13%	31.4%	24.2%
2006	6.1	6%	13%	26.9%	19.6%
2007	9.0	8%	18%	9.8%	-0.9%
2008	9.9	11%	28%	-12.7%	-19.3%
2009	10.0	10%	24%	-2.8%	11.3%
2010	12.0	11%	25%	19.0%	7.1%
2011	12.2	10%	24%	16.8%	-0.2%

	4-year returns annualised	
Year	TPC	Benchmark
2003	14.6%	1.2%
2004	16.0%	2.8%
2005	23.8%	12.2%
2006	33.3%	21.4%
2007	23.1%	13.6%
2008	12.0%	4.1%
2009	3.9%	1.3%
2010	2.6%	-1.2%
2011	4.2%	-1.0%

Annualised internal rate of return (IRR) since 1990 on the TPC portfolio was 23.0% in year 2000 and 19.3% in year 2011.

Source: Ontario Teachers' Pension Plan Annual Reports from 1990 to 2011

Exhibit 2.8

Ontario Teachers' Pension Plan – Risk-adjusted Returns

	TOTAL FUND			
RISK-ADJUSTED RETURN	**1995–2000**	**2001–2005**	**2006–2011**	**1995–2011**
Mean excess return	0.4%	3.8%	1.3%	1.7%
Std Dev of excess return (Tracking error)	1.8%	0.7%	4.5%	3.2%
Information ratio (Excess return/Tracking)	0.22	5.16	0.29	0.53

Source: Ontario Teachers' Pension Plan Annual Reports from 1990 to 2011.

Information ratio is a risk-adjusted measure of investment performance. It is the ratio of excess returns generated above the benchmark return to the standard deviation of those returns.

Information ratio = Excess return/Tracking error

Excess return refers to the excess return generated above and beyond that generated by the relevant benchmark. Tracking error is the variability of the excess return, measured by its standard deviation.

The information ratio (IR) measures a portfolio manager's ability to generate excess returns relative to a benchmark, but also attempts to identify the consistency of the investor. The higher the IR the more consistent a manager is at outperforming versus his/her benchmark.

Source: Investopedia.com

Exhibit 2.9

Annualised Net Returns from Fund Investments and Direct & Co-Investments by Teachers' Private Capital

ANNUALISED NET RETURNS	**1990–2000**	**2000–2006**	**2006–2011**	**1990–2011**
Fund Investments	34.3%	13.8%	7.1%	16.0%
Direct & Co-Investments	20.9%	31.6%	4.5%	21.0%

Figures are comparable to net of fee returns

Source: Teachers' Private Capital

Exhibit 2.10

Teachers' Private Capital's Fund Investments

Fund	Vintage	Status	Fund Size ($Mn)	Type	Called (%)	Distr. (%) DPI	Multiple (X)	Net IRR (%)	Benchmark (%)	Difference (%)	Quartile	Date Reported
BC European Cap V	1994	Liquidated	530.6	Buyout	93.3	519	5.19	58	30.5	27.5	1	31-Dec-12
BC European Cap VI	1998	Liquidated	1,212.8	Buyout	86.4	231.3	2.31	20.8	13.8	7.1	1	31-Dec-12
Providence Equity Partners IV	2001	Closed	2,764.0	Buyout	92.1	229	2.41	24	22.9	1.1	1	30-Jun-12
Wellspring Capital Partners III	2002	Closed	675.0	Buyout	98.7	184.1	2.2	27.6	16.1	11.5	1	30-Jun-12
Ares Corporate Opportunities Fund II	2006	Closed	2,065.0	Buyout	107.2	97.9	1.6	14.7	7.8	6.9	1	30-Jun-12
Technology Crossover Ventures VI	2006	Closed	1,411.0	Expansion / Late Stage	97.4	92.6	1.34	10.5	3.1	7.4	1	30-Jun-12
Frazier Healthcare V	2005	Closed	475.0	Venture (General)	97.3	81.2	1.34	9.3	0.5	8.8	1	30-Jun-12
Abingworth Bioventures V	2007	Closed	587.6	Venture (General)	57.2	51.3	1.92	19.6	1.1	18.5	1	31-Mar-12
Actera Partners	2007	Closed	693.6	Buyout	97.7	49.1	1.57	20.9	7.7	13.2	1	30-Jun-12
MBK Partners II	2008	Closed	1,600.0	Buyout	63.3	9.8	1.56	19.6	9.1	10.6	1	30-Jun-12
BC European Cap IV	1991	Liquidated	166.2	Buyout	100	215.3	2.15	25.9	25.3	0.6	2	31-Dec-12
MidOcean Partners	2003	Closed	1,800.0	Buyout	98.5	210.2	2.17	n/a	14.3	n/a	2	30-Jun-12
Phoenix Equity Partners IV	2001	Closed	422.3	Buyout	122.1	188.8	2.11	32.1	28.8	3.2	2	30-Jun-12
Providence Equity Partners III	1999	Closed	950.0	Buyout	101	149.8	1.53	14.5	10.7	3.8	2	30-Jun-12
Ares Corporate Opportunities Fund	2003	Closed	750.0	Buyout	120.7	131.8	1.66	14.3	14.3	0	2	30-Jun-12
Glencoe Capital Partners III	2003	Closed	200.0	Buyout	108.5	113.4	1.53	40.6	14.3	26.3	2	30-Jun-12
Doll Capital IV	2004	Closed	375.0	Venture (General)	95	47.9	1.4	6.4	0.7	5.8	2	30-Jun-12
Chrysalix Energy II	2005	Closed	70.0	Early Stage	87.9	19	1.01	n/m	-0.4	n/m	2	30-Jun-11
FountainVest China Growth Partners	2008	Closed	942.0	Growth	65.3	17.7	1.11	6.5	2.7	3.8	2	30-Jun-12
BC European Cap VII	2000	Closed	4,077.9	Buyout	100	203.8	2.1	17.9	24.9	-7	3	30-Jun-12
DLJ Merchant Banking Partners II	1997	Closed	3,000.0	Buyout	98.5	140.1	1.43	6	9.3	-3.3	3	30-Jun-12
Lighthouse Capital Partners V	2003	Closed	366.0	Venture Debt	93	112	1.2	4.4	11	-6.6	3	31-Mar-12
Silver Lake Partners II	2004	Closed	3,600.0	Buyout	88.4	84.8	1.56	10	12.3	-2.3	3	30-Jun-12

Fund	Vintage	Status	Fund Size ($Mn)	Type	Called (%)	Distr. (%) DPI	Multiple (X)	Net IRR (%)	Benchmark (%)	Difference (%)	Quartile	Date Reported
CCMP Asia Opportunity Fund II	2005	Closed	1,575.0	Buyout	127.1	62.1	1.23	5.1	9	-3.9	3	30-Jun-12
Escalate Capital	2005	Closed	195.0	Mezzanine	89.7	61.4	1.3	5.8	8.4	-2.6	3	31-Mar-12
Wind Point Partners VI	2006	Closed	715.0	Buyout	92	56.4	1.1	2.7	7.8	-5.1	3	30-Jun-12
BC European Cap VIII	2005	Closed	7,651.7	Buyout	93.1	39.9	1.19	5.6	9.1	-3.5	3	30-Jun-12
Alta BioPharma Partners III	2003	Closed	300.0	Venture (General)	95	39.3	0.95	-1	2.6	-3.6	3	31-Mar-12
Oak Investment Partners XI	2004	Closed	1,500.0	Venture (General)	100	39.2	0.99	-0.2	0.7	-0.8	3	30-Jun-12
Diamond Castle Partners IV	2005	Closed	1,850.0	Buyout	91.4	28	1.15	3.9	8.5	-4.6	3	30-Sep-12
Providence Equity Partners VI	2007	Closed	12,099.0	Buyout	98.2	24.2	1.17	4.8	10	-5.2	3	30-Jun-12
Sanderling Venture VI Co Investment	2004	Closed	190.0	Co-investment	100	13.6	1.23	4.6	7.1	-2.5	3	30-Jun-12
Wind Point Partners V	2002	Closed	476.0	Buyout	118.4	93.4	1.15	6.3	16.1	-9.9	4	30-Jun-12
Phoenix Equity Partners II	1996	Liquidated	206.5	Buyout	96.5	86.9	0.87	-2.9	21	-23.9	4	31-Dec-12
Providence Equity Partners V	2005	Closed	4,259.0	Buyout	91.2	68.1	1.17	2.9	8.5	-5.6	4	30-Jun-12
Hicks, Muse, Tate & Furst Latin America Fund I	1998	Closed	934.9	Buyout	100.1	66.3	0.76	-3	8.8	-11.7	4	30-Jun-12
Ethos Private Equity Fund V	2005	Closed	750.0	Buyout	85.6	34.2	1.06	1.7	9	-7.3	4	31-Dec-11
Heartland Industrial Partners	2000	Closed	1,300.0	Buyout	97.2	25.4	0.41	-9.2	13.4	-22.6	4	30-Jun-12
CCMP Asia Opportunity Fund III	2008	Closed	1,200.0	Buyout	53	21.8	0.96	-4	9.1	-13	4	30-Jun-12
Phoenix Equity Partners 2006	2006	Closed	652.2	Buyout	92.4	19.1	n/a	-4.5	6.5	-11	4	31-Dec-11
Exxel Capital Partners V	1998	Liquidated	866.8	Buyout	100	5.8	0.06	-45.4	8.8	-54.2	4	31-Dec-12
Advent Central & Eastern Europe IV	2008	Closed	1,582.6	Buyout	58.4	0	0.64	-23.1	8	-31.1	4	30-Jun-12
Phoenix Equity Partners 2010 Fund	2010	Closed	649.4	Buyout	22.4	0	n/a	-23.6	-2.8	-20.8	4	31-Dec-11
Newport Global Opportunities Fund	2007	Closed	500.0	Distressed Debt	96.6	0	0.86	-19	7.9	-26.9	4	31-Dec-11
BC European Cap IX	2011	Closed	8,575.2	Buyout	10.6	0	1.22	n/m	n/m	n/m	n/a	30-Jun-12
EQT VI	2011	Closed	6,514.9	Buyout	9	0	1	n/m	n/m	n/m	n/a	31-Mar-12
Thoma Bravo Fund X	2012	Closed	1,250.0	Buyout	25.8	0	0.98	n/m	n/m	n/m	n/a	30-Jun-12

Note: This listing has been extracted from Preqin database and may not be a comprehensive list of all the fund investments made by Teachers' Private Capital.

The benchmark used for each fund i s chosen based on the type of fund, the fund's vintage year and its geographic focus. For example, 1994 / Europe / Buyout for the BC European Cap V fund.

Source: Preqin Database

CASE 3 PRO-INVEST GROUP
HOW TO LAUNCH A PRIVATE EQUITY REAL ESTATE FUND

SYNOPSIS

The case describes how the Pro-invest Group—a boutique investment firm that specializes in private equity real estate, real estate asset management and private equity—built its business and raised a first-time private equity fund. While Pro-invest founders bootstrapped the business since its launch in 2013, in-house funds are running out by mid-2014 and third-party capital is needed to take the venture to the next level. After deciding on a suitable fund structure, the team hits the fundraising trail. Yet, Pro-invest is cast into turmoil when a potential investor pulls out at the last minute. The Pro-invest team must reevaluate its approach and select other fundraising options to move forward; the case explores the pros and cons of each fundraising option in detail.

PEDAGOGICAL OBJECTIVE OF THE CASE

The case gives an overview of the different options available to private equity firms when raising a new fund. It helps students to evaluate the various choices and understand in detail the dynamics involved in fundraising, especially for first-time funds. They will be able to:

- Understand the central elements, e.g. control versus economics, that private equity fund managers consider when raising capital.
- Gain insights into the fundraising dynamics in the real estate private equity industry.
- Step into the shoes of a fund manager's management committee and evaluate the pros and cons of the various fundraising options.
- Appreciate the questions and due diligence requirements from large institutional investors before allocating funds to a real estate private equity fund.
- Appreciate the challenges of balancing the efforts of fundraising and executing investments in parallel, in particular when raising a first-time fund.

SUGGESTED ASSIGNMENT QUESTIONS

1. Complete the chart in Appendix 1. Draw up the criteria for ranking the different options and then rate them on a scale of one to three.
2. Which option would you choose and why?
3. What are your key take-aways from the case with regards to private equity fundraising?

ADDITIONAL RESOURCES

To make the most of this case study, we suggest the following additional sources to provide context and background information:

- In particular, we recommend the following chapters from *Mastering Private Equity—Transformation via Venture Capital, Minority Investments & Buyouts*
    - Chapter 1 Private Equity Essentials
    - Chapter 5 Alternative Strategies
    - Chapter 17 Fundraising
    - Chapter 19 Performance Reporting
- You may also refer to the book website for further material:
  www.masteringprivateequity.com

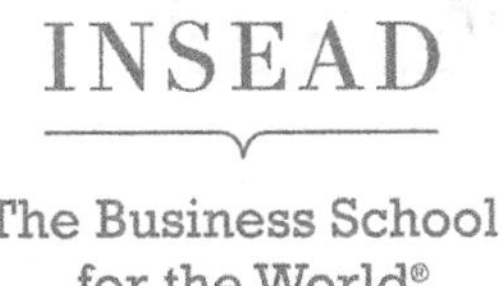

Pro-invest:

How to Launch a Private Equity Real Estate Fund

01/2017-6221

This case was written by Anne-Marie Carrick, Research Associate, Bowen White, Associate Director Global Private Equity Initiative (GPEI), Claudia Zeisberger, Affiliate Professor of Decision Sciences and Entrepreneurship & Family Business, all at INSEAD. It is intended to be used as a basis for class discussion rather than to illustrate either effective or ineffective handling of an administrative situation.

Additional material about INSEAD case studies (e.g., videos, spreadsheets, links) can be accessed at cases.insead.edu.

April 2015

"They are not coming in," announced Ronald Barrott, CEO of Pro-invest, on his return to the board room where the weekly Management Committee meeting was taking place. His remark was met with an astonished silence. Minutes earlier, he had rushed out to take the long-awaited call from Adriana Star Capital – the culmination of months of painstaking effort to find an external solution to the group's short-term funding needs. It hadn't worked.

The infusion of equity was urgently required to advance with Pro-invest's strategy to design and construct a chain of 3-star hotels in Australia and New Zealand that would address the needs of an expanding market. Since 2013, Pro-invest had made huge strides: refining its investment thesis; building its team; beginning construction; and holding a first fund closing. With three projects underway, funding was tight and meeting the group's obligations and payroll each month was becoming a challenge.

The news that Adriana Star Capital was backing out at such a late stage came as a complete shock. The Pro-invest team had spent countless nights preparing the necessary background information, financial scenarios and documentation for the investor's local team . . . and countless meetings, phone calls and conferences with the investor's industry experts reviewing Pro-invest's case with a fine-tooth comb. With sign-off from both the firm's Australian and Asia boards, approval from the investor's Investment Committee in New York seemed a mere formality. Even Adriana Star Capital's own team in-country, who had championed the opportunity, was at a loss.

Devastated but determined not to give up, Ron asked the team to consider an alternative source of funding. The clock was ticking . . .

Background Pro-invest Group

The Pro-invest Group, a boutique investment firm specialised in Private Equity Real Estate (PERE), real estate asset management and private equity, was co-founded by Ronald (Ron) Barrott and Sabine Schaffer in the wake of the global financial crisis in 2010. As asset values plunged and liquidity seized up, the only cash generated from many portfolios was through the yield on real estate assets. Recognizing a golden opportunity, Ron and Sabine moved to raise funding for a focused strategy investing in Australian real estate.

However, steady cash flow was not the only thing that investors sought in a private equity investment: they wanted to see real value creation. By 2010 investors were increasingly attracted to tangible bricks-and-mortar opportunities as they watched their "paper" fortunes disappear in the financial downturn. In the real estate market it was also 'back to basics': creating value through operational management rather than financial re-engineering, which had frequently resulted in overleveraged real estate projects before the crisis and created a number of distressed opportunities in the market.

Creating value in real estate investment meant one thing: the operational involvement of a team with hands-on experience of building hotels from scratch and managing properties on a daily basis. "Standard" fund managers generally did not wish to be involved in operational aspects of managing assets, so to differentiate their fund Ron and Sabine aimed to add a team with deep sector expertise to leverage this unique selling point.

Finding an Opportunity, 2012: Holiday Inn Express – Going 'down under'?

The asset class the team focused on was the 3-star business hotel segment. There were several reasons for this. First, it provided investors with a good risk/return ratio. Second, the CEO, Ronald Barrott, a serial entrepreneur, had built and run some of the largest integrated development and real estate asset management firms in the UK as well as the Middle East. Ron explained:

> *I had a vast amount of experience in the sector. In my previous company I had assisted InterContinental Hotel Group (IHG) with the introduction of their 3-star business hotel brand to Europe in the late 1990s. Within five years one of my smaller companies had built the first Holiday Inn Express portfolio of 15 hotels throughout England, achieving a net IRR for its investors of more than 25%, from 1997 to 2003 and pre-leverage running yields in the early teens.*

When, in 2012, the Pro-invest team studied the markets that the Holiday Inn Express brand had not yet conquered, they were surprised to learn from IHG's head of Asia, that Australia and New Zealand were among them. This was a revelation: IHG had been present in Asia for more than 30 years and active with their full-service hotel brands in Australia but apparently the select-service brand had not been introduced to Australia or New Zealand. Input from local government officials and a private research firm engaged to explore the opportunity supported the case for investment: research had shown that Australia required more hotel bedrooms, with the highest demand in the 3-star segment.

Realising what an incredible opportunity they had before them – in effect a whole continent (Australia) as a market – Pro-invest re-joined forces with IHG in early 2013, and signed a master development agreement for a Holiday Inn Express for Australia soon afterwards.[1]

First Steps – Building a Team

Finding the right people for the core team was of utmost importance. However, given their limited financial resources, not all the members could be hired from the outset. Sabine and Ron found themselves in a chicken-and-egg situation: they needed funding to build a team, but some investors would not meet them until they had at least a core team in place.

1. New Zealand would be added at a later date.

From the beginning, the founding partners made a conscious decision to fund most of the operations themselves until they reached scale. They adopted a bootstrap approach, with creative thinking to attract the right talent. According to Ron:

> *We knew who we wanted to hire – industry experts that we had previously worked with who had excellent proven track records (Exhibit 3.1). We had to find creative solutions for hiring the team, by either offering a certain level of flexibility on their engagement at the beginning – a part-time role growing full time – or structuring compensation with a lower salary and a higher equity component.*

This approach mitigated the cash-flow burn to an extent and suited some of Pro-invest's early hires, who were leaving large corporate jobs and didn't want to jump right back into a 60-hour work week. More importantly, offering an equity-heavy compensation structure incentivized Pro-invest's key people and ensured alignment of interest within the team (which can sometimes be tested when times get difficult in the early years).

The first people the group hired were senior operating professionals considered key to both executing its investment strategy and establishing credibility with the investment community. To round-out the senior management team, Ron and Sabine engaged a head of developments and earmarked a head of hospitality (Exhibit 3.2).

With the core team in place, Pro-invest was in a position to start discussing its value proposition in the market. They had identified a market where hotel rooms were under-supplied and the penetration level was low. They had partnered with IHG and developed a solid master development agreement for the continent. Their strategy and master plan had been substantiated by third-party research…and now they had the team in place to execute. As Sabine recalled:

> *It was an exciting time as we built the core team and looked for our first site to acquire. However, what was less fun was financing the project. We had to ensure that we had sufficient funds at the end of each month to meet pay-roll. With our belts tightened, business class tickets for travel were out of the question and we all used our air miles that fortunately we had accrued over the previous years. Remember, wherever you travel to from Australia, it is still long-haul.*

Progress had come at a cost: it was clear that in-house funds would soon run out and external capital would be required to take the venture to the next level. Ron and Sabine estimated that they had a maximum of 12 months remaining. It was time to fundraise.

Which Structure?

First, they needed to decide what type of fundraising would be most suitable. They considered finding small family offices to fund one hotel at a time, but felt that such a perpetual state of fundraising would be a managerial nightmare. In addition, this approach would likely lead to each investor wanting a "say" in the hotel asset which would make employing a consistent approach across all assets a true challenge: Said Phil Kasselis, Head of Pro-invest Hotels Group:

In my experience, most people believe that staying in a hotel makes them experts in the industry, and have an opinion on all aspects of the hotel's development, from interior design to cutlery.

Moreover, they had always planned to sell a portfolio of standing hotel assets for which institutional investors would pay a premium. With a first portfolio target of 12–15 hotels, Pro-invest's goal was to eventually roll out up to 50 prime Holiday Inn Express hotels throughout Australia. Funding each hotel on a standalone basis could result in a large number of owners with their own agendas, which would make selling the portfolio and achieving consensus unlikely.

A second approach was to raise a typical 'blind pool'[2], private equity fund to finance the first portfolio of hotels and provide Pro-invest with full control of investment decision-making. This would also allow several investors to diversify risk across a portfolio of assets in different Australian localities, and avoid any potential conflict of interest by eliminating investors' ability to cherry-pick Pro-invest's best assets. Finally, with capital committed for at least seven years, a fund structure would allow Pro-invest to build a team focused on building value across a portfolio of hotels rather than looking sporadically for single assets. Tim Sherlock, Head of Pro-invest Developments, said:

Although the team we had built by this time counted only a handful of members, given their wealth of expertise and experience we were convinced we had 'the secret sauce' for a successful project. As a team we had an incentive on the upside of the overall portfolio exit which investors were happy with, as our interests were aligned until the actual exit occurred and our investors would see returns.

Although market trends were for direct single-deal investments, the more Ron, Sabine and the Pro-invest team considered their goals and interests, the more they felt a closed-end fund[3] would be the most appropriate structure.

Anchor Investor – First Commitment

Starting mid-2013, the founding members spent months traveling the globe meeting with potential investors. They called on investors they had worked with previously, as well as new investors who had demonstrated an interest in Real Estate as an asset class such as hotels or PERE.

Although Pro-invest generated interest from the investment community, finding an anchor investor who would sign a first commitment, validate their investment thesis, and help them 'take off' was a different matter. After countless conversations with potential investors, Sabine crossed paths with a senior partner from an investment firm at a PERE conference:

2. 'Blind pools', typically structured as limited partnerships, are long-term investment vehicles raised by fund management companies that have full investment decision-making authority. Investors in these vehicles have no impact on the investment decision-making process, and thus participate in the vehicle's investments 'blind.'

3. 'Blind pools' are more technically referred to as closed-end funds, in which a fund management company secures long-term commitments from investors to execute a investment strategy. At the end of the fund's term, all invested capital – and the majority of profits generated through that investment activity – must be returned to fund investors.

We had tried to contact him for some time, but as he was a well-known investment professional it had proved almost impossible. After attending a PERE conference where we tried, unsuccessfully, to speak with him, I decided to cold e-mail him. Given his senior position, I didn't expect to receive an answer. So I was delighted a few days later, when he wrote to confirm his interest in our investment strategy and suggested a meeting next time I was in Hong Kong.

When the day arrived, Sabine had only 30 minutes with him, which she was determined to maximize. Afterwards, as he escorted her to the lift, he explained: "I am not sure how your portfolio could fit into our structure but I have a friend who may be interested." Convinced that he meant 'Nice meeting you but no thanks', she left with little hope.

However, four weeks later she received an email from him, requesting a meeting with his friend the next time they were in Singapore. 'The friend' turned out to be one of the principals of an Asian family office, with a wealth of experience in the hotel industry. He immediately understood the group's proposition. Following a face-to-face meeting with Ron, they engaged a third-party real estate service provider to run due diligence on Pro-invest, resulting in a first commitment signed for AUS$40 million by the end of 2013. As Ron observed:

For us, this was a sign of the family's trust in us which we were both honoured and humbled by. With this first external funding we could execute on our first three projects – one hotel site in Sydney and one in Brisbane.

The Search for Funding Options – Looking for the Right 'Fit'

With an anchor investor on board, the next six months were spent exploring other sources of funding to continue the roll-out plan. Time was of the essence as the growing team uncovered more and more attractive investment opportunities that required judicious funding. As the summer of 2014 rolled around, Pro-invest had engaged closely with seven funding sources:

The UHNWI

An Ultra-High Net Worth Individual (UHNWI) based in Singapore offered Pro-invest an AUS$200 million investment, but it was clear from the outset that it would be on his terms – he would be running the show. Being 'employees' – albeit glorified ones – was not what they wanted, so the offer was rejected. The individual concerned was known to be a shrewd business person and they weren't convinced that sharing any economic upside would be high on his agenda.

The IPO

Another opportunity came through an investment banker who suggested that Pro-invest consider raising funds from public markets. He was convinced that they could easily float the first three assets and, thanks to the deal flow pipeline Pro-invest had developed, was confident they could raise funds from the Australian stock market. His firm would assist the Pro-invest team with the listing but stopped short of offering to underwrite it. With no guarantee of a successful listing and considerable resources required to prepare the business for public sale, this option was also put aside.

The Mezzanine

The team entered into detailed discussions with an international investment firm interested in Pro-invest's strategy. The firm conducted three months of due diligence with a promise of matching the anchor investor's capital commitment in exchange for a seat on Pro-invest's Investment Committee. However, the investment firm's principal in Australia had little experience in the hotel industry, and members of the Pro-invest team were reluctant to include an external voice in the investment decision-making process. The investment firm eventually proposed a mezzanine structure with an equity-kicker to protect both the firm's downside exposure and provide the potential for upside participation. Crucially, the structure would provide the international investment firm a senior position in relation to Pro-invest's anchor investor. Said Sabine Schaffer:

> *We weren't convinced that our existing anchor investor would be happy that his equity investment would now become inferior to another incoming mezzanine investor. So we didn't pursue this option either.*

Project Pony

An Australian investment house with global operations also came to the table. Its team instantly understood the opportunity and was eager to work with Pro-invest to strike a deal it dubbed 'Project Pony.' Its capital markets team quickly offered its services to help raise AUS$200 million in funding through a private placement with an Australian institutional investor and several international PERE investors. In return, the Australian house demanded an equity stake in the Pro-invest management company so that the house could directly participate in the upside generated by Pro-invest. Insisting "This is real life post 2008," the house listed a number of asset managers for whom they had done exactly the same in the past year, assuring the Pro-invest team that they were more than capable of raising the required funds. Pro-invest was not convinced as the team did not want to share the upside with what – in the end – was the role of a placement agent, with no value add to the actual day-to-day business. Also, it would make discussion with any further incoming investor more complicated as they preferred to see the actual team 100% incentivized and as a result aligned with the investors' interest.

The Managed Account

Another idea arose while talking to a well-known pension fund: Why not create a managed account? The investor had previously had a bad experience in 'co-mingled' funds with multiple investors providing capital for a single project. The pension fund offered to commit AUS$300–500 million to the account, for which it would maintain full investment approval rights. Far from a 'blind pool,' the pension fund would vet each opportunity on a case-by-case basis before deciding whether or not to invest its capital. The scale and certainty of funding was attractive to the Pro-invest team, but the inability to control investment decision-making and potentially be forced to pass on opportunities it deemed attractive, gave them pause.

The Private Bank

For some months, Pro-invest mulled over the opportunity to engage with the private banking arm of an international investment bank. A number of the bank's clients had expressed interest in the fund's investment thesis, and the bank was willing to explore a possible collaboration. However, the bank's clients requested that the Pro-invest vehicle be structured as an Australian Managed Investment Trust (MIT), which enabled preferential tax treatment (a tax rate of 15% rather than 30%) and hence higher returns. Implementing such a structure would not only require the establishment of an Australian Financial Service Licensed (AFSL) onshore fund manager, but a complete restructuring of the existing investment fund – a process that would require time and resources.

Reverse IPO

The seventh opportunity was to use an existing AIM-listed investment vehicle and execute a reverse IPO. IPOs on AIM had been used in the past for investments in the mining sector but with the mining bubble coming to a burst, there were a number of listed AIM entities that were interested in changing their activities and become active in other more promising sectors, hospitality being one of them.[4] By offering the AIM listed investment vehicle for a reverse IPO, Pro-invest could benefit from an existing infrastructure as well as investor base interested in seeing their funds invested in Australia and, who could help push the price to new heights in a short time through a secondary offering of securities.

* * *

Throughout discussions with each investor, it was clear that all parties wanted to see both the Pro-invest team and IHG invest into the forthcoming investment vehicle, to have 'skin in the game'. The fundraising process received additional credibility when, after detailed due diligence, IHG confirmed an AUS$20 million commitment to the fund; the Pro-invest team followed suit. The additional funding allowed construction to begin on a third Holiday Inn property in Adelaide. With the additional commitments, Pro-invest held its first official fund closing in November 2014 at over AUS$60 million.

Adriana Star Capital Appears . . . and Folds

With the process firing on all cylinders, Pro-invest leadership received a call from Adriana Star Capital; they wanted to learn more. They had been impressed by the first

4. Commodity prices hit record highs in the early 2000s, but tanked around the time of the global financial crisis. In a country (Australia) with a strong mining industry, many companies and individuals got stung.

official closing, the three assets in various development stages, IHG's participation as an investor in the fund and the Pro-invest team, now grown to a team of seven professionals. As a result serious discussions with regards to investing began in late 2014. Five months of gruelling due diligence followed, in which no stone was left unturned. Sabine noted:

> *Over the last two years, we had found an anchor investor and completed the fund's official first closing. With some first assets under management (AUM) and projects underway we were confident that we would pass the Adriana Star Capital's rigorous due diligence process. It proved to be one of the most thorough I had ever experienced in my finance career so far.*

Once completed, the investment team's head of Australia believed that the deal being signed off by head office in New York would be a formality when the investment case was presented to the Investment Committee for approval. It appeared to be perfect timing for the group to invest in the Australian dollar, which had weakened significantly against the US dollar, making fundraising "cheaper" and more attractive to US dollar investors.

However, despite all the different elements falling into place, the Investment Committee response from the New York based investor was negative. Even more frustrating for those involved, there was no apparent explanation.

Back to the Drawing Board

Having announced the devastating news, Ron addressed the disappointed team.

> *We have three assets but we need to execute quickly on additional ones to 'keep face' with our stakeholders. We've just spent five months passing all due diligence questions with a party who has finally decided to bail out without any wrongdoing from our side. We have everything in place: the team, the sites, the banks for the debt. All we need is the equity. Any ideas?*

Although stunned by the 'no', they were determined to find another solution. It was clear to both Ron and Sabine that they should revisit the seven funding opportunities considered previously. Were the investors still interested in the project? If so, which one should they pursue? "None of the options were perfect," he admitted, "but we didn't have much choice."

Onwards and Upwards

The next day, the team was more subdued than usual. Ron called the principal directors to the boardroom at 9.00am, where Sabine laid out the various fundraising options and the pros and cons of each. The criteria for judging the alternatives were as follows:

- *Pro-invest keeps control*: One of the main concerns for the Pro-invest team was how much, if any, input into the investment decision-making process an incoming investor would be given. While the interests of Pro-invest and its existing fund stakeholders would generally align with an incoming investor, on occasion they might differ. Allowing an incoming investor to have a seat on ProInvest's Investment Committee, or otherwise have a say on investment decision-making, could curtail the Pro-invest team's ability to control its own fate.

- *Pro-invest team to keep upside:* Several investors were looking to capture a portion of the upside generated by the Pro-invest management company in exchange for their capital commitment. Some investors and advisors indicated an ability to write 'bigger tickets' if upside was granted. At the same time, Pro-invest's senior management had to maintain sufficient upside to incentivize its team.
- *Certainty of Funding:* Pro-invest had just gone through an exercise that demonstrated how fickle fundraising could be. Selecting a fundraising option that provided a high certainty of success was a priority for the team.
- *Investor fit*: Investors came in various forms. High Net Worth/family offices invested their own capital while institutional investors invested on behalf of clients. In general, UHNWI and FO could maintain an investment as long as they wished, whereas an institutional investor required clear exit timing.[5] Pro-invest ideally needed to select the investor whose characteristics would best fit their investment strategy.
- *Additional costs*: Costs were at the forefront of every first-time fund founder's mind, and keeping a tight rein on cash and expense was crucial. Next to the traditional set-up costs of a fund (legal, structuring, etc.), the Pro-invest team had to bear in mind the potential cost of any restructuring, particularly placement fees and fees linked to receiving certain licenses.
- *Investor value-add*: Some investors might bring a specific skill set (e.g. knowledge of the industry, networking, etc.) which the fund manager may be able to leverage. Also, in addition to tangible skills, securing investment from a well-known, leading institutional investor would send a strong signal to the market regarding the quality of the Pro-invest team and their investment strategy and hence potentially ease the path for further fundraising.
- *Future fundraising*: Getting the right investor mix on board the first time around was important for raising future funds. Pro-invest had to bear in mind an investor's capacity to re-up in a follow-on fund. Setting up the 'wrong' investor pool from the outset could be detrimental to future fundraising.

Challenges

As Pro-invest's senior management team considered their options, each of the seven criteria was weighed equally. However, as the discussion progressed, it became clear that control and financials were core considerations for all team members. Sabine summed it up: "Once the key criteria were agreed, we had the task of applying these to all the different options. Would any of the funding options fit the criteria or should we consider alternatives. The clock was ticking, we needed to act quickly, and only time would tell whether we had made the right decision."

5. Known as a sunset clause.

Appendix 1

Options Criteria	The UHNWI	The IPO	The Mezzanine	Project Pony	The Managed Account	The Private Bank	Reverse IPO
TOTAL							

Exhibit 3.1

Pro-invest Team Members and Advisors (May 2014)

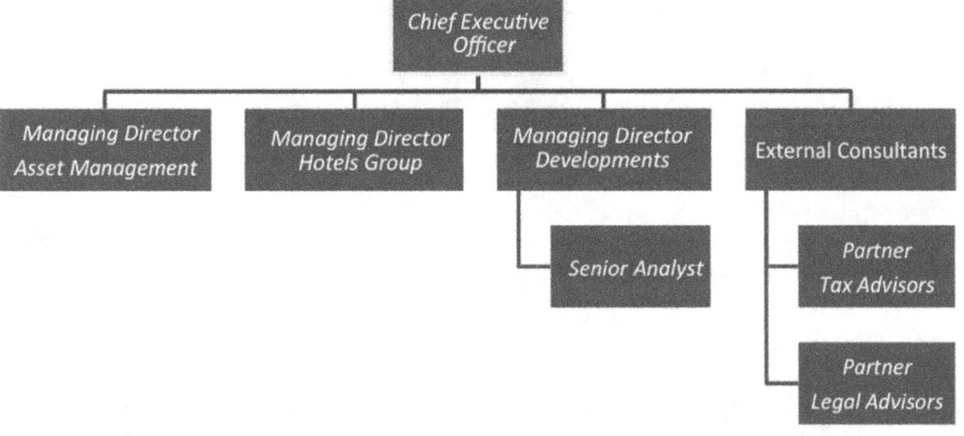

Source: Pro-invest

Exhibit 3.2

Pro-invest Senior Management Team

RONALD BARROTT

- A serial entrepreneur with over 40 years of real estate investment, development and project management experience.
- CEO of ALDAR Properties which developed the world renowned Yas Island, home to Formula 1 in Abu Dhabi.
- Primary involvement of transactional real estate projects in Europe, GCC, and Asia totalling USD75 billion.
- Founder, CEO and Chairman of Stannifer Group, an integrated development and real estate company with assets across the world.
- Under Stannifer Group, Ron established the Holiday Inn Express brand the UK in partnership with IHG.
- Fellow of the Royal Institute of Chartered Surveyors.

SABINE SHAFFER

- 17 years of experience in funds management, private equity, hedge funds and capital markets.
- Integral involvement in the incubation of three Private Equity Funds and advised a Private Equity Real Estate fund focusing on Quality Limited Services hotels in the Middle East.
- Lead team working on an IPO in London, AIM market, as well as establishment of companies within the Dubai International Financial Centre.
- Extensive experience in structuring and asset managing of investment vehicles.
- Master's degree from Harvard University and PhD in Economics from University of Austria.

TIM SHERLOCK

- 18 years' experience in Australian Real Estate.
- Strong track record in acquisitions, development and asset management.
- Broad national network of property agents, owners and development consultants.
- 5 years as Head of Acquisitions within the Property Investment Banking team at Investec Bank.
- 5 years with International agency firm Savills managing the sale of development sites and investment properties.
- Involvement in $400m worth of residential development sites and $300m worth of commercial, industrial and retail investments.
- Expertise in Australian real estate market and extensive network of property owners and agents.

PHIL KASSELIS

- Fourth generation hotelier with over 30 years' experience in the hotel industry.
- 8 years' experience with hospitality consulting firms Horwath Asia Pacific and Arthur Andersen.
- 13 years spent in senior hotel development roles with IHG based in Sydney, Dubai and Singapore.
- Negotiated in excess of 100 hotel deals comprising hotel management agreements and franchises throughout Asia Pacific, the Middle East and Africa.
- Previous roles include Director, Hotel Investments with Knight Frank Expotel and Development Director for Accor Asia Pacific.
- Board member: Tourism Accommodation Association (NSW).

CASE

4 HITTING THE TARGET
OPTIMIZING A PRIVATE EQUITY PORTFOLIO WITH THE PARTNERS GROUP

SYNOPSIS

In 2011, Partners Group is nearing the end of a year-long process for a new mandate from a European pension fund called Future Plan. The pension client had serious problems with its 6-year-old PE program, consistently falling short of its target allocation to the asset class, while generating poor returns—seemingly always a step behind the opportunities in the market. To date, Future Plan had invested purely through PE fund-of-fund products offered by two managers, one focused on European markets the other on global markets. The fallout from the global economic crisis had wreaked havoc in its portfolio, and Future Plan's PE strategy was in need of serious change. Expanding its PE mandate to include secondary and direct investment strategies, Future Plan begins a competitive manager search process with one single goal: achieve its target allocation to the asset class by 2014. The case charts the Partners Group's path in the manager selection process and details how the firm's expertise and services—along with a novel holding structure—offered a solution to Future Plan's goals.

PEDAGOGICAL OBJECTIVE OF THE CASE

This case provides readers a ringside seat to the actions taken by a medium-sized pension fund when managing its private equity portfolio allocation. Students will explore the rationale behind making investment decisions, key challenges faced by institutional investors when constructing and managing a private equity portfolio, and the different characteristics of primary, secondary and direct PE investments. The case provides data and a step-by-step guide for students to develop a commitment strategy—across primary, secondary and direct PE investments—that will enable Future Plan to hit its target allocation to PE by year-end 2014.

SUGGESTED ASSIGNMENT QUESTIONS

1. Why was Future Plan dissatisfied with its PE programme? What was missing or lacking?
2. What were the key challenges faced by Future Plan when they sought an additional external manager for PE? What were they looking for?
3. What impact would adding secondary and direct investments have on Future Plan's PE programme?

Modelling the Portfolio

4. Using the information in Exhibits 4.4 and 4.8a, model the expected NAV for Future Plan's existing portfolio of PE investments through year-end 2011. Was the evolution of Future Plan's actual exposure to the asset class in line with this? If not, what may have contributed to the deviation?
5. Assuming Future Plan maintains its 5% target allocation to PE and a steady growth in total pension assets, determine its target allocation to PE (in € terms) at year-end 2012, 2013 and 2014.

6. Based on the return expectations for Future Plan's PE programme and the information provided in Exhibits 4.9 and 4.11, determine Future Plan's long-term target allocation by segment (i.e. the percentage of the total portfolio allocated to private equity, private debt, private infrastructure and private real estate). Calculate the expected return for this target allocation.
7. Based on Future Plan's risk appetite and strategic priorities as described in the case, determine a long-term target allocation by investment type (i.e. the percentage of the total portfolio allocated to primary, secondary and direct investments).
8. Based on your answers Question 4.7 and Exhibits 4.8a–c, determine the commitment (in € millions) to primary, secondary and direct investments required for Future Plan to hit its target allocation to PE by year-end 2014. What annual commitment capacity (in € millions) to primary, secondary and direct investments is required for Future Plan to maintain its target allocation to PE beyond year-end 2014?

ADDITIONAL RESOURCES

To make the most of this case study, we suggest the following additional sources to provide context and background information:

- In particular, we recommend the following chapters from *Mastering Private Equity – Transformation via Venture Capital, Minority Investments & Buyouts*
  - Chapter 1 Private Equity Essentials
  - Chapter 5 Alternative Strategies
  - Chapter 18 LP Portfolio Management
  - Chapter 21 LP Direct Investment
  - Chapter 24 Private Equity Secondaries
- You may also refer to the book website for further material:
  www.masteringprivateequity.com

Hitting the Target

Optimizing a Private Equity Portfolio with Partners Group

01/2017-6256

This case was written by Anne-Marie Carrick, Research Associate, Bowen White, Associate Director of Global Private Equity Initiative (GPEI), and Claudia Zeisberger, Senior Affiliate Professor of Decision Sciences and Entrepreneurship & Family Business, all at INSEAD. It is intended to be used as a basis for class discussion rather than to illustrate either effective or ineffective handling of an administrative situation.

Additional material about INSEAD case studies (e.g., videos, spreadsheets, links) can be accessed at cases.insead.edu.

December 2011: It was the eve of Partners Group's final presentation to build a bespoke private equity (PE) portfolio for a European pension fund – Future Plan. After spending nearly a decade tending the relationship and recently participating in Future Plan's year-long search for an additional PE manager, the pieces were falling into place. Michael Studer, Partner, Head of Portfolio & Risk Management at Partners Group, was reviewing the proposed strategy for the last time.

The challenges presented by Future Plan's PE allocation were not uncommon among small- to medium-sized pension funds. Since launching its PE programme in 2005, Future Plan had struggled to achieve its target allocation to the asset class and returns had been disappointing. Understanding and addressing these issues dominated the Investment Committee's agenda – the PE allocation regularly took up half of their meeting time, despite its sub-5% allocation in the overall portfolio.

Partners Group's presentation was near completion. Its investment track record and broad expertise in private markets was highly regarded, and its proposed innovative holding structure promised to streamline and simplify Future Plan's reporting and decision making. Nonetheless, there had been stiff competition. Partners Group needed to present a superior option to that of the other remaining PE manager in the final pitch. How could Michael Studer demonstrate that Partners Group was the best company to help Future Plan achieve its target allocation by 2014?

Future Plan and the Legacy Portfolio, 2005–11

Pension Fund Background

In 1999, HM Domestic, a global logistics provider, established Future Plan to formally manage its €4.5 billion pension assets. Initial funding for the plan consolidated a small pool of pension assets managed externally that drew directly from the HM Domestic's balance sheet. With a young and expanding workforce, minimal payouts were expected in the next decade, leaving a long "runway" to grow pension assets before worrying about distributing capital.

The task of managing the pension fund fell to an Investment Committee (IC) consisting of three HM Domestic employees assigned by the board, and three representatives nominated by the company's pension plan holders. With no dedicated investment professionals to oversee the day-to-day activity of the fund, and minimal support from the nominees, the vast majority of the work fell to the three HM Domestic employees on the IC, led by the company's treasurer, Thomas Meier.

Thomas and his colleagues all had full-time roles at HM Domestic and therefore could devote only 10% of their time to managing the pension fund, adding to the challenge for a team that was understaffed compared to similarly sized pension funds. To compensate for its lack of manpower, the IC elected to invest fund capital via external managers. Future Plan engaged investment consultants Aaklan Advisors to assist in due diligence and manager selection, working within the target allocations set by the IC.

In June 1999, the IC approved a conservative portfolio that consisted of a 60% allocation to (predominantly domestic) government bonds, an allocation to domestic and emerging market public equity, and a small allocation to domestic real estate (Exhibit 4.1).

Magnifying Returns – Allocating to Alternatives

At year-end 2004, following five years of steady performance and a continued stream of policyholder premiums, Future Plan's asset base had grown to €6.8 billion (Exhibit 4.2). However, the pension fund's performance had been decidedly unspectacular (Exhibit 4.3), largely due to the conservative allocation of its investment portfolio.

Spearheaded by Thomas Meier, the IC launched an investigation into how it could increase the fund's risk/return profile. During their mid-year review of the portfolio in 2005, it was decided that Future Plan would expand its mandate and allocate capital to a diversified portfolio of alternative investments consisting of private equity, hedge funds and commodities. The target allocation for each alternative asset class was set at 2.5%. Thomas explained Future Plan's approach to alternatives as follows:

> *We were looking for better returns and were convinced that alternatives were the way forward, particularly since we could afford to lock up our capital. Our first forecast payouts were a long way off, and we wanted to take advantage of the illiquidity premium offered by certain alternative asset classes. The success of large US pension funds and endowments in the alternative space also influenced the decision. We were attracted to private equity because returns are derived from fund managers' hands-on management of portfolio companies.*

At the time, a golden era was dawning on the PE industry, with robust performance, fundraising, and access to cheap debt driving industry activity. For Future Plan, the asset class promised to add incremental returns to its overall investment portfolio: while the target return from its existing portfolio was 9%, the returns expected for a PE programme were between 12% and 16%. Despite this benefit, the IC members remained cautious in their approach, conscious of their limited understanding of the mechanics of a PE portfolio.

Future Plan was not alone in this regard. PE was an unknown quantity for many small- to medium-sized pension funds, which principally invested in liquid market strategies such as fixed income and public equity. The complexity of managing cash flows in and out of a PE fund, the lack of control over investment decision making and timing, and the 10-year commitment required for most PE funds were uncharted territory.

Given these challenges, Future Plan followed the guidance of the Aaklan Advisors and selected two fund of fund (FoF) managers to build its allocation to PE: one with a focus on European growth and buyout funds (Bellex Capital), the other with a broad, global mandate (Arkridge Capital). These FoF managers would allocate capital to a portfolio of primary PE fund offerings, which would in turn invest in and manage a portfolio of privately-held companies.

Evolution of Future Plan's PE Portfolio

Future Plan made its first PE commitment to a closed-end FoF managed by Bellex Capital in October 2005, and followed up with a commitment to an Arkridge closed-end FoF vehicle in June 2006 (Exhibit 4.4). In November 2006, Future Plan made its first commitment directly to a primary PE fund offering: an infrastructure fund targeting European assets.

While Future Plan quickly exceeded its target allocation to hedge funds and commodities, its PE allocation grew more gradually as the FoFs called and deployed capital (Exhibit 4.5). Nevertheless, by the end of 2007 the net asset value (NAV) of its PE portfolio had risen to just short of €70 million, and at its year-end meeting the IC raised its target allocation to 3%.

No sooner had Future Plan gained some traction in PE, than international markets began to wobble then plunge into the depths of the global financial crisis. The headline-grabbing PE investments executed during the 2006–07 peak morphed into reports of PE-backed companies filing for bankruptcy, as fund managers scrambled to cope with overextended portfolios. Thomas Meier recalled the early years of Future Plan's PE programme (Exhibit 4.6):

> *We expected that it would take time to build up our allocation to PE, but we were underwhelmed with the execution at the fund of funds. We were slightly under-committed from the start, so the total amount of invested capital was constantly below what we hoped for... then we went into the crisis, and capital was invested even slower than before.*

The fallout for Future Plan was even greater as private infrastructure was particularly hard hit by the crisis. The fund in which it had invested saw several of its investments blow up, exacerbating the dismal performance generated by the rest of Future Plan's PE portfolio (Exhibit 4.7).

In addition to the poor performance—which was magnified by the multiple layers of fees associated with FoFs—addressing the issues generated by the PE allocation imposed a significant administrative strain. The process through which the fund met its capital calls became particularly burdensome: every call had to be dealt with individually by accountants at HM Domestic. The challenge of raising cash and meeting these capital calls within the required 10-day window was further hampered by Future Plan's custodian bank, which required original, hard copy transfer orders before it would move any funds. As a result, PE consistently took up 50% of the time in IC meetings – the operational burden far exceeded the benefits delivered, particularly when compared to Future Plan's portfolio of traditional asset classes.

Bruised and battered by the impact of the global financial crisis on its PE portfolio, Future Plan faced a reckoning: either the PE allocation had to start performing in line with expectations or be terminated.

Repositioning the PE Portfolio

Given the mediocre performance of Future Plan's PE allocation, action had to be taken, but what path should the IC take? They could increase commitments further with their existing managers, seek an additional manager, or wind down the programme over a number of years – multiple options had to be considered. After numerous discussions late into the night, their decision was unanimous: find a solution rather than abandon the PE programme. As Thomas recalled:

> *I continued to have faith in the PE strategy – we just needed to improve on execution. And our existing portfolio also supported fixing the portfolio: we couldn't just sell it. We were hearing the right ideas from our FoF managers, but we were behind the trend and missing the "sweet spot" in the market. What we needed was simply more flexibility and better execution. But we had to find it.*

A major strategy review concluded that Future Plan's current programme was too narrow: investing solely in primary fund offerings via closed-end FoFs did not provide the flexibility to capitalize on opportunities in the market. To be more nimble, Future Plan decided to broaden its mandate with its external managers so that they could act on opportunities as they arose.

With its focus on primary PE funds offerings (via the FoFs), Future Plan had so far overlooked two strategic tools to more proactively manage its allocation to the asset class, namely secondary and direct investments. Purchasing LP interests in existing PE funds on the secondaries market would provide exposure to funds with more mature portfolios, accelerating NAV development and providing higher visibility than a primary fund commitment (Exhibits 4.8a and b). Direct investments, including co-investments, would eliminate any lag or ambiguity regarding a Future Plan investment (Exhibit 4.8c), as capital would flow directly into the shares of a PE-backed company with the additional benefit of eliminating the fees associated with a typical PE fund. Looking for a manager with the capability to execute on both strategies was the declared goal.

Incorporating secondary and direct investments into its portfolio was not without risk, however. Unlike primary fund offerings, secondaries and directs were decidedly transactional: while PE firms first pre-marketed and then formally marketed a primary fund offering over one to two years, secondary and direct opportunities were unpredictable and required the ability to assess complex transactions within months or even weeks. Managers executing such transactions therefore required a different skill set to that of a team with experience investing in primary funds. Direct investments also presented a risk profile that differed from primary and secondary fund investments, as Thomas noted:

> *We didn't want our portfolio to be too concentrated in a single vintage year, and with direct investments the investment of capital is less gradual: managers invest in deals over a few vintage years, and that's it. We were also wary of information asymmetries in the context of co-investments, and that managers often only offered a co-investment for deals that were too large for their main funds... thus outside of their comfort zone.*

In mid-2010, Future Plan made fresh commitments to Bellex Capital and Arkridge Capital. However, rather than closed-end fund vehicles, Future Plan committed capital to separately managed accounts (SMAs) and extended each manager's mandate to invest across primaries, secondaries and directs. However, as Bellex and Arkridge were only just expanding into secondaries and directs, the majority of the capital deployed via these accounts was expected to flow into primary fund offerings. To gain immediate exposure to secondaries and directs, Future Plan would need an additional manager.

Enter Stage Left: Partners Group and the Pitch

Thomas led the search for a manager with an established track record in secondary and direct investment as well as primaries. Partners Group was one of the first firms Thomas contacted as he had built a relationship over the years with Robert Lustenberger, a senior client relationship manager who looked after Partners Group's Swiss pension fund relationships. They first met in 2002 and had remained in touch through various investment conferences. Robert had been a source of support in the challenging post-crisis environment, sharing information and helping Thomas understand the finer points of PE. His input had opened Future Plan's eyes to the idea of broadening (rather than cancelling) its PE mandate.

Ten other managers (in addition to Partners Group) responded to Future Plan's initial Request For Information (RFI) in the search for ideas on how to address the challenges in its PE portfolio. After a two-month screening process, the group was narrowed down to six managers, who were invited to respond to a more detailed Request For Proposal (RFP), providing background information on their track record and proposed solution. Robert described Partners Group's approach to the RFP:

> *The RFP was an important step for us. In the proposal we highlighted the challenges Future Plan faced and described how we would help them reach their goals. We explained how Partners Group's multi-asset class and integrated 'relative value' approach to private markets provided the flexibility to invest in the strategy presenting the best opportunity for our clients at any given time. We particularly highlighted that including direct and secondary investments in the portfolio would result in lower fees compared to a traditional FoF given the absence of the double-fee layer. We also demonstrated how we could support Future Plan beyond investment management, with our suite of client services including portfolio management and best-in-class reporting.*

From the pool of six, two providers were shortlisted to make a final presentation for the mandate: Partners Group and another well respected firm in the sector. In August 2011, members of Future Plan's IC were invited to Partners Group's headquarters in Zug for a full-day in-house due diligence session. As Robert recalled, the focus at this point was to share Partners Group's current view of the market (see Exhibit 4.9) and its experience:

> *We showed the potential partners our general investment strategy for the next two years. We explained the secondary and direct side, which at the time were very attractive as many LPs were looking to sell existing stakes in private equity funds. We then showed them how we would continue to manage the allocation over time and provided examples of how we had built up other clients' portfolios over a short period of time.*

Robert also presented a solution to address the administrative burden presented by Future Plan's PE portfolio: an innovative holding structure that would consolidate all of their PE investments in a single offshore entity (see Exhibit 4.10). As part of the proposition, Partners Group offered to administrate the holding company for Future

Plan and manage cash flows to and from its existing PE fund, FoFs and SMAs; Future Plan would only need to meet capital calls from the holding company. Reporting would also be simplified, as the NAV of its entire PE programme would be consolidated into a single line on the balance sheet. Furthermore, capital calls could be netted by capital distributions at the holding company level, thus reducing Future Plan's tax bill.

The presentation included Partners Group's provision of investment-level "steering" on future commitment decisions for Future Plan's entire PE allocation, aided by consolidated statements from the holding structure. This would be exclusively in the form of advice, the final decision remaining with the IC. While a specific commitment plan was not shared during the meeting, Robert described in broad strokes how Partners Group's Portfolio & Risk Management team engaged with clients to help them achieve their target allocation to PE.

The Task at Hand

Impressed with the findings of its first in-house due diligence, Future Plan scheduled a second meeting on 3rd December 2011. In addition to Alfred Gantner, one of Partner Group's Founding Partners, the group heads of Private Equity Directs & Primaries, Real Estate, Infrastructure, and Portfolio & Risk Management would attend the meeting.

Crucial to the Partners Group's proposition was a robust strategy that would enable Future Plan to hit its target allocation to PE by year-end 2014. While the holding company structure was the 'icing on the cake', Michael Studer and his team still had to bake the cake.

Exhibit 4.1
Future Plan Total Portfolio Asset Allocation

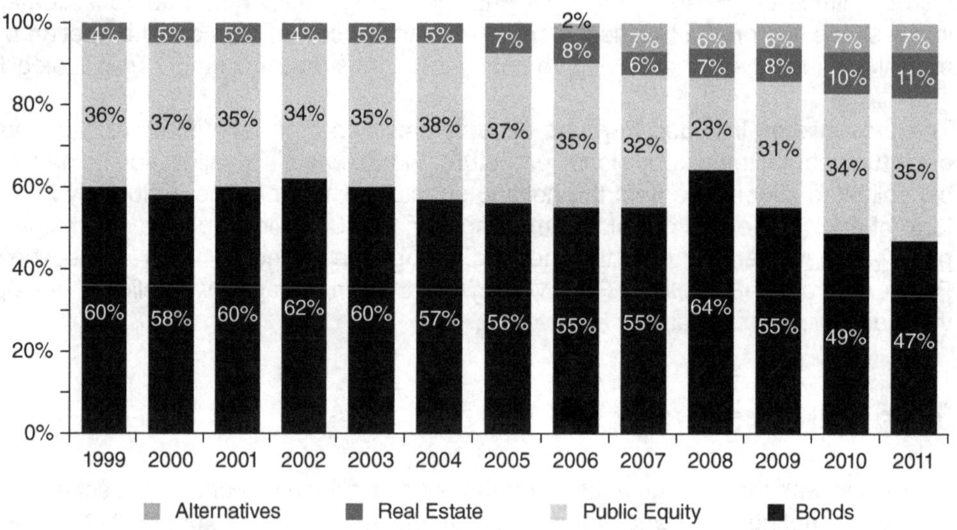

Exhibit 4.2
Future Plan Historical Assets under Management

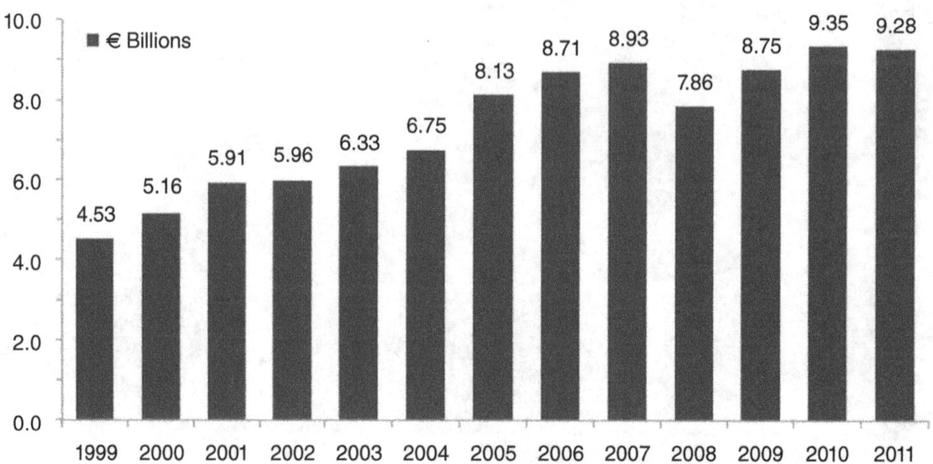

Exhibit 4.3
Future Plan Total Portfolio Performance

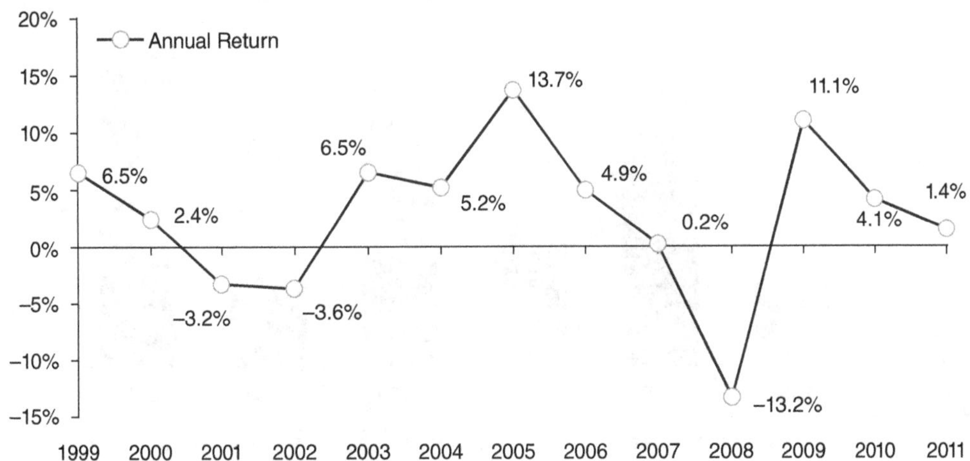

Exhibit 4.4
Future Plan PE Commitments (in € millions)

	Bellex Capital	Arkridge Capital	Infrastructure Fund	Total
H2 2005	93.54			**93.54**
H1 2006		82.13		**82.13**
H2 2006			68.64	**68.64**
H1 2007				
H2 2007	61.24			**61.24**
H1 2008				
H2 2008				
H1 2009				
H2 2009				
H1 2010	106.47	59.82		**166.29**
Total	**261.25**	**141.95**	**68.64**	**471.83**

Exhibit 4.5
Future Plan Alternative Investment Asset Allocation

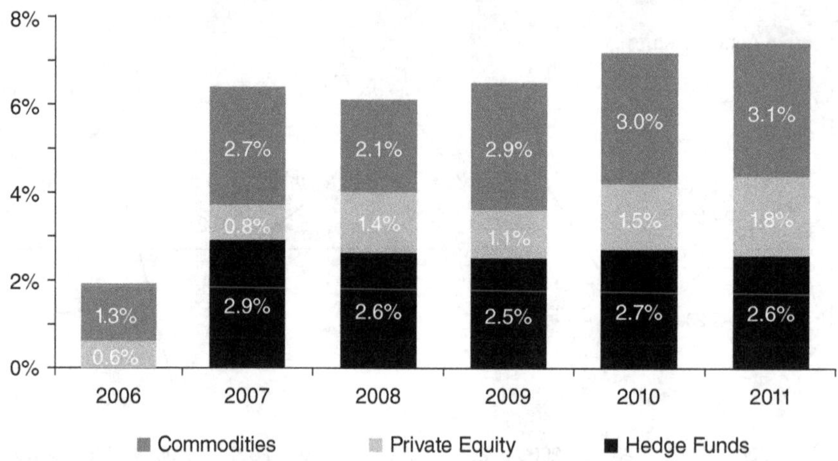

Exhibit 4.6
Future Plan PE Target Allocation vs. Actual Exposure

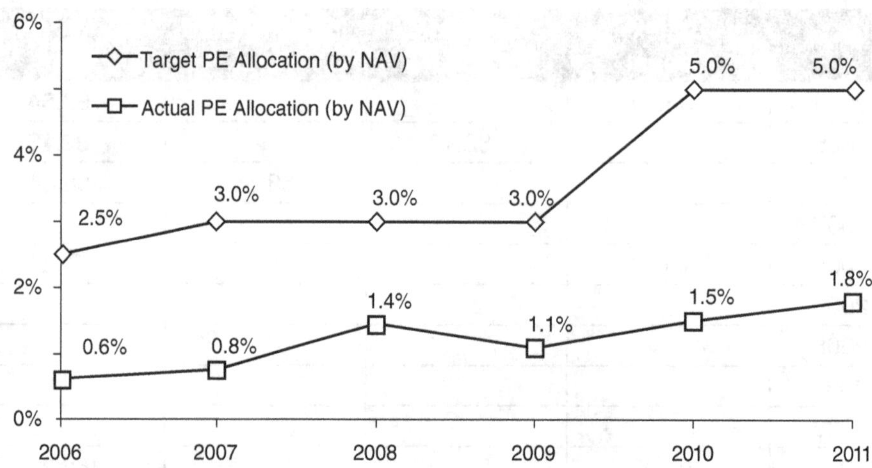

Exhibit 4.7
Future Plan PE Portfolio Performance

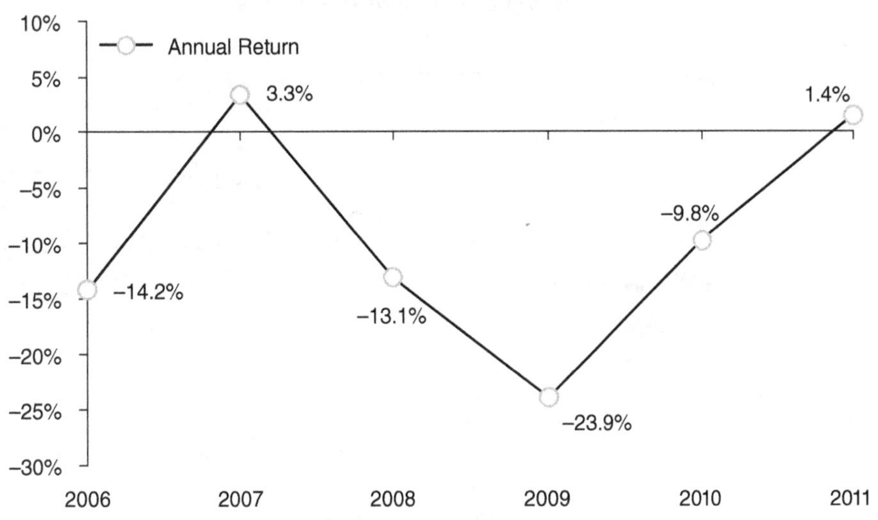

Exhibit 4.8a
Evolution of a Primary PE Fund Offering
(€10 million commitment, net of fees)

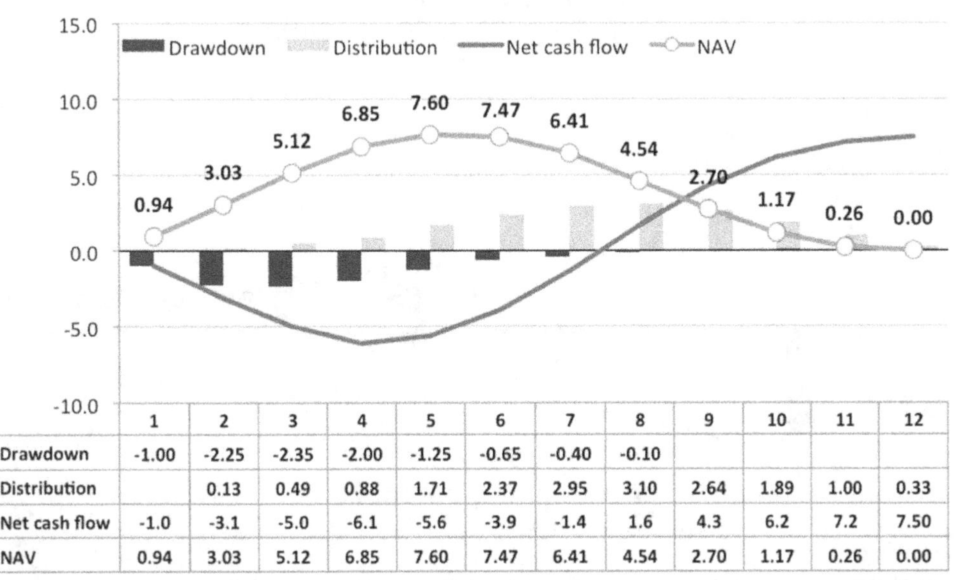

	1	2	3	4	5	6	7	8	9	10	11	12
Drawdown	-1.00	-2.25	-2.35	-2.00	-1.25	-0.65	-0.40	-0.10				
Distribution		0.13	0.49	0.88	1.71	2.37	2.95	3.10	2.64	1.89	1.00	0.33
Net cash flow	-1.0	-3.1	-5.0	-6.1	-5.6	-3.9	-1.4	1.6	4.3	6.2	7.2	7.50
NAV	0.94	3.03	5.12	6.85	7.60	7.47	6.41	4.54	2.70	1.17	0.26	0.00

Exhibit 4.8b

Evolution of a Secondary PE Investment

(€10 million commitment, net of fees)

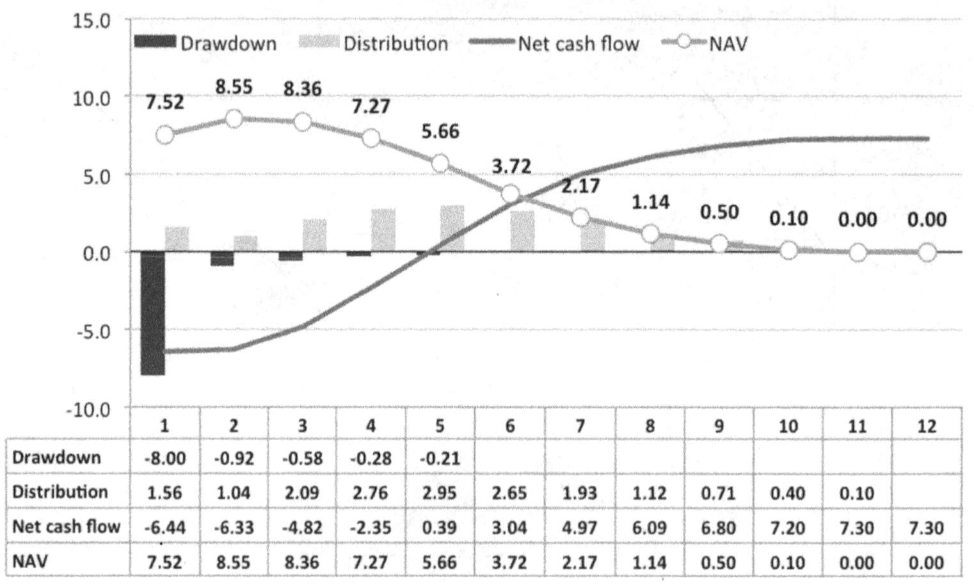

	1	2	3	4	5	6	7	8	9	10	11	12
Drawdown	-8.00	-0.92	-0.58	-0.28	-0.21							
Distribution	1.56	1.04	2.09	2.76	2.95	2.65	1.93	1.12	0.71	0.40	0.10	
Net cash flow	-6.44	-6.33	-4.82	-2.35	0.39	3.04	4.97	6.09	6.80	7.20	7.30	7.30
NAV	7.52	8.55	8.36	7.27	5.66	3.72	2.17	1.14	0.50	0.10	0.00	0.00

Exhibit 4.8c

Evolution of a Direct PE Investment

(€10 million investment)

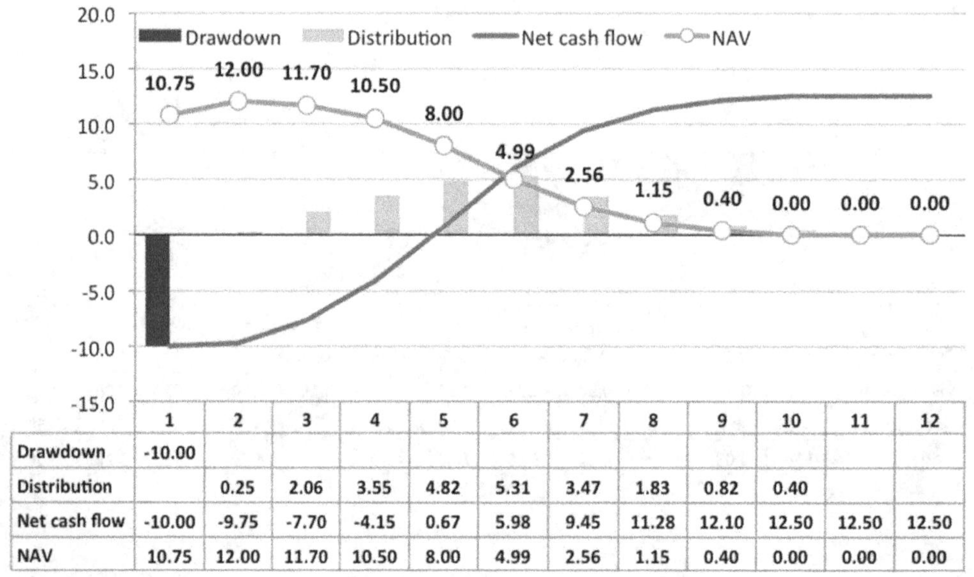

	1	2	3	4	5	6	7	8	9	10	11	12
Drawdown	-10.00											
Distribution		0.25	2.06	3.55	4.82	5.31	3.47	1.83	0.82	0.40		
Net cash flow	-10.00	-9.75	-7.70	-4.15	0.67	5.98	9.45	11.28	12.10	12.50	12.50	12.50
NAV	10.75	12.00	11.70	10.50	8.00	4.99	2.56	1.15	0.40	0.00	0.00	0.00

Exhibit 4.9

Partners Groups' Relative Value Matrix – H1 2012

<table>
<tr><th></th><th colspan="12">North America</th><th colspan="12">Europe</th><th colspan="12">Asia/emerging markets</th></tr>
<tr><td>Private equity</td><td colspan="4">Directs</td><td colspan="4">Secondaries</td><td colspan="4">Primaries</td><td colspan="4">Directs</td><td colspan="4">Secondaries</td><td colspan="4">Primaries</td><td colspan="4">Directs</td><td colspan="4">Secondaries</td><td colspan="4">Primaries</td></tr>
<tr><td>Growth capital</td><td colspan="4">Directs</td><td colspan="4">Secondaries</td><td colspan="4">Primaries</td><td colspan="4">Directs</td><td colspan="4">Secondaries</td><td colspan="4">Primaries</td><td colspan="4">Directs</td><td colspan="4">Secondaries</td><td colspan="4">Primaries</td></tr>
<tr><td>Private debt</td><td colspan="4">Directs</td><td colspan="4">Direct Secondaries</td><td colspan="4">Primaries</td><td colspan="4">Directs</td><td colspan="4">Direct Secondaries</td><td colspan="4">Primaries</td><td colspan="4">Directs</td><td colspan="4">Direct Secondaries</td><td colspan="4">Primaries</td></tr>
<tr><td>Private infrastructure</td><td colspan="3">Brownfield</td><td colspan="3">Greenfield</td><td colspan="3">Directs</td><td colspan="3">Secondaries</td><td colspan="3">Brownfield</td><td colspan="3">Greenfield</td><td colspan="3">Directs</td><td colspan="3">Secondaries</td><td colspan="3">Brownfield</td><td colspan="3">Greenfield</td><td colspan="3">Directs</td><td colspan="3">Secondaries</td></tr>
<tr><td>Private real estate</td><td colspan="3">Value-added</td><td colspan="3">Opportunistic</td><td colspan="3">Directs</td><td colspan="3">Secondaries</td><td colspan="3">Value-added</td><td colspan="3">Opportunistic</td><td colspan="3">Directs</td><td colspan="3">Secondaries</td><td colspan="3">Value-added</td><td colspan="3">Opportunistic</td><td colspan="3">Directs</td><td colspan="3">Secondaries</td></tr>
<tr><td>Listed strategies</td><td colspan="6">Listed private equity</td><td colspan="6">Listed infrastructure</td><td colspan="6">Commodities</td><td colspan="6">Fixed income</td><td colspan="6">Insurance-linked securities</td><td colspan="6">Opportunistic</td></tr>
</table>

Exhibit 4.10

Partners Group Proposed Holding Structure & Services

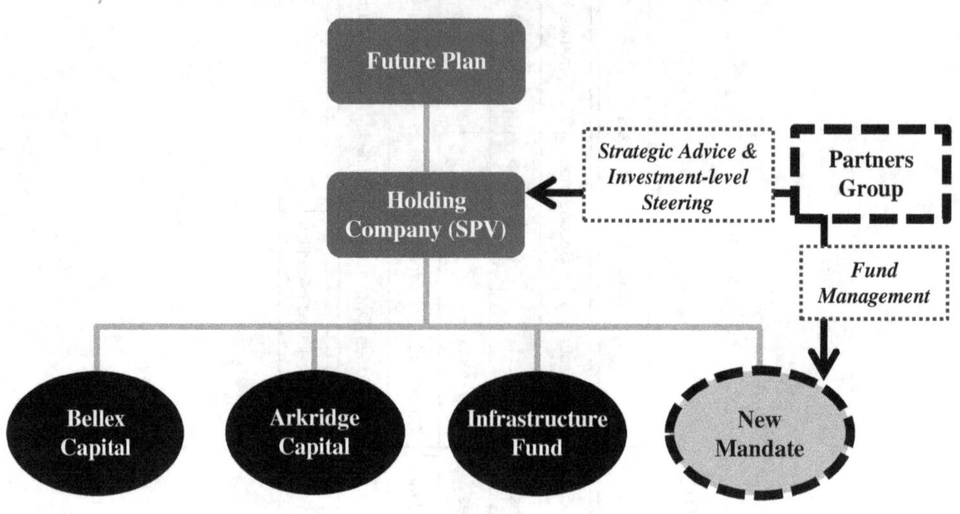

Exhibit 4.11

Private Market Expected Returns and Volatility (by segment)

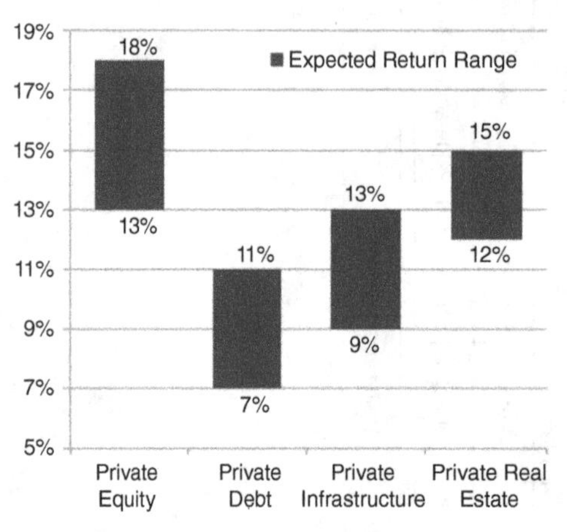

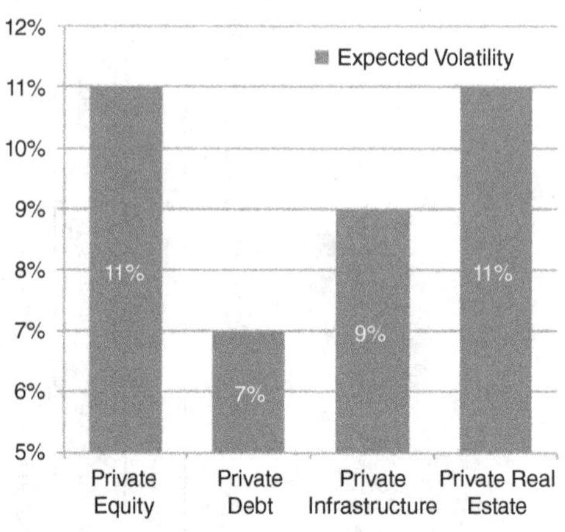

SECTION II
Venture Capital

The venture investor must always be on call to advise, to persuade, to dissuade, to encourage, but always to help build. Then venture capital becomes true creative capital—creating growth for the company and financial success for the investing organization.

—**George F. Doriot,** INSEAD Founder, Architect and Founder of the first venture capital firm (ARD) and often referred to as the "Father of Venture Capital"

CASE

5 SULA VINEYARDS
INDIAN WINE?—CE N'EST PAS POSSIBLE!

SYNOPSIS

The case focuses on early-stage and seed investments in an emerging-markets setting. After winning a 19% market share in the Indian wine market in less than four years, Sula Vineyards' founder Rajeev Samant is looking for an external investor to expand its business and further scale operations. Enter Deepak Shahdadpuri who founded Gem India Advisors (GIA) in 2004 to invest very early in young, up-and-coming start-ups in India. The case describes the opportunities, risks and assumptions associated with this investment, and asks students to arrive at a valuation for the fledgling business.

PEDAGOGICAL OBJECTIVE OF THE CASE

The case is designed to step students through the valuation and deal structure of a venture capital investment in India, using the Sula Vineyards example. Can a valuation using discounted cash flow (DCF) and comparables be a meaningful way to arrive at a fair price for the venture capitalist's stake? What deal structure can protect the investor from the inherent risks in this deal? The case allows for a detailed discussion of the critical questions venture investors need to answer pre-investment as well as an exploration of post-investment growth initiatives.

SUGGESTED ASSIGNMENT QUESTIONS

1. What are the key investment risks for Shahdadpuri in GIA's investment in Sula? Suggest ways to mitigate each.
2. Using comparables and DCF analysis, decide how GIA should determine the enterprise value of Sula at January 1, 2005. What are the key assumptions regarding growth, capex, and so on?
3. What share of Sula should GIA ask for and at what valuation? Why?
4. How should GIA structure the shareholders' agreement to protect against downside risks?
5. What role should GIA play in Sula post-investment? How do you propose GIA should scale the business? What constraints are currently limiting Sula's growth?

ADDITIONAL RESOURCES

To make the most of this case study, we suggest the following additional sources to provide context and background information:

- In particular, we recommend the following chapters from *Mastering Private Equity—Transformation via Venture Capital, Minority Investments & Buyouts*
  - Chapter 1 Private Equity Essentials
  - Chapter 2 Venture Capital
  - Chapter 7 Target Valuation
  - Chapter 9 Deal Structuring
- You may also refer to the book website for further material:
  www.masteringprivateequity.com

Sula Vineyards

Indian Wine – "Ce n'est pas possible !"

03/2015-5668

This case was written by Dhruv Narain and Romain Kapadia, research associates, and Liz Scott, case writer, at INSEAD Case Development Centre, Abu Dhabi, under the direction of Claudia Zeisberger, Senior Affiliate Professor of Decision Sciences and Entrepreneurship and Family Enterprise at INSEAD. It is intended to be used as a basis for class discussion rather than to illustrate either effective or ineffective handling of an administrative situation.

This case was developed with the financial contribution of the Abu Dhabi Education Council, whose support is gratefully acknowledged.

Additional material about INSEAD case studies (e.g., videos, spreadsheets, links) can be accessed at cases.insead.edu.

Introduction

It was January 2005 and Deepak Shahdadpuri, Managing Director of GEM India Advisors (GIA), swirled his glass of Shiraz carefully as he let his mind wander for a couple of minutes. He was thinking about his year in Fontainebleau, France, where he had started to develop a keen and intricate knowledge of fine wine whilst studying for his MBA at INSEAD. He smiled to himself as he wondered whether that knowledge was about to prove a more valuable investment than the tuition fees paid at the time. As he raised his pen to sign the shareholders' agreement on his latest investment, his mind wandered back to his first meeting with Rajeev Samant, CEO of Sula Wines, six years earlier in December 1998. Introduced through mutual friends while on vacation in Goa, Shahdadpuri and Samant had formed an immediate bond through their shared passion for "the good life", as Samant put it. Since that time, the friendship had continued to develop on periodic vacations and Shahdadpuri had acted as an informal advisor on Samant's business.

From its introduction into the Indian market in 2000, with an initial production capacity of just 30 acres, Sula had grown to become India's second-largest wine producer, distributor and retailer in just four and a half years. Differentiating the brand from other domestic growers, Sula was the first wine to vaunt its Indian heritage and local production as a positive marketing attribute, reflecting a new pride in Indian products and confidence that its quality was comparable to Californian, Australian and European wines.

Shahdadpuri's interest and involvement in Sula had grown along with the business. Yet despite the brand's successful track record and favourable economic conditions, he still had several concerns. Owing to a lack of relevant market data and previous transactions in India's wine and spirits industry, Shahdadpuri's first concern was whether he was appropriately valuing his investment in Sula. Secondly, he worried about the legal uncertainty surrounding wine-making and alcohol distribution in India, which was separately regulated by all 22 Indian states. Adding to his uncertainty was what he felt were growth assumptions based on very little information, as well as potential competitive pressures from India's largest spirits companies, including United Breweries, which was known to aggressively target new products and markets. Moreover, although steep import duties had effectively curtailed competition from imported wines in the past, how long would this continue going forward? Above all, Shahdadpuri was concerned about his friendship with Samant. He knew a strained business relationship could potentially ruin their longstanding friendship – the old adage "business and friendship don't mix" resonated in his head.

Sula Wines

The CEO of Sula had not followed a conventional path to establishing Sula Vineyards as one of India's leading winemakers; it was more the outcome of a handful of other ideas pursued before eventually settling on winemaking. After leaving India in the early 1990s to pursue degrees in Economics and eventually Industrial Engineering from Stanford University, Samant had been hired by Oracle in San Francisco. He soon became one of the company's youngest finance managers. However, with his professional and family ambitions focused on India, he left Oracle after two years to return to Mumbai.

More than a year had passed since his return when he decided to visit his family's estate in Nashik, a region two hours north of Mumbai. Located in the foothills of India's western mountain ranges, the picturesque setting inspired Samant to convince his family not to sell their 30-acre plot so that he could use the land to grow mangoes. However, as he pursued that idea, he became less convinced about the long-term viability of a mango business: there appeared to be plenty of local competition and an extremely fragmented retail market. Ultimately, he was not convinced that the export market for mangoes had the sort of margins that would make the business sustainable. He was, however, more familiar with the favourable economics of winemaking. While at Stanford he had often been struck by the similarities in climate and vegetation between California's wine country and the Nashik region. Hence, Samant eventually settled on the idea of using the land to grow grapes.

A lot of climatic data later and a chance encounter with his future business partner, Kerry Dempskey, a leading winemaker from California's Sonoma Valley, led Samant to form Sula Vineyards in 1998. The two eventually established Nashik Vinters Limited (NVL) in 2002, to take advantage of favourable government regulations and a growing demand for Sula products. Initially incubated with Rs30 million in seed capital that was used to construct a state-of-the-art winery on the family estate, Sula entered India's wine market when both the market and domestic competition were nearly non-existent. In addition, wine imports were rarely distributed as steep tariffs and high prices kept them beyond the reach of most Indians. As a result, consumer interest and knowledge of wine products were low.

Since its creation, Sula's product portfolio had grown to include the *Sula* and *Madera* brands of domestically produced wine at its Nashik vineyards. (See Exhibit 5.1 for Sula's product range and pricing as at 1 January 2005.) The company also imported and distributed brand name wines from leading producers around the world, including Taittinger Champagne (France), BRL Hardy (Australia) and Taylor's Port (Portugal), as well as imported bulk wines for distribution under Sula brands in India. Sula's bulk import, Chilean Merlot, sold under the *Satori Merlot* brand, established a leadership position in the red wine market in India's metropolitan capital Mumbai.[1] By 2005, Sula was commanding a 19% share of the market for all wine sold in India, irrespective of origin, and had doubled its output each year since 2000, with growth in demand still outpacing the increase in supply.

Sula had successfully lobbied the state and federal government on the economic benefits of the development of India's wine regions. As a result, several government initiatives had been taken to nurture the wine industry, including the Maharashtran state government announcing an excise and sales tax reduction after reclassifying wine as an agro-product. The regulatory structure in other states was also encouraging; rules regarding retail wine sales (i.e., through grocery stores) continued to be relaxed and further easing was expected in the future.

To date the company had raised a total of US$1.3 million from the original founders and business angels. Since setting up NVL, revenues had grown from US$620,000 in the year ending 31 March 2002 to US$2.5 million for the year ending 31 March 2004. The company forecasted revenues of US$4.3 million and an EBITDA of US$890,000 for 2005. Sula was now seeking additional investment from outside investors to increase

1. Satori Merlot would later be produced locally by Sula and no longer imported.

its production capacity and distribution, strengthen its marketing efforts, fortify its management team and introduce new product extensions to meet its growth projections.

GEM India Advisors

GEM India Advisors, an Indian private equity fund focused on India's blossoming consumer sector, was led by Shahdadpuri, a private equity veteran with over 16 years of private equity and strategy consulting experience. Despite focusing on the technology sector for the past four years, his numerous annual visits to India had convinced him of the investment opportunity that India's consumer space represented, and which had been largely overlooked by most funds at that time. Seeking to capitalise on this opportunity, in 2004, and in conjunction with GEM Advisors New York, Shahdadpuri set up GEM India Advisors with a clear mandate to invest in consumer-related businesses in the country. Although he had considered investing in several other initial transactions prior to Sula, according to Shahdadpuri the deciding factor was the ease and comfort he felt in dealing with Samant, and the mutual trust and respect that existed between the two. Nevertheless, Shahdadpuri's future reputation would rely on the success or failure of GIA's first investment in India.

The Indian Wine Industry

Although India was the largest consumer of spirits in the world by volume and the second largest consumer of alcoholic beverages after China, its wine sales in 2004 accounted for less than 0.20% of all alcoholic beverages sold. On a per capita basis, India lagged behind other countries with an average wine consumption of 0.1 litres annually, compared with the global average of 6 litres.

GIA estimated the size of the Indian wine market in 2004, based on consumption, to be in the vicinity of 2.7 million litres annually (see Exhibit 5.2). This was expected to double to over 5 million litres in the next three years, and to increase tenfold to reach well over 20 million litres annually by 2014. Between 2000 and 2004, the percentage of domestically produced wine was estimated to have taken market share from imported wines, increasing from 44% to 69% of the total wine market over the period. Compared with sales of hard liquor such as whisky, brandy and rum, however, wine consumption remained relatively low, with annual consumption of hard liquor estimated to amount to over 500 million litres. Nevertheless, as wine increased in popularity it was expected to take away market share from spirits.

At the time of Sula's development in the late 1990s, the domestic Indian wine industry was almost non-existent. Steep tariffs on imported wines kept the price of imported wines high and out of the reach of most citizens. Meanwhile, a lack of domestic production and of the expertise needed to cultivate and distribute wine hindered the growth of domestic vineyards. Cultural factors also constrained demand. Following several centuries of British colonial rule, the market for alcoholic beverages had been influenced by British tastes, and consumption of whisky, beer, rum and gin far exceeded demand for other types of alcohol with origins in continental and Eastern Europe such as wine and vodka. Equally, alcohol consumption in India was culturally more acceptable among men than women, while wine was perceived to be more of a "female" drink. As a result, the number of wines offered within the country, imported or domestically produced, was extremely limited.

Sula faced initial competition from two domestic growers, Champagne Indage and Grover Vineyards. Champagne Indage was India's oldest wine producer, commanded a 60% market share, and was largely credited with developing the wine industry within the country. Indage produced three categories of wine: white, red and sparkling, and marketed a total of 25 products under various brand names. Its top brand alone, *Riviera*, accounted for 15% in volume and 12% of the value of India's total wine market. Indage owned 200 acres of land and utilised an additional 750 acres under contract, with plans to add an additional 1,000 acres to its capacity in the near future. The company had a unique strategy of marketing its products through restaurants and bars owned by the Indage Hotel Group, which owned numerous upscale properties in India's major metropoli. Although a publicly traded company, 60% of the company was still controlled by the founding family. For the year ending 31 March 2004, Indage reported sales of Rs254 million (US$5.9 million), EBITDA of Rs59 million (US$1.4 million) and a net profit of Rs34 million (US$0.8 million).

Sula's other competitor, Grover Vineyards, had been established in 1988 at the foot of the Nandi Hills on the outskirts of Bangalore by promoters Kanwal and Kapil Grover, who had made a personal mission of reviving India's wine industry. By 2005, Grover had over 200 acres under cultivation and used only French wine grapes, selected exclusively from the original 35 varieties of the *Vitis Vinifera* species. Grover also marketed several varieties of wine under its signature brand names but did not import any.

Several factors supported the growth of the Indian wine industry starting in the early 2000s, namely favourable government regulations and India's changing consumer demographics. State wine policies were increasingly liberalised to the advantage of India's wine producers. Maharashtra, home to India's largest city, Mumbai, announced plans to reduce the sales tax on wine from 20% to 4%. Rajasthan, close to Delhi, also liberalised its regulations governing wine distribution, the largest state to do so thus far. Further, a new measure was passed that completely eliminated excise duties from wine manufactured in new wineries in India after 2001.

In addition to looser regulations, changes in consumer attitudes and behaviour were impacting the market for Indian wines. With a booming economy, increased media exposure to the west and a young, globally-minded population, alcohol consumption (including wine) was increasingly part of the new urban lifestyle. It was not uncommon for young adults in India to aspire to lifestyles portrayed by American movies and media.

As a result of these factors, since the 1990s the wine industry had grown 22% per year and had an expected compound annual growth rate (CAGR) of 25% for the coming decade.[2] Due to the limited number of producers and weak brand recognition outside India for domestically produced wines, the export market remained small but was expected to expand in the coming years.

The Global Wine Industry

By 2005, the global wine industry was estimated to be worth US$87 billion in sales, growing at 5% annually.[2] The United States led in New World vineyards based on production; it tied with China with regard to the size of new wine-growing areas.[3]

2. Source: GIA, Investment Memorandum, April 2005.
3. Source: CIES, countrywide bodies, ABN AMRO estimates.

Australia was reported to be leading New World wine exports, and in 2003, excluding intra-EU trade, was estimated to be the world's largest exporter in terms of volume. Chile, the US, South Africa and New Zealand were other New World producers also experiencing rapid growth in exports.[4]

The leading wine-producing countries globally in order of litres produced were France, Italy, Spain, the US and Argentina, while the largest consuming countries were France, Italy, the US, Germany and Spain[5] (see Exhibit 5.3). Although the global wine industry continued to grow, Old World producers were becoming less influential and experienced slower growth than New World producers and emerging markets. However, consumers in older markets continued to trade up to higher quality products, resulting in increased overall sales despite steady or even declining volumes of consumption.

Over the past decade, China had become the fastest growing market in terms of total wine consumption, admittedly starting out from an initial low base. More interestingly, the volume growth in wine consumption far exceeded that of other alcoholic drinks. This was partially driven by the affordability of wine in comparison with other alcoholic beverages in the country. Other factors affecting wine consumption in China, which were also relevant to the Indian market, included the influence of western eating and drinking habits and rising average incomes.[6] By 2005, China ranked 11 in terms of grape wine production. Many industry experts thus saw China as one of the greatest opportunities for both production and consumption globally.

India's growth as a wine producer could be compared to New Zealand in the late 1960s and early 1970s, when that country underwent similar legal, political and social changes that had encouraged the growth of the domestic wine industry. The late 1960s marked the end of the "Six o'clock swill" in New Zealand, where bars were forced to shut at 6 o'clock in the evening and remain closed on Sundays. Concurrent legislative reforms permitted "bring your own" licenses for restaurants, allowing customers to bring their own alcohol when dining out. Both of these changes had had a profound effect on New Zealand's attitudes towards alcohol consumption, and wine in particular. It was also a time when many New Zealanders began travelling, living and working in Europe, and were thus exposed to Europe's distinctive wine-drinking culture.

In 1973 Britain had entered the European Economic Community, ending a longstanding trade partnership in meat and dairy products between Britain and New Zealand. Losing its biggest meat and dairy trade partner forced New Zealand's government to rethink agricultural policy and consequently focus on the development of alternative industries such as viticulture, which encouraged the growth of vineyards and wine production in New Zealand. From 1995 to 2004, total annual wine production in New Zealand had grown from 56.4 million litres to 119.2 million, with productive vineyard hectares growing from 6,110 to 18,112 over the same period. New Zealand had a thriving export business and its Sauvignon Blanc was considered by many wine experts to be the best in the world. In contrast to India, however, New Zealand's small

4. Wittwer, G. & Rothfield, J. "Projecting the world wine market from 2003 to 2010", Centre of Policy Studies, Monash University, Australia; *Australasian Agribusiness Review* – Vol.13 – 2005, Paper 21, ISSN 1442-6951.
5. "Global Wine Production, Consumption and Trade, 1961 to 2001, A Statistical Compendum", CIES, University of Adelaide, Australia.
6. http://www.wines-info.com/Newshtml/200907/2282009072811164753.html.

population limited domestic consumption and the vast majority of production was for the export market.

Parallels could be drawn between the Chinese, New Zealand and Indian wine industries in terms of changing consumer attitudes towards wine consumption, influenced in part by increasing exposure to western lifestyles, the correlation observed between rising per capita GDP and wine consumption, and changing government policies promoting the wine industry.

Valuation

One of the real challenges for Shahdadpuri remained the valuation of the company itself. Although comparable transactions were often the best metric for valuing venture investments, there was little meaningful information available on comparable companies within India. With growth assumptions based on very general demographic data and trends, he was extremely conscious of the risks to valuation that came from demand issues as well as production and distribution.

These included any number of operating risks, such as disagreements with or disengagement by wine-making expert and equity partner Kerry Damskey with Samant, pest infestations in the vineyards, problems with the barrelling process, costs rising on any of the inputs, falling consumer demand in the event of a deterioration in brand image or quality, and the emergence of a strong competing brand. Furthermore, there was always the potential threat of greater competition from foreign wines as the local market expanded, tastes became increasingly sophisticated, and the attractiveness of gaining a larger share of the expanding market for wine in India grew, bringing competition from foreign exporters. Added to this was the possibility of the government reducing tariffs on imported wine in the future.

Shahdadpuri asked his team to probe the assumptions underlying their estimates of future market growth and the ability of Sula to retain or grow market share. If the market had grown 22% on a CAGR basis in the last 10 years, was this alone a reasonable basis for future growth, and, if so, how much market share could Sula hold on to? His first task was then to develop a "base case" scenario using historical financial and market data to make a pre-money enterprise value valuation:

Figure 5.1

Sula Wines – Historical Performance

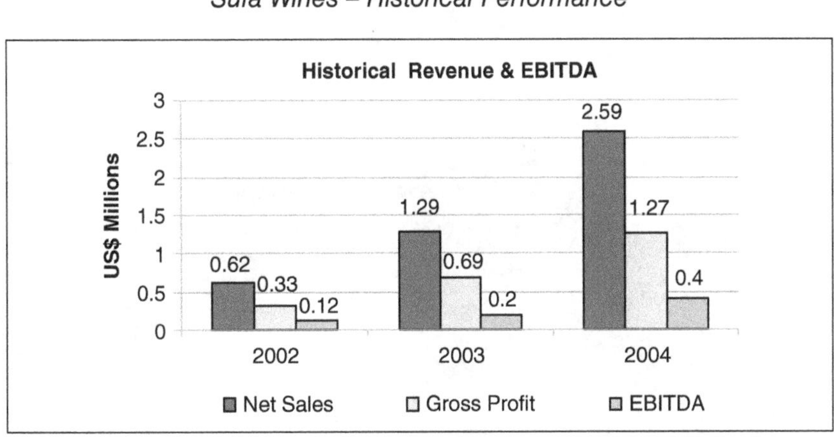

Even after making all the growth rate and cost assumptions to get to this point, several serious questions had perplexed the team at GIA:

- What period should they amortize the assets over?
- What discount rate should they use?
- What was the terminal value of the business?

In addition, Shahdadpuri and his team needed to examine how much equity they would seek to put into the company, what equity and voting share they would be able to negotiate, and what representation and control they could exercise in the company. In preparing their analysis, Shahdadpuri's team also asked for guidance on a potential exit strategy from the investment in the future.

Conclusion

Despite these many concerns, Shahdadpuri wanted to pursue the investment in Sula. The key to this was correctly analysing and determining the value of the investment, identifying the key areas of risk in the transaction and mitigating them. As he penned his signature on the shareholders' agreement, solidifying his company's investment in Sula, he took another sip of the Shiraz. "Life is risky," he thought, "but without risk it would be extremely boring."

Exhibit 5.1

Product Positioning, 1 January 2005

Product Positioning	Low (< Rs 150) (< $3.30)	Middle (Rs 150–250) ($3.30–5.60)	Premium (Rs 250–350) ($5.60–8.00)	Super Premium (Rs 350–500) ($8.00–12.00)	Super Premium (> Rs 500) (> $12.00)
Red		Madera Red (Rs180) ($4.00)	Satori Merlot (Rs 350) ($8.00)	Sula Cabernet Shiraz (Rs 395) ($9.00)	Sula Dindori Shiraz Reserve (Rs 550) ($13.00)
White		Madera White (Rs180) ($4.00)	Sula Chenin Blanc (Rs 350) ($8.00) Pacifica Chardonnay (Rs 350) ($8.00)	Sula Sauvignon Blanc (Rs 450) ($10.00)	
Rose		Madera Rose (Rs 180) ($4.00)	Salu Blush Zinfandel (Rs 350) ($8.00)		
Sparkling			Sula Seco (Rs 340) ($7.75)	Sula Brut (Rs 475)	
Dessert					Sula Late Harvest Chenin Blanc (Rs 550) ($13.00)

Source: Sula Wines

Exhibit 5.2

The Indian Wine Market

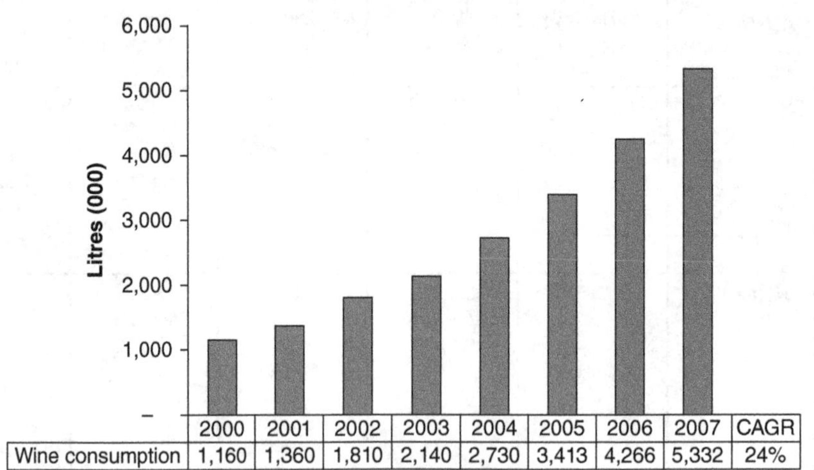

Between 2000 and 2004, the percentage of domestically produced wine has increased from 44% of the market to 69% of the market.

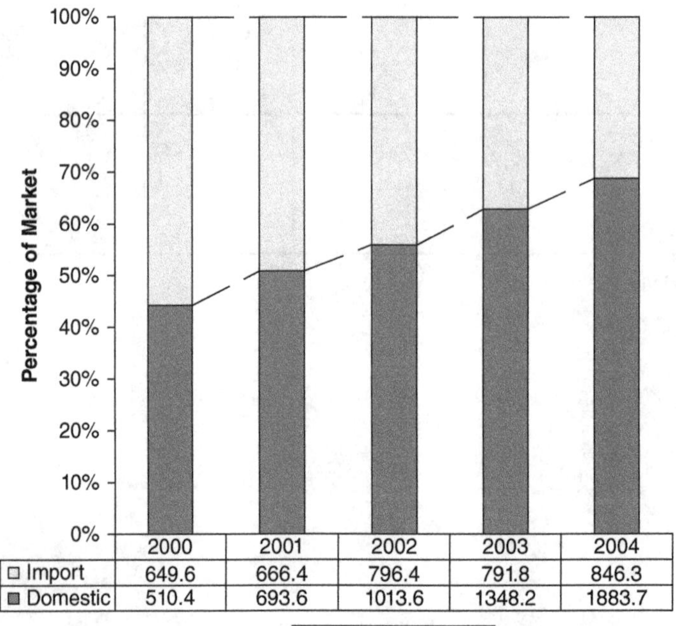

Source: GEM India Advisors

Exhibit 5.3

The Global Wine Industry

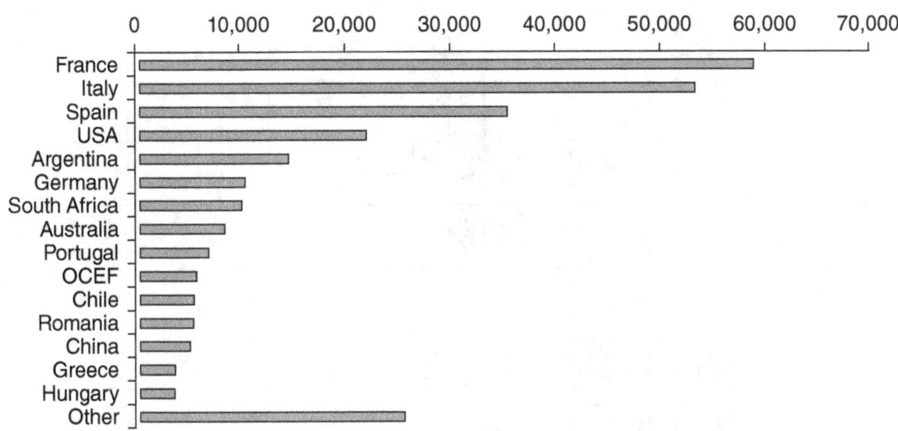

Source: Global Wine Production, Consumption and Trade, 1961 to 2001 A Statistical Compendium, CIES, University of Adelaide.

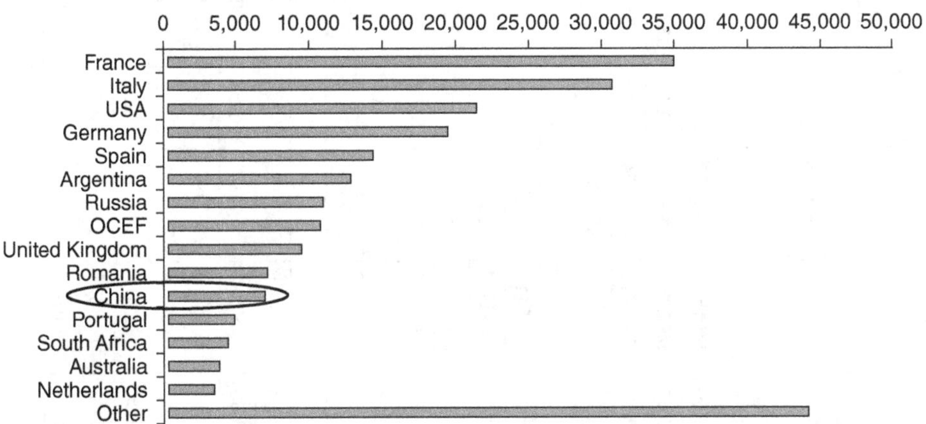

Source: Global Wine Production, Consumption and Trade, 1961 to 2001 A Statistical Compendium, CIES, University of Adelaide.

Exhibit 5.4

Industry Comparables

GLOBAL ALCOHOLIC BEVERAGES VALUATION

	TKR	FY Mon	ML Rtg	Crncy	Local Price	Local Mkt Cap (mm)	Mkt Cap US$(mm)	EPS			PVE		EPS Growth			5 YR EPS%	5 YR PEG	05* EW EBITDA	05* CP MGN
								2004	2005	2006	2005	2006	2004	2005	2006				
NORTH AMERICA																			
ANHEUSER-BSCH	BLD	Dec	A-2-7	US$	$48.55	$39,354.6	$39,155	$2.56	$2.35	$2.95	17.7	16.5	4%	7%	7%	10.0	1.8	11.3	21.8%
BROWN FRMAN	BFB	Apr	NR	US$	$50.56	$6,158.2	$6,158	$2.19	$2.44	$2.68	20.7	18.9	20%	11%	10%	10.0	2.1	NA	17.2%
CONSTELLATION	**STZ**	**Feb**	**B-2-9**	**US$**	**$53.64**	**$6,233.0**	**$6,233**	**$2.65**	**$3.21**	**$3.70**	**16.7**	**14.5**	**6%**	**21%**	**15%**	**15.0**	**1.1**	**10.3**	**13.4%**
VINCOR	YVN	Mar	C-2-9	CAD	$32.69	$1,091.5	$874	$1.43	$2.25	NA	14.5	NA	–13%	57%	NA	11.0	1.3	10.0	15.3%
AVERAGE							**$52,620**				**17.4**	**16.6**	**–1%**	**24%**	**11%**	**11.5**	**1.6**	**10.5**	**17.7%**
EUROPEAN WINE & SPIRITS																			
ALLIED DOMECQ	ALDQF	Aug	B-2-7	GBP	515.00	5,541.4	$962	35.54	36.35	40.37	14.0	12.8	6%	4%	10%	10.3	1.4	10.4	23.3%
DIAGO	DGEAF	Jun	A-3-7	GBP	738.00	21,984.4	$3,778	48.19	46.58	49.77	15.8	14.8	1%	–3%	7%	6.2	2.5	11.2	23.3%
LVMH	LVMHF	Dec	B-1-7	EUR	55.00	26,948.6	$4,631	2.80	3.08	3.13	17.8	16.0	8%	10%	11%	0.6	1.0	10.2	19.5%
PERNOD RICARD	PDRDF	Dec	A-3-7	EUR	107.60	7,584.10	$1,303	6.62	7.08	7.79	15.2	14.0	6%	7%	9%	8.0	1.9	10.7	21.3%
REMY CONTR	REMYF	Mar	B-3-7	EUR	31.68	1,402.5	$241	1.66	1.61	1.69	10.7	18.7	.24%	–1%	6%	8.1	2.4	12.8	17.0%
AVERAGE							**$10,906**				**16.5**	**15.3**	**–1%**	**3%**	**8%**	**8.5**	**2.0**	**11.1**	**21.1%**
EUROPEAN/LAT AM BEER																			
CARLSBERG	CABJF	Dec	B-2-7	DMK	283.50	21,624.8	$3,716	15.8	21.15	25.94	13.4	10.9	–34%	33%	23%	9.7	1.4	7.7	7.2%
FEMSA	FMK	Dec	C-2-7	USD	56.35	5,970.1	$1,026	3.36	4.08	4.75	13.8	11.8	27%	22%	17%	14.4	1.0	8.3	15.9%
GRUPO MODELO	GPMCF	Dec	C-1-7	MDN	30.74	99,959.1	$127,643	1.72	1.92	2.05	16.0	14.9	15%	12%	7%	9.2	1.7	7.3	29.4%
HEINEKEN	HINKF	Dec	A-3-7	EUR	26.99	13,225.1	$16,914	1.51	1.58	1.69	17.1	16.0	–8%	4%	7%	4.9	3.5	9.9	13.4%
INBEV	IBRWF	Dec	B-1-7	EUR	29.00	17,284.0	$22,105	1.64	1.90	2.14	15.2	13.6	14%	16%	13%	12.9	1.2	7.9	11.5%
SABMILLER	SBWRF	Mar	B-2-7	USD	$15.40	18,387.6	$16,388	$0.76	$1.04	$1.15	14.9	13.4	44%	24%	11%	8.0	1.9	7.5	15.4%
SCTTISH & NWC	SNCNF	Dec	A-2-8	GBP	455.50	4,074.4	$7,570	29.31	32.00	34.54	14.2	13.2	.25%	9%	8%	7.0	2.0	11.6	19.9%
AVERAGE							**$197,562**				**15.0**	**13.4**	**5%**	**19%**	**12%**	**9.4**	**1.8**	**8.3**	**14.9%**

AUSTRALIAN WINE & BEER																			
FOSTER'S	FBRWF	Jun	A-2-7	AUD	5.45	10,864.1	$8,343	0.26	0.29	0.32	19.0	17.1	.13%	10%	11%	10.0	1.9	11.2	21.4%
SOUTHCORP	STHHF	Jun	–6-	AUD	4.41	3,255.3	$2,500	0.15	0.16	0.29	27.8	22.4	41%	9%	24%	5.0	5.6	16.2	15.1%
LION NATHAN	LNNTF	Sep	B-2-7	AUD	7.54	4,129.7	$3,171	0.42	0.46	0.59	16.2	15.0	8%	11%	9%	8.0	2.0	10.1	22.3%
AVERAGE							**$14,014**				**21.0**	**18.2**	**12%**	**10%**	**14%**	**7.7**	**3.2**	**12.5**	**19.6%**
ASIAN BEER																			
TSINGTAO	TSGTF	Dec	C-3-7	CNY	8.45	8,957.0	$1,148	0.22	0.26	0.23	33.0	30.0	9%	14%	16%	15.0	2.2	8.2	6.7%
ASAHI	ASBRF	Dec	B-2-7	JPY	1249.00	608,950.0	$5,761	50.30	94.10	84.30	14.9	14.0	1%	67%	0%	16.0	0.9	6.4	6.5%
KIRIN BREWERY	KNVWF	Dec	A-2-7	JPY	1022.00	993,129.5	$9,395	44.40	45.20	45.90	22.6	22.3	33%	2%	2%	8.1	2.8	6.5	6.5%
SAPPORO	SODBF	Dec	B-2-7	JPY	468.00	166,322.8	$1,573	18.20	24.51	25.12	10.0	18.6	162%	35%	2%	31.1	0.6	9.9	4.3%
AVERAGE							**$17,377**				**22.4**	**21.4**	**53%**	**30%**	**3%**	**17.6**	**1.6**	**7.5**	**6.0%**
GLOBAL ALCOHOLIC BEVERAGE AVERAGE							**$292,979**				**17.8**	**16.4**	**8%**	**15%**	**10%**	**9.6**	**1.9**	**9.3**	
S&P 500 (First CII)	**SPX**				**$1,192.0**			**$66.42**	**$70.33**	**$75.00**	**16.9**	**15.9**	**20%**	**6%**	**7%**				

Source: Merrill Lynch BLD's EPS includes option expenses. 'For those companies with fiscal year-ends in February or March we used forecast FY06 operating margins and EVBITDA estimates.

Exhibit 5.5
Transaction Comparables

Recent Industry Wine Acquisitions

Date	Acquiror	Asset		EBITDA (x)
12/95	Foster's	Mildara Blass	AUS	11.8
4/96	Foster's	Rothbury	AUS	11.0
4/96	Southcorp	Coldstream	AUS	19.4
4/97	Simeon	Australian Vntg	AUS	20.1
8/00	Vincor	RH Phillips	USA	9.0
8/00	Foster's	Beringer Wine	USA	11.5
1/01	Southcorp	Rosemount	AUS	13.0
2/01	Lion Nthn	Montana Wines	NA	12.0
8/01	Allied Dorn	Montana Wines	NA	12.4
8/01	Vincor	Hogue Cellars	USA	6.5
9/01	Allied Dorn	Bodega y Bbds	Spain	10.0
9/01	Lion Nthn	Banksia Wines	AUS	12.4
9/01	Vincor	Hogue	USA	11.5
10/01	BRL Hardy	BlackStone	USA	11.2
10/01	Lion Nthn	Petaluma	AUS	16.5
2/02	McGuigan	Simeon Wines	AUS	8.3
11/02	Vincor	Goundrey	AUS	9.6
3/03	Wine Grp	Glen Ellen	USA	4.2
6/02	Cranswick	Evans & Tate	AUS	8.8
7/02	Simeon	McGuigan	AUS	8.3
9/02	Lion Nthn	Wither Hills	NZ	10.4
1/03	Const Brnd	BRL Hardy	AUS	12.0
5/03	Vincor	Kim Crawford	AUS	6.0
7/04	Vincor	Western	AUS	10.6
7/04	Wine Grp	Golden State	USA	NA
12/04	Const Brnd	Robert Mondavi	USA	15.0
12/04	Diageo	Chalone Wine	USA	17.1
12/04	Const Brnd	Ruffino	Italy	NA
1/05	Foster's	Southcorp	AUS	15.4
1/05	EJ Gallo	Barefoot Cellars	USA	NA
	Average			11.6x

Source: Company reports and Merrill Lynch

Exhibit 5.6

Press Clipping

Indian Vintage Rivals New World

By Ian MacKinnon

The Times: London, UK September 8, 2003

Of all the hurdles that Rajeev Samant knew he would encounter when he decided to become one of only a handful of Indian wine-makers, there was one he never counted on: being able to keep pace with demand.

Yet Mr. Samant's Sula Vineyards, which recently pressed the fifth vintage of their flagship Sauvignon Blanc, have won higher praise than simply the enthusiasm of the Indian consumer. One prominent wine critic declared the wine "floral crisp and dry", well able to hold it's own with the New World offerings.

Wine has long been around in India, even getting a passing mention in the Kama Sutra. But in Hindu culture most are teetotal, while those who do indulge prefer something stronger - invariably whisky.

Mr. Samant, 36, likes to do things differently. With an engineering degree from Stanford University, he got a job at Oracle in San Francisco. He left after two years. After wondering what to do next the shipping entrepreneur's son set out to make his own wine on a piece of family land in Nasik after discovering that the climate there was ideal when teamed with the light, well-drained soil.

Production has doubled every year and will reach 500,000 bottles by December, but Sula cannot keep up with demand. Its success reflects how India's tastes are changing fast, especially among the newly affluent middle classes.

Wine consumption is increasing at 20 percent annually. Hip young professionals who travel abroad regularly are bringing home new habits and shunning hard liquor. "Shops in Bombay say that a decade ago wine was only a small fraction of their business. Now it's up to 10 percent", Mr. Samant said.

Sula is also winning a vote of confidence from foreign buyers. Last year 7,000 cases were shipped overseas, sold in shops and restaurants in San Francisco's Bay Area and imported by one of Italy's leading wine merchants. Orders also came from France this year.

"It 's great fun now and we're turning a small profit", Mr. Samant said. "But it was hard going at the start. All my friends thought I was crazy. They said it wouldn't work."

Indeed it took Mr. Samant 18 months to gather more than 100 official signatures needed to open the winery."I had a bundle of papers more than a foot thick", he said.

Others are now jumping on the bandwagon. Five wineries have opened in Nasik in the past year and officials have had expressions of interest from 40 others. Land that could not find a buyer a decade ago now goes for 14,000 an acre.

Sula's outgoings remain high because of so much of its raw materials have to be imported. Bottles come from France, yeast from Australia and wire cages for the methode champenoise from Spain. The grapes, however, are Indian and Mr. Samant believes they are the key ingredient that will ensure that he can keep the competition at bay.

CASE 6

ADARA VENTURE PARTNERS

BUILDING A VENTURE CAPITAL FIRM

SYNOPSIS

This case examines a critical decision the partners of a venture capital firm, Adara Venture Partners, need to take in June 2013. While raising their second fund, the partners face the prospect of an anchor investor pulling out because Adara has not yet assembled sufficient capital to meet the end-of-month deadline to complete the fund's first closing. Consequently, the partners are evaluating the possibility of the general partner (GP) itself underwriting a portion of the gap in the fund's total capital commitment—which involves weighing a host of critical issues at the heart of venture capital fund management: GP economics, fundraising strategy, investor relations and the fund's investment strategy.

PEDAGOGICAL OBJECTIVE OF THE CASE

An overarching objective of the case is for participants to understand the entrepreneurial challenge of building a venture capital firm from the ground up. The specific decision addressed in the case—whether or not the partners should proceed with underwriting a portion of the firm's second fund—allows participants to explore a host of issues that relate to the management of a venture capital firm.

SUGGESTED ASSIGNMENT QUESTIONS

1. What factors should the GP consider when deciding whether to underwrite a significant portion of a follow-on fund?
2. How much, if any, of the first closing commitments should the GP be willing to underwrite?
3. What are the implications of not underwriting, apart from the obvious risk of not closing the fund ahead of the anchor investor's deadline?

If they do decide to underwrite:

4. How should the GP position its decision to underwrite a larger stake in the fund with limited partners (LPs) that have already committed to participate in the first closing? What would you expect the reaction from LPs would be to the possibility of a larger GP stake in the fund?
5. How would you assess the probability of the partners being capable of placing their underwritten stake after the first close, both in terms of amount and in terms of timing?
6. How would you suggest the GP market its own underwritten portion to potential investors? Should the placement approach change over time?
7. Should the GP prioritize (a) placing the underwrite or (b) increasing the size of the fund as it has conversations with potential LPs following the first closing?
8. Are there any potential conflicts of interest in the ongoing management of the fund resulting from a stake underwritten by the GP? How can the partners mitigate these?

9. What are the potential interrelationships between the structure of the first closing (underwritten or not) and the implementation of the investment strategy?

ADDITIONAL RESOURCES

To make the most of this case study, we suggest the following additional sources to provide context and background information:

- In particular, we recommend the following chapters from *Mastering Private Equity—Transformation via Venture Capital, Minority Investments & Buyouts*
  - Chapter 1 Private Equity Essentials
  - Chapter 2 Venture Capital
  - Chapter 16 Fund Formation
  - Chapter 17 Fundraising
- You may also refer to the book website for further material:
  www.masteringprivateequity.com

Adara Venture Partners

Building a Venture Capital Firm

10/2015-5822

This case was written by Vikas A. Aggarwal, Assistant Professor of Entrepreneurship and Family Enterprise at INSEAD, and Anne-Marie Carrick-Cagna, Research Associate with the INSEAD Centre for Entrepreneurship. It is intended to be used as a basis for class discussion rather than to illustrate either effective or ineffective handling of an administrative situation.

Additional material about INSEAD case studies (e.g., videos, spreadsheets, links) can be accessed at cases.insead.edu.

"After an intense ride full of highs and lows, we faced the prospect of either bailing out or doubling up on the bet, the effort and the risk ..."

It was late on a Friday afternoon at the beginning of June 2013. Nico Goulet and Alberto Gómez, co-founders of Adara Venture Partners, had just spent hours in a meeting discussing the dilemma the firm faced. They had successfully raised a first fund in 2006, and were inches away from closing a second. However, the pressure was mounting as the anchor investor had imposed a deadline of 30 June 2013, and they were short on commitments to meet the €30 million target for the fund's first close. The two partners had a stark choice: either underwrite the shortfall themselves or cancel the second fund.

The latter option would severely limit the prospects of the fledgling venture, jeopardizing nine years of intensive effort for the firm and its partners. However, the implications of underwriting the commitment themselves were equally daunting. Both Managing Partners faced a weekend of reflection, knowing that they needed to take a decision within the first days of the upcoming week.

Starting Out: The Origins

Upon graduation from INSEAD in 1992, Nico had begun work as a consultant at Monitor Company, based primarily in Madrid, Spain. During his eight years there he gained valuable experience in various sectors including information technology, telecommunications, pharmaceuticals, healthcare and defence. By 1999, however, he had grown weary of the consulting career path and was convinced that there was an opportunity in Spain to create a venture capital fund focused on early-stage technology firms. With so many new firms being started in the technology sector, early-stage capital to fund new ventures was hard to find.

In 2000, he had left the relative safety of his job at Monitor to start a venture fund, NetFractal. Over the next two years he raised over $18 million in equity and limited partnership commitments from financial institutions such as Deutsche Bank Asset Management, and proceeded to invest in three different projects:

"We worked on these three projects through 2002. By then two had already tanked with the dotcom collapse, and one was doing fine, but it was clear that a larger, more robust vehicle would be necessary to be sustainable in this market."

At the end of 2002, Nico met and teamed up with Alberto Gómez and Roberto de Saint-Malo, with whom he had a common interest in starting a venture capital fund in Spain (see Exhibit 6.1). With a vision of creating a firm that replicated the institutional features of the traditional venture capital model, the three founded Adara Venture Partners.

Convincing potential investors that technology in Spain was an attractive investment, however, was an entirely different matter. Nico and his partners had already identified many of the drivers of changes taking place in Spain, but it would take longer than they expected to get enough investors on board.

One of the team's first decisions was where to locate the fund. After looking into the possibility of Spain, they found that it was too complex – its burdensome regulations added to the operational constraints of funds. As a result, they looked at other possibilities, notably Belgium and Luxembourg. They finally settled on Luxembourg, where the fiscal and supervisory framework was already in place, and offered greater flexibility as compared to equivalent structures in Spain. Overall, its regulatory environment made it easier to replicate the limited partnership model.

Next, they needed to decide what form the fund would take, together with its investment strategy. It was agreed that Adara would aim to attract institutional money, and to focus on early-stage companies.

> *"We really wanted more institutional money than money from private individuals, without excluding these. The advantage of institutional funds is that they have a more systematic and longer-term approach to their investments. Their view is generally more objective, but also less personal."*

First Fundraising: Tough but Straightforward

The partners were convinced that they had the arguments to persuade investors that Spain was an attractive opportunity for a new fund targeted at early-stage technology firms. However, despite the breadth of their combined experience, they had no shared track record in this domain.

Two and half years later, in June 2005, Adara Ventures SICAR was officially created as an investment vehicle in Luxembourg. The first closing was on July 18, 2005 for a total of €40 million, and the final closing took place on March 30, 2006, bringing in total commitments of €50 million. Nico explained their approach:

> *"We had thought it would take just a year. It was true we didn't have a track record, but what we could say was that we had been working to find companies to invest in. We showed potential partners that we had sourced a real pipeline of potential portfolio companies. When we talked to the target companies we indicated that our aim was to be one of the largest venture capital funds focused on technology, and operating in Spain. We acted very much like an entrepreneurial start-up. We had to convince the LPs—but we had to find creative ways for them to share our complete conviction."*

It was during this first fundraising that the "statistical" hurdle became clear: to close one investor the team had to talk to almost ten prospects, a proportion that persisted in their future fundraising efforts.

The lead investors in Adara Ventures (Fund I) included the European Investment Fund through the European Communities Growth and Employment Initiative: MAP-ETF Start-Up Facility, pension funds from Telefónica, and several other institutions and family offices. In total there were 24 Limited Partners (8 institutional, representing 63% of commitments, and 16 private). Approximately 45% of the commitments came from Spain and the remainder were evenly split between Europe and the rest of the world. In 2007, another €5 million was added to the pool in the form of a co-investment agreement with NEOTEC, to be managed by Adara Venture Partners.

Investing the First Fund: Off to the Races

The deal flow turned out to be even better than the firm had expected, with a stream of high-quality, attractive investment opportunities. Adara reviewed almost 200 potential candidates during the fund raising process, and from these selected a pipeline of deals that were available for investment in the short term. The prospects had already been analysed and their development monitored for many months, so it was reasonably quick to finalize the due diligence process and enter into negotiation of the definitive investment agreement. This allowed the fund to deploy its capital rapidly. As a result, the investment period was shortened from five to three years. Alberto explained:

> *"In effect, we had been bootstrapping the fund, working for two years at no cost to the investors. This was consistent with the values which drive our entrepreneurial spirit and the interests of our investors and entrepreneurs we support. Our feeling is that investors were able to get a concrete feel for the manner in which we would be investing, and thus become comfortable that we would be capable of configuring a productive portfolio with their money.*
>
> *We began investing. These were exciting times. We had raised $55 million! We had a fund in a market where not many other funds were active. We were able to complete 13 investments during the three-year period until the end of the investment period."*

The shortened investment period ended in December 2008. By that time more than 500 opportunities had been screened and 13 investments completed across a variety of sectors including enterprise software, mobility, semiconductors, cyber security and collaboration. One of the investments had already experienced a swift exit with good investment performance (145% gross IRR), and the rest of the portfolio was evolving positively. There had only been one write-off (on one of its smaller investments).

Second Fund: First Attempt

The traditional view is that general partners (GPs) raise a successor fund at the time they finish configuring the portfolio of the initial fund—i.e. at the end of the investment period. Given that the management fee structure generally decreases at that time, the successor fund ensures that the GP maintains an adequate stream of revenue to support the team and its management activities on the live portfolio at the same time that it is deploying the successor fund.

So in mid-2008 the team set out to raise the firm's second fund… but soon hit a wall. It began with the series of events that included the collapse of Lehman Brothers, the bursting of the subprime bubble, and the initial phases of the global financial crisis and recession. At the same time, the portfolio was just not mature enough to provide visibility to interested LPs as to the potential returns that could be expected from the first fund.

Realizing that there was no way they were going to succeed in raising the second fund in these conditions, the partners decided to retreat and to focus their efforts on the first fund's portfolio. At this stage, investments had been made, but the fund had not yet completed a full cycle. As a result, it was nearly impossible to assess the companies' true potential—i.e., which ones would ultimately succeed or fail. As Nico put it:

> *"We hit a double whammy when we tried to raise the second fund. Second funds are always more difficult because of the need to demonstrate a track record, and given the exogenous conditions at the time this was no exception. Our portfolio was still very young and very difficult to assess, so we quickly realized that we had to buckle down and make things happen for the first fund before even entertaining the idea of raising a second fund."*

The 'Dark Ages'

Between 2008 and 2011 the firm endured a series of difficulties in which several trends came home to roost.

First, the natural evolution of the portfolio generated a series of write-offs. Between 2008 and 2011, three companies were sold back to the founders, and two larger investments were liquidated completely, resulting in full write-offs. These absorbed an inordinate amount of partner time. Despite reasonable progress on the more positive stories in the portfolio, it was difficult to judge which would be the winners among the six surviving companies.

Second, the financial performance of the fund in terms of its net asset value (NAV) was deep in the traditional J-curve, prompting nervous reactions from LPs and even a couple of small defaults among minor investors who decided to take the losses and cease supporting the fund.

Finally, the GP itself faced a shrinking budget, which led to the realization that the team could not sustain three full-time partners. Combined with discussions on the appropriate strategy for the eventual second fund, the situation prompted Roberto Saint Malo's exit from the management company after protracted negotiations.

Renaissance

In 2011, amid rumours that the euro (currency) might disappear, and as unemployment in Spain rose from 6% to 26%, the portfolio had wound down to five remaining companies. However, despite the turbulence, there were some successes in the portfolio, with one significant exit in 2011.

On entering 2012, the first fund had two exits with meaningful returns that it could show to investors. The portfolio was looking healthy, with no companies at imminent risk of failure, and two beginning to show promise. AlienVault and LoopUp began to exhibit the potential to become "dragons" in their own right.[1] The evolution of the portfolio sent a powerful message about the strategy of the next fund on the back of this emerging track record, in particular the performance of AlienVault.

1. "Dragons", or "Fund Returners" are investments that generate distributions equal to or greater than all investor commitments in one single exit. They require a combination of meaningful investment size and a very healthy multiple performance.

Founded in 2007 by Julio Casal in Madrid, AlienVault was the creator of a pre-eminent Open Source Security Information Management (OSSIM) security platform under the name *AlienVault Unified Security Management* (*AlienVault USM*). The OSSIM market had a 21.9% CAGR, and was likely to surpass $2.3 billion in 2014. Adara Ventures invested in its Series A in 2008, and helped drive the internationalization of the company, including a move to Silicon Valley in 2011. From there it went on to raise Series B, C and D funding rounds from blue chip Silicon Valley funds such as Trident Capital, Kleiner Perkins and Intel Capital. The company also attracted senior executives from HP and used its venture funds to expand its sales and marketing and R&D, becoming the global market leader in the SME segment.

In January 2013, AlienVault reported a doubling of its revenues as compared to 2012, with strong continuing growth metrics. The company also gained visibility with its community-sourced threat intelligence feed and database, the AlienVault Open Threat Exchange. It had successfully closed its Series D round of funding with GGV Capital, bringing total funds raised to more than $70 million. Given its market, team, investor base, board composition and the growth in revenues and valuation, this investment was quickly becoming one of the mainstays of the returns for Adara's first fund. It had the potential to radically alter the performance profile of the firm. Alberto commented:

> *"AlienVault obviously provided us with a strong message on the potential performance of the first fund, but it also provided another very strong component to us as we tried to raise the second fund. It was the perfect illustration of our strategy to invest early in local companies that leveraged the high quality and low cost of engineering resources, followed by a global expansion and move to Silicon Valley, where top-tier investors could lead the subsequent rounds. In this process our capital was deployed in a highly capital-efficient environment and enabled us, when successful, to generate very high gross returns on individual investments."*

The other portfolio companies also continued to see healthy growth and gross margin metrics (see Exhibit 6.2). Specifically, the balance between write-offs and successful investments and the mix of return profiles within those positive outcomes sent an important message to LPs, as Nico explained:

> *"Traditionally a major portion of our message had focused on the types of investments we made. We began to gradually incorporate an increasing focus on the portfolio management aspects, where the overall outcome of the fund is heavily influenced not only by the initial investment choices but also the manner in which the follow-on investment choices are made.*
>
> *Essentially it is as important to choose portfolio companies well as it is to maximize the amount of money deployed in good investments and minimize the amount of money sunk in underperformers. Given the very high level of uncertainty associated with early-stage venture investing, this can only be achieved through a progressive investment strategy where the initial ticket is a small proportion of the total investment in any company.*
>
> *Therefore, the two variables that define the overall performance of the fund are the failure rate as a percentage of commitments and the average gross multiple on performing investments. Both of these can be actively managed by the GP through strategic and tactical decisions in all phases of the fund."*

At this stage the team was clear that it had a winning strategy with the leverage provided by the high-quality and low-cost Spanish engineers in the early stages of the investment. It had demonstrated the capability to globalize its companies with a view to bringing on board blue-chip Silicon Valley investors, and ultimately to exit there. They now felt that that they had a powerful story to take to investors for the next fund, as summarized by the mission statement and investment strategy described in Exhibit 6.3.

Second Fund: All or Nothing

Alberto summarized the situation as the two Managing Partners decided to hit the fund raising trail again:

> *"The first fund's portfolio was showing real promise when we went hit the road in mid-2012 to once again attempt to raise the firm's second fund. This time we were ready. Our gross investment activity yielded a healthy multiple, with a lot of potential in the portfolio, so we were on positive ground. We now had some metrics that made sense and were consistent with our fundraising pitch."*

Everything was beginning to line up nicely, and Nico and Alberto secured an anchor investment in December 2012. They negotiated an agreement with the European Investment Fund (EIF) and NEOTEC (a Spanish public-private Fund-of-Funds), who provided Adara Venture with an anchor investment for a little less than half of the projected €30 million first close. The commitment came with a deadline to execute the first close by the end of June 2013, given the constraints of one of the vehicles used by NEOTEC to make the investment. The EIF was a returning investor from the first fund, and NEOTEC was a new LP for Adara. The deal also included a commitment of €2 million from the team (see Exhibit 6.4).

Based on that anchor investment, the team was able to secure approximately 10 additional LPs during the following six months. Nonetheless, as the deadline approached, the pressure to close also intensified, as Nico explained:

> *"We had gone through a tough period from 2008–2011 with the NAV of the fund dropping to almost 0.6x. While some of the investors from Fund I were supportive and committed to the next fund (albeit with lesser amounts), others decided to postpone their decision until the returns had actually materialized.*
>
> *By the middle of the second quarter we still had many conversations with interested parties open, but we could clearly tell that we would have difficulties achieving the target closing by the deadline of June 30. The pressure was rising, and we had to begin to explore alternatives."*

On the one hand, Adara could cancel the closing and lose the anchor commitment, hoping that the team would be able to maintain the fundraising momentum to compensate for the loss of the anchor. This would inevitably lead to a significantly longer fundraising timeline and also add a very real risk that the second fund would never materialize, with subsequent implications for the firm.

On the other hand, the partners could move to underwrite the first closing themselves, with a view to placing the underwrite amount with investors that were secured after the first closing. In practice this meant that the partners would need to assure themselves and the anchor investors that they were capable of sustaining the foreseeable capital call schedule for a period of time until they were able to place the underwritten commitments, while maintaining sufficient resources in the GP in order to build the portfolio of Fund II. Last but not least, they also needed to evaluate their ability to place the underwritten commitments should they go down this avenue.

"If we decided to proceed with the plan to underwrite the first closing, we needed to be certain that we were able to execute on the espoused strategy and begin to make investments. If our ability to build the portfolio was constrained by the ability of the GP to meet its capital calls, then we could easily fall into a conflict of interest situation."

Additionally, the first fund would cease to provide fees to the GP in 2015, or possibly even earlier given that it was fully called by mid-2013. From then on, the only revenue to the GP and the partners would be the fees emanating from the second fund:

"There are several interesting twists in relation to this concept of underwriting: the GP already has a base commitment of €2 million, which is an irrevocable minimum. The 'steady state' capital call schedule should be on the order of 10% of commitments per annum. Underwriting thus implies that for every €1 million of underwrite there will be €100k per annum in incremental drawdowns for the GP, with the resulting impact on the operating budget of the GP.

The commitments are channelled through the GP, but the partners are obliged to respond for them, so the call schedule ultimately impacts the operating economics of the GP very significantly. While there are still fees coming in from the first fund, there is more room to assume greater commitments. But time once again plays against us, because there is a lot of pressure to place the commitment early, with the time and effort implications that that has for the deployment of the fund."

The ability to place the underwrite and the speed at which it can be placed also drove the context around this decision:

"Obviously one would only underwrite if one has a strong conviction that it can be placed in a reasonable timeframe, or that the GP can in effect sustain itself with a higher level of commitment than the minimum already negotiated and included in the Term Sheet. Therefore there is a very important piece of the equation which relates to the pipeline of potential investors, and the conviction we had that we would be able to convince investors to subscribe to at least our own underwrite, and hopefully even increase the overall size of the fund.

In addition, there was always the fall-back option to start discounting the underwrite after a period of time. When a piece of underwrite is placed, the GP recovers the commitments drawn down up to that date, which is a number that increases with time as the fund makes its calls. Technically we could start discounting that amount, effectively providing an incentive to inbound investors to subscribe, but that would obviously not fare too well with those investors that did sign up at the beginning."

The only outcome that was clearly disastrous was where the GP defaults on part of its commitments because it simply cannot front the calls—a scenario to be avoided at all costs:

"A default scenario would effectively be a definitive sentence for the GP. In all probability, the LPs would vote to remove the GP and hand over the management of the fund to another GP that could honour its commitments. This would effectively terminate all future expectations for the firm."

Last but not least, an underwrite scenario needed to be carefully crafted and communicated to those investors that had committed to the first closing. The anchor investors[2] with broad experience investing in other GPs would have a strong view as to the validity of the different scenarios and the limits that the GP should respect.

June 2013: A Time to Decide

> *"As the deadline of June 30 loomed, it became clear to us that we were in an 'all or nothing' dilemma: we either needed to cancel or delay Fund II, or underwrite the first closing."*

To support the decision process, Alberto and Nico needed a clear view of the overall economics they were facing as a GP, including the various sources of revenue (fees, carry) but also the ongoing cash costs to manage both funds together with the capital calls generated by the commitment. As almost all of their personal wealth was already tied up in the GP, they knew that the economics of the GP would drive the decision of whether to underwrite or not, and if underwriting, how much.

While the underwrite decision was critical for the future of the firm and the team, it was also clear to the partners that the implications of the decision not only concerned the GP itself but also affected diverse elements of the fund raising strategy, communication with investors, the investment strategy of the fund, the roll-out of the investment programme, and several other operational and strategic issues.

2. The EIF has more than 350 GP relationships throughout Europe, nurtured during more than 20 years of activity.

Exhibit 6.1

Managing Partners (from investor presentation mid 2013)

Education

MIT Massachusetts Institute of Technology — Harvard University — INSEAD — École Centrale Paris

Corporate

Telefonica — Merrill Lynch — McKinsey & Company — Andersen Consulting

Morgan Stanley — Booz Allen Hamilton — Monitor Group

27 years

Venture Capital

- 3 investment vehicles
- $100Mn in managed funds
- 1000 deals addressed
- 18 investment decisions
- 12 complete cycles
- 5 acquired
- 3 sold back to founders
- 4 Liquidations

22 years

Governance

4 entrepreneurial executive positions

	Alberto Gomez Age 49	Nico Goulet Age 47	Combined
Academic Background	MIT: BSc. (VI: Electr. Eng.) Harvard: MBA	Centrale Paris: BSc. (Air Espace) MIT: MSc. (XVI: Aero & Astro) INSEAD: MBA	5 graduate degrees | 4 global institutions
Corporate experience	16 years: Booz Allen (3) McKinsey (2) Morgan Stanley (4) Merrill Lynch (4) Telefonica (3)	11 years: Andersen Consulting (2) Monitor Company (9)	27 years | 7 major corporates
Investing experience			
Years experience	10 years	12 Years	22 Years
Total funds managed	$80Mn	$100Mn	$100Mn
Investment vehicles managed	3	3	4
Total deal flow addressed	> 1000	> 1000	> 1000
Total investment decisions	15	16	18
Completed investment cycles	10	11	12
Acquired companies	4	4	5
Sold back to Management	3	3	3
Liquidations	3	4	4
Entrepreneurial involvement			
Direct executive involvement	2 ventures	3 ventures	4 ventures
Formal Directorships (Total/Tech Ventures)	8 total 7 tech. ventures	15 total 11 tech. ventures	19 total 16 tech. ventures
Total director tenure	> 35 years	>55 years	>90 years
Academic involvement			
Teaching, seminars & conferences	IdE ESIC	INSEAD Stanford IFAES AENOR	

Exhibit 6.2

Adara Ventures (I) Portfolio as of mid-2013

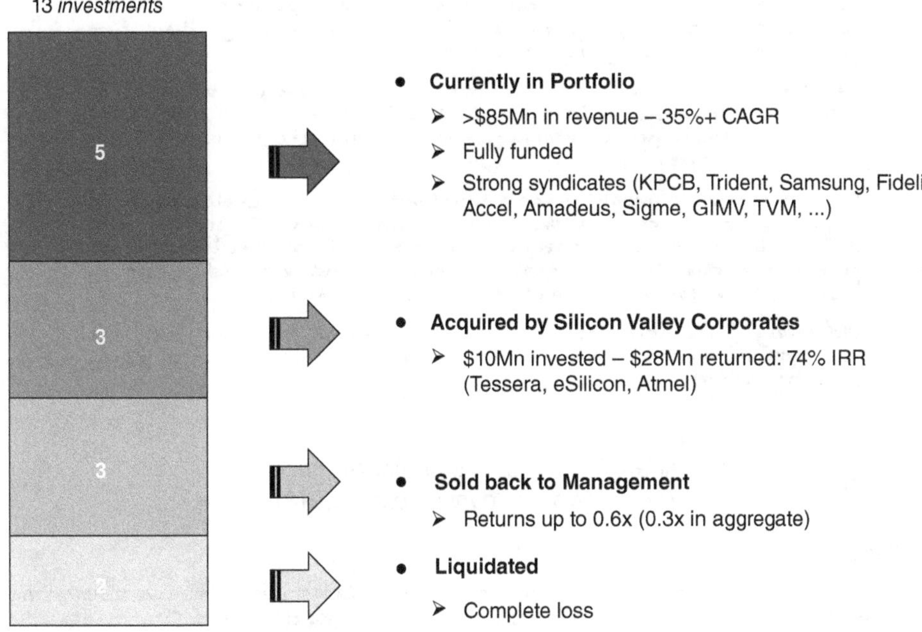

Growth Track in Current Portfolio (Synthetic view – weighted – as of early 2013)

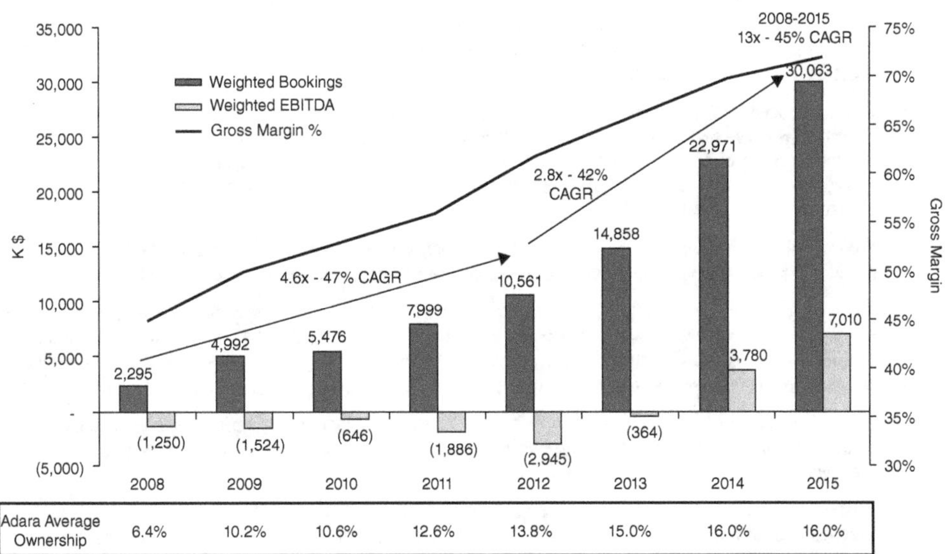

Adara Average Ownership	6.4%	10.2%	10.6%	12.6%	13.8%	15.0%	16.0%	16.0%

Exhibit 6.3

Adara Ventures Mission Statement (2013)

Our mission is to provide our investors with superior long term returns on their capital. We achieve this by creating diversified portfolios of technology based ventures.

We strive to help build great companies that have the potential to create lasting value. To do so, we back entrepreneurs with a powerful vision, the excellence to execute their plan and the courage to risk failure in its pursuit.

Our portfolio companies are involved in the development of innovative products and services for the Digital Enterprise, with differentiated business models and the potential for rapid growth. We push our companies to globalize quickly and establish a strong presence in major technology hubs such as Silicon Valley.

Ultimately , we look to exit our investments, together with the founders we have backed, through the sale of our stakes to global industry players.

Adara Ventures Investment Strategy
(From its pitch to investors in 2013)

The Strategy

By launching its third investment vehicle, Adara will continue to build its position as a reference Venture Capital firm in Europe with strong ties to Silicon Valley. We will focus on early stage companies in the Digital Enterprise areas in which we have deep knowledge (Software, IT Security, Mobility, Semiconductors, Cloud infrastructure, Communications, etc.), with particular emphasis on selecting and supporting the entrepreneurs leading them.

The strategy is based on the following premises:

- Build a portfolio of 12-15 companies, which compete for investment in their follow on rounds. We will invest small amounts of money initially and then increase our exposure to those companies that achieve or exceed their milestones. The target is for successful investments to generate gross returns of 4x+, and to quickly cut-off our exposure to non-successful companies.
- Select advanced technological teams, which are led by exceptional entrepreneurs with deep technical talent; These companies will have revenues (in some case up to €1Mn) and reference customers at the time of our first investment, and the proceeds of our investment will typically be destined towards refining the value proposition so that it can address a global niche, "productizing" the offering so that it can scale, and complementing the team with the talent needed to compete globally.
- Focus on those entrepreneurs that are receptive to coaching, organizational growth and involved support. Only opportunities with a clear path to globalisation and presence or impact in Silicon Valley will be pursued.
- Actively support the international go-to-market efforts of our portfolio, emphasizing: (i) North America, the largest global market for technology and a necessary "proof point" for successful exits; (ii) Asia, where the technology consumption trends are very strong and (iii) Latin America, a large and growing market for enterprise technology where portfolio companies can leverage local sales traction with large Spanish multi-nationals that are present there.
- Proactively position portfolio companies in the Silicon Valley ecosystem, leveraging our experience, credibility and network of resources that includes investors, professionals/executives, partners, service providers and potential acquirers.
- Build on our experience in Digital Enterprise (B2B) markets, and our insights into the long-term trends that support technical innovation and disruption in the large and mid-sized enterprise market. We plan to avoid consumer plays in the local market that may be subject to short-term trends, instead focusing on unique product and go-to-market advantages that address a global niche. We believe the potential capital appreciation in a strategic M&A exit for such companies is superior to most other options.
- Provision sufficient funds for follow-ons so that Adara can continue to participate alongside international investors in future rounds, thereby protecting and enhancing our returns.

Exhibit 6.4

Adara Ventures II Term Sheet (Q1 2013)

THE FUND	• Adara Ventures II SCA SICAR ("Adara II"). • *Société en Commandite par Actions*, incorporated in Luxembourg as per *SICAR* regulations.
SIZE	• Target € 40-50 million (minimum first closing of €30 million).
RETURN OBJECTIVE	• A net return to investors of 2-3x committed capital, or approximately 20% IRR
INVESTMENT STRATEGY	• Investments in high-growth, technology-intensive companies, initially in their early stages of development. Follow-on investments in selected cases during their growth phase. • Majority of companies originating in Spain, with the potential to address global markets and seek an exit in leading global markets for technology, such as Silicon Valley. • Focus on companies serving the Digital Enterprise, with significant engineering content and intellectual property (e.g.: Enterprise SW, IT security, Mobility, Semiconductors, Communications, Cloud Infrastructure,...).
GENERAL PARTNER	• Adara Venture Partners II S.àr.l. will have management responsibility and exclusive authority over investment decisions.
INVESTOR REPRESENTATION	• Investor Advisory Committee (comprised of investors committing over € 2 million) to review matters pertaining to investment policy, valuations, potential conflicts of interests, etc.
ANCHOR INVESTORS	• European Investment Fund, Neotec Capital Inversión S.C.R., and Axis Participaciones.
CUSTODIAN BANK, CENTRAL ADMIN.	• Royal Bank of Scotland – Luxembourg. • Alter Domus – Luxembourg.
LEGAL ADVISORS	• Arendt & Medernach.
INDEPENDENT AUDITOR	• Deloitte.
CLOSING	• First Closing Date prior to June 30, 2013.
MINIMUM COMMITMENT	• € 500,000 per investor.
CAPITAL CALLS	• Approximately semi-annual basis, representing 6-12% of capital commitments each year. • Upon capital calls from the General Partner (10 Days Notice).
TERM	• Investment period: 5 years (until 30-June-2018 approximately). • Total Duration: 10 years (until 30-June-2023, approximately) unless extended.
MANAGEMENT FEE	• 2.5% per annum on total capital commitments, during the investment period. Subsequently reduced to 2.5% of invested capital.
COMMITMENT BY GENERAL PARTNER	• Capital commitment of € 2,000,000.
ESTABLISHMENT COSTS	• One time set-up costs, not to exceed 1.0% of total commitments.
DISTRIBUTIONS	• 100% of commitments plus 20% absolute hurdle return (one-time) to Investors as priority. • 20% carried-interest on total capital gains to the General Partner, provided hurdle is achieved.
DIVERSIFICATION	• No more than 15% of total commitments on a single portfolio company.
INVESTOR REPORTING	• Quarterly non-audited reports. Annual audited Financial Statements.
JURISDICTION	• Grand Duchy of Luxembourg. • Both the SICAR and the General Partner are regulated by the Luxembourg *CSSF (Commission de Surveillance du Secteur Financier)*.

CASE

7 SIRAJ CAPITAL

INVESTING IN SMEs IN THE MIDDLE EAST

SYNOPSIS

In 2009, Siraj Capital, a Saudi Arabia-based fund investing in small and medium-sized enterprises (SMEs), is deciding whether to invest in Tower United Contracting Company ("Tower"), a Saudi telecom infrastructure provider. One of the current shareholders, Alpha Media Group, is keen to divest its holdings in the company: they had invested in the company two years earlier in a bid to diversify their activities from broadcast networks and to tap into the fast-growing telecom network marketplace. They had, however, underestimated the financing requirements of the firm and are thus eager to liquidate their stake in the company.

The case provides an opportunity to step into the role of an investment professional in a Middle Eastern private equity firm. From that perspective, it is critical to not only close the right deal at the right price, but to also pay attention to the risks associated with the investment, and consider risk mitigation. Linked to the investment decision is the question of what value Siraj could bring to Tower post-investment.

PEDAGOGICAL OBJECTIVE OF THE CASE

This case helps to develop an understanding of the particular challenges associated with investing in the Middle East. More broadly, it emphasizes a set of issues relevant to evaluating deals in emerging markets. Areas of analysis include evaluating Tower as a business, including its opportunities and bottlenecks for growth; the investment climate in the Middle East North Africa (MENA) region and the pros and cons of investing in a growth setting with relatively immature capital markets; and the investment approach of Siraj Capital, including their potential value-added to portfolio companies.

SUGGESTED ASSIGNMENT QUESTIONS

1. What is the biggest bottleneck for Tower's growth?
2. What sources of value-add can Siraj bring to Tower?
3. What are the biggest risk factors Siraj must consider in a Tower investment?
4. What items should Siraj pay attention to as it conducts due diligence on this investment?

ADDITIONAL RESOURCES

To make the most of this case study, we suggest the following additional sources to provide context and background information:

- In particular, we recommend the following chapters from *Mastering Private Equity—Transformation via Venture Capital, Minority Investments & Buyouts*
  - Chapter 3 Growth Equity
  - Chapter 6 Deal Sourcing & Due Diligence
  - Chapter 13 Operational Value Creation
- You may also refer to the book website for further material:
  www.masteringprivateequity.com

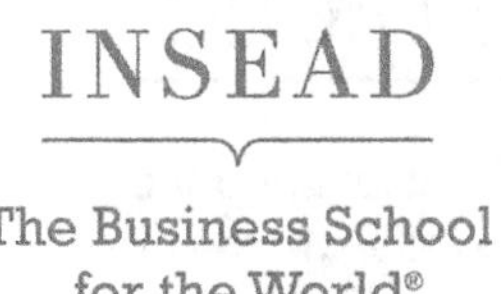

Siraj Capital

Investing in SMEs in the Middle East

02/2012-5862

This case was written by Pascale Balze, Case Writer, Case Development Centre, Middle East Campus, under the supervision of Vikas A. Aggarwal, Assistant Professor of Entrepreneurship and Family Enterprise at INSEAD. It is intended to be used as a basis for class discussion rather than to illustrate either effective or ineffective handling of an administrative situation.

This case was developed with the financial contribution of the Abu Dhabi Education Council, whose support is gratefully acknowledged.

It was July 2009. Tarek Kabrit and Hisham El-Farouki, respectively Principal and Vice President of Saudi-based holding company Siraj Capital, had to decide whether or not to invest in Tower United Contracting Company (Tower), a telecom infrastructure provider based in the Kingdom of Saudi Arabia (KSA) and part of the Alpha Media Group. Kabrit and El-Farouki had little time ahead of them. They knew that Alpha's shareholders needed cash urgently to fund the media business and were on the lookout for the best offer. Two years ago they had invested in Tower in a bid to diversify their activities from broadcast networks and tap into the fast-growing telecom network marketplace. But they had underestimated the financing requirements of the firm and were now eager to liquidate their stake in the company.

The proposed transaction entailed the purchase of a 65% stake of Tower. Tower's founder and managing director, Aziz H. Assi, who was to retain the remaining shares, had estimated that Tower needed an extra SAR20 million (US$5.3 million) over the next five years to realise all the projects in its pipeline and capitalise on the growth of the ICT sector. He had initially sought to raise debt financing, but failed to do so in the challenging financing context of the time. By the end of 2008, the global financial and economic crisis had started to unfold in the region and bank loans had become increasingly expensive, when accessible.

Considering the positive market outlook for the telecom industry, Kabrit and El-Farouki thought that Tower could be a valuable addition to Siraj's portfolio of companies. This primarily included Saudi-based SMEs that operated in expansionary and non-cyclical sectors. By streamlining business operations and leveraging its extensive regional network, the holding company had turned its portfolio of SMEs into national/regional players, generating operational value in excess of US$5 billion across its portfolio.

Yet the two investors were unwilling to make a hasty decision. The global downturn had started to negatively impact Siraj. The holding company had plans to expand its investment spree and raise its first PE fund of US$200 million, but fund-raising had turned out to be more challenging than expected. Individual and institutional investors had become risk averse. Attempts to raise funds among Siraj's existing shareholders also proved unsuccessful. Made up of high-net-worth individuals, they had already invested a total of US$65 million and were unwilling to inject more capital in the current context. Regional banks had also stopped lending. Eventually, Siraj had just managed to increase its shareholder base and raise US$25 million. Meanwhile, its portfolio of companies had started to show signs of distress and now Kabrit and El-Farouki were worried that they might be forced to partially exit some of their success-stories-in-the-making for lack of financing.

More than ever they realized that there was no room for mistakes, and that there was a lot to consider. They had to close the right deal at the right price. What were the risks associated with the investment, and how would they manage these? And ultimately, what added value could Siraj bring to the table?

Private Equity in the Middle East North Africa (MENA) Region

Private equity in the MENA region got off to a late start. While the petrodollars of the early 2000s had supported many leading global PE players, PE activity in the region was paradoxically largely undeveloped. In fact, the cumulative value of PE investments between 2002 and 2006 in the MENA region accounted for a mere 0.2% of regional GDP.

In 2007, the vast liquidity surplus of the region had nonetheless started to find its way home, given the favourable economic prospects driven by high oil prices, sound demographics and rising public and private investment. (Exhibit 7.1 Oil prices, July 08 – July 09). Returns on the region's nascent stock exchanges had also become attractive for investors. As a result, the number of funds under management in the MENA region peaked to 107 and totalled US$14 billion as the year ended, compared with 74 funds and US$7 billion worth of commitments in 2006. (Exhibit 7.2 PE funds in MENA, 2001–07).

Yet the region's lack of corporatisation and its unsophisticated financial markets still hindered PE investments and exits. In particular, the prominence of traditional family businesses posed a challenge to the emerging PE industry. Largely uneducated on the benefits of having PE investors, business owners were reluctant to surrender their shares and control to PE firms, or to implement structural changes. They were equally unwilling to improve corporate governance – a requirement for the degree of transparency sought by PE firms, and a prerequisite to prepare companies for exit.

The shallow capital markets coupled with the unsophisticated banking sector had also impeded the leveraging of transactions. Access to acquisition finance was restricted as bank loans were mainly based on balance-sheet assets, collateral and personal guarantees rather than on non-recourse cash flow. As a result, PE investments primarily translated into equity stakes in growing, poorly capitalized, underleveraged and poorly financially-structured businesses rather than on turning around underperformers or improving the operations of highly leveraged businesses. Access to growth capital was equally limited for PE minority stakeholders as banks were reluctant to grant loans to investors with limited control over operational and strategic decisions as well as cash flows. In addition, a paucity of financial information obstructed PE investments, making comparability of financial performance across companies and countries difficult and unreliable. A shortage of human capital with knowledge of the local market and world-class skills to fill senior positions in PE firms, as well as in portfolio companies, was a further obstacle to PE development. On account of this, only half of the total funds raised in the region had been invested by end 2008, and just 5% of these investments had been realised on exit.

The global economic and financial crisis would present an additional challenge for the emerging PE industry as fund-raising became anaemic, leveraging became expensive (if accessible), and investment opportunities became even thinner on the ground. Meanwhile, stock market corrections would force the PE industry to reconsider exit routes.

Siraj Capital

Background

Founded in 2006 by Dr Ghassan Al Sulaiman, Siraj was operated as a merchant investment and finance holding company. Headquartered in Jeddah, the economic heart of the Kingdom of Saudi Arabia, Siraj was also present in the Saudi capital Riyadh, and had two other offices in the leading regional economic hubs of Dubai (UAE) and Beirut (Lebanon). Since its inception, the group had established a significant regional presence in business development and incubation, structured finance markets and PE (Exhibit 7.3 Siraj's Investment Practice Breadth).

Siraj's PE investments focused on the MENA region, in particular the KSA. For Siraj, Saudi Arabia presented strong macroeconomic fundamentals. In recent years, the country had enjoyed a period of sustained growth driven by government reforms including privatisation of the telecom and power industries, along with a surge in oil prices. Further, the majority of the Saudi population was young, allowing for a potentially larger addressable market in the future (Exhibit 7.4 KSA Macro Economic Outlook, 2006–13).

Within Saudi Arabia, Siraj invested in SMEs operating in non-cyclical industries which stood to primarily benefit from the strong demographic and macroeconomic fundamentals, notably consumer goods, food and beverage and retail. Siraj also considered sectors that were best positioned to take advantage of the rapidly evolving Saudi regulatory environment, such as TMT (telecom, media and technology).

Unlike other regional players who invested US$30–40 million stakes in pre-IPO companies, Siraj invested in smaller deals between US$5 and US$20 million. Siraj believed that regional SMEs provided vast opportunities for proprietary deal flow. From experience, El-Farouki knew that many SMEs lacked the financial resources and business expertise to grow into national and regional champions. Given the immature capital and financing markets, banks traditionally shied away from lending to SMEs who lacked 3–5 years of historical financials and sufficient fixed assets to serve as collateral. At the same time, most SMEs had been used to operating in a growth market and were unprepared for the economic downturn. PE funds with expertise in enhancing business efficiency were therefore in high demand as small business owners were more inclined than larger family businesses to surrender some of their stakes to PE investors.

El-Farouki thought that such a positioning was unique in the KSA. Indeed, other PE houses operating in the country were either focused on larger transactions or on a specific sector. The leading PE house, Abraaj Capital, had only just started to venture into the SME sector. Yet Siraj's management remained confident. First, they had a head start, having operated in this segment three years longer than anybody else. Second, while Abraaj Capital and others who followed suit might in some cases be competing for deals, El-Farouki knew that they might also invest in transactions originated by Siraj.

Network & Expertise

Connections play a key role in the region as the business landscape is made up of powerful, tight-knit and opaque merchant families that are difficult to penetrate for outsiders. Siraj's powerful shareholders consisted of high-net-worth individuals and provided valuable access points to source deals and grow portfolio companies. Al Sulaiman had high-profile connections within the Saudi private and public sector, which had helped him bring on board a powerful line-up of shareholders made up of prominent family groups in the region. Siraj's CEO, Ibrahim Mardam-Bey, was also well connected within the upper echelons of society and enjoyed personal relationships with most of the regional commercial banks, thanks to his extensive experience in structured Islamic finance. As one of the first members of Saudi's fast-growing

Entrepreneurs Organisation, El-Farouki also regularly mingled with the close circle of young western-educated Saudis who had returned to the Kingdom to take over their family businesses or set up their own. Besides leveraging its own resources to source deals, Siraj also took part in several business initiatives enabling priority access to the fastest-growing SMEs in the KSA.

To support and grow its investment portfolio, Siraj had hired a talent pool of 16 seasoned investment professionals for its Jeddah and Dubai offices. The team was mainly made up of MBA graduates of Middle East origin with extensive experience in finance and operational management. A graduate of INSEAD, Kabrit had over nine years of professional experience in MENA investment banking and strategic consulting. Having graduated from INSEAD/Wharton, El-Farouki had worked in syndicated finance for JP Morgan before setting up his own business in the KSA. Along with other members of the investment team, Kabrit and El-Farouki had strong business pedigrees and understood the major hurdles to running small businesses in the region.

The Investment Approach

By July 2009, Siraj had screened hundreds of companies and undertaken a total of nine acquisitions. The company had also fine-tuned its investment process and value-creation approach by learning the hard way that acquiring stakes in regional SMEs required a much higher level of due diligence and a more hands-on approach than investing in larger players. Kabrit elaborated:

> *"Investing in regional SMEs is a very different game than investing in larger players. SMEs in the region are really unstructured as compared to their western counterparts. They have been operating for several years in a growth market and have paid little attention to establishing accounting and financial procedures. Numbers cannot be trusted and controls are not at the same standard as with larger companies."*

Reflecting on this, Siraj had established a rigorous assessment process to close the right deals at the right price. The primary assessment would typically focus on the company's financials, growth prospects, market, the quality of management, and the value of the firm. Apart from accessing the right information, the main challenge lay in determining a fair value for the company. The limited number of publicly quoted companies, coupled with a lack of financial disclosure, made it difficult to base the valuation on market metrics. In line with other PE houses in the region, Siraj would value companies using the discounted cash flow (DCF) model. Yet determining the present value of future cash flows was far from straightforward. Estimating the risk-free rate was particularly tricky. In the West it was assimilated with the coupon rate on government bonds. In the Middle East, the number and variety of government bonds issued were limited and therefore could not be used as a proxy. Likewise, calculating the beta, based on the local stock market index, and equity risk premium, determined by the historical premium earned by stocks over default-free securities over the long term, was also difficult due to the relatively immature equity market in the region. Revising management projections also proved challenging as company finances could often not be trusted. Based on historical data, the industry outlook and the anticipated growth of the firm, Siraj would often slash the management's original forecasts by as much as 70%.

The committee process also adhered to non-negotiable "deal breakers", such as never going into a deal above five times net earnings unless the company presented exceptional growth potential, and avoiding an internal rate of return (IRR) below 30%. Entry multiples, however, could often be renegotiated, as SMEs in the region had few growth options due to their limited access to loans. They lacked the means to hire an international investment bank to do the valuation. Securing control of the board was a prerequisite and of paramount importance to Siraj. Although they always sought a minority stake in the company, they took control of the board either by appointing a member of the investment team as chairman, or by holding the majority of board votes. This would ensure control of the budget and of the pace and scope of change. The due diligence process was conducted by renowned international companies to uncover any legal, commercial or financial risks associated with the investment.

Beyond the acquisition phase, operational activism was crucial to Siraj's value-creation success. Kabrit noted:

> *"SMEs must be monitored on a daily basis, and PE firms must be ready to do the dirty work, from crunching the numbers to drafting presentations to banks and major clients."*

To this end, Siraj had established an internal investment monitoring unit to work specifically for the first six months following any addition to its portfolio. Composed of accountants, the unit would support the work of the investment team by installing accounting and financial procedures, and by controlling the company accounts on a daily basis. To further monitor its investments, Siraj would require the board to meet monthly and the CEO to present detailed quarterly reports. (Exhibit 7.5 provides an example of Siraj's value creation in several of its portfolio companies).

Beyond controlling and monitoring the company, Siraj would focus on leveraging its network, its access to capital, and its expertise to build up processes to create a platform for growth. To advise on the strategic direction of the company it would usually establish a sound advisory board. Kabrit explained:

> *"Entrepreneurs in this part of the world are very much on their own. They have little understanding of finances, and hardly anyone to talk to regarding the strategic direction of their company. Establishing a sound advisory board provides the strategic support for these entrepreneurs."*

Except for their first investment, Siraj's investment process and value creation model had proved successful. This was estimated to have created operational value in excess of US$100 million across its portfolio companies since the first acquisition. Siraj had also exited Janayen I Real Estate through a management buy-back with returns of over 80%.

Tower

Background

Established in 2005, Tower United Contracting Company was a KSA-based infrastructure outsourced service provider for telecom operators and original equipment manufacturers (OEMs). By early 2009, Tower's activities were threefold. (1) The GSM division was responsible for providing services to the wireless markets. This department typically got involved in the erection of greenfield and rooftop towers and the associated infrastructure. These activities had quickly expanded with the entry of new competition in the wireless markets and related spending on the roll-out of infrastructure in the form of transmission towers. By the end of 2008, the GSM division accounted for 80% of total company revenue. (2) The Outside Plant (OSP) division undertook all projects related to the laying of fixed wire cables (copper, fibre-optic, etc.), including any associated civil work, and accounted for 15% of Tower's total revenue in 2008. (3) The Telecom Instrumentation division sourced and installed all equipment required by the other two divisions. Examples of such equipment included the instrumentation needed within shelters and the various receivers installed on top of the wireless towers. Each of the three divisions provided end-to-end civil and electrical work, including planning, engineering, design, implementation, construction and procurement.

Tower's Marketplace

Despite its small size, Tower had recognized expertise and a solid track record in the telecom infrastructure industry in the KSA. It was well known for responding proactively to its clients' needs and for providing timely and efficient execution. The heads of both the GSM and OSP divisions were actively involved in monitoring Tower's daily activity. Field engineers were asked to send written and visual updates of their work on a daily basis so that clients could be updated as and when required. The management team and execution team had many years of telecom experience. Assi, a managing partner and one of the founding members of Tower, had extensive experience in the industry and a hands-on approach to running the company's operations.

On the back of its strong reputation, the company had established long-term relationships with a small number of major international equipment vendors and telecom operators in the Kingdom. By mid-2009, Tower had a long list of projects in the pipeline (Exhibit 7.6 Tower's Revenue Contribution by Customer 2007–08. Exhibit 7.7 Tower's Pipeline/Announced Projects). Thanks to its reputation, the company had also managed to climb the value chain. By the end of 2008, it often bid directly with telecom operators as the main contractor on most of its projects, either alone or in partnership with other equipment vendors.

Only a few other industry players were as well positioned as Tower to support telecom providers with an end-to-end service. In addition, the sector presented barriers for new players, who had to be able to offer a full spectrum of services to compete. This implied having a large, technically-experienced workforce available off-the-shelf for project execution, along with substantial working capital.

Financial Performance

In 2008, Tower's net revenue amounted to SAR8.5 million (US$2.3 million), representing a 118% rise compared to a year earlier. The leap in revenue derived from the fact that telecom providers and telecom equipment vendors were increasingly outsourcing the bulk of their infrastructure build-up activities to companies like Tower, which could enable timely and efficient execution of their roll-out plans.

Along with revenue growth, the company's top-line and bottom-line margins averaged respectively 26.4% and 10.6% of net revenue during the same year. The preliminary financial results for 2009 suggested that Tower had withstood the global financial and economic crisis, with net revenues increasing by 12.2% to SAR9.5 million (US$2.5 million), and top- and bottom-line margins of 20.8% and 5.3% respectively. Nonetheless, the company required an increased cash injection to fund the working capital needed to support accounts receivable related to the completed and work-in-progress projects typical of the industry (Exhibit 7.8 Tower's Key Financials, 2007–09).

Growth Potential

Looking ahead, Tower stood to benefit from the growth the KSA telecom sector, notably in the 3G and broadband Internet market (Exhibit 7.9 Saudi Telecom Operators' revenue, 2008–12). The expansion was fuelled by a number of factors. Since its accession to the World Trade Organization, the KSA government had committed US$3–4 billion to private telecom operators to deliver connections nationwide and transform Saudi cities into connected, digitally-enabled metropolitan centres, with internet access and e-services through the widespread installation of telecom equipment, including analogue and fibre-optic cables.

The rise in purchasing power of Saudi consumers, coupled with the country's young population, was expected to drive the increase in mobile and broadband penetration in years to come (Exhibit 7.10 Market prospect in 3G technology, internet and fixed line).

As telecom operators continued to add subscribers, they were expected to focus on network quality and to upgrade their networks. The new competition within the telecom industry was anticipated to lead to the compression of margins and a reduction in price levels, forcing operators to look at ways to reduce operating expenses and unlock value from their existing balance sheets to finance future projects. Tower-sharing and the rise of third-party tower companies were to emerge as a result.

These market dynamics had far-reaching implications for the provision of telecom infrastructure and services. Telecom infrastructure needed to be upgraded or built to support the technological, geographic and service-wise expansion of the telecom industry. Further growth potential in the region existed, particularly in countries where Tower's telecom clients were launching international/regional expansion programmes.

In addition, opportunities also existed for Tower to move further up the value chain by offering to build, maintain, own and lease network sites and infrastructure to telecom operators. This asset management model had been popular for over a decade in the US and in Europe but was largely unheard of in the Middle East. Beyond increasing the margins of telecommunications infrastructure services companies, the model also generated attractive annuity income under long-term agreements with blue chip customers. At the same time, telecom operators benefited from these deals as they allowed them to rapidly increase coverage with limited Capex requirements. Industry experts forecasted Capex spending to increase significantly in the following four years (Exhibit 7.11 Telecom Capex Spending in KSA market, 2009 and Exhibit 7.12 Tower's Management vs. Siraj Revenue Projections).

Exhibit 7.1
Oil prices July 08 – July 09

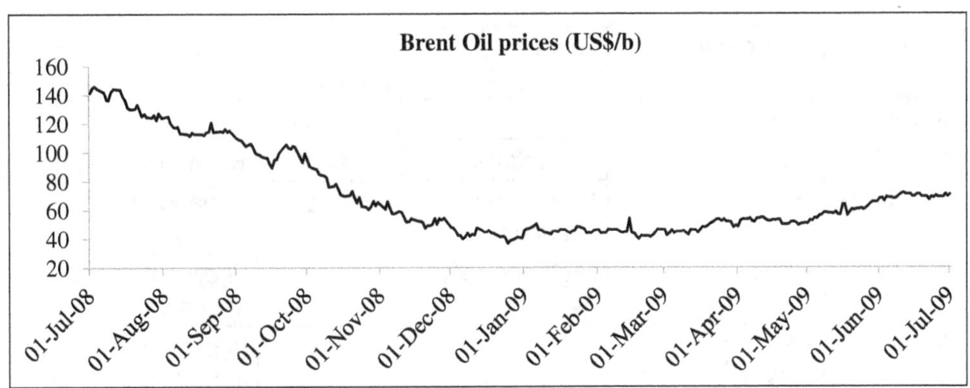

Source: Zawya Private Equity Monitor

Exhibit 7.2
PE Funds in MENA 2001–07

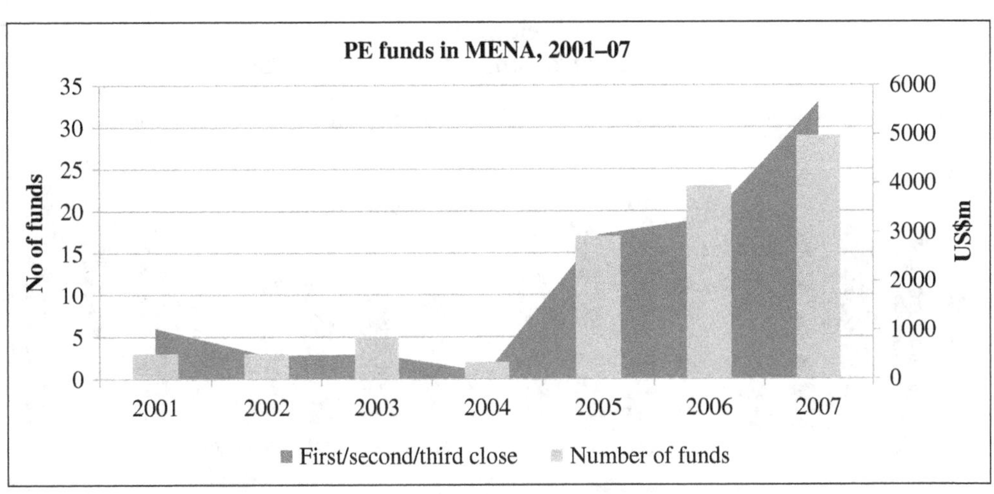

Source: Zawya Private Equity Monitor, MENA Private Equity Association

Exhibit 7.3

Siraj's Investment Practice Breadth

Date	Company	Sector	Siraj's equity (%)	Current Status
July 2007	Morpheus IT	IT	16.7%	Bankrupt
April 2008	Salata	Agriculture	80%	Expanding into KSA
April 2007	Reidin.com	Real estate services	25%	Expanded into Turkey
May 2009	Lomar	High end retail	30%	Grew number of shops by 200%
July 2007	RE Janayen I, II, IV	Workers accommodation	30%	In process of listing in Singapore
Nov 2010	Saudi Holiday Inn Express	Hospitality lodging	10%	First three sites in KSA identified

Source: Siraj Capital

Exhibit 7.4

KSA Macroeconomic Fundamentals, KSA, 2006–13

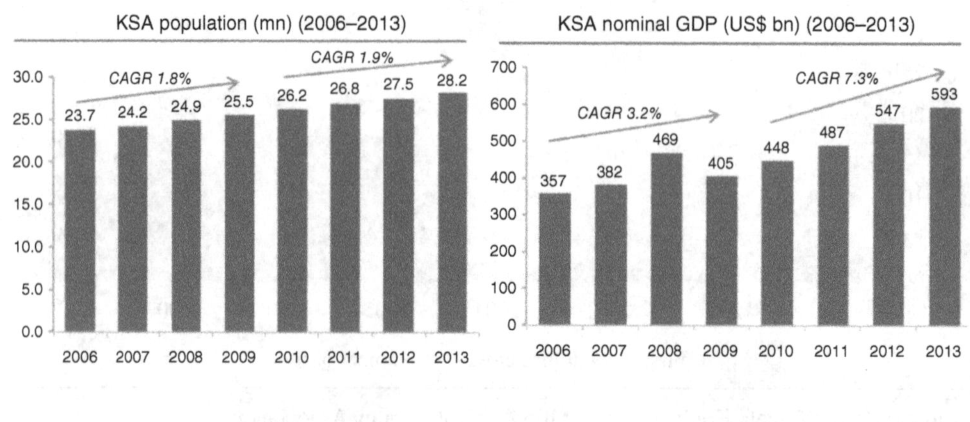

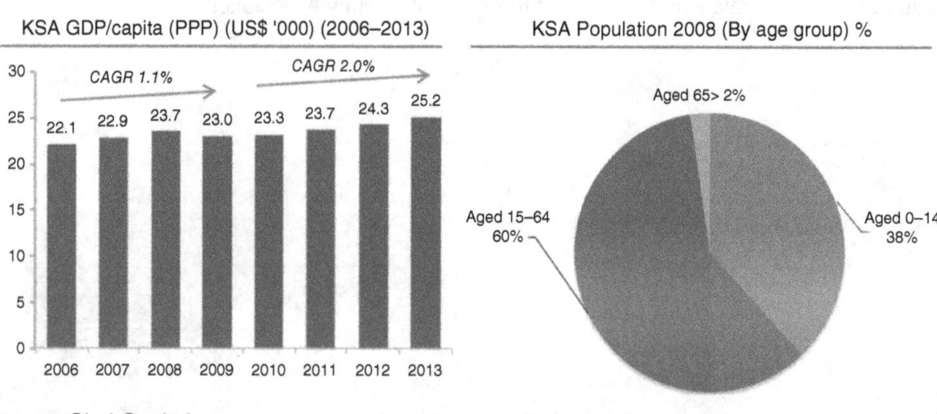

Source: Siraj Capital

Exhibit 7.5

Examples of Siraj's Value Creation

Company	Strategy	Finance	HR	Sales/Marketing	Operations
Salata	- Worked with sector specialist management team to formulate overall development strategy - Developed comprehensive Management Presentation with Lazard laying out plans for expansion with strategic partners in KSA and Bahrain - Partnered with Bidwells, UK based agriculture consultancy, to provide assistance with technical due diligence, management expansion, marketing, supply chain and sustainability strategy - Working with Lovells to ring-fence and register Salata IP	- Retained Lazard as lead financial advisor raising US$20m capital across GCC institutional investors - Deployed interim CFO to develop financial statements in preparation for company's first major audit by KPMG - Injected US$1m in additional shareholder loans to support short-term working capital. Currently working on securing additional US$3m in working capital facility - Developed comprehensive forecasting model for monthly reporting - Appointed KPMG as company auditors	- Successfully drove recruitment efforts for Finance Manager (who replaced Siraj IMU team member) and Marketing Manager - Developed HR roadmap across all functions as part of company's expansion plans	- Working with advertising agency, developed Salata brand, logo and tag line - Worked with agency to build Salata's first website - Prepared marketing message for interviews with BBC and articles on Emirates 24/7 - Supported business development efforts to secure off take agreement with Unifrutti - Nominating Salata for 2011 "Arabia 500" initiative	- Negotiated terms with Ras Al Khaimah Investment Authority for land, electricity and water rights - Supported CEO on securing exclusivity agreements with technology suppliers in EU - Facilitated key introductions to leading food and beverage client base in KSA

(Continued)

Exhibit 7.5 (*Continued*)

Company	Strategy	Finance	HR	Sales/Marketing	Operations
Lomar	- Set annual Balanced Scorecard to monitor company performance - Quarterly board meetings - Target B/B+ market segment with launch of "Hemza" 2nd tier brand - Lead discussions with high-end female brand acquisition target - Company targeting to "own" outlets in KSA; "franchise" to regional MENA markets - Working with legal counsel to ring-fence and protect IP & brand rights	- Introduced budgeting and cash flow planning system - Revised company cash payment process, providing net improvement of 20+ days in WC cycle - Bank introduction leading to approval of SR 1m LC line versus purchase orders - Switched company auditors to KPMG	- Seconded Siraj IMU member as CFO; upgrading internal processes & controls, training company accounting team - Created job description and interviewed 20+ "brand managers"; in process of finalizing with short-listed candidates - Worked with management to create store salesman retention and career-development plan - Held regular training sessions with Lomar CEO covering finance, budgeting, cash management	- Nominated company to Saudi Fast Growth 100 list, ranked #13; Lomar CEO has become "face" of initiative - Introductions to regional director of Fairmont Group for strategic Lomar location in Fairmont Mecca retail plaza - Introductions to directors of regional airlines and hotel groups to develop bespoke Lomar gift solutions - Based on successful Siraj Capital pilot project, new "corporate client" initiative launched	- Identified major bottlenecks – production – and worked with mgmt and govt agencies to push for completion of new production facility and new worker visas - Recommended and led initiative to create Saudi female production capability (12 staff currently), alleviating "Saudization" problem

Tower	- Set Balance Scorecard to monitor company performance - Shifted strategy towards the higher growth broadband segment and recurring revenue - Launched partnership discussions relating to the expansion into the Bahraini market, along with a move towards owning and leasing back telecom towers	- Injected close to US$2m into the company as shareholder loans - Secured US$2.5m credit line from Lebanese Bank; expanded to US$5.0m - Launched capital raising initiative for the company to provide it with the required financing to achieve growth targets (in process) - Switched company auditors to KPMG & revised revenue recognition process	- Sourced and interviewed over 50 CFO and head of HR candidates - Installed Siraj IMU team member as CFO; upgrading internal processes & controls, training company accounting team - In discussions to hire a new COO to transition into CEO as part of a succession plan as current CEO is nearing retirement age	- Redesigned company logo - Re-launched website - Assisted in the financial sections of various bids that the company was engaged in - Led a number of contract negotiations - Nominated the company for the Saudi Fast Growth 100 list, it won 11th place 2 years in a row - Nominating company to Arabia 500 2010 list	- Installed new accounting software - Installed ERP systems - Streamlined a number of key processes including budgeting, cash flow management, billing and collections - Replaced local 3rd tier auditors with KPMG
Reidin	- Designed and led annual strategy and action planning workshop to help refine company's growth focus and product strategy - Supported H2T, Macquarie Capital and Deutsche bank capital raising efforts - Evaluated partnership and alliance opportunities with complementary technology companies and M&A candidates	- Injected US$0.5m in convertible debt to support company's operations as a bridge financing - Currently guiding Finance Manager on structure for forecasting monthly earnings - Enhanced company's financial reporting standards to ensure GAAP compliance	- Successfully drove recruitment efforts for Head of Direct Sales	- Guided management on inside sales best practices and incentive compensation plan	- Improved corporate governance through expansion of board to include 2 non-executive directors - Facilitated new market-entry roadshow with Macquarie Capital driving key introductions in Saudi Arabia including Mayor of Jeddah

Source: Siraj Capital

Exhibit 7.6

Tower's Revenue Contribution by Customer

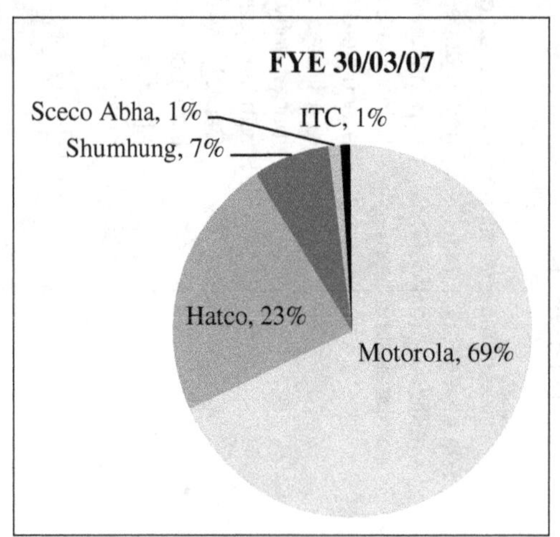

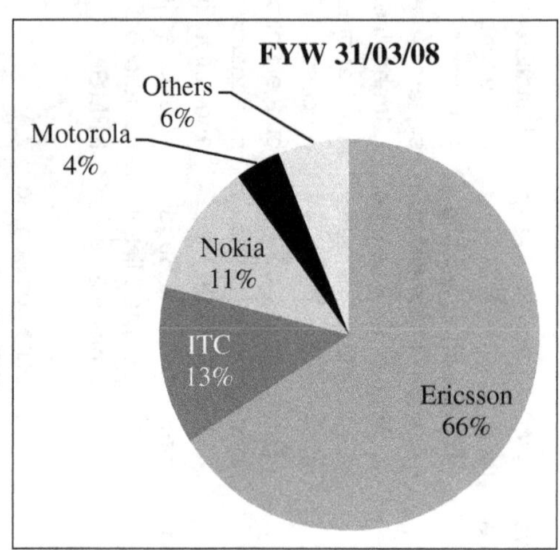

Source: Tower's accounts

Exhibit 7.7

Tower's Pipeline/Announced Projects

Division	Project	Vendor	No. of Sites	Status	Estimated Value (SAR)	Expected Commencement	Expected Completion
GSM	Green Field Site Construction	Ericsson	25	Won	9,375,000	1st January 2010	31st December 2010
GSM	Green Field Site Construction	STC (Ahad)	40	Shortlisted	17,400,000	31st May 2010	30th March 2011
GSM	Green Field Site Construction	NSN/Zain	14	Shortlisted	5,600,000	31st May 2010	30th March 2011
GSM	Rooftop Installations	Ericsson	36	Won	3,780,000	31st January 2010	31st December 2010
GSM	Rooftop Installations	STC (Ahad)	17	Shortlisted	5,355,000	31st May 2010	30th March 2011
GSM	Rooftop Installations	NSN	20	Shortlisted	5,600,000	31st May 2010	30th March 2011
GSM	Telecom Installations	NSN	34	Shortlisted	850,000	31st May 2010	30th March 2011
GSM	Telecom Installations	STC	74	Bidding	1,850,000	31st May 2010	30th April 2011
GSM	Site Acquisitions	Ericsson	20	Shortlisted	230,000	31st May 2010	1st April 2011
GSM	Site Acquisitions	SITC	74	Bidding	851,000	31st May 2010	30th March 2011
OSP	OSP Installations	STC (Ahad)	11	Shortlisted	7,425,000	31st May 2010	30th March 2011
OSP	OSP Installations	SITC	266	Bidding	99,750,000	31st May 2010	30th March 2011
				Total	158,066,000		

Source: Tower's management

Exhibit 7.8

Tower's Key Financials, 2007–09
(Millions of SAR, Financial Year Ending March 31st)

	10/10/05–31/03/07	31/03/08	31/03/09	31/01/10 10 months	31/03/10
Revenue – net	**3,92**	**8,552**	**9,597**	**21,033**	**24,498**
Growth rate (%)		*118%*	*12%*		*155%*
Cost of Revenue	–2,604	–6,291	–7,601	–14,723	–17,434
Gross Profit	1,318	2,261	1,996	6,31	7,064
Gross Margin %	*34%*	*26%*	*21%*	*30%*	*29%*
General and administration expenses	–1,573	–0,785	–0,752	–2,001	–2,12
% of revenue	*40%*	*9%*	*8%*	*10%*	*9%*
EBITDA	**–0,256**	**1,477**	**1,244**	**4,308**	**4,944**
EBITDA Margin (%)	*–7%*	*17%*	*13%*	*21%*	*20%*
D&A	–0,038	–0,514	–0,621	–0,207	–0,215
Operating Profit (EBIT)	**–0,294**	**0,962**	**0,622**	**4,101**	**4,729**
Finance costs	–0,008	–0,055	–0,117	–0,681	–1,104
Profit before Zakat	–0,302	0,962	0,505	3,42	3,625
Transfer to Statutory Reserve	0	–0,061	–0,051	0	0
Retained earnings	0,302	0,545	0,998	4,291	4,533
Zakat	0	0	–0,077	NA	–0,091
% of profit before Zakat	*0%*	*0%*	*7.7%*	*2.5%*	*2.5%*
Net profit for the year	**–0,302**	**0,907**	**0,505**	**4,291**	**3,534**
Profit Margin (%)	*–8%*	*11%*	*5%*	*20%*	*14%*

Source: Siraj Capital

Exhibit 7.9

Saudi Telecom Operators' Revenue, 2008–12

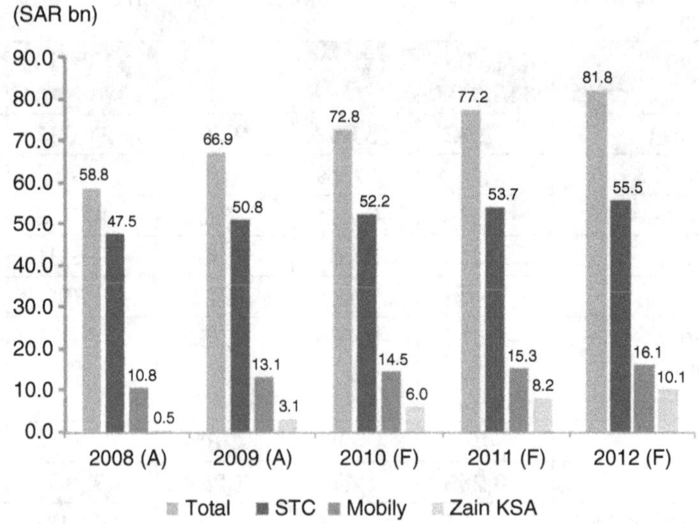

Source: Company Audited Financial Statements. Forecasts are based on financial projections made by Global Investment House from the research reports dated April 2009.

Exhibit 7.10

Market Prospects in 3G technology, Internet and Fixed Line

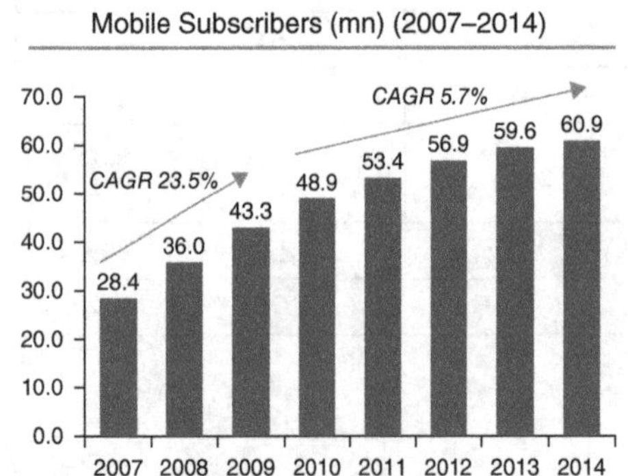

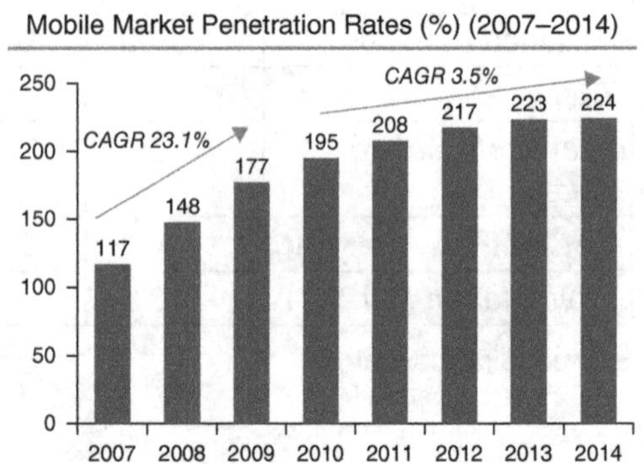

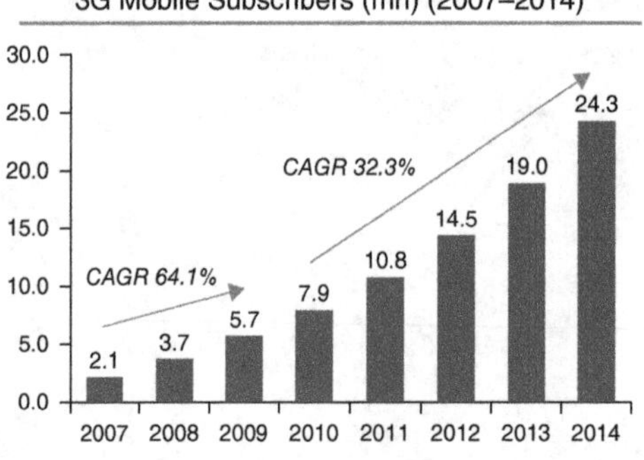

Exhibit 7.10 (*Continued*)

Internet Subscribers (mn) (2007–2014)

CAGR 16.5%
CAGR 7.7%
2007: 7.5, 2008: 9.0, 2009: 10.2, 2010: 11.3, 2011: 12.5, 2012: 13.5, 2013: 14.4, 2014: 15.2

Internet Market Penetration Rate (%) (2007–2014)

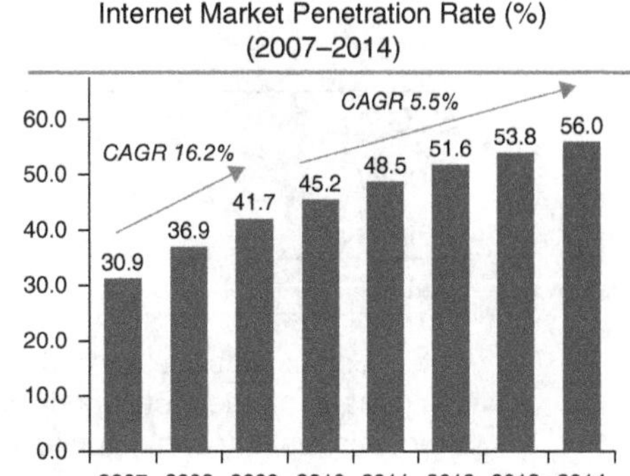

Broadband Internet Subscribers (mn) (2007–2014)

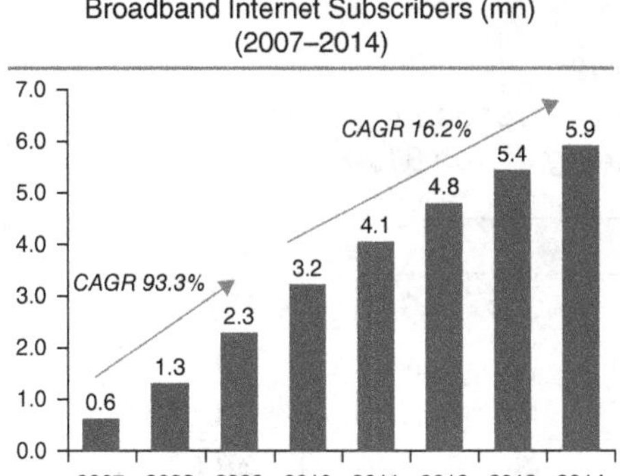

Broadband Internet Market Penetration Rate (%) (2007–2014)

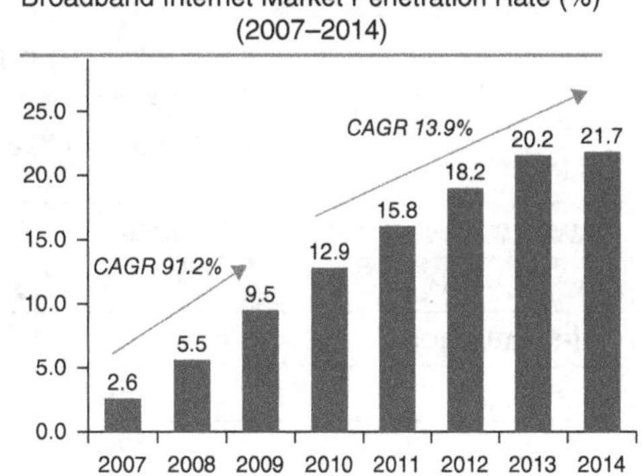

Fixed Line Subscribers (mn) (2007–2014)

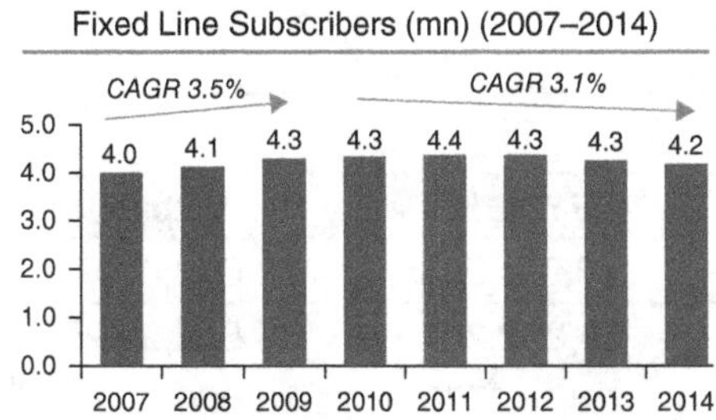

Fixed Line Penetration Rates (%) (2007–2014)

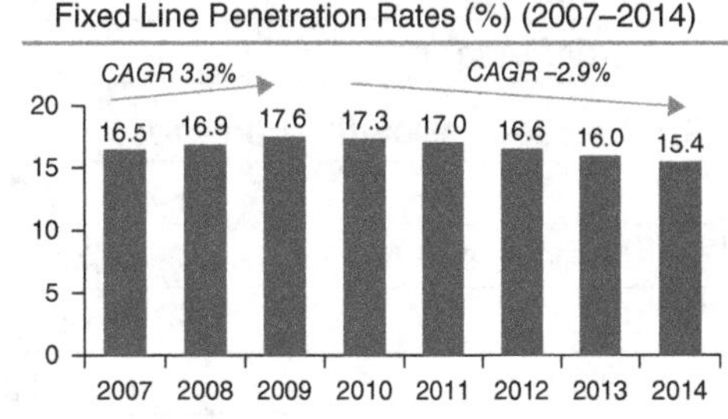

Source: BMI Saudi Arabia Telecommunications Report Q1 201

Exhibit 7.11

Telecom Capex Spending in KSA Market, 2009
(SAR '000)

STC	15,925,731
Mobily	3,292,112
Zain KSA	1,840,393
Total	**21,058,326**

Note: Capex passive spending includes expenditure on passive component of the network including steel tower/antenna mounting structures, battery bank, power supply, security cabin among others.

Source: Tower's management

Exhibit 7.12

Tower's Management vs. Siraj's Revenue Projections
(SAR, Financial Year Ending March 31st)

Tower's based growth scenario			
	FY 2011	**FY 2012**	**FY 2013**
Total Revenue	65,081,000	85,126,000	103,990,000
Total cost	46,403,000	60,696,500	73,846,000
Project cost	28,600,000	36,300,000	43,800,000
Non project cost	17,803,000	2,439,500	30,046,000
Net profit	18,678,000	24,429,500	30,144,000
Net profit margin	*29%*	*29%*	*29%*
Siraj's based growth scenario			
	FY 2011	**FY 2012**	**FY 2013**
Total Revenue	33,556,280	46,674,588	68,000,000
Total Cost	30,053,942	39,232,231	55,855,291
Project cost	18,791,517	26,137,770	38,080,000
Non Project cost	11,262,425	13,094,461	17,775,291
Net Profit	3,502,338	7,442,358	12,144,709
Net Profit Margin	*10%*	*16%*	*18%*

Source: Siraj Capital

SECTION III
Growth Equity

For us, the fun of what we do is both identifying superb, high-growth companies and rolling our sleeves up and working closely with them to help take their businesses to the next level.

—**William E. Ford,** Chief Executive Officer, General Atlantic

CASE

8 PRIVATE EQUITY IN EMERGING MARKETS
CAN OPERATING ADVANTAGE BOOST VALUE IN EXITS?

SYNOPSIS

In April 2008, Mekong Capital (MC), a private equity firm based in Ho Chi Minh City, Vietnam, took a minority equity stake in Golden Gate, one of the few restaurant chain operators in the country at the time. Within five years, Golden Gate has expanded aggressively, growing from a single restaurant concept with five locations to nine concepts and 58 locations. By 2013, Mekong is considering an exit as it is eager to deliver a timely and healthy return to its limited partners. Yet the exit route and the valuation of Golden Gate are far from certain. There are no publicly traded multi-concept restaurant groups in Vietnam and few private competitors that can serve as a benchmark. Equally concerning, Golden Gate's operating performance weakened in 2012; the chain missed its targets for earnings and same-store sales growth in a number of its outlets. MC must evaluate the options and the best avenue for an exit and decide what operational improvements are required to attract trade buyers or create the foundation for a successful initial public offering (IPO).

PEDAGOGICAL OBJECTIVE OF THE CASE

The case demonstrates how private equity firms with operational capabilities have a distinct advantage in sourcing investments in emerging markets. Students examine how minority investors can dynamically shape a portfolio company's operational strategy to position a company for IPO or match potential buyers' needs, thus maximizing value for the current owners. Additionally, the case offers a unique opportunity to study the investment allure of Vietnam, an emerging market that is quickly becoming one of the private equity hotspots in Asia. The case is rich and versatile, allowing instructors to emphasize certain components depending on their teaching objectives.

SUGGESTED ASSIGNMENT QUESTIONS

1. How do you win the best deals at the lowest prices through *advantaged sourcing*?
   - Discuss MC's deal-origination strategy as it is portrayed in the Cozy Tea scenario and compare it to deal sourcing in the US or Europe.
   - What might MC do to differentiate itself from other PE firms in the eyes of Vietnamese business owners?
2. Considering the fragility of the growth equity structure, how do operation-centric PE firms influence direction and execution as minority owners?
   - Emerging markets entrepreneurs are often convinced of their vision and can be quite stubborn in clinging to their views, especially if they enjoy initial success. What are the ways growth equity investors in emerging markets can assess a business owner's willingness to partner in decision making?
   - Mekong owned this business for five years before deciding to make a strategic shift and take operating actions. These strategic changes and insights weren't

identified in the pre-acquisition due diligence process, nor were they addressed in the first five years of Mekong's ownership.

3. The Golden Gate board of directors has gathered to discuss the company's plan to realize value as it shapes an exit strategy. Which exit option should be pursued? And what are the differences in operating strategies in the two exit paths?

ADDITIONAL RESOURCES

To make the most of this case study, we suggest the following additional sources to provide context and background information:

- In particular, we recommend the following chapters from *Mastering Private Equity—Transformation via Venture Capital, Minority Investments & Buyouts*
  - Chapter 1 Private Equity Essentials
  - Chapter 3 Growth Equity
  - Chapter 6 Deal Sourcing & Due Diligence
  - Chapter 15 Exit
- Case website for faculty and lecturers: http://cases.insead.edu/mekong-capital
- You may also refer to the book website for further material:
  www.masteringprivateequity.com

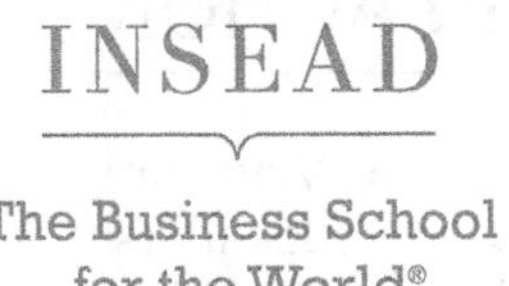

PE in Emerging Markets

Can Mekong Capital's Operating Advantage Boost the Value in its Exit from Golden Gate Restaurants?

03/2016-6162

This case was written by Peter Goodson, Professor at UC Berkeley-Haas School of Business, Distinguished Fellow of INSEAD's Global Private Equity Initiative and Fellow of Dartmouth's Tuck Private Equity Center, and Kimberly McGinnis, case writer and Haas School alumnus, under the supervision of Claudia Zeisberger, Professor of Entrepreneurship at INSEAD and Academic Director of INSEAD's Global Private Equity Initiative (GPEI). It is intended to be used as a basis for class discussion rather than to illustrate either effective or ineffective handling of an administrative situation.

Note: This case contains fictionalized material for a board meeting to deepen the problem-solving perspective.

Additional material about INSEAD case studies (e.g., videos, spreadsheets, links) can be accessed at cases.insead.edu.

On a balmy evening in July 2013, Chad Ovel, a Partner at Mekong Capital, Vietnam's first private equity firm, sat at his desk in the firm's Ho Chi Minh City headquarters. The air-conditioned comfort of the office was a far cry from how the day had started. At 4 am he had been in the central kitchen of the Golden Gate Group, a restaurant chain operator, observing a manager taking shipments of produce and checking inventory levels. Over the previous two days, he had visited the kitchen of every Ho Chi Minh City outpost owned by Golden Gate.

Mekong Capital had held a 15% growth equity stake in Golden Gate for the past five years, during which the group expanded profitably from one restaurant concept with five locations to 10 concepts and 58 locations. By 2013, Golden Gate was on track to generate $6.3 million in EBITDA, representing a 34% annualized increase in traffic and a 33% annualized increase in EBITDA since Mekong Capital's initial investment. The window to realize a return on its stake in Golden Gate was fast approaching.

Private equity fund limited partners (LPs), which typically consist of pension funds, sovereign funds, family-office capital and fund-of-funds investors, expected to exit their investments within five to seven years, if not sooner. Chad found himself thinking that although growth was impressive at Golden Gate, were the restaurant operations optimized sufficiently? Was the management team ready to show a new owner that a solid platform for future growth was in place? These were the questions the team needed to focus on, but being new to the restaurant trade and from an operational background, he wondered whether Golden Gate management – much less the team at Mekong – would pay heed to his concerns.

When a business grows substantially (as was the case with Golden Gate), LPs expect cash-on-cash returns to increase. Despite Golden Gate's expansion, it was still subject to the usual emerging market investment challenges – an addiction to growth, elusive profits and even rarer exits. Indeed in 2012 Golden Gate had disappointed in terms of both profitability and same-store sales in many of its locations. If I were the acquirer or an underwriter, Chad asked himself, would I believe that this past success would continue or not? Would I be comfortable bidding for the restaurant chain? And if I did, would I pay full price?

Fifteen years running Vietnamese businesses and a successful experience as a turnaround CEO led Ovel to question the restaurant chain's 'readiness' before its investor's exit. After what he had seen in the kitchen that morning, he was convinced that it was not positioned to maximize value. More importantly, he could see how operations could be enhanced in a relatively short period of time to attract multiple buyers and warrant a premium offer, or persuade an underwriter to launch an IPO and support serial sales of Mekong-held shares.

Until now, the management team had championed continuation of its expansion plans as the best way to create value for shareholders. Tomorrow morning, Ovel would propose a radical shift in Golden Gate's strategy—to stop opening outlets. He would call for a moratorium on new locations and hone in on back-of-the-house improvements, convinced that incremental improvements in the supply chain and kitchen would drive the most value – not only for Mekong before exit but the remaining Golden Gate shareholders over the long term.

As this was his first major initiative since joining Mekong Capital as a partner and assuming the role of deal leader on Golden Gate, Ovel knew he was taking a risk by going against the prevailing pursuit of 'growth for growth's sake'. Golden Gate's board consisted of five members – Ovel, one other outside director, and three members of the Golden Gate management team. Golden Gate management was passionate about finding new locations and developing new concepts – it was their main strength. Would they, he wondered, be willing to listen to him, being new to the situation and having an operational rather than an investment eye? With the right incentives in place it might be possible, but he would have his work cut out for him in the coming months as he managed the exit process.

Ovel took a deep breath as he left the office and hailed a cab to the airport for his trip to attend the Golden Gate Board meeting in Hanoi. He hoped the overnight flight would be uneventful – tomorrow was going to be a test.

Private Equity in Asia

Investment tends to take a different form in emerging markets. Over 88% of the deals done across Asia to date have been "growth equity", a term denoting a minority investment in which the invested capital is used primarily to fund growth rather than buy out existing shareholders. As a growth equity investor, a PE firm must persuade the management team to take them seriously (as opposed to control investments where PE firms can force decisions if necessary). While agreed-upon rights exist for minority investors, their enforceability is questionable. This is in contrast to US management buyouts, where gaining control is the model on which the PE phenomenon is built. And different from the venture capital industry, where an entrepreneur's ownership is diluted, often to less than 50%, by multiple investment rounds as the start-up grows. The popularity of growth equity in emerging markets was in part a product of the business culture – founders and owners (often families) were extremely averse to giving up control.

Exiting such investments could prove challenging. Markets tended to be less liquid and less developed, making public offerings difficult, and there were fewer trade buyers capable of executing a third-party sale. Often a family was reluctant to sell its entire business to a trade buyer because of the family legacy embedded in it, preferring an IPO which left family members in charge and enhanced their prestige in the community. In 2008 when Mekong first invested in Golden Gate, the relatively young PE firm had no track record of exiting investments. Later it developed one of the best track records in achieving realizations from all of its emerging market investments, exiting or partially exiting 19 of its 26 investments by 2014.

Background: Mekong Capital

Founded by Chris Freund in 2001, Mekong Capital was an early mover as a local Vietnam-focused private equity firm. Like many emerging market investment sponsors, the early days involved trial-and-error experiments. Mekong's first fund invested primarily in the low-cost manufacturing sector, with limited success.

Shift to a Consumer-Focused Strategy

Mekong's 2008 investment in Golden Gate was part of its second investment vehicle, MEF II. After studying Mekong's previous successes and failures, Freund saw that the majority of his achievements had come from investments in consumer-facing businesses. Over time the firm would focus entirely on this segment, in part because Vietnam had the fastest growing middle class and affluent consumer base in the region (see Exhibit 8.1).

Another key consideration was that exit possibilities in the consumer segment were more robust: acquirers and stock markets had proved to favour consumer-driven businesses. Also, there was very little government intervention in the sector and ample investible opportunities. As Mekong continued to develop sector know-how and operational expertise, it believed it could offer entrepreneurs incremental capabilities as distinct from investors that simply offered capital.

Evolution to a Hands-on Operating Improvement Strategy

Over the years, the firm had grown the depth and breadth of its operating involvement. Helping businesses improve operationally had become the cornerstone of Mekong's value-creation strategy. At first, Mekong provided assistance with accounting normalization, governance structure, enhanced reporting measures and goal setting. Little by little, it added other services as the need arose. It began to recruit executives for portfolio companies, as finding talent became increasingly challenging. As of June 2015, over 65 executives recruited by Mekong's talent team were deployed at its portfolio companies. In turn, operating advisors were engaged with functional or sector expertise.

Recruiting Chad Ovel was an extension of Mekong's operating-centric vision. Although Ovel joined Mekong in 2013, Chris Freund had met him in 2004. A native of Iowa, Ovel had been in Vietnam since 1996, learning fluent Vietnamese while working in a number of managerial and business development roles. When Mekong founder Chris Freund first met Ovel, he was running the largest furniture exporter in the country. Freund appreciated Ovel's depth of experience and practical leadership, and recruited him to lead the turnaround of AA Corporation, a Mekong portfolio company. In six years as CEO of AA, he revived the struggling company, growing revenue twelvefold and generating a 50%-plus EBITDA annualized growth rate. When Freund asked Ovel to join Mekong Capital in 2013, he did not realize how fruitful the relationship would be.

VOB is Formed

To formalize the structure, with the help of a retired partner from Clayton, Dubilier & Rice (CD&R), the first US-based operating-centric PE firm, Mekong Capital created a value optimization board (VOB). The VOB structure gave Mekong and its portfolio companies access to world-class expertise that was otherwise unavailable in the local market (see Exhibit 8.2). For example, around the time of Mekong's Golden Gate realization, Pete Bassi, former CEO of Yum! International joined the VOB board. As chairman and president of Yum!, he had overseen more than 12,000 restaurants (60% KFC, 38% Pizza Hut, 2% Taco Bell) spread across 100 countries, representing over $10 billion of sales and $500 million in profits annually. Bassi had personally led the expansion of KFC and Pizza Hut across Asia, opening over 1,100 new units each year around the globe.

A VOB director's responsibilities can be broad—they range from sourcing new investments, providing and evaluating operating initiatives to increase value, and working with the firm's management teams to drive operating gains throughout the life of the investment. Moreover, to ensure VOB directors' are compensated in a way that aligns their interests with those of Mekong Capital, each member of the VOB earns carried interest and is accountable for results. Ovel explained:

> *"Our VOB has decades of experience between them. It would be difficult to recruit this level of talent on the ground, or find a consultant with the same credibility. Also, unlike working with a consultant, we have a long-term relationship with our VOB directors and they want to see us succeed."*

Deal Origination

Reading the Tea Leaves

Mekong Capital's deal origination strategy evolved towards a top-down approach, looking for the best management teams and potential sector winners while developing long-term courtships. Its calling card was its reputation for building the best-managed businesses in Asia, while the firm provided wealth-creation opportunities for managers and co-owners. This went a long way to creating preferred positions when investment opportunities arose. At the time of Mekong's investment in Golden Gate, however, intuition played a key role in identifying the opportunity. Freund recalled how, in July 2007:

> *"I was in our Hanoi office, drinking tea. I looked at the label – Cozy Tea – and on a whim I thought there might be an investment opportunity in the tea company… their website redirected to Ashima [which became Golden Gate's first restaurant brand]. Vinh was the founder of both the restaurant and the tea company. We did a bit of research and thought the restaurant looked like a more interesting opportunity… The sector was attractive to us but there was not a lot of validation in Vietnam because there were no public restaurant groups. There was really only one other fairly big chain and it wasn't profitable."*

Courtship Inspires a Deal

Following up for Freund, Tran Thu Hong, Mekong Capital's Hanoi-based deal leader, reached out to the founder Vinh (see Exhibit 8.12 for an index of names). At the time, Vinh was not looking for equity investment and had rebuffed several other suitors, as Tran Thu Hong explained:

> *"Although Vinh was not interested in an investment, we had a mutual friend so Vinh was willing to meet me just to chat. We started discussing his business on a regular basis. We talked about his vision, what he wanted to achieve. He already had another concept in mind…. I encouraged him to think bigger and we spoke about expanding to 50 locations."*

Through their weekly conversations, Vinh started to refine his vision for Golden Gate's growth and to realize he might need an equity partner. But it wasn't until he spoke to a fellow entrepreneur that he decided to move forward with Mekong Capital. The firm introduced Vinh to Nguyen Duc Tai, CEO of another portfolio company, Mobile World. Vinh recounted:

> *"[Tai] told me his story. After speaking with him I believed that going with a private equity fund was the right thing to do. I also knew that Mekong Capital was interested in more than just making money on its investment. They would help me build my business and lend outside credibility. Another thing that attracted me was Chris Freund's reputation for integrity. I felt that while we may have disagreements over direction in the future – as is true in any venture – his word was good. Having a firm I could trust as a partner was critical to me."*

Negotiations were short and sweet (see Exhibit 8.9 for an overview of negotiations in Asia). According to Vinh,

> *"I didn't see valuation as the primary issue… I was selling a stake to bring in a partner that could help me grow faster than I could on my own. That was the bet. I was more interested in whether or not Mekong Capital could help me make my business better or not than I was in selling a minority position for the highest price. We would make far more from our remaining ownership if they were as good as I thought they were in helping me develop the business to its full potential."*

After several months of due diligence, Mekong Capital purchased a 15% stake for US$1.5 million in January 2008.

Golden Gate and Growth

The Opportunity

Despite a lack of viable restaurant chains, the Vietnamese dining sector was aided by attractive economic and demographic trends: it was the 13th most populous country in the world, with 89 million[1] people as of 2013 with an average age of 29. (See Exhibits 8.3–8.5 for additional economic and demographic data.) Since initiating economic reforms in 1986, Vietnam had been slowly transitioning from a centrally-planned economy to a free-market economy. With the transition had come strong growth in exports, as well as in the industrial and consumer sectors. According to the World Bank, in 2014, GDP grew 6% in 2014 and the rate was expected to continue through the next year and accelerate in 2016. Vietnam had also managed to improve its macroeconomic stability, curbing inflation to a manageable 4.1% in 2014.

The food service sector had grown 9.2% between 2006 and 2011, one of the fastest rates in the region.[2] Yet competition in the seated casual dining space was limited. While KFC had been present in Vietnam since 1997, McDonald's did not open its first location in the country until 2014. Nearly 80%[3] of local Vietnamese restaurants outlets were kiosks or food stalls with little indoor seating.

1. World Development Indicators, World Bank.
2. East West Hospitality Group Report.
3. *Ibid.*

Successful examples from other parts of developing Asia had shown the restaurant business to be highly scalable. Hotpot restaurants like Ashima were especially attractive, with relatively low start-up costs and limited kitchen equipment required. In Thailand, local restaurant companies such as Thai-Chinese-Japanese hotpot restaurant Coca Group and multi-concept Syndicate Public Group had each established over 50 locations. Syndicate Public was even traded on the Thai Stock Exchange. In China, by 2007 the Forever Pride (Little Sheep) hotpot chain was ranked the number two retail chain with over 400 company-owned outlets (see Exhibit 8.6).

Even within the restaurant segment, Golden Gate stood out for its strong management team and modest start-up costs. "Vinh and his co-founders were clearly A-players," said Freund. "There was a real leadership team, and the decision-making process was very collaborative."

Meagre Beginnings

In 2003, Vinh started a teabag company in Vietnam marketing directly to consumers. Although Cozy Tea became Vietnam's second largest teabag brand, stiff competition from Lipton made it difficult to translate market share into profitability. In 2005 while still managing the tea business, Vinh decided to open a restaurant in Hanoi that served mushroom hotpot and featured vibrant interior design and exotic ingredients.

Even though the price point initially seemed beyond the reach of the average Vietnamese consumer, Ashima became a huge success overnight. It took only three months for the restaurant to pay back the initial investment (compared to an average of 2-3 years for quick-service restaurants in the USA). He quickly shifted his attention from the struggling tea business to the restaurant sector, opening additional locations. When Tran Thu Hong first contacted him, the company had five Ashima restaurants in Hanoi and Ho Chi Minh City.

Adaptability and Expansion

After Mekong's investment (2008), Mekong and Golden Gate agreed on two priorities: First, they decided to continue building out locations to reach an ambitious expansion target of 50 locations by 2012. Second, to strengthen the management team.

Golden Gate was already planning to launch a second concept, Kichi Kichi, a conveyor belt hotpot chain with an average ticket of US$11, less than half that of Ashima. Freund commented:

> *"At the onset, one of my biggest concerns was the leap to multiple concepts. Golden Gate had always been excited about multiple concepts and at the time they had only had one."*

Launched in 2009, Kichi Kichi was not an immediate success. Its first outlet, located inside a mall, failed. After revisions to the initial concept and the decision to choose street-front locations, Golden Gate was able to open several successful branches of Kichi Kichi, as Freund affirmed:

> *"Golden Gate proved to be really good at experimenting. They were always tinkering with décor, menus, and concepts."*

Golden Gate's adaptability was well-suited to the changing tastes of Vietnam's rising middle class. Diners were hungry for new experiences, many having limited travel experience outside of Vietnam. According to market studies, the Vietnamese consumer was value driven (focused on both quality and price), with a preference for Asian cuisine while open to new concepts. Younger consumers were rapidly developing brand awareness and loyalty. Golden Gate played to these trends. A year after the Kichi Kichi launch, it started Sumo BBQ, a Japanese table-side grilling restaurant. A year later, it introduced Vuvuzela's, an upscale Western-style sports bar offering draught beer and Asian and Western food (see Exhibit 8.7 for its restaurant concepts).

This rapid expansion was not without growing pains, as Vinh recounted the story about his failure to dig roots in Singapore:

> *"After we got investment, we started to think we were a big company and had to think global. We made the decision to go to Singapore. We thought it would be a great market to bring a Vietnamese concept to a global audience, but we simply were not ready."*

After the failure in Singapore, Golden Gate refocused its attention on the domestic market, where it now had to keep pace with the ultra-competitive market for real estate and talent in Vietnam's two largest cities, where all its restaurants were located. In 2013, its home city of Hanoi had 6.9 million residents and per capita income of US$2,985. Ho Chi Minh in the south boasted 7.8 million residents and per capita income of US$4,513, more than twice the national average. The relatively strong buying power of Vietnamese consumers in these "tier-one" cities made them attractive, but their robust economies also made competition for locations and people particularly fierce. It was difficult to procure sites suitable for restaurants, as Ovel explained:

> *"Vinh had specifically asked for the authority to take locations whenever he could. Taking locations is very opportunistic... he didn't want to have to take it to the board; he needed to make decisions quickly."*

Building Talent

Finding talent also was an issue, especially in Ho Chi Minh City. With Hanoi and Ho Chi Minh City more than 700 miles apart, each required its own central kitchen and managerial staff. Vinh and his cofounders, all natives of Hanoi, found that "the experience in Ho Chi Minh was totally different [than Hanoi]. We struggled for five years to find the right management." Freund recalled how Golden Gate needed talent to fuel its expansion strategy:

> *"Early on, I worried about the management team. Are they going to recruit professionals? They had fairly junior marketing and finance staff. It was a slow build, but eventually they were able to create a great team."*

With Mekong's help and suggestions, Golden Gate recruited a new COO, CFO, and HR director. A big breakthrough came in 2011, when Golden Gate recruited Nguyen Cao Tri, a food service veteran from KFC, to run its Ho Chi Minh operations. Vinh explained:

> *"[Tri] saw everything wrong with the structure, marketing, operations. He brought best practices from KFC, and he was motivated."*

Missed Target

In 2012, despite growing from four to eight concepts and increasing the number of outlets from 36 to 41, Golden Gate's customer traffic slid (see Exhibit 8.8). While still profitable, it missed its earnings targets in 2012 and same-store sales growth declined across many of its established outlets.

Adding to the tensions, Freund had verbally agreed to Vinh's proposal made earlier in the year, that the company would buy back 11% of its shares from one of his co-founders based on a US$27 million valuation at a P/E ratio of 6x, which in turn was based on the expected 2012 net profit target. As the year progressed, net profit performance was significantly off track, such that the P/E of the buy-back at the agreed valuation ultimately looked to be a P/E ratio of 10–12x – nearly double that of what was previously agreed. Expecting the buy-back proposal to be submitted to the board and that the terms would not be finalized until approved, Freund then learned that the agreement had already been executed and board approval was merely a formality.

The resulting deadlock took several months of discussions to resolve. Ultimately, Freund took responsibility for not having communicated clearly with Vinh that his initial support for the plan was "on principle," and that the final terms would have to be approved by the board before the buyback was executed. Freund ultimately agreed to do the buy-back at the $27 million valuation. Vinh acknowledged:

> *"Chris's reputation for integrity was impeccable. He did not disappoint. While we may have different opinions, we could trust that his intentions and objectives were for the good of the company."*

Maximizing Value and Creating a Profitable Pathway for Future Owners

Growth vs. Value: Changing Tack?

By 2013, Golden Gate had 10 concepts and 58 restaurants. The company had grown into one of the only multi-concept chains in Vietnam and had a professional management team. But needless to say, the cloud of the 2012 performance still lingered on in the mind of Chris Freund. He and his new partner Chad agreed that Ovel should take over as Mekong's deal leader for Golden Gate:

> *"We had agreed that Mekong Capital's exit from Golden Gate was to be imminent. It was surprising… here was a very good business, yet no one here could generate what a clear investment thesis for a new buyer looked like."*

In order to create a compelling value proposition for the next owner or for public shareholders, Ovel's first order of business was to understand Golden Gate from top to bottom, from customers to suppliers:

> *"None of my predecessors at the firm had been to the central kitchen or looked into the supply chain in great depth. Interactions had been limited to the board room, the head office, and casually visiting some of the restaurants."*

While Ovel was new to restaurants, he was well-versed in working capital and supply chain management. After a few days visiting Golden Gate kitchens, he believed fundamental changes in the back-of-the-house could make Golden Gate a more profitable and desirable acquisition target:

> *"There is a tendency to focus on what is going well: great interior design, great locations, and great menus. The front of the house was working well but everything else was delegated to someone else. I was convinced the back of the house was the number one driver for margin expansion. We could increase profitability, improve working capital and improve the customer experience – ensure faster service times and deliver every item on the menu – if we focused on the kitchen and supply chain, and created the right KPIs...."*

> *"At the time, there was no demand forecasting from restaurants to the central kitchens. All communication was paper and email. With nearly 60 stores, I couldn't believe there wasn't an IT system in place. And then there was the supply chain. If a vendor would turn up with a truck full of lettuce and the kitchen didn't need it that day, they'd say they were rejecting the shipment due to poor quality. This kind of practice just amplified the inefficiencies."*

To date, Golden Gate's success formula had emphasized top line growth. Vinh's team were considered 'tastemakers', skilled at launching new concepts. Managers were rewarded based on store traffic and footprint expansion. Ovel believed that if Mekong's exit were to occur via a trade sale, it would be efficiency, not topline growth, which would command a higher price. He was convinced that implementing a new set of operational value key performance indicators (KPIs) around wastage, spoilage, input costs and optimizing payment terms with vendors was a critical first step. In order to measure KPIs at a store level, he would have to work with Golden Gate's CFO to design an adequate cost-accounting system and establish a basic enterprise resource planning (ERP) system.

Ovel also believed a supplier education programme could improve the quality of ingredients. In Vietnam there were few farms large enough to be Golden Gate's sole supplier, so Golden Gate had to work with many small suppliers for every ingredient, reducing consistency. By working closely with farmers, he thought Golden Gate could get produce and other key ingredients delivered to its own specifications.

Operating Advisors and External Visits

Mekong Capital brought in a number of its operating advisors to present to Vinh, including prominent restaurant consulting groups from the US and Hong Kong. Ovel explained the tactic:

> *"We couldn't be relevant in the same way [as restaurant experts]; we couldn't provide companies best practices from their industry. For Golden Gate, we could tell them how to make an investment report, build a company culture ... but we couldn't tell them to restructure their kitchen or cook a sauce.... So we looked for consultants who could provide sector insight, operational depth, and had the credibility to drive change."*

'Seeing is believing' for many management teams in an emerging market. Most are very inward-facing with little exposure to best practices and formal training. Golden Gate's senior management team visited Hong Kong-based Maxim's, Thailand's Central Group, and Chicago-based Lettuce Entertain You. Said Vinh:

> *"Visiting restaurants overseas gave me new ideas… it helped to see it for myself. After my trip to Chicago [to visit Lettuce Entertain You], I wanted to change [Golden Gate's organizational] structure. Golden Gate had a 'top-down' system, where regional and store managers reported to headquarters. As Golden Gate grew in size and complexity, it was increasingly difficult to maintain the centralized structure. Lettuce Entertain You had more than 40 concepts. They could have more concepts because they were organized with a bottom-up profit sharing structure. The back office just supported them, it didn't command them. People at the restaurant level became decision makers and were able to develop their creativity."*

Ovel's proposed change in KPIs dovetailed with Vinh's proposed organizational shift as both required new reporting processes and systems in order to move accountability to the restaurant level.

One of Mekong's operating advisors, Joel Silverstein of East-West Hospitality Group, was brought from Hong Kong to review operations. Silverstein's verdict was that "Golden Gate was a pretty well-run chain before I walked in the door. We were making incremental improvements… nothing that would double or triple their income overnight." He outlined additional measures to consider:

- **Buying "the whole cow":** Golden Gate sourced its beef from North America and Australia, and used this as a key part of its advertising around quality ingredients. Beef accounted for nearly 40% of Golden Gate's costs, since most of their businesses were beef-related and beef prices were at a 25-year high. Silverstein recommended they buy "the whole cow" and increase the yield to 90–95% of each cow using special butchering techniques.
- **Developing a recipe management system:** This would allow Golden Gate to see critical operational metrics (such as waste and cost of each menu item) on a dish-by-dish basis, even more granular than the systems Ovel was proposing.
- **Lowering pricing:** All of Golden Gate's concepts had an average ticket of over $10, which Silverstein believed killed scalability. By contrast, the average ticket at a competing Vietnamese chain, Al Fresco's, was US$5, while Pizza Hut's was $6–7.
- **Expanding beyond Tier One cities:** Silverstein believed Tier Two Vietnamese cities were under-penetrated. Comparing his experience in Thailand and China, he foresaw good development opportunities in the next 5–10 years, although affordability would be key.

More Expansion Now?

Expanding beyond Hanoi and Ho Chi Minh (Tier One cities) had been in the back of everyone's mind for some time. Over 80% of Vietnam's population lived outside of Hanoi and Ho Chi Minh City. In the second tier were two cities with over one million inhabitants, as well as several other larger conurbations. Few international or national restaurant chains operated in these markets, leaving them relatively untapped.

An expansion strategy seemed especially timely in early 2013. Golden Gate management had heard rumours that the largest property developer in Vietnam, VinGroup, was about to announce the building of 22 new shopping malls in Tier Two cities throughout Vietnam by the end of 2016. VinGroup's malls would focus on entertainment and dining to drive traffic. Aside from fast food companies, Golden Gate and its multiple brands would be the perfect tenant for VinGroup. The potential could be anywhere from 50-75 new restaurants, as each mall could easily house 2–4 different Golden Gate concepts. Once Golden Gate had a reason to reach into Tier Two cities, they could piggyback on the new supply chain to add high-street locations in each major Tier Two city, easily resulting in 200-plus restaurants by the end of 2017.

But this strategy was not without its risks. Urbanization was only slowly chipping away at the rural population and per-capita income was significantly lower in these secondary markets, as Ovel explained: "Expanding operations in Tier Two was unique and different in many respects than toiling in the Tier One markets where managers had been concentrating on to date." The logistics of supplying restaurants hundreds of miles apart could be challenging, and recruiting and training talent might be difficult.

Preparing to Exit

Ovel started working with Golden Gate's CFO to get the books in order. He had been working in parallel with Golden Gate leadership to put together a stock incentive plan for key employees, as he believed certain employees, such as Tri (director of Ho Chi Minh City operations) were the key value-builders of the business. No matter which avenue – optimization or expansion – Golden Gate pursued, these were necessary steps before an exit could be completed. Just as Ovel had brought in operational advisors to help formulate a plan, he sought their counsel as to the efficacy and value that could be achieved by both exit pathways to hear their recommendations before the upcoming board meeting.

The Board Meeting

Exit Advice Prior to the Board Meeting

Ovel spoke with Nguyen Son Duy, who covered the consumer sector for Hanoi Securities, a leading local investment bank, to get his assessment of taking Golden Gate public 12 months out. Enthusiastic at the possibility of underwriting the IPO, Duy met with Ovel and several Golden Gate board members, sharing a brief pitch outlining the process and considerations for taking Golden Gate public. In it, he explained how Mekong could sell all of its stock in the IPO offering, or sell a portion in the IPO and hold out for a higher valuation later, offering secondary shares down the road. It was Duy's opinion that the highest ultimate value for the business was through public ownership, given the emerging bull market in Vietnam. He believed that after going public, Golden Gate could gain a premium over the market price as part of a trade sale down the road, in essence double dipping on value. If Golden Gate were to continue on its aggressive growth path, Duy estimated that the company could be worth at least $300 million if ownership was retained and the company sold to a strategic acquirer in five years (Exhibit 8.10 summarizes his valuation).

The Hanoi Securities pitch was circulated to the entire Golden Gate board. Several members had already indicated agreement with the bank's analysis that an IPO and aggressive growth strategy represented the best avenue for value maximization.

In terms of operating strategy—the dilemma whether to focus on either expanding units or focusing on margins in existing locations over the near term—Duy was unequivocal in recommending footprint expansion as a priority. Moreover he was a strong advocate for entering the Tier Two market in full force, explaining it would make a better story for the IPO. Privately, Duy shared that the glamor of being a first mover in these huge untapped population clusters would make their job easier in attracting growth-minded investors; the IPO buyer in this market was conditioned to favour aggressive growth stories and loved 30%+ growth rates. Although there were no major restaurant group IPOs he could cite as an example, Duy mentioned several recent listings of consumer goods companies that had experienced major pops in value, and referred to the success of food & beverage listings on the neighbouring Thai Stock Exchange, such as S&P, a quick-service restaurant with a market cap of over US$100 million.

Ovel was not so sure. From informal conversations at a recent Asian Food & Beverage Convention he believed a number of international restaurant groups and possibly private equity firms with existing restaurant chains in their portfolio would be interested in Golden Gate. In order to get a complete perspective on a sale to another industry player or PE buyer, he contacted several global investment banks with food sector expertise.

One Hong Kong-based banker took the view that unit profitability and same-store sales growth would be the cornerstone of value for an acquirer, and sent along a research note on the food service sector which seemed to support this idea. If Golden Gate were sold in a trade sale, recent disappointing same-store results would be a deterrent to maximizing value, he explained. Moreover, while the Tier Two expansion was an attractive part of the Golden Gate value proposition for a trade or PE buyer, they would likely appreciate the potential growth without Mekong Capital having to actually prove it. Indeed, the risks of opening a small sample of Tier Two locations might be too great to make this a viable short-term strategy.

Finally, Ovel sought the advice of selective restaurant leaders who had bought other chains like Golden Gate. Exhibit 8.11 includes examples of acquirer criteria from industry expert Pete Bassi, based on his extensive acquisition experience when expanding Yum! International's Pizza Hut and Kentucky Fried Chicken across all of Asia.

Anxious Moments Preparing for the Debate

Settled in his hotel room in Hanoi, Ovel began to gather his thoughts for the meeting ahead. He mulled over the exit alternatives. Were the pros and cons of each option laid out sufficiently? Were the risk/reward assessments clearly identified by the board from the conversations with the underwriter and acquisition experts from the global firms? (See Exhibit 8.12 for index of names.)

An IPO was intriguing, but was the Hanoi Securities' assessment focused more on current market conditions than longer term profitability fundamentals? Stock market sentiment was fickle: sooner or later the underlying existing unit underperformance – if not rectified – would detract from the value on the stock market.

Could the management team handle at the same time growth in new markets and improving efficiency? Was it more prudent to focus on improvements first and look to an acquisition as the most likely and timely route to exit? How convinced should he be that Tier Two expansion was the right move before fixing existing units? How big of an operational leap was involved in opening in more rural locations? Was postponing near-term cash realization the right thing for his investors?

From stimulating same-store sales growth, to introducing new KPIs, to creating a supplier education program, there had to be priorities. Many of these improvements were worthwhile and could be part of a compelling value proposition for an acquirer, but Golden Gate would have to prioritize. It simply did not have the resources to undertake them all at once.

Ovel was hoping for board buy-in the next morning but realised it would be difficult to get. These were two very promising exit pathways with diametrically opposed operational implications. "How should I frame my presentation?" he wondered.

Exhibit 8.1

Middle Class and Affluent Population of Vietnam

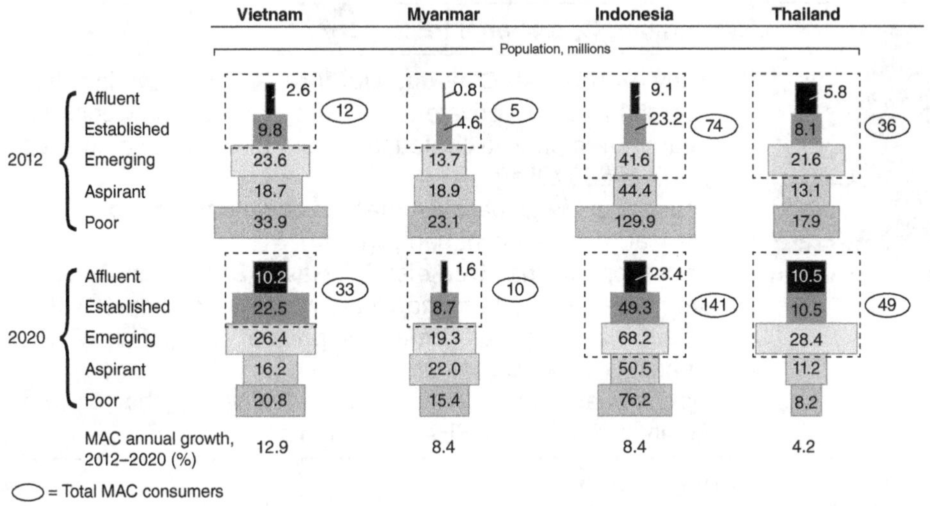

Population, millions

		Vietnam	Myanmar	Indonesia	Thailand
2012	Affluent	2.6	0.8	9.1	5.8
	Established	9.8	4.6	23.2	8.1
	Emerging	23.6	13.7	41.6	21.6
	Aspirant	18.7	18.9	44.4	13.1
	Poor	33.9	23.1	129.9	17.9
	(Total MAC consumers)	12	5	74	36
2020	Affluent	10.2	1.6	23.4	10.5
	Established	22.5	8.7	49.3	10.5
	Emerging	26.4	19.3	68.2	28.4
	Aspirant	16.2	22.0	50.5	11.2
	Poor	20.8	15.4	76.2	8.2
	(Total MAC consumers)	33	10	141	49
MAC annual growth, 2012–2020 (%)		12.9	8.4	8.4	4.2

⬭ = Total MAC consumers

Source: BCG CCCI models; BCG analysis.

Note: In Vietnam and Myanmar, the MAC population comprises the affluent and established segments. In Indonesia and Thailand, the MAC population also includes the emerging segment; this is owing to differences in the point at which consumer spending takes off in these markets. The MAC cutoff is monthly per capita income of $190 in Vietnam, $120 in Myanmar, and $150 in Thailand. For Indonesia, the MAC cutoff, which is expressed in spending rather than income, is $40 per month.

Exhibit 8.2

Value Optimization Board at Mekong Capital (May 2015)

 **Peter Goodson**	**Chairman: Operational PE Expert** • Early Partner at **Clayton, Dubilier & Rice**, world's first operating centric private equity firm focused on achieving returns by improving operating performance in 52 companies worth of $80 billion • Founder of the global M&A practice at **Kidder, Peabody**, and co-head of investment banking • Professor at the **Berkeley - Hass Business School**; prominent in turnaround leadership, operational value creation and emerging markets private equity. Fellow- PE Center @ Tuck / Dartmouth • Operational Focus: Distinguished Fellow- Global Private Equity Initiative @ INSEAD Singapore
 **Bob Willett**	**Retail Expert** • Former CEO of **Best Buy International** for 10 years, where he led Best Buy's most profitable non-U.S. operations, including **CarPhone Warehouse** in Europe, **Five Star Electronics** in China, **Geek Squad** in Europe, and the launch of **Best Buy Mobile** in the U.S. • Former Managing Partner of **Accenture's global retail practice** • Rose through the ranks at **Marks & Spencer** • Chairman **Meta Pak**, **Occahome**, **Eagle Eye Solutions**
 **Pete Bassi**	**Restaurant Expert** • Clearly one of the world's leading restaurant executives • At Yum International as Chairman and President ran more than 12,000 restaurants (60% **KFC**, 38% **Pizza Hut**, 2% **Taco Bell**) spread over approximately100 countries representing over $10 billion of sales and $500 million of profits annually • Personally led the famous and successful expansion of **Kentucky Fried Chicken** and **Pizza Hut** across Asia opening over 1100 new units each year globally • Boards: **Potbelly**, **BJ Restaurants**, and **AmRest** restaurant chain HQ in Poland
 **Paul Lageweg**	**FMCG Expert** • Leading expert in brand and marketing development • Currently Regional Marketing Director Asia Pacific for British American Tobacco and previously led the global launch of the e-cigarette • Former Group Managing Director at Kimberly Clark for several Asian countries, including Vietnam • Former General Manager for Unilever in Vietnam

Exhibit 8.3
Gross National Income per Capita (Thousands USD, PPP), 2005–2013

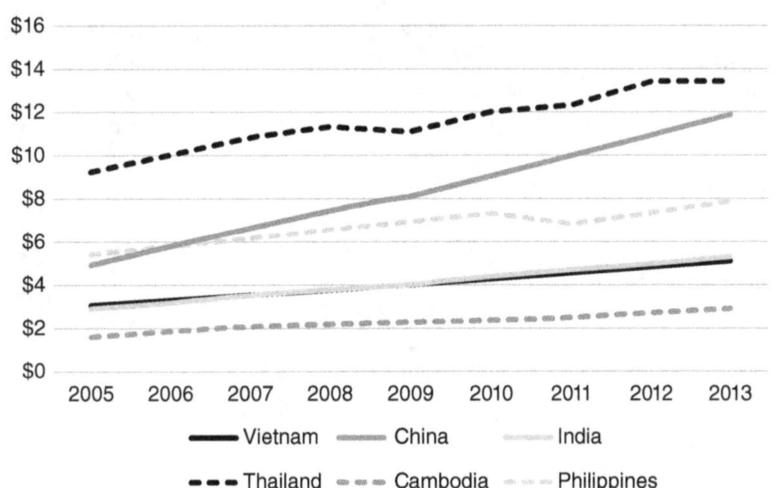

Exhibit 8.4
2013 Population (in millions) for Select Countries

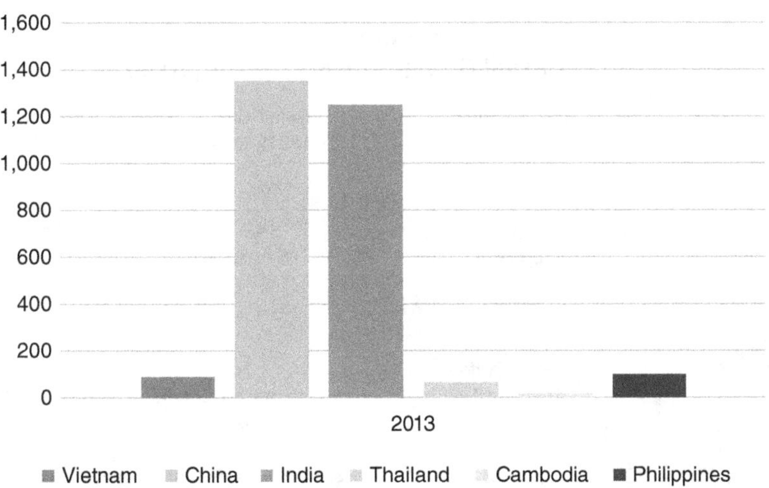

Exhibit 8.5

Real GDP Growth of Southeast Asia, China and India (annual percent change)

	2012	2018	2014-18	2000-07
ASEAN-6 countries				
Brunei Darussalam	1.0	2.4	2.3	–
Indonesia	6.2	6.1	6.0	5.1
Malaysia	5.6	5.3	5.1	5.5
Philippines	6.8	5.9	5.8	4.9
Singapore	1.3	3.1	3.3	6.4
Thailand	6.5	5.3	4.9	5.1
CLMV countries				
Cambodia	7.2	7.1	6.8	9.6
Lao PDR	7.9	7.5	7.7	6.8
Myanmar	–	7.0	6.8	–
Vietnam	5.2	6.0	5.4	7.6
Average of ASEAN 10	5.5(*)	5.6	5.4	5.5(**)
2 large economies in Emerging Asia				
China	7.7	7.5	7.7	10.5
India	3.7	6.1	5.9	7.1
Average of Emerging Asia	6.4	6.9	6.9	8.6

Source: OECD Development Centre

Exhibit 8.6

Asian Casual Dining / Hot Pot Chains (2008)

China	Little Sheep 715 outlets	Ajisen Ramen 185 outlets	Little Lively Sheep 413 outlets
Thailand	Coca Suki Restaurant 50 outlets	S&P 278 outlets	The Pizza Company 120 outlets
Vietnam	Highlands Coffee 40 outlets	Pho24 Vietnamese Pho Noodle 60 outlets	KFC 40 outlets

In Thailand, the Coca Group – a Thai-Chinese-Japanese hotpot cuisine restaurant group – had firmly established a position with more than 50 outlets nationwide and internationally. S&P, a 278-outlet chain of quick-service restaurants, listed on the Stock Exchange of Thailand, had a market capitalization of US$100.9M in October 2007. In China, the 200-outlet Ajisen (China) chain was among the nation's top five restaurant chains with estimated revenue of $121M in 2007.

In Vietnam, there were no multi-concept restaurant chains at the time of Mekong Capital's initial investment in Golden Gate. KFC was the only major Western quick-service restaurant active in the market.

Exhibit 8.7
Golden Gate Concepts (2013)

ASHIMA Avg. Check: $23	KICHI KICHI Avg. Check: $11	SumoBBQ Avg. Check: $18	Vuvuzela Avg. Check: $13	i Sushi Avg. Check: $22
Hotpot serving mushroom and other speciality items that are traditionally perceived only for the royalty and the wealthy	Extensive hotpot options delivered via rotating conveyor – at a fixed price	Japanese BBQ, served tableside, featuring imported beef from Australia/USA	Lively western style bar offering various types of food and draught beer	Authentic Japanese-style food including Sushi and Tepanyaki
# of units: 5	# of units: 22	# of units: 12	# of units: 6	# of units: 2
Ba Con Cùu' Avg. Check: $13	**35th Street Avg. Check: $7**	**Daruma Avg. Check: $9**	**GoGi house Avg. Check: $10**	
Mongolian lamb hotpot featuring speciality soup and imported lamb from Australia	A modern interpretation of traditional street food capturing the spirit of the 36 quarters of old Hanoi	Japanese Bistro offering a novel Japanese fast food serving style	Traditional Korean-style BBQ	
# of units: 4	# of units: 1	# of units: 1	# of units: 5	

Source: Company Data, # of units as of 2013 year end, excluding one unit to be closed in Q4 2013

Exhibit 8.8
EBITDA Growth, 2008–2014(e)

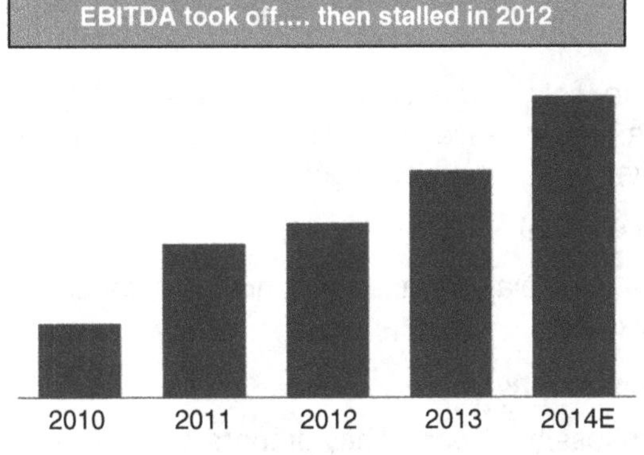

Exhibit 8.9

The Eight Keys to Successful Negotiations in Asia (adapted from The Chinese Negotiation, John L. Graham and N. Mark Lam, October 2003, Harvard Business Review)

1. **Personal Connections**

   Asian business people prize relationships among friends, relatives and close associates. Favours are always remembered and returned, though not necessarily right away. Ignoring reciprocity is considered immoral.

2. **The Intermediary**

   Introductions are essential during meetings with strangers. This trusted business associate connects you with his trusted associate, creating a personal link to your target organization or executive. Intermediaries interpret negotiators' moods, body language and facial expressions. They—not the negotiators—first raise business issues for discussion, and often settle differences.

3. **Social Status**

   Casualness about social status doesn't play amount people who value obedience and deference to superiors. Sending a low-level representative to a high-level negotiation can kill a deal.

4. **Interpersonal Harmony**

   Relationships of equals are cemented through friendships and positive feelings, generated during months of visits and long dinners. Any attempt to do business without first establishing harmony is rude.

5. **Holistic Thinking**

   Asians discuss all issues simultaneously in apparently haphazard order—emphasizing the whole package over details. Nothing is settled until everything is. This holistic thinking contrasts with the linear approach of some Westerners—and spawns the greatest tension between negotiating teams.

6. **Thrift**

   Asians bargain intensely over price, padding offers with room to manoeuvre and using silence and patience as tactics. They expect both sides to make concessions—often after weeks of haggling.

7. **"Face" or Social Capital**

   A broken promise or display of anger or aggression causes mutual loss of face—disastrous to any deal.

8. **Endurance, Relentlessness**

   Asians prize relentless hard work. They prepare diligently for negotiations and expect long bargaining sessions. Demonstrate your endurance by asking many questions, doing your research and showing patience.

Exhibit 8.10

Hanoi Securities' IPO Suggested Valuation

	IPO-HOLD *New growth Trade Sale Year 5*	SALE *Exit Now*
Proceeds	Reinvested	Distributed
# of Restaurants	300	60
Revenue	$350 million	$70 million
EBITDA	$ 30 million	$10 million
EBITDA Multiple	10x	10x
Value: PV in 5th year sale vs exit now	**$300 Million**	**$100 million**

Exhibit 8.11

Restaurant Acquirers' Perspectives on Value[4] (adapted from interview with Pete Bassi, Retired Chairman and President Yum! International)

When a buyer enters a new market like Vietnam, there are several key criteria they might use to determine both level of interest and to define the value of an acquisition target. A buyer will want to see that the existing business is on a stable footing, and unit profitability is fully developed, with credible plans for future growth. Some of the questions/metrics the buyer might emphasize include:

Unit Economics and Forecasting Assessment

- **Same-Store Sales Growth (SSS):** How are the existing locations trending? A buyer might conduct an analysis of comparable stores and in the process isolate those that are going through the usual "honeymoon" period experienced by new stores. A buyers' analysis might be categorized by relevant mix issues: region, vintage, management spans, turnover etc. He might compare base SSS to like duration to better determine how each development program is actually performing and will most likely perform in the future.
- **New Unit Returns:** This includes detailed tracking/analysis of opening results. It is important to quarantine the pattern of a new store's "trial period," as well as understanding the pattern of sales erosion. A buyer might develop a new unit return model based on empirical data: Sales erosion, margin stabilization, unit cash-on-cash returns in terms of investment payback, etc.

4. Notes from Professor Goodson's Interview with Pete Bassi

- **Stability of Unit Margins:** What is the stable-state margin and how long does it take to achieve it? Usually this is a couple of years out from opening and the acquirer is looking for 20%-plus cash margin. This is important to a buyer because if it takes a year or more to reach a stable margin the company needs to absorb the incremental hit in its costing of its development program. A buyer will want to understand the fixed and variable cost components, and their influence on margin and price elasticity. Again a buyer might segment this analysis by relevant mix issues: region, vintage, management span, turnover etc. are fundamental. What are the patterns: are there key performance differences; are there location inferences or operational mix implications?
- **Capital Efficiency:** What is the cash-on-cash payback period for new site openings by mix? Is it on average under 12 months or can it be brought to this standard? How much new capital investment from the acquirer, if any, will be required to support buyers forecast? What local capital is available from franchising, lending sources to fund growth internally, if any?
- **Supply Chain Effectiveness:** How much of the supply chain is localized, and what are the foreign exchange and pricing implications? What is imported? What is the historical cost of goods sold inflation rate? How concentrated is supply? Any scale issues with suppliers? What ERP process or simple planning systems exist? A buyer would look to review the distribution system in terms of quality, efficiency and scale. What are the processes on contracts: duration, terms and approvals? Are there sufficient back-up suppliers to offer steady supply if needed and keep the pressure on costs?

Strategic Efficacy

- **Customer Knowledge:** Does a seller use customer analytics or do they rely on seat-of-the-pants judgments? What attracts customers? How does the customer view the restaurant in the marketplace? How do they develop customer feedback: process used and accuracy history? What creates frequent customers?
- **Incentive linkage to value drivers:** Do they create actionable KPIs that measure the right stuff? Are a few high-impact metrics linked to compensation in a meaningful manner?
- **Footprint-Growth Potential:** What is the opportunity for expansion by theme? How tough is the competitive landscape for talent and location. Does the customer's pocket-book and preference indicate strong future demand for the restaurant concept and price point? Is the supply chain capacity enough to support the growth? Are there aggregation or central kitchen opportunities?
- **Multiple Concept Capability:** Does management have the bandwidth to innovate, develop and support more themes or are they limited to existing concepts? Do they jump to new themes before they develop what they have to stable and profitable levels? Who are the key taste/menu/site entrepreneurs and how good are they? Have they shown innovation in menu creation and introduced new entrées successfully over time?
- **Key Talent Retention/Development:** Most emerging market teams require significant gap-filling. How willing is management to bring in real talent? Who are the "must-have talents" throughout the organization? How are they locked in if a deal takes place? From employee conversations and triangulating answers: Who is continuously referenced as the best at developing supply chain sources/buying? Who is the best menu innovator? Who is the best at training staff, and why? Who are the best site managers, and why?

Exhibit 8.12

Cast of Characters

- Chad Ovel: Mekong Capital's newest Partner and Deal Leader for Golden Gate Group
- Chris Freund: Founder of Mekong Capital, who initially sourced the Golden Gate investment
- Pete Bassi: Former CEO of Yum! International; serves on Mekong Capital's Value Optimization Board
- Dao The Vinh (Vinh): Founder and CEO of Golden Gate Group
- Tran Thu Hong (Hong): Mekong Capital Deal Leader, who built relationship with Golden Gate
- Nguyen Duc Tai (Tai): CEO of another Mekong portfolio company, Mobile World
- Nguyen Cao Tri (Tri): a manager recruited from KFC to run Golden Gate's Ho Chi Minh operations
- Joel Silverstein: Operating advisor from East-West Hospitality Group, who was engaged to review Golden Gate's operations
- Nguyen Son Duy (Duy): Hanoi Securities investment banker

Golden Gate Restaurant Themes

- 37th Street – a modern-oriented but traditional street food restaurant
- Ashima – the pioneer mushroom hotpot restaurant chain in Vietnam
- Ba Con Cuu – Inner Mongolia hotpot restaurant chain
- City Beer Station – an affordable beer garden
- Daruma – Japanese sit-down restaurant
- Gogi House – Korean BBQ restaurant chain
- iCook – a Japanese fast-food
- Isushi - buffet à la carte of Japanese cuisine
- Kichi-Kichi – rotary express hotpot restaurant chain
- Sumo BBQ – grill & hotpot restaurant chain
- Vuvuzela – beer club chain, delivery concept

Restaurant Management Training Visits

- Central Group –Thailand-based restaurant group
- Lettuce Entertain You – US-based restaurant group
- Maxim's – Hong Kong-based restaurant group

[illegible]

CASE

9 SLALOM TO THE FINISH

CARLYLE'S EXIT FROM MONCLER

SYNOPSIS

In late 2010, Carlyle is considering an exit from its investment in the European fashion brand Moncler, in which it holds a minority stake. With the capital markets opening up in the aftermath of the global financial crisis, the shareholders in the business begin to prepare the company for a public listing. However, by spring 2011, volatility in the financial markets (as the Euro crisis unfolds) is increasing, prompting Carlyle to start a low-key secondary sales process as a back-up option. The dual-track process comes to a decision point in early June, when Carlyle must commit to one of its options—or develop alternatives.

The case focuses on the complexities of preparing and executing an exit under rapidly changing market conditions, taking various stakeholder interests and potential outcomes into consideration. As a true growth-equity investment, despite the involvement of a large global buyout investor, it comes with the additional challenges of ensuring alignment of interest with other stakeholders.

PEDAGOGICAL OBJECTIVE OF THE CASE

The case shows how private equity firms think from the outset about a suitable exit and how they position a portfolio company for a successful exit through various strategic decisions. It gives students a chance to evaluate different exit options for a private equity firm and to discuss how optionality and negotiation leverage in a sales process can be created and maintained. The case also demonstrates how private equity firms make decisions under uncertainty and time constraints, taking a variety of financial and nonfinancial factors into account.

SUGGESTED ASSIGNMENT QUESTIONS

1. Describe the constraints Carlyle faced when preparing its exit from Moncler.
2. In fall 2010, what were the main exit options available to Carlyle? List the respective advantages and disadvantages for each option.
3. Fast forward to Thursday, June 2, 2011: compare the two main options on the table for Carlyle and discuss the alternatives by addressing the following questions:
   - What are the expected returns for Carlyle under the different exit scenarios? Please differentiate between immediate realizations and outstanding value.
   - What are the advantages and disadvantages of each alternative? Describe the risks to realizing those returns.

ADDITIONAL RESOURCES

To make the most of this case study, we suggest the following additional sources to provide context and background information:

- In particular, we recommend the following chapters from *Mastering Private Equity—Transformation via Venture Capital, Minority Investments & Buyouts*
  - Chapter 1 Private Equity Essentials
  - Chapter 3 Growth Equity
  - Chapter 12 Securing Management Teams
  - Chapter 15 Exit
- Case website for faculty and lecturers: http://cases.insead.edu/slalom-to-the-finish
- You may also refer to the book website for further material:
  www.masteringprivateequity.com

Slalom to the Finish

Carlyle's Exit from Moncler

03/2015-5969

This case was written by Rishika Agrawal, Researcher for INSEAD's Global Private Equity Initiative (GPEI), and Michael Prahl, Executive Director of GPEI, under the supervision of Professor Claudia Zeisberger, Affiliate Professor of Entrepreneurship and Family Enterprise at INSEAD. It is intended to be used as a basis for class discussion rather than to illustrate either effective or ineffective handling of a particular situation or for any other purpose.

The information in this case is derived from publicly available sources.

The case originated from a class project by Borja Aparicio, Beat Braegger, Lukas Gayler and Gerd Wipplinger, all MBA class of December 2012, carried out under the supervision of Professor Vikas Aggarwal, Assistant Professor of Entrepreneurship and Family Enterprise at INSEAD.

This case was sponsored by INSEAD's Private Equity Club (IPEC) and was the winner of its annual case writing competition for MBA students.

Funding for this case study was provided by INSEAD's Global Private Equity Initiative (GPEI).

Additional material about INSEAD case studies (e.g., videos, spreadsheets, links) can be accessed at cases.insead.edu.

> "The Moncler down puffa is to the alpine sports scene what denim is to streetwear: it is legendary and at the same time current."
>
> Retailer Club 21

Marco De Benedetti, group managing director of Carlyle, was sitting in his office on Friday January 14th 2011, after another meeting with the board of directors at Moncler. Browsing through the news headlines, he saw that Fitch had become the last of the big rating agencies to downgrade Greece's credit rating to junk status. According to its statement, Fitch had taken the decision despite support from the EU and IMF for Greece's austerity programme.

Our investment in Moncler has been doing great so far, he thought, but there is one important question for us at Carlyle: Will the increased uncertainty and volatility in the European markets due to the European debt crisis cause the IPO market to close again after it looked so promising in 2010, and should we therefore broaden our exit approach towards a dual track strategy with a possible IPO on one side and a trade sale through an auction on the other?

Moncler: Background

Moncler is an abbreviation of Monastier-de-Clermont, a mountain village near Grenoble, France, where the brand was born in 1952. In the decades that followed Moncler became famous for its stylish down jackets and was often credited with inventing the down-filled ski jacket, which it supplied to French Winter Olympic teams from the 1960s. The jackets became a must-have fashion item and could be seen on the slopes of St. Moritz in Switzerland, Megève in France, as well as Cortina d'Ampezzo in Italy where the company opened its own stores.

Besides the Moncler brand, the company managed the brands of Henry Cotton's, Marina Yachting, and Coast Weber & Ahaus. It also licensed Cerruti's sportswear brand 18CRR81.

Remo Ruffini, an Italian entrepreneur, bought the 50-year-old brand in 2003, taking full control of all the company's operations in 2005 with the help of three local Italian private equity (PE) firms. His goal was to reposition Moncler and turn it from a sports casual active line into a contemporary urban outerwear collection. With a clear vision, referred to as his "global down jacket strategy", he started by changing the strategy for the product, the range (*gamme*) and distribution.

On the product side, everything that was not down-filled was dropped from the Moncler line. The range was expanded by adding higher-end, designer and archive collections through collaborations with the likes of Balenciaga and Fendi, and by creating high-end collections such as "Moncler Gamme Rouge" for Women, designed by Giambattista Vialli and "Moncler Gamme Blue" for Men, designed by Thom Browne. Moncler's distribution, after consolidating within the world's most exclusive mountain resorts, reached for the first time specialty stores and high-end retailers in major cities.[1] Moncler opened its first urban store in Paris' Rue du Faubourg Saint Honoré

1. *Women's Wear Daily*, 6/7/2007, Vol. 193 Issue 121, p. 14.

in 2007, followed by a store on Milan's Via Spiga in 2008. Thanks to an innovative communication strategy and its uniqueness, the brand began attracting celebrity clients and a following for its ultra-chic puffa jackets.

Carlyle's Investment in Moncler: The 2008 Transaction

By 2008, Ruffini had spent five years reshaping the company. The collections were now more contemporary and innovative, and significant investment had been made in rebuilding the wholesale distribution business. Ruffini was convinced that Moncler could make the leap from an iconic brand known only in a few European countries to a global luxury brand. At the time, it was an upmarket brand but not associated with the luxury market. Its products were mostly distributed through department stores and a few retail outlets of its own. Ruffini's vision was to expand its retail network globally and make Moncler an international luxury symbol, paving the way for a public listing of the company in the future.

With his original private equity partners keen to see returns from their well-performing investment and the need for a strong partner to support his global vision, Ruffini began talks with various international PE firms, aiming to find the one who had the experience, capability and the network to achieve his goals.

Carlyle (Exhibit 9.2 & 9.3) stood out among the PE firms interested in Moncler due to its global footprint and willingness to pay a fair price for a minority stake. Ruffini felt that their vision and interests were well aligned to realize his ambitions for taking Moncler global and public.

In October 2008, Carlyle announced a deal which valued the Italian company at €468 million. In a statement after the signing of the deal,[2] De Benedetti commented, "Moncler is a historic sport luxury garment brand that has returned to play a relevant and prestigious role in the market." Looking to the future, he added, "Starting from today, as shareholders of the company we will support Moncler with strategic vision and the means necessary to maximize the important global development opportunities for Moncler and the other brands of the group."[3] Moncler's chairman, creative director and shareholder, Remo Ruffini, commented: "I am now very enthusiastic to have Carlyle as a shareholder to face the new challenges of growth together."

The investment in Moncler was made from Carlyle's third pan-European buyout fund, the €5.35 billion Carlyle Europe Partners III fund (vintage 2007). After losing out to Permira for Valentino Fashion Group S.p.A. in 2007, and an unsuccessful bid for Roberto Cavalli in July 2008, Carlyle had finally found the promising luxury garment brand they were looking for. Carlyle acquired a 48% stake in Moncler from Ruffini's original PE partners, Mittel S.p.A. (a Milan-based financial company), Progressio Sgr (a Milan-based PE firm), and Isa S.p.A. (a Trento-based financial institution). In 2007, Moncler had a turnover of €259 million and EBITDA of €40 million, and it

2. http://www.luxist.com/2008/08/08/carlyle-group-buys-stake-in-luxe-sport-label-moncler.
3. *Women's Wear Daily*, 8/7/2008, Vol. 196 Issue 28, p. 4.

was expected that turnover would increase to €300 million in 2008, with EBITDA of €53 million. Based on these fundamentals, Moncler's enterprise value represented an 8.8x 2008 EBITDA multiple (see Exhibit 9.4 and 9.5 for transaction details). However, although Carlyle was now the largest shareholder, the shareholder agreement clearly stipulated that the major governance rights would stay in Ruffini's hands.

Carlyle's Investment in Moncler: Value Creation

With the support of Carlyle at Moncler, the expansion of the directly managed retail business became the main objective. Carlyle had invested in a healthy and solid company with a highly competent management team. However, to prepare the firm for international expansion a new retail director from Gucci was added, and the first steps were taken towards reorganizing the company into regional hubs by enlarging its local management teams on the ground in Asia, the US and different parts of Europe.

Moncler took charge of its distribution channels by converting distribution agreements into joint ventures over which it had full control. Several product licences were brought back in-house, either direct or through newly established joint ventures, as in the case of the Moncler children's line.

The corporate organization was restructured to adopt a division-based model to better manage each business according to its specific characteristics, needs and development stage. The new structure consisted of two distinct divisions (Exhibit 9.6) one for the Moncler brand contributing 66% of 2010 group sales, and one for the lesser known brands in its portfolio – Henry Cotton, Marina Yachting, Coast Weber & Ahaus and 18CRR81 Cerruti.

From the beginning, Carlyle shared Ruffini's view that the opening of new stores and markets was the key to further growth. At the beginning of 2008, the company operated only six stores, and revenues were heavily dependent on Europe, especially Italy. International expansion was therefore crucial to diversify revenues, reduce risk and realize the revenue and EBITDA growth potential which Carlyle had bought into.

The strategy was quickly implemented and 33 new Moncler stores opened between 2008 and 2010 in fashion capitals around the world, including Hong Kong, Beijing, Shanghai, Tokyo, Osaka, London, Munich, Rome, Copenhagen, New York, Chicago and Geneva. With strong overall sales growth, dependency on the Italian market decreased from 61% of total sales in 2008 to 52% in 2010. Sales in Asia and the US increased by more than 150% during this period and accounted for 15% and 4% respectively of global sales in 2010 (Exhibit 9.7).

From 2008 to 2010 the share of the wholesale business dropped from 89% to 78% of group revenues as retail sales increased. Overall, revenues grew by 38.6% and EBITDA by 92.5% between 2008 and 2010 (Exhibits 9.8 and 9.9).

With the company performing beyond expectations and abundant future growth opportunities still to be explored, the Carlyle team started to consider its options for a timely exit. Whatever the avenue chosen, careful planning and timing would be the key to success.

Carlyle Exit Considerations

Given Moncler's size, the company was a viable candidate for an initial public offering (IPO). Yet its growing global presence and image as a luxury brand made it an equally attractive candidate for a trade sale to a strategic buyer, such as the large brand conglomerates (e.g. LVMH, PPR, or PVH). Likewise, other PE firms might be interested given the continued strong growth potential and successful history of PE ownership in the company.

Moncler had turned out to be an important investment for the Carlyle group and its European ambitions. The company's strong performance and the swift response to the changes implemented created an opportunity for a potentially quick and attractive exit – the first for Carlyle's Europe III fund. This would allow Carlyle to return money to investors with an above-average performance early in the fund's life, setting the stage for successful future fundraising rounds.

And there were plans to take Carlyle itself public. Its partners had debated an IPO since the mid-2000s and the discussion was tabled again at the end of 2010. A successful exit from Moncler would, in a small way, contribute to this effort by helping to validate Carlyle's global business model.

Therefore Marco De Benedetti was keen to lead the investment in Moncler to a successful exit, ideally in line with the vision and desires of Ruffini, who had been clear from the start that he wanted his company to join the group of publicly listed fashion brands. De Benedetti's career prior to Carlyle – including several years as CEO of Telecom Italia – had allowed him to build a strong business network in Italy which he was willing to leverage to achieve a high-profile exit for this investment.

The IPO Option

When thinking through his options, De Benedetti was aware of the influence that Ruffini's preference would have on the choice of exit. While the most common exit route for private equity was a trade sale whereby a strategic or financial investor acquired the company, Ruffini had always envisioned a public listing at an opportune time for Moncler, and was strongly against his company being acquired by a strategic buyer. In line with the owner's vision and the agreement in 2008, an IPO was also the preferred choice of exit for De Benedetti – the challenge was to find the right time to start the process.

After a difficult market in 2008 and 2009 following the global financial crisis, hopes were raised for 2010. Yet the year started with a string of failed IPOs across Europe, among them CVC's planned sale of Belgian chemicals business Taminco, Blackstone's listing attempts for two of its portfolio companies, the UK entertainment business Merlin and the travel reservations company TravelPort, as well as Apax's and Permira's failed exit from retail chain New Look. Although the volatility of the economy was blamed for these events, it was suspected that high levels of debt on the balance sheets of the listing candidates had also put off potential investors.

Later that year, the IPO markets finally started coming to life and PE firms began actively pursuing this exit route (Exhibits 9.10 and 9.11). Positive signals came from the listing of German cable business Kabel Deutschland backed by Providence Equity Partners and Ontario Teachers' Pension Plan, as well as Apax Partner's successful listing of Promethean World. In both cases the sponsors preferred an IPO over several good offers from other private equity firms, some of them at higher valuations than the IPO pricing. It was anticipated that these transactions would jump-start the IPO market for PE-backed companies. Overall the public equity markets had stabilized by mid-year 2010 and were moving upwards again, providing potentially attractive valuations for private equity owned IPO candidates.[4]

Encouraged by the positive market outlook, management started working towards preparing Moncler for an IPO in the fall of 2010. Milan seemed a natural choice for the listing given Moncler's long history and strong presence in Italy. Initially, energies were focused on reorganizing the company in terms of governance, structure, reporting and implementation of IFRS accounting principles, along with the necessary legal and audit aspects as per the Borsa Italiana's compliance guidelines.

As advisors on the IPO process, two international banks (Merrill Lynch, Morgan Stanley) and two local banks (Mediobanca, Intesa Sanpaolo) were retained. One local bank was needed to advise on procedures with the Italian Stock Exchange, while a second was engaged for marketing to Italian institutional investors. The foreign banks would sell the Moncler story to international investors in the UK and US and provide credibility.

As the team deliberated over the right time to IPO, they also had to take into account plans by other fashion companies to go public. Most prominent among them were the major Italian luxury groups Prada and Salvatore Ferragamo, which were planning to list in Hong Kong and Milan respectively. As both companies had a higher profile than Moncler, and were both timed to IPO in summer 2011, there might be less interest in an offering for Moncler from investors who obviously had a finite amount of money to allocate to the Italian fashion segment. Furthermore, if one of the IPOs performed poorly, valuations for the segment could drop significantly. On the other hand, most big Italian fashion houses like Armani and Dolce & Gabbana were still private, so investors looking for exposure to the Italian luxury market had a limited choice. On balance, Carlyle felt that an IPO was feasible but that getting to market before Prada and Ferragamo was crucial to achieve sufficient uptake from investors.

"An Italian company needs around 100 days to complete the listing process on the Italian Stock Exchange from when it files the documents with the regulator," said Domenico Siniscalco, head of Italian mutual fund association Assogestioni and chief of Morgan Stanley's Italy operations, adding that this was twice as long as in other European markets. In view of this regulation and the buoyant IPO markets in early 2011 (and the fact that Prada's IPO was slated for mid-June and Ferragamo's for July), Moncler filed for an IPO on 11th March, with the stated goal of going public in early June.

However, shortly after the IPO registration in April, the stock markets started to look less promising. Some companies chose to reconsider planned listings. Others like Rhiag-Inter Auto Parts Italia S.p.A. pulled its planned offering from Borsa Italiana, citing adverse market conditions. Grupo T-Solar Global SA and Renovalia Energy SA also dropped IPOs in April and May respectively.

4. http://realdeals.eu.com/article/15571-kabel-deutschland-becomes-europes-biggest-ipo-of-2010_15571.

De Benedetti was concerned about the IPO valuations for Moncler. All along the banks had pitched an enterprise valuation of €1.17 billion to €1.37 billion, which translated into a multiple of 11.4x to 13.4x 2010 EBITDA. Despite recent market developments they were sticking to their original valuation, but with the market losing momentum a downward revision of the price range closer to the listing time looked likely. Given the increasing uncertainty around the IPO, De Benedetti felt that he had to create alternative options for Carlyle in order to ensure a profitable exit.

The Trade Sale Option

In line with private-equity-backed IPOs, trade sales had been recovering since 2010 (Exhibit 9.12). Potential strategic buyers had low net debt (Exhibit 9.13) and could easily finance a transaction such as Moncler. The large fashion conglomerates such as LVMH, PPR and PVH had been less acquisitive recently; Moncler could be an interesting target for them to leverage their know-how in expanding sales in emerging markets and licensing (see Exhibit 9.14 for recent branded apparel transactions over $US300 million). However, they typically preferred to purchase businesses in full, or at least acquire a controlling stake which would allow them to consolidate the business and realise synergies more easily.

Selling to a large strategic buyer would be the end of the IPO road for Moncler. Given his close association with Remo Ruffini, De Benedetti knew it would not be a palatable exit route for him. He therefore started considering an alternative: a sale to a private equity firm. Given Ruffini's long and mostly positive experience with Carlyle and his initial Italian backers, he felt he could be convinced to accept another private equity firm (in the event an IPO could not be executed).

Many PE firms had raised large funds at the peak of the market prior to the financial crisis, but had been slow to deploy them given the subsequent turmoil in the financial markets and drying up of debt financing. This pressure to invest and a relatively more benign economic outlook had led to a strong rebound in investment activity. At the same time, PE firms were eager to return money to investors, prompting interest in transactions between PE funds. Despite this alignment of interests between PE funds as buyers and sellers, of late few large secondaries had been closed in Europe (see Exhibit 9.15 for PE secondaries in Europe with EV above €400 million).

The Dual Track Process

In a 'dual track process', sellers initiate a public offering *and* a trade sale process in parallel. Some of Carlyle's competitors had actively pursued this exit route in recent months. For example, Vestar Capital Partners had sold its portfolio company Birds Eye Foods to a strategic buyer; Kabel Deutschland had been listed by Providence Equity Partners; and Takko had been sold by Advent to Apax Partners, all using a dual track process.

Studies showed that companies acquired after filing for an IPO commanded a premium as high as 26%,[5] although this might in part result from a selection bias reflecting the

5. http://blogs.wsj.com/venturecapital/2010/07/06/ipos-it-seems-are-key-to-ma-success/.

relatively higher quality of these companies. Conversely, the dual track process clearly increased the complexity of a transaction, with associated costs and management time escalating significantly.

This last point was a major concern for Moncler, where management was busy expanding the business. A dual track process would bring with it significant distractions from the operating business, which were likely to undermine the company's growth momentum and its financial results mid-term, as well as potentially reducing ongoing performance ("current trading"), even during the exit process.

So when De Benedetti initiated a dual track process, he structured it in a low key way. Carlyle started sounding out prospective buyers without involving any banks or even the management of Moncler. However, without their support it was not possible to run a traditional wide auction process with multiple bidders. Instead, preliminary discussions were held with a few select buyers. The team prepared information decks and set up a limited number of focused meetings. But the complexities of the deal (with an IPO lurking in the background and only a minority stake on offer) deterred many interested buyers. Casting the net more widely might have brought in more potential buyers, but aside from lacking an advisor to manage the process it was mainly the need to keep the sales process out of the public domain that stopped Carlyle from pursuing this course.

If news of the sales process had leaked to the market it would cause a lot of concern. Investors would question the seriousness of the IPO, in particular whether Moncler's owners were convinced of their ability to float the company, or whether they were just using the public market option as a threat to keep possible buyers honest. A failed sales process would also have repercussions on the IPO pricing; investors would likely question why they were being asked to pay more than supposedly sophisticated buyers with full access to company information. Carlyle even kept the existence of the sales process from its IPO advisors so as not to discourage them, and reduce the risk of leakage to the market.

Despite all the challenges that the parallel IPO process involved, the potential IPO provided Carlyle with negotiating leverage over prospective buyers. Conversely, bidders were assured of the reliability of the financial information as the seller had gone through stringent due diligence and compliance for the IPO. However, given the time constraints imposed by the impending IPO, De Benedetti was eager to put the negotiations on a more substantial footing. In the month prior to the IPO listing, Carlyle limited discussions to one private equity firm – Eurazeo, a leading French PE firm, which emerged as the sole contender.

Throughout the process De Benedetti remained convinced that an IPO was the better exit option, which was why the IPO process was maintained at full speed and given first priority. For a long time the dual track was simply a way to create optionality in case of adverse conditions for a public listing.

Meanwhile, the banks were busy with the road-show/pre-marketing for the IPO. While they broadly stuck to their valuation and offering size, other banks in the market were markedly less confident about investor sentiment and valuations for upcoming IPOs. As Dan Cummings, head of global equity capital markets at Bank of America Corp, said at the time:

> *"Sellers who want to go ahead with their offerings will be faced with the potential trade-off of a more modest valuation or a smaller-sized deal. Because stocks have been marked down by a fair number of sell-offs lately, the valuations at which investors are willing to accept new issues have come down."*

Klaus H. Hessberger, co-head of Equity Capital Markets for EMEA at JPMorgan, said:

> *"We also noticed that investors were even more selective about IPO quality and the story behind the business. In 2010 they would at least look at most deals; in 2011 they took a binary approach — they would scrutinize a deal in great detail or not even consider it."*[6]

As more uncertainty around the IPO developed, Carlyle accelerated negotiations with Eurazeo.

Decision Time

On Thursday, 2nd June 2011, the IPO banks proposed an enterprise valuation of €0.96 to €1.06 billion for Moncler, which translated into a multiple of 9.5-10.5x 2010 EBITDA. This was €200-300 million short of their initial pitch, with the EBITDA multiple correspondingly 2.0-3.0x lower. In their defence the banks claimed that the market was facing more volatility as a result of the European debt crisis, which had undermined overall investor morale. The valuations at which investors were willing to accept new issues had come down, and, since Moncler had only recently emerged as a luxury brand and was relatively new in the market, they demanded a further discount. Given the state of the market, the banks were proposing an offering of maximum 30% (all secondary shares) of which 10% would come from the original Italian PE investors and 20% from Carlyle. Neither Ruffini nor management would sell into the initial offering.

While the company valuation had been drastically revised downwards, the IPO process was still underway and would soon reach a point of no return. Moncler was required to officially announce the price on Monday, 6th June, with a price range for the IPO. Once the price was made public it would be the end of the dual track since it would imply that the decision to go ahead with the listing had been made. Were the IPO to be withdrawn after the price release the reputation of both Moncler and Carlyle in the capital markets would be negatively impacted.

The official price announcement would also communicate a substantially lower valuation expectation to Eurazeo, which was certain to reduce its bid in light of this new information. Eurazeo had proposed an equity value of €1,079 million, subject to documentation and some final points for negotiation. While Eurazeo was willing to acquire a majority stake and provide a full exit for Carlyle, Ruffini was wary of giving any party a majority stake, so discussions had settled on a 45% proposal (30% from Carlyle, 10% from the Italian PE houses, just under 5% from Ruffini, and a small amount from Sergio Buongiovanni, the Group's long-serving CFO and COO). While Eurazeo's current non-binding offer seemed attractive in light of the reduced IPO pricing, how realistic was it to try and close a deal with Eurazeo before the

6. http://www.ey.com/Publication/vwLUAssets/Global_IPO_trends_2012/$FILE/Global_IPO_trends_2012.pdf.

announcement date, and at what point in the intense negotiations would power shift from the seller to the buyer? PE firms were savvy negotiators and known to use every advantage to obtain a reduced price or extract other concessions.

Marco De Benedetti knew he had to act quickly with less than four days until a decision had to be made. Ruffini was less sensitive to the downward valuation and the public market discount, but De Benedetti believed the value they had created in Moncler was much higher than was currently being offered. He felt that the company had a strong balance sheet and great potential which the public markets were discounting due to overall market uncertainty. Knowing that the owner's preference was for the IPO, if De Benedetti chose another route he would have to find a way to monetize and realize some value for both Carlyle and Ruffini, while ideally keeping the ultimate objective of the IPO alive.

If Carlyle was not confident that the timing of the exit was right, or that there was still enough upside to keep the IRR at high levels, Carlyle could consider partially exiting the business and keeping some of the upside. This could be accomplished through an IPO and a secondary sale to Eurazeo, although the IPO provided better liquidity for a later exit. In addition, if the average first-day price spike (resulting from under-pricing designed to entice investors to buy into a new offering) of around 12% for the last 12 months was taken into account, the valuation gap between IPO and trade sale would narrow quickly on the outstanding stake.

A sale to Eurazeo would likely offload a larger stake from Carlyle than an IPO, but it would make the subsequent sale of a remaining stake more difficult. Eurazeo would expect Carlyle to stay in until a joint exit, prolonging the lifetime of their investment by another three to five years. Yet staying in for a longer period could provide Carlyle with an opportunity for further upside, especially in the public markets, although it would also expose it to company- and market-specific risks.

Moncler's balance sheet was healthy, with €160 million in debt and further substantial paydowns expected by the year end. In May 2010, Carlyle had already received dividends of €14.5 million from a small recapitalisation. This time around there was substantially more room for re-leveraging the balance sheet. The exact amount would mostly depend on the exit route. In the event that Carlyle kept everything as it was, the banks had indicated a debt multiple of up to 4.5x 2010 EBITDA, although both Carlyle and management preferred to go with a slightly lower figure of 4.0x to provide Moncler with some safety margin given the risks associated with its high growth and the fashion industry it was operating in. In the event of a sale to Eurazeo, the debt multiple would be lower – probably around 3.0x, as Eurazeo (similar to Carlyle at the time of its investment) would prefer to leverage only moderately until it had a better feel for the cash flow volatility in the company. The public markets, on the other hand, would not look favourably on the idea of a pre-IPO recapitalisation, hence Carlyle had not pursued this option.

With less than four days to go, what should Marco De Benedetti do?

Exhibit 9.1

Biographical Information

Marco De Benedetti, Managing Director of the Carlyle Group and co-head of its European Buyout Fund

Born 1962 in Turin. Married with two children. After completing high school in Switzerland, he graduated in History and Economics from Wesleyan University in 1984. He attended the Wharton Business School, where he obtained an MBA in 1987. From 1987–89 he worked for Wasserstein, Perrella & Co., a merchant bank in New York, in M&A. In 1990 he joined Olivetti as assistant to the CEO of Olivetti Systems & Networks, and was later appointed Group Director of Marketing and Services. In 1992 he was appointed GM of Olivetti Portugal. In September 1994 he became CEO of Olivetti Telemedia, part of the Olivetti Group, with responsibility for developing telecommunications and multimedia activities. In October 1996 he became Chairman of Infostrada, a company that rapidly became the main Italian alternative fixed-line carrier for voice services and the market leader in internet access. Following Olivetti's takeover of Telecom Italia, in July 1999 he was appointed CEO of TIM. Following the merger between Telecom Italia and TIM, in July 2005 he was appointed CEO of Telecom Italia, but resigned in October 2005. Since November 2005 he has been Managing Director of the Carlyle Group where he co-heads the European Buyout Fund. He serves on the board of Cofide S.p.A., Moncler S.p.A., NBTY, Inc., CommScope, Inc. and Save the Children Italia.

Source: European Private Equity and Venture Capital Association

Remo Ruffini

Remo Ruffini started his career working for his father's company, Gianfranco Ruffini Ltd, in the US. The company handled the stylistic designing and marketing of a series of clothing ranges. Mr Ruffini returned to Italy in 1984, where he founded the New England Company, and in 1993 the Ingrose women's wear collection, which he sold to Stefanel Group in 2000. He worked as a consultant for various companies between 2000 and 2003.

In search of a new challenge, Mr Ruffini took over the Moncler brand in 2003 and was involved from every angle, focusing on advertising strategy, image, product and distribution. The strategy of the "global down jacket" (a jacket for all occasions) was conceived by him and restored Moncler to its former glory. His ultimate dream was to create the perfect equation: Moncler equals quilted jackets and quilted jackets equal Moncler.

Source: *Financial Times*

(http://www.ftconferences.com/luxury2012/speakerdetails/3197/?PHPSESSID=c31079326f70a5d1855edc1671900740)

Exhibit 9.2

Carlyle: Background

William E. Conway (formerly CFO of MCI), David M. Rubinstein (a former aide to President Carter) and Daniel A. D'Aniello (formerly at Marriott Corp.) founded the Carlyle Group in Washington DC in 1985 with $5 million, naming it after the hotel in New York where the founders used to meet. They decided on Washington DC as their headquarters, not only to differentiate themselves from the mass of New York investment firms but to stay close to the political decision makers in the US.

The company spent the first years leveraging its founder's previous experiences to make investments primarily in restaurant and food-service companies. But in 1989, after Frank Carlucci (former US Secretary of Defense) joined the group, the firm redirected its focus to other sectors including manufacturing, consumer products and defence. Carlyle started to engage in high-profile deals and its reputation quickly grew along with the number of its partners and associates. With the help of its strong network, Carlyle also closed deals in the Middle East and Western Europe from the mid-1990s onwards.

Carlyle's network of advisors and deal makers was impressive. Over time it included former heads of state, politicians, regulators and royalty: a British prime minister, a president of the Philippines, a South Korean prime minister, US secretaries of state and of defence, a White House budget director, a head of the SEC, a Bundesbank president, as well as a Saudi prince and George Soros.

Carlyle expanded its operations to Europe in the late 1990s with a string of office openings in London, Munich and Paris, raising its first European buy out fund, Carlyle Europe Partners, in 1998. Offices in Milan and Barcelona where added shortly after. By 2011 the Carlyle Group had grown into a diversified global alternative asset manager with 1,300 employees, operating from 32 offices across six continents, with $156 billion in assets under management.

The company established itself as a "private global investment firm that originates, structures and acts as lead equity investor in management-led buyouts, strategic minority equity investments, equity private placements, consolidations and build-ups, and growth capital financings."[7]

7. Carlyle Group website.

Exhibit 9.3

The Carlyle Group[8]

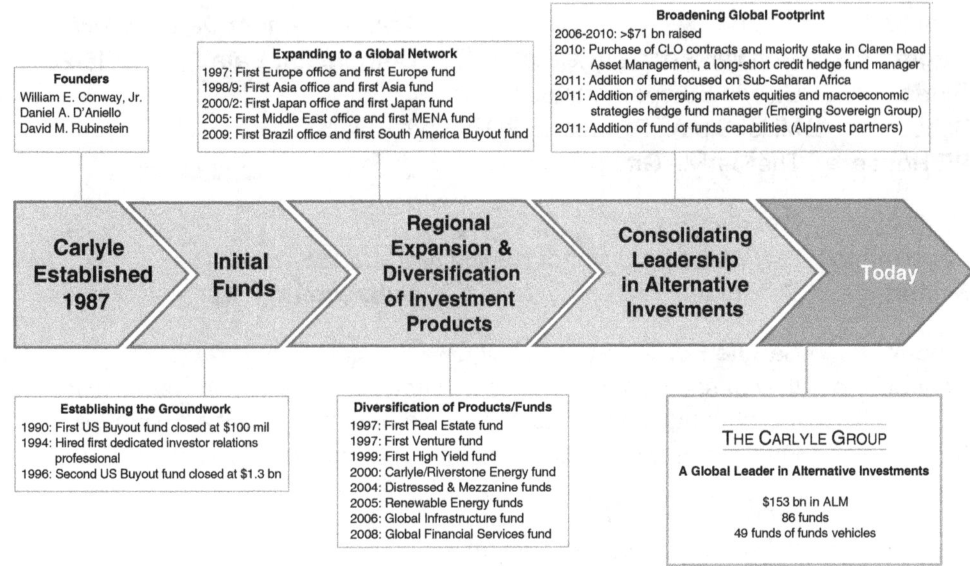

Assets under Management[9]

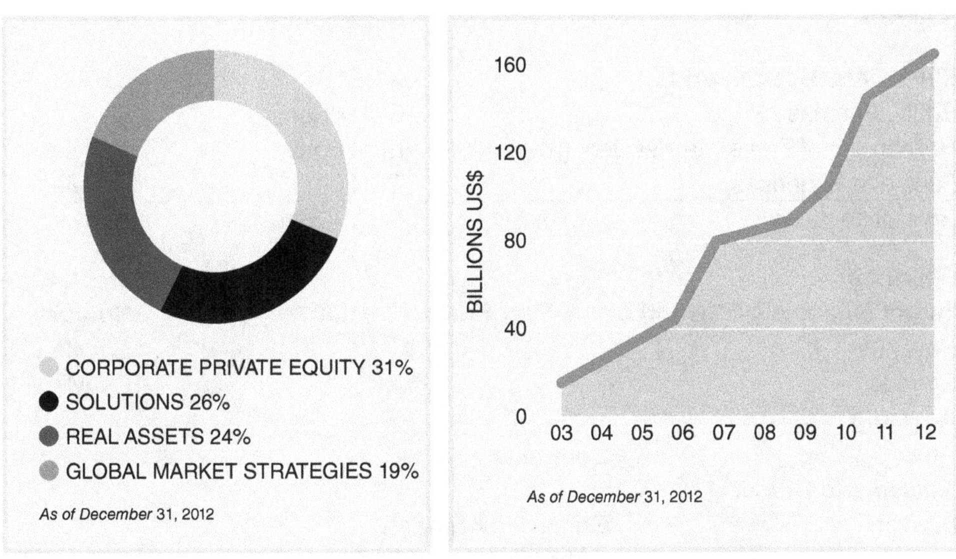

8. The Carlyle Group SEC Registration Statement: (http://www.nasdaq.com/markets/ipos/filing.ashx?filingid=7858907).
9. http://www.carlyle.com/about-carlyle.

Exhibit 9.4
Transaction Details

Deal ID	191563	**Announcement Date**	05/08/2008
Target	Moncler S.p.A. (48% Stake)	**Completion Date**	12/10/2008
Bidder	Carlyle Europe Partners III LP		
Seller	Mittel S.p.A., Progressio SGR S.p.A., Isa S.p.A.		
PE House	The Carlyle Group, LLC		

Target	**Moncler S.p.A.**		
Description	Italy based producer of fashion and sportswear products		
Sectors	Consumer: Retail	**Subsectors**	Apparel, Clothes

Bidder	**Carlyle Europe Partners III LP**		
Description	Italy based financial services company, engaged in private equity investments, and in real estate and operating finance businesses		
Sectors	Financial Services, Real Estate	**Subsectors**	Investment banking

Seller	**Progressio SGR S.p.A.**		
Description	Italy based private equity firm		
Sectors	Financial Services	**Subsectors**	VC/PE
Seller	**Isa S.p.A.**		
Description	Trento based financial institution active in Private Equity		
Sectors	Financial Services	**Subsectors**	

Financials (Use of Funds)		**Source**
Equity Purchase Price	EUR 408m	Carlyle
Refinancing of Pro-forma Net Debt (31.12.2008)	EUR 60m	Carlyle
Fees and Expenses	EUR 8m	Carlyle
Enterprise Value	EUR 476m	Carlyle

Reported		
Target Financials EUR (m)	**Year Ending 31/12/07**	**Source**
Revenue	259	Carlyle
Earnings	18	Carlyle

Advisors	
Role	**Company**
Advisors to Bidder	
Lawyer	Grimaldi e Associati
	Latham & Watkins LLP
	Studio Pedersoli e Associati
PR	MS&L Italia (Publicis Groupe)
Advisors to Mittel S.p.A.	
Lawyer	Agnoli Bernardi e Associati

Source: Mergermarket (Moncler S.p.A. – Carlyle Europe Partners III LP – Mittel S.p.A.; Progressio SGR S.p.A.; Isa S.p.A.)

Exhibit 9.5

Transactional Details – Source of Funds

2008 Deal	Signing 5 August 2008 - Closing 12 October 2008
Sources of Funds	**€mm**
Acquisition Debt	129
Operating Net debt rolled over	43
Total Net Debt (31.12.2008)	**172**
Equity	304
Total Sources	**476**

Equity	
Carlyle	48.0%
Remo Ruffini	38.0%
Brand Partners	13.5%
S. Buongiovanni (CFO)	0.5%

Source: Carlyle

Exhibit 9.6

Moncler Corporate Structure

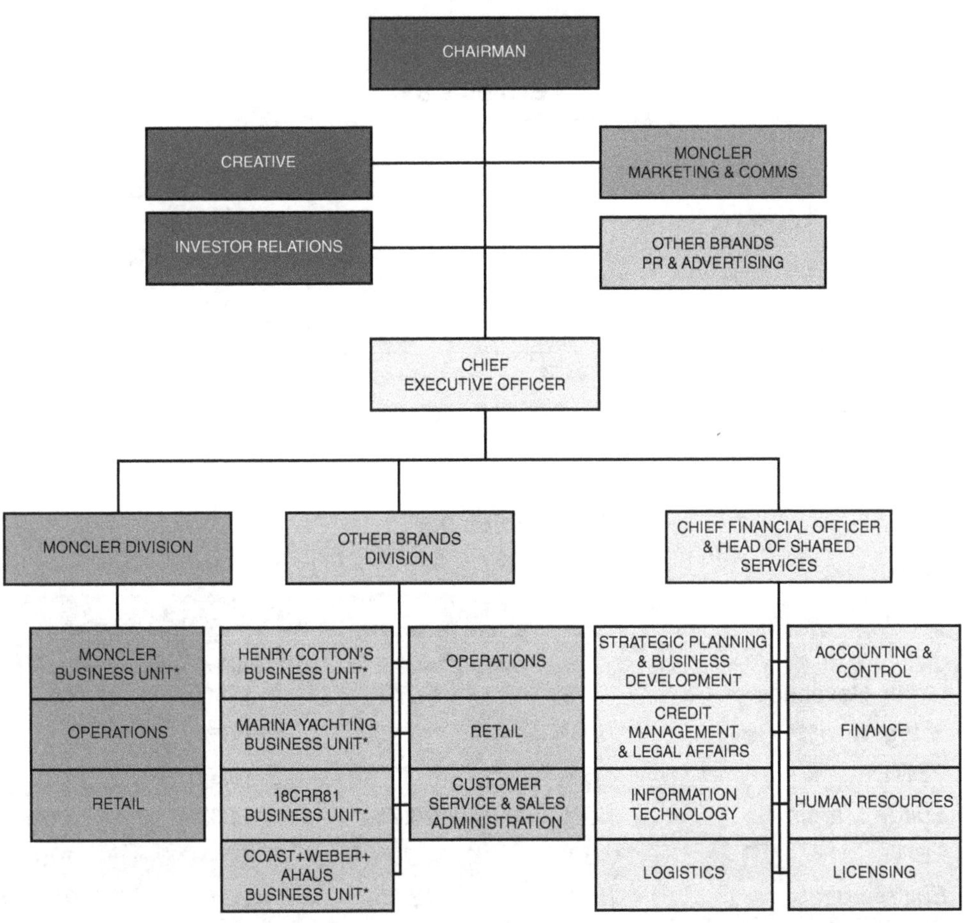

© MONCLER 2011- P,IVAIT04642290961

Exhibit 9.7
Moncler Revenue by Geographies

€ million; %	2008A	2009A	2010A
Italy	187	216	221
% on total	*61%*	*58%*	*52%*
Other EU	88	108	127
% on total	*28%*	*29%*	*30%*
Asia and Japan	25	40	63
% on total	*8%*	*11%*	*15%*
North America	7	9	18
% on total	*2%*	*2%*	*4%*
RoW	2	0	0
% on total	*1%*	*0%*	*0%*
Group Revenues	**309**	**373**	**428**

Exhibit 9.8
Moncler Revenue by Channel

€ million; %	2008A	2009A	2010A
Retail	34	54	96
% on total	*11%*	*14%*	*22%*
Wholesale	274	319	332
% on total	*89%*	*86%*	*78%*
Group Revenues	**309**	**373**	**428**

Exhibit 9.9
Moncler Group Consolidated Key Financials

€ million; %	ITA GAAP 2008A	IFRS 2009A	IFRS 2010A	IFRS 2011E
Group Revenues	309	373	428	487
YoY growth%	*19.4%*	*20.9%*	*14.6%*	*13.9%*
EBITDA	53	77	102	115
Ebitda Margin %	*17.2%*	*20.7%*	*23.8%*	*23.6%*
EBIT	39	70	92	100
Ebit Margin %	*12.6%*	*18.8%*	*21.5%*	*20.4%*
Net income	18	35	52	60
Net Debt	172	124	143	110
Net Debt/EBITDA	3.2x	1.6x	1.4x	1.0x

Source: Carlyle

Exhibit 9.10
Global PE backed IPOs by Region

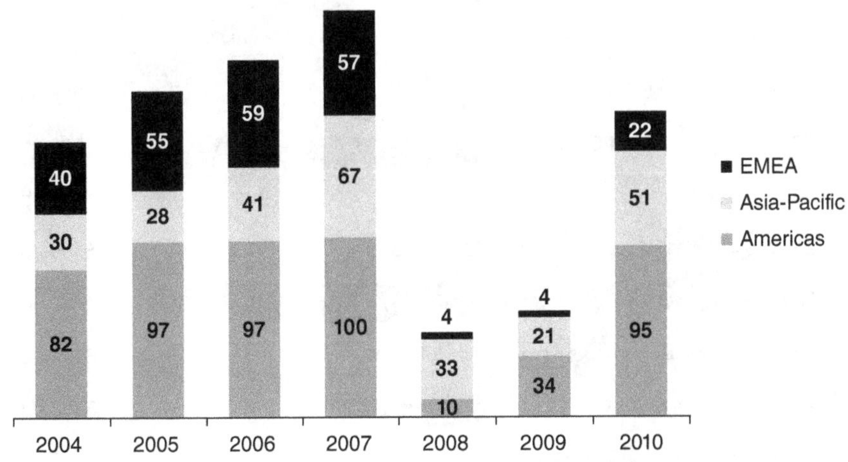

Source: Ernst & Young Global IPO trends
http://www.ey.com/Publication/vwLUAssets/Global_IPO_trends_2012/$FILE/Global_IPO_trends_2012.pdf

Exhibit 9.11
Top 10 PE-backed European IPOs in 2010

Date	Company	Seller	Industry	Volume (EURm)
5-Oct-10	Pandora A/S	Axcel	Fashion Jewellery	1,336
18-Apr-10	Amadeus IT Holding	BC Partners, Cinven	IT Solutions	1,317
9-Jul-10	Vallar	N. Rothschild	Investment Trusts	808
2-Jun-10	Christian Hansen Holding	PAI Partners	Chemicals, Biotechnology	674
19-Mar-10	Kabel Deutschland Holding	Providence Equity Partners	Telecommunications	660
26-Mar-10	Brenntag AG	BC Partners	Chemical Distribution	650
11-Nov-10	Mail.ru Group Ltd.	Elbrus Capitals	Internet Investment	648
29-Oct-10	AZ Electronic Materials SA	Carlyle, Vestar Capital	Chemicals	441
20-Jul-10	Ocado Group	J.L. pension fund, others	Internet retail	436
14-Jul-10	Stroeer Out-of-Home Media	Cerberus	Media	358

Source: Bloomberg

http://www.rolandberger.de/media/pdf/Roland_Berger_European_Private_Equity_Outlook_20110419.pdf

Exhibit 9.12
Global PE Exits by Deal Value

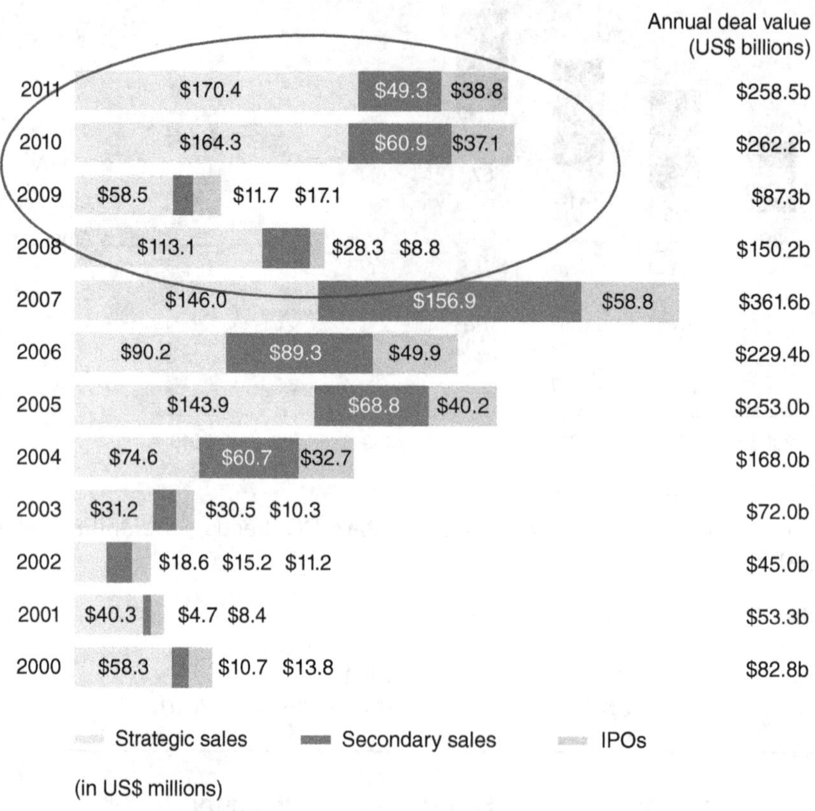

Source: Ernst & Young Global IPO trends
http://www.ey.com/Publication/vwLUAssets/Global_IPO_trends_2012/$FILE/Global_IPO_trends_2012.pdf

Exhibit 9.13

Comparable Trading Companies

Company	Country	MV (EUR m)	EV (EUR m)	EV/Sales 2010	EV/Sales 2011	EV/EBIDTA 2010	EV/EBIDTA 2011	EV/EBIT 2010	EV/EBIT 2011
Hermes	FR	27,907	27,120	11.3x	9.9x	35.3x	29.9x	40.6x	34.3x
LVMH	FR	56,743	61,717	3.0x	2.7x	12.1x	10.6x	14.3x	12.3x
PPR	FR	13,248	18,173	1.2x	1.2x	9.7x	8.8x	11.9x	10.8x
Ralph Lauren	US	9,377	8,903	2.2x	1.9x	12.1x	10.3x	14.9x	12.6x
Burberry	UK	6,575	6,255	3.8x	3.1x	15.9x	12.6x	19.3x	15.4x
Hugo Boss	DE	4,527	4,842	2.8x	2.4x	14.5x	10.9x	18.3x	13.2x
PVH	US	3,132	4,638	1.4x	1.1x	13.2x	8.1x	18.5x	9.9x
VF Crop	US	9,572	9,843	1.7x	1.5x	11.4x	9.5x	13.1x	11.2x
Abercrombie & Fitch	US	4,156	3,780	1.5x	1.2x	11.4x	7.6x	23.2x	12.5x
Timberland	US	1,640	1,469	1.4x	1.2x	11.7x	10.6x	13.8x	n.a.
Columbia	US	1,261	1,043	1.0x	0.8x	10.0x	8.2x	13.8x	10.9x
Gerry Weber	DE	1,064	992	1.6x	1.4x	9.6x	8.5x	10.9x	9.7x
Mean				**2.8x**	**2.4x**	**13.9x**	**11.3x**	**17.7x**	**13.9x**
Median				**1.7x**	**1.4x**	**11.9x**	**9.9x**	**14.6x**	**12.3x**

Source: Bloomberg

Exhibit 9.14

Recent Branded Apparel Transactions over US$300 Million (including buybacks)

Date Announced	Target Name	Acquiror Name	% of Shares Acq.	Deal Value inc. Net Debt (USD m)	EV (USD m)	EV/EBITDA
05/02/2011	Volcom	PPR SA	100.00	516.43	516.43	14.59
08/05/2010	Pepe Jeans	Arta Capital, L Capital	27.90	112.05	401.608	-
06/15/2010	Quicksilver	Creditors	-	74.50	1,325.36	6.98
02/11/2010	VF Corp	VF Corp	-	724.40	8,488.85	8.92
11/10/2009	Esprit Holdings	Esprit Holdings	-	855.89	7,934.40	9.34
06/17/2009	Eddie Bauer Holdings	Golden Gate Capital	100.00	286.00	505.26	9.58
02/10/2009	Gerry Weber	Gerry Weber	58.05	325.13	652.41	12.28
01/28/2009	Link Theory Holdings	Fast Retailing	61.39	362.83	458.53	14.13
Median						**9.58**

Source: ThomsonOneBanker

Exhibit 9.15

Recent PE Secondaries in Europe with EV > €400 Million

Date	Firm	Acquiror	Seller	EV (EURm)	Firm Industry
May-11	SPIE	AXA Private Equity, Caisse de depot et placement du Quebec, Clayton Dubilier & Rice	PAI Partners	2100	Engineering
May-11	Gruppo Coin	BC Partners	PAI Partners	1300	Retail
May-11	Compagnie Europeenne de Prevoyance	JC Flowers & Co	PAI Partners	800	Insurance
May-11	Environmental Resource Management PLC	Charterhouse Capital Partners	Bridgepoint Advisers	662.34	Environmental Services
May-11	Metroweb	F2i SGR, Sanpaolo IMI Private Equity	A2A, Stirling Square Capital Partners	436	Telecoms
Apr-11	Evonik Industries	Rhone Capital	CVC Capital Partners	900	Chemicals
Apr-11	Metallum	First Reserve Corporation	Groupe Alpha	670	Materials
Apr-11	Tomkins plc	Eigen Capital	CPP Investment Board, Onex Corporation	622.81	Engineering
Apr-11	Kiloutou	PAI Partners	Sagard Private Equity	535	Industrial
Apr-11	DYWIDAG-Systems International	Triton	CVC Capital Partners	400	Industrial
Mar-11	Phones4U	BC Partners	Doughty Hanson, Providence	805.55	Retail
Feb-11	Gerflor	Intermediate Capital Group	AXA, Equistone , Intermediate Capital , iXEN, Natixis	500	Manufacturing
Feb-11	Amadeus	AXA Private Equity, Permira	Air France, BC Partners, Cinven, Deutsche Lufthansa, Iberia	450	IT
Feb-11	Zabka	Mid Europa Partners	Penta Investments	400	Retail
Jan-11	Capio	CVC Capital Partners	Apax France, Apax Partners, Nordic Capital	900	Healthcare
Dec-10	Takko Fashion	Apax Partners	Advent International	1250	Retail
Dec-10	IMCD Group	Bain Capital	AAC Capital Partners	650	Industrial
Dec-10	Falcon Group	Macquarie Group	Mid Europa Partners	574	Telecoms
Dec-10	Falcon Group	MIRA	Al-Bateen Investment Co., Lehman Brothers, Mid Europa Partners	574	Telecoms
Dec-10	Hyva	Unitas Capital	3i, Groupe Alpha	525	Industrial
Nov-10	Britax Childcare	Nordic Capital	Carlyle Group	528.4	Manufacturing
Sep-10	TDC A/S	CVC Capital Partners	Apax , Blackstone , KKR, Permira, Providence	2540.62	Telecoms
Sep-10	Visma	Kohlberg Kravis Roberts	HgCapital	1442.52	Software
Sep-10	B&B Hotel	Carlyle Group	Eurazeo	480	Leisure
Aug-10	Autobar Group	CVC Capital Partners	Charterhouse Capital Partners	1200	Food
Aug-10	TeamSystem	HgCapital	Bain Capital	565	Business Services
Jul-10	Picard	Lion Capital	BC Partners	1500	Food
Jul-10	Ontex	Goldman Sachs, TPG	Candover Partners	1200	Consumer Products
Jun-10	Sebia	Cinven	Astorg Partners, Montagu Private Equity	800	Healthcare
Jun-10	Cerba European Lab	PAI Partners	Astorg Partners, IK Investment Partners	500	Healthcare

Source: Preqin

CASE 10 INVESTOR GROWTH CAPITAL
THE BREDBANDSBOLAGET INVESTMENT

SYNOPSIS

Bredbandsbolaget is a Swedish broadband provider founded in the midst of the dot-com bubble in the late 1990s. With very high capital expenditure requirements and having struggled to meet its business plan objectives in previous years, its majority investors—including Investor Growth Capital (IGC)—are now faced with the dilemma of whether to extend further funding to the business. The main complicating factor is the search for a way to circumvent antidilution provisions which protect co-investors unable to match the company's additional funding needs.

IGC is the venture capital and growth equity arm of InvestorAB, a Swedish investment company founded in 1916 and to-date controlled by the Wallenberg family.

PEDAGOGICAL OBJECTIVE OF THE CASE

The case presents a late-stage, multi-round venture investment and the accompanying opportunities and challenges that shareholder turbulences can cause. The objective is to provide a basic understanding of the problems, questions and deliverables typical in a late-stage venture capital or growth equity investment. Readers will gain an understanding of the following:

- The need of balancing the investment's attractiveness and the necessary risk assessment
- Portfolio fit and investment horizon
- Investment valuation based on discounted cash flow and comparables
- Term sheet structuring

SUGGESTED ASSIGNMENT QUESTIONS

1. Assist the IGC partner and the investment committee with the decision. What should they do about this faltering portfolio company?
2. What will be the consequences of not investing new capital? What is the downside?
3. Which risks need to be considered before injecting new money into this portfolio company?

ADDITIONAL RESOURCES

To make the most of this case study, we suggest the following additional sources to provide context and background information:

- In particular, we recommend the following chapters from *Mastering Private Equity—Transformation via Venture Capital, Minority Investments & Buyouts*
  - Chapter 1 Private Equity Essentials
  - Chapter 2 Venture Capital
  - Chapter 3 Growth Equity
- You may also refer to the book website for further material:
  www.masteringprivateequity.com

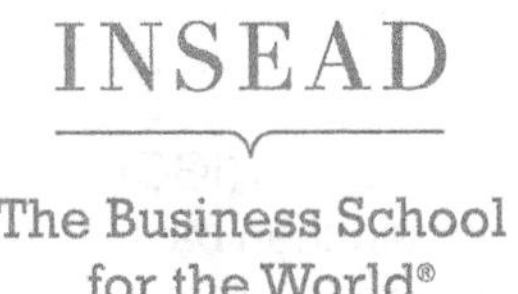

Investor Growth Capital

The Bredbandsbolaget Investment

05/2013-5653

This case was written by David Piehl, INSEAD MBA 2009, under the supervision of Claudia Zeisberger, Affiliate Professor of Decision Sciences and Academic Co-Director of the Global Private Equity Initiative (GPEI) at INSEAD. It is intended to be used as a basis for class discussion rather than to illustrate either effective or ineffective handling of an administrative situation.

Additional material about INSEAD case studies (e.g., videos, spreadsheets, links) can be accessed at cases.insead.edu.

On 17 March 2003, Johan Röhss, Managing Director at Investor Growth Capital's (IGC) Stockholm office, looked out towards the Swedish capital's archipelago and then back to the financials and business plan of B2 Bredband AB (branded "Bredbandsbolaget" or "B2"). Like the Swedish spring, the B2 investment had shown glimmers of hope lately, but it was too early to celebrate a new season. Bredbandsbolaget was facing a number of tests, the first one being the investment committee meeting in a week's time.

In 2003, Bredbandsbolaget was competing for the position of leading alternative broadband operator in Sweden. The company operated an expanding proprietary national broadband network using Ethernet LAN and DSL technology. Bredbandsbolaget had been one of IGC's investments since 1999. Measured by capital contributed it was the biggest investment in IGC's portfolio due to the CAPEX -intensive nature of creating a broadband infrastructure. As a consequence, by the beginning of 2003 funds that had initially been expected to last up until break-even were coming to an end.

There was, however, some light at the end of the tunnel. First of all, over the last two years a new Chairman, Jan Stenberg, and a new CEO, Peder Ramel, had been appointed and the company had started meeting its quarterly business plan targets. Secondly, the company was not wholly to blame for the liquidity issue. A main source of the problem was the fact that one of the principal investors, UK cable operator NTL, had been unable to provide the SEK 157.5 million ($21 million) it had committed to in 2002. Instead, NTL had gone into Chapter 11 in early 2002, creating an opportunity for IGC, along with some of the other investors; Carlyle Group, Access Industries and potentially Continuum Group, to increase their share of the company by acquiring NTL's 29% share.

There were a number of questions facing the remaining investors. First of all, would an additional investment create value? This depended on several factors such as the investors' core belief in the business and whether the improving operational situation was an affirmation of the business model or just a temporary upswing. Secondly, Bredbandsbolaget would most likely require more funds than the outstanding NTL commitment before it reached break-even. Investors thus had to determine whether their fund characteristics could withstand a further substantial capital commitment. Equally important would be to determine, what the consequences would be if they did not participate, i.e., how diluted they would become? For investors who did intend to participate, the question was, on the contrary, what the best structures would be for diluting non-participating investors given the existing anti-dilution terms.

With these questions in mind, and with the anti-dilution provisions of the Shareholders' Agreement in front of him, Johan Röhss had until the end of the week to finalise his proposal on whether to participate in the add-on investment, and, if so, what the structure and terms should be.

The Swedish Broadband Market

Broadband can be defined as a telecommunications access service which has sufficient bandwidth to carry multiple voice, video and data channels simultaneously. In 2003, broadband access represented one of the fastest growing segments in the telecommunications industry. Estimates at the time predicted that the number of broadband subscribers globally would be 97.2 million by the end of 2003, growing by 45% to 140.6 million by the end of 2004.[1] The broadband penetration rate (defined as broadband subscriptions as a percentage of households) in Western Europe was expected to hit 20% on average by the end of 2003; it had already reached over 50% in a number of Asian countries (See Exhibit 10.2).

Sweden, with a population of approximately 9 million, had opened up its telecom monopoly to competition in 1993.[2] Approximately one-third of the population lived in three metropolitan areas around Stockholm, Göteborg and Malmö, 90% lived in communities with more than 2,000 residents. The country enjoyed a comparatively high penetration of PCs and internet subscribers but was on a par with the European average broadband penetration of 15% in 2002 and an expected penetration rate of 23% by the end of 2003.

Growth rates in Sweden were, however, expected to accelerate more quickly than those of other European countries as infrastructure investments by both market participants and the government would increase accessibility in and outside the major cities. Equally important was an improving legal situation for alternative operators to make use of the incumbent Telia's nationwide copper network at a fair price. Access to the network was essential as it enabled any operator to deploy ADSL technology wherever there was a fixed telephone line. In 2003, Sweden had a 96% fixed-line penetration and it was therefore expected that these developments would increase competition and lower prices. By 2005, broadband penetration was therefore expected to have almost doubled to around 43% (See Exhibit 10.2).

In 2003, Bredbandsbolaget estimated the market potential as follows:

- Sweden had 4.5 million households, almost all of them fixed telephony subscribers.
- Only 4.05 million households were located in towns and villages with more than 1,000 households, constituting the financially viable market for DSL services.
- Of these, 65%, or 2.6 million, had internet connections.
- By the end of 2003, it was estimated that 23%, or 0.9 million, would be connected to broadband.
- It was assumed that an ARPU* of SEK 300 a month there was a potential broadband market worth SEK 2.2 billion a year ($293 million).
- Given the high broadband growth rates, in 2008 the market could be expected to be worth SEK 8 billion a year ($1.07 billion).

(See Exhibit 10.3)

Competitors

In 2003, 84% of Sweden's residential broadband market was held by the five largest operators: Telia, Bredbandsbolaget, Com Hem, Bostream and UPC. The remainder of the market was fragmented with around 90 internet service providers (ISPs) mainly

1. Informa, 2003.
2. "FÖRHANDLINGAR" Nationalekonomiska Föreningen 2001-03-27.
* ARPU = Average Revenue Per User.

acting as service providers on Telia's wholesale platform or operators of small regional broadband networks. The most significant players in this segment included Tele2, Glocalnet and Spray (See Exhibit 10.4). B2, along with the small ISPs, were estimated to have increased their market share by growing at about 5% more than their "fair share" during 2002, whilst the market shares of Telia and the cable operators Com Hem and UPC had declined somewhat.

With the rapid market expansion, Bredbandsbolaget expected to be able to continue acquiring brand new customers as opposed to mainly "stealing" them from the competition for another two to three years. The market consensus was, however, that size and thereby economies of scale were becoming increasingly important given the large investments in the fairly limited market, and that the market participants would therefore be heading towards consolidation sooner rather than later.

The Offering

Bredbandsbolaget's offering had initially focused almost exclusively on providing high-speed broadband at speeds of up to 100 Mbps through B2's proprietary network. Around the year 2000, this offering was widened as two things became apparent. Firstly, it became clear that higher-speed broadband only addressed a small proportion of the market. Secondly, Bredbandsbolaget, which was still intimately linked to an initial promise its founders had made, of "Broadband for everyone at 200 kronor (SEK) per month", started to differentiate its offering as a way to move away from this promise. From then on, consumers were offered connections over Ethernet LAN or DSL (i.e., the phone line), whereas corporate customers were offered connections via DSL or direct fibre access. (For more details on the offering and pricing points, see Exhibit 10.5).

Building the Company, 1998–2002

At the height of the high-tech bubble, a handful of companies and entrepreneurs became icons of the new economy. Dressed in his characteristic orange fleece jacket, one of the more widely known of these entrepreneurs was Jonas Birgersson, dubbed "Broadband-Jesus" by the press because of his ability to share his vision of broadband internet access as a cornerstone of the new economy and society (See Exhibit 10.13 – Media gallery).

With his soon-to-be-famous tag line "Broadband for everyone at 200 kronor (SEK) per month)" Birgersson, along with other entrepreneurs, had started B2 Bredband AB (Bredbandsbolaget) in 1998, as a subsidiary of their primary start-up, web-development company Framtidsfabriken ("the Future Factory"). Bredbandsbolaget was first incorporated as an internet service consultancy company with a view to developing technology for an IP/Ethernet consumer broadband network, but soon shifted towards actually creating a broadband infrastructure. In 1999, B2 Bredband AB was therefore incorporated as a separate company.

The early days of Bredbandsbolaget were characterised by bold plans and significant deals but also by a substantial cost base increase. With a view to creating a proprietary consumer broadband network, the company raised equity capital of SEK 1.7 billion

($226 million) from a group of investors including Investor Growth Capital, the Carlyle Group and Intel.[3] Shortly thereafter, Bredbandsbolaget signed a contract with major housing association HSB for the installation of Ethernet LAN broadband connections in all HSB's properties throughout Sweden (approximately 0.5 million members). The first customers were connected in December 1999.

In 2000, UK cable operator NTL made a significant investment in B2 and the cumulative invested capital in the company reached SEK 2.4 billion ($320 million). Bredbandsbolaget also established a presence in Norway through the acquisition of Bredbåndsfabrikken AS, and joined the Swedish 3G consortium Orange Sverige as a minority investor when the Swedish state auctioned off Swedish mobile phone frequencies.

The same year saw the appointment of a new Chairman, Jan Stenberg, previously CEO of Scandinavian Airlines (SAS) and a former member of Ericsson's Corporate Executive Committee. Finally, Bredbandsbolaget entered into a SEK 4.1 billion ($547 million) vendor financing agreement[4] with Cisco for the ongoing development and construction of a high-speed broadband network.

In 2001, the market abandoned many investments made in the previous five years as the dot-com hype gave way to a crash. Bredbandsbolaget was however not one of these investments. Instead, Bredbandsbolaget received, in 2001–2002 a renewed mandate to implement its ambitious investment plan, seriously competing with the incumbent, Telia, the former state-owned operator.

Under its new chairman, the company did react operationally to the changes in the environment and a strategic reorganisation was commenced in early 2001. Staff numbers were cut from an average of 420 in 2001, to 217 in 2002. The pace of expansion slowed down and the company started focusing on increasing customer penetration within its existing base of connected buildings. In October 2001, it sold its share in Orange Sverige in order to focus on its core broadband business. At the same time, Access Industries and Continuum Group Ltd. became shareholders and joined the ownership structure following a SEK 2.4 billion ($320 million) private placement, while the investments started rendering traction and B2's customer base reached 50,000 in November 2001.

To grow its sources of revenue, in 2002 B2 launched an IP telephony service and began marketing broadband services to the corporate market while the company continued its organisational restructuring and appointed Peder Ramel as CEO. With the combined skills of the new Chairman and CEO, extensive operational experience was brought on board and had a positive effect. Cash flow and the rate at which cash was burnt, however, remained a major issue.

---

3. Note: Intel would later discontinue its active investor role.

4. The Cisco vendor financing agreement was structured as preferential, non-subordinated debt, with the credit limit continually extended by 1.5x the total accumulated purchase value. The *de facto* credit line did not accrue any interest.

Investor Growth Capital

Investor Growth Capital (IGC) was formed in the mid-1990s as the VC arm of the Swedish Wallenberg family's investment vehicle 'Investor AB'. Investor AB had been formed in 1916 as the holding company for the Wallenberg's interests in some of Sweden's best-known companies such as LM Ericsson, Atlas Copco, ABB, Electrolux and SEB. With the founding of IGC, Investor AB's focus on large, established companies was accentuated, while IGC covered the early to growth stage mandate of the sphere.

By 2003, 30 IGC investment professionals were managing a portfolio whose value exceeded $1 billion, from offices located in New York, Menlo Park, Hong Kong, Tokyo, Stockholm and Amsterdam.[5] In contrast to a traditional VC fund, IGC had some flexibility on investment size and timeframe on investments. In all other aspects it functioned as a regular VC fund.[6]

Sentiments Among Investors

At the beginning of 2003, Bredbandsbolaget had five major shareholders: NTL, IGC, Carlyle Group, Access Industries and Continuum. In the course of time it became clear that there were going to be significant changes to this structure, driven by investor-specific circumstances affecting any one party's ability to participate in a new round of financing.

Founded in 1993, British cable operator NTL had embarked in the late 1990s on an aggressive acquisition strategy targeting European assets in the industry. The company's acquisitions included the consumer cable division of Cable and Wireless, bought for $10 billion, and the 2000 acquisition of a 29% stake in Bredbandsbolaget.

The collapse of the telecommunications market in mid-2000, however, dealt a serious blow to NTL. This, combined with its rapid acquisition of local cable operators, led to severe problems with both operations and finances. Devalued and struggling with debts of around $18 billion, NTL, which by 2000 had become a US-registered company, sought Chapter 11 bankruptcy protection in May 2002 in order to organise a refinancing deal. NTL would not emerge from protection until January 2003, having converted around $11 billion of debt into shares. Technically, this amounted to the largest debt default in US corporate history.

One of its obligations, entered into in 2000, committed the company to a SEK 157.5 million ($21 million) second-round investment in Bredbandsbolaget, a commitment it could not fulfil due to its dire situation. By the end of 2002, NTL therefore preliminarily agreed to a deal whereby other key investors would acquire its share of Bredbandsbolaget for SEK 375,000 in exchange for waiving any claims on the outstanding commitment.In March 2003, however, the deal had not yet been closed.[7]

5. www.investorab.com/en/InvestorGrowthCapital/Default.htm. Note: An IGC office in Beijing was opened in 2005.
6. In the case of Bredbandsbolaget, a cost of equity of 20% was applied.
7. http://en.wikipedia.org/wiki/NTL:Telewest#NTL_.281993.E2.80.932006.29.

Investor Growth Capital had made its first investment in Bredbandsbolaget in 1999 and had gradually increased its share in each round of financing since (See Exhibit 10.7). In line with this strategy, IGC committed to fund one third of the NTL share and urged the other two majority owners to follow suit.

Given the Carlyle Group's position as one of the world's largest private equity firms with more than $84.5 billion under management, the Bredbandsbolaget investment was a medium-sized deal but with a different risk profile from many of its other more mature investments. In 2003, the group was running 64 funds across four investment disciplines (buyouts, growth capital, real estate and leveraged finance), with a team of over 495 investment professionals operating out of offices in 20 countries working in North America, Europe, Asia, Australia, the Middle East/North Africa and Latin America.[8] When the NTL situation arose, Carlyle chose to participate in the deal, agreeing to purchase one third of NTL's A-, B- and C-shareholdings.

Continuum Group was founded in 2000 by two investment bankers in London. In 2003, it managed a fund of $75 million. Through a cornerstone investment in Continuum by Swedish PE firm Novestra, Continuum came into contact with the B2 investment.[9] After investing a total of SEK 307 million ($41 million) of its funds into B2, problems that arose in other parts of its portfolio meant that it had limited funds to participate in additional rounds. With such a large proportion of the fund invested in B2, exiting the investment was not an optimum scenario for Continuum, but neither could it participate in the NTL buy-out.

Access Industries was founded by Russian-American investor Len Blavatnik in 1986 as a privately held, US-based industrial group with long-term holdings worldwide. In 2003, the group focused on holdings in three sectors: natural resources and chemicals, media and telecommunications, and real estate.[10] Bredbandsbolaget brought Access on board in 2001 through a private placement.

In 2003, it became clear that Access was aiming for a significantly larger stake in the company as it came to IGC and Carlyle with the following proposal:

- Access agreed to participate for the remaining one third of shares in the NTL deal.
- It proposed to make an offer to buy out four fifths of all Continuum shares, with IGC to assume the remaining fifth. The total consideration of Continuum's exit would be for $20 million.
- Access indicated that it was ready to make an offer for 36.5% of A-, 32.7% of B- and 7.2% of C-shares of minority investors (Framfab and Novestra) at a 97% discount.

Anti-Dilution Provisions in the Shareholders' Agreement

Johan Röhss realised that there were opportunities waiting to be seized in the investor turmoil. Firstly, there were clear corporate governance benefits in concentrating the

8. http://www.carlyle.com/Company/item1676.html.
9. http://www.highbeam.com/doc/1G1-61689633.html.
10. http://www.accessindustries.com/about.html.

ownership further. Secondly, IGC might be able to do so at a favourable price. The chances were high, of course, that minority investors would not agree.

Access Industries, which had not yet disclosed its proposal to minority investors, was valuing B2's A- and B-shares at a very significant discount. On the one hand, Continuum and the other minority investors knew they did not have the funds to participate in additional rounds and could rightfully expect Access, IGC and Carlyle to attempt to wash them out of the investment in the new round of financing by putting a low valuation on the company and thus a low value per existing share. This would in turn entitle the new round of funding to claim a large portion of the post-money shareholding. Those were the rules of the game and also the majority owners' fiduciary duty, provided they believed that a further investment would generate the highest return. If the three main investors were able to go ahead with this plan, the discount proposed by Access was simply driven by market rationale and it would be worth considering.

On the other hand, there were obstacles. Continuum and minority investors rightfully felt that they had some protection: in the anti-dilution provisions of the Shareholders' Agreement, a minimum value-per-share had been agreed. Shares could not be valued at less than SEK 5.54, the level at which the share price was already set. Even if a low valuation was obtained, there was no room to *de facto* value the company any lower by lowering the price of current shares. Any room for additional shareholdings claimed by a new round would thereby be entrenched by this minimum threshold or come in at a valuation that was too high. Needless to say, this was a headache for the majority owners.

Options Facing the Majority Investors

Summarising the situation, Röhss concluded the following. Bredbandsbolaget's expansion had required substantial amounts of capital and to date (2003) it had raised SEK 4,289 million ($620 million) of which SEK 700 million ($93 million) had been contributed by IGC for a current shareholding of 17.65%. As illustrated by Exhibit 10.9 and 10.10 (P&L and BS), funds were now running out, although – provided the NTL situation was resolved in the sense that money was transferred to B2 – the company would be able to operate for a number of months.

The board and investors were faced with three main options:

Option 1: If operations continued "as is" but without any capital injection, the company would simply face bankruptcy. This would mean a distressed sale or, at best, a hasty trade sale. In such a scenario, IGC could not expect more than SEK 100 million to 400 million in total for Bredbandsbolaget, and the best option would be a last-minute cancellation of the NTL buyout.

Option 2: The second option was to radically bootstrap the company, terminate all CAPEX investment and cut company costs, thereby limiting the runway left to break-even. This was generally seen as a risky option in that it required a commitment to the NTL deal, while at the same time there was uncertainty about how quickly costs would be able to come down. There was also uncertainty in terms of how competitive Bredbandsbolaget would be if it did not reach its targeted scale quickly. Furthermore, there was also the question of the type of exit Bredbandsbolaget's investors would subsequently be able to obtain.

Option 3: The third option was, of course, to commit further capital. All three majority investors agreed that if Bredbandsbolaget were to receive funding, it would have to be sufficient to see it through to break-even. At the same time, putting more money in would need to be rewarded with a substantial share of additional shareholding. The anti-dilution provisions, however, prevented this. From the majority shareholders' viewpoint, this posed a major obstacle at a point which, given the required returns, was crucial in determining B2's survival.

Operationally, the additional investment option also required that the business plan be executed. For this to be the case, B2 had to position itself as the leading alternative broadband provider in the market. The upside, of course, was that if B2 managed to do so, it would become a very attractive strategic and cash-flow generating acquisition target for either one of the current market participants or a new entrant, or possibly fulfil the prerequisites for a standalone IPO.

Choosing between these options boiled down to the valuation of the company, the burn rate of funds, how much shareholding could be obtained given the Shareholders' Agreement structure, and what the value created but also risks associated with an additional investment were. What also somehow needed to be taken into account was the upside lost if investors decided to go for bankruptcy and liquidation, which, once again, threw Röhss back to the fact that with the anti-dilution provisions as they were, bankruptcy seemed to be the more realistic outcome.

It was apparent that Access was betting that the new round would indeed obtain a fair share of ownership, i.e., that IGC, Carlyle and Access would find a way to dilute the minority investors. With the investment meeting approaching, Röhss could do nothing but investigate the foundation for this optimism. For the valuation there were, luckily enough, a number of comparables available (see Exhibit 10.11), but was there a way of circumventing the anti-dilution provisions?

Exhibit 10.1

Forecast Broadband Penetration by Country 2004

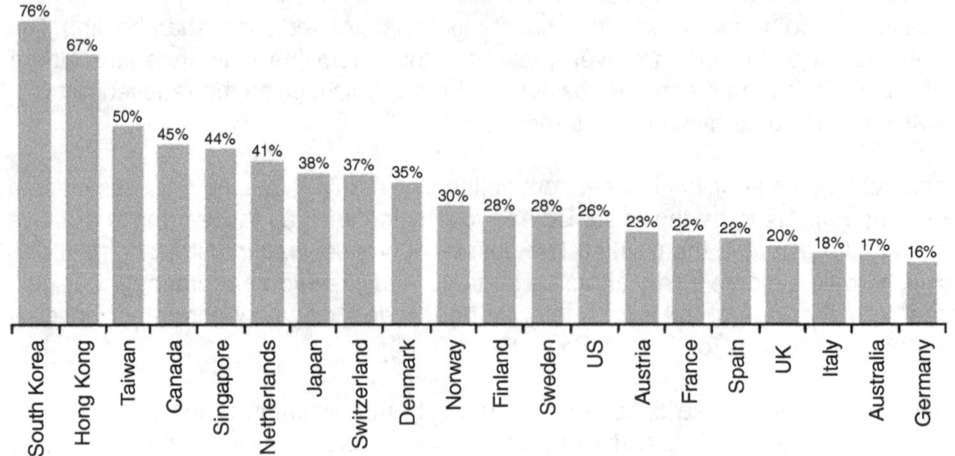

Note: defined as total number of broadband subscriptions as a % of households

Source: Informa

Exhibit 10.2

Broadband Penetration in Sweden 1999–2002, Actuals 2003–2009 Forecast

Swedish Internet Market	1999	2000	2001	2002	2003	2004	2005	2006	2007	2008	2009
Swedish Population ('000)	8,861	8,883	8,909	8,941	8,976	9,011	9,048	9,113	9,183	9,256	9,330
Computer penetration	4,874	5,507	5,791	5,990	6,642	6,759	7,148	7,473	7,714	7,960	8,024
Computer penetration %	55%	62%	65%	67%	74%	75%	79%	82%	84%	86%	86%
Internet penetration	2,658	4,530	4,722	5,007	5,834	6,128	6,514	6,835	7,163	7,498	7,744
Internet penetration %	30%	51%	53%	56%	65%	68%	72%	75%	78%	81%	83%
Broadband penetration	-	266	802	1,341	2,064	2,523	3,891	4,921	5,969	6,850	7,278
Broadband penetration %	0%	3%	9%	15%	23%	28%	43%	54%	65%	74%	78%

Sources: World Internet Institute – Internet och bredband i svenska hushåll 2009. Statistiska Central Byrån (SCB).

Exhibit 10.3

Telecommunication End User Market Revenue 2001–2004

End-user market for telecommunications, total revenue (SEK billion)

SEK billion	H1 2001	H2 2001	H1 2002	H2 2002	H1 2003	H2 2003	H1 2004
Total	24.1	25.2	25.1	25.4	25.4	24.6	24.9
Internet access*	1.0	1.1	1.4	2.1	2.1	2.3	2.4
Data communications	2.1	2.2	2.2	2.4	2.1	2.2	2.0
Mobile telephony	7.9	8.4	8.4	8.4	8.6	8.7	8.4
Fixed telephony	13.1	13.5	13.0	12.5	12.7	11.3	12.1

*Excludes dial-up traffic revenues, which is included under "Fixed telephony"

Source: PTS

Exhibit 10.4

Market Share 2002 – Swedish Broadband Market

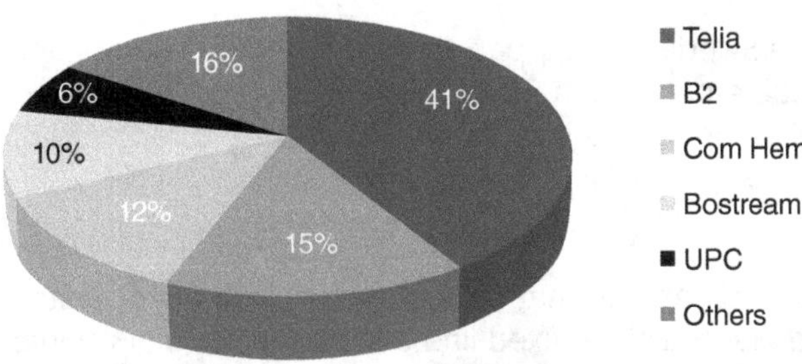

Source: B2 Estimates

Telia

Telia is the national incumbent telecommunications operator and the Swedish arm of TeliaSonera. The company is active in all segments of the telecom market other than cable TV, following the initiated divestiture of its previous subsidiary Com Hem. Telia offers broadband services over DSL and Ethernet LAN networks, and reported 420,000 subscribers at the end of 2002. At the same time, it reported that 144,000 broadband subscribers were connected to its network via service providers. At the beginning of 2003, TeliaSonera was 45% owned by the Swedish State.

Com Hem

Com Hem is the largest cable TV operator in Sweden, serving 1.4 million homes and a market share of around 55%. In addition to TV services, the company offers broadband services to those homes connected to its upgraded two-way network (currently 810,000 homes) and recently launched an IP-telephony service. Com Hem reported 139,000 broadband subscribers at the end of Q4, 2004. The company is a former subsidiary of TeliaSonera and was acquired by private equity fund EQT in 2003.

Bostream

Bostream was founded by Swedish real estate company Riksbyggen, but was acquired at an undisclosed price by Regency Capital, a UK private equity firm, in 2001.

A pure broadband internet service provider, it had 95,000 subscribers by the end of 2002 (65,000 ADSL wholesale subscribers, 12,000 DSL direct subscribers, 17,000 LAN subscribers, and 3,500 SME customers). Geographically, Bostream and its customers were active in different regions from Bredbandsbolaget, which meant that direct competition between the two had so far been limited.

A large proportion of Bostream's customers (two-thirds) had access based on Telia's network as "wholesale" subscribers, meaning that Bostream did not have its own network or equipment in the telestations, resulting in lower capex but also lower gross margins.

Bostream had strong financials: fiscal 03/04 (end by 31/03) showed SEK 372 million in revenues (up from SEK 222 million), EBITDA of SEK 56 million (up from SEK 32 million) and positive net income of SEK 35 million (02/03 SEK 21 million). On the balance sheet, total assets were SEK 194 million, but net assets only SEK 11 million and equity SEK 11 million (See Exhibit 10.12).

In 2003, Bostream had 105 employees, 60 of whom worked in their customer call centre. Management was led by three partners at Regency Capital, including two English citizens with little connection to Sweden other than Bostream. The CEO was Richard Burston, an ex-Morgan Stanley banker.

Exhibit 10.4 (Continued)

UPC

UPC Sverige is the Swedish arm of pan-European cable TV operator UnitedGlobalCom and operates a cable network in Stockholm serving 287,000 homes. UPC also offers broadband services under the brand name "Chello" and reported 65,000 broadband subscribers at the end of 2002.

Tele2

Tele2 is one of the largest alternative telecommunications operators in Europe, with 28 million customers, mainly in fixed-line telephony and dial-up internet. In Sweden, Tele2 also operates mobile and cable networks under the brand names "Comviq" and "Kabelvision". Tele2's Swedish operations reported revenues of SEK10.4 billion during 2004.

Glocalnet

Glocalnet is an alternative telecommunications operator targeting the residential market and is active mainly in the fixed-line telephony and broadband segments. The company is 37% owned by Norwegian national incumbent operator Telenor. Glocalnet reported 35,000 broadband customers at the end of 2002.

Spray

Spray Network operates one of the largest internet portals in Sweden and also offers broadband and fixed-line telephony services. The company is a subsidiary of Lycos Europe.

Corporate market

In the market for corporate broadband access, incumbent operator Telia was, at beginning of 2003, the largest operator with a market share around 40%. Tele2 was the second largest operator with an estimated 11% share of all connections, followed by Telenor with an 8% market share. B2 was the fourth largest provider in the market with a 6% market share, closely followed by Song Networks. The remaining part of the market was fragmented, with a large number of ISPs including MCI and Bahnhof.

Telenor

Telenor is the national incumbent telecommunications operator in Norway. Internationally, Telenor was primarily focusing on mobile telephony although the company had a broad service portfolio for the Swedish market and was actively acquiring to extend it. For example, Telenor's Swedish fixed-line business was a combination of the former subsidiaries Utfors, Telenordia and Telenor Business Solutions and targeted the corporate market with fixed line telephony and data communications solutions. Telenor also acted as a wholesaler of DSL connectivity. In the residential segment, the company was active through its 37% shareholding in Glocalnet. Telenor's Swedish fixed line operations reported revenues of approximately NOK 1.2 billion during 2002.

Song Networks is a business-focused telecommunications operator active in all the Nordic countries. In 2003, the company was offering telephony, internet access, hosting, and data communications services such as IP-VPN, as well as carrier services to other telecom operators. Song Networks' Swedish operations had an estimated annual turnover of around SEK 0.8 billion.

Exhibit 10.5

Pricing Points by Offering in the Swedish Broadband Market

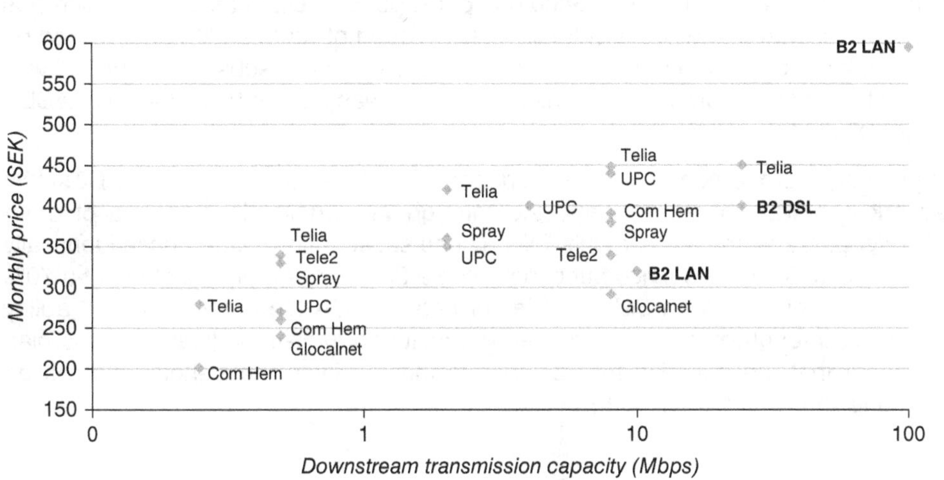

The Broadband Offering

Broadband can be defined as a telecommunications access service having the bandwidth sufficient to carry multiple voice, video or data channels simultaneously. It is sometimes defined as an access service capable of delivering transmission speeds of 2Mbps or more, but typically the term includes all forms of "always-on" access services capable of delivering transmission speeds higher than that of traditional dial-up access services over the public telephone network.

Broadband connections enable a wide range of services and applications over and above high-speed internet access and all the applications that come with it such as quick downloading of large files, instant messaging, music and video streaming, online gaming and eCommerce.

Starting in the early 2000s, broadband operators were also able to deliver sufficient transmission capacity to offer carrier class IP-telephony and video services such as digital TV and Video-on-Demand.

Ethernet LAN (Ethernet Local Access Network)

Subscribers connected through an Ethernet LAN network had the choice of two different subscriptions; one giving bi-directional transmission speeds of 10 Mbps and the other giving 100 Mbps both downstream and upstream. The monthly fee for the 10 Mbps service was SEK 320, whereas the 100 Mbps connection was available for an additional SEK 275 per month, i.e., at SEK 595. Both connections were subject to a SEK 495 installation fee.

Exhibit 10.5 (Continued)

DSL

A DSL subscription – Digital Subscriber Line – meant being connected to the internet via a telephone line. B2 only marketed one package to its DSL customers, which was a connection with a downstream transmission speed of up to 24 Mbps, provided on a "best-efforts" basis and the actual speed varied. The initial subscription period was six months and the monthly fee for the DSL access was SEK 399 in addition to a SEK 495 installation fee.

An increasing proportion of DSL subscribers was located in areas outside B2's own network and was therefore connected through the wholesale platforms of other network operators, most commonly Telia. These subscriptions were priced identically to the regular 24 Mbps service but contributed a 30% gross margin instead of a 70% margin for subscribers on B2's proprietary network. On the other hand, the ability to connect through other networks was not included in B2's original business plan but meant that the potential market grew to include every household with a fixed telephone line (See Exhibit 10.5).

Exhibit 10.6

Cap Table Pre & Suggested Post NTL Buyout

SHARE CLASSES AND SHAREHOLDINGS IN B2 - PRE NTL BUYOUT

Shareholder	Number of shares ('000)				Shareholding
Preference	A	B	C	Total	%
NTL	76,558	90,973	7,037	174,568	29.00%
Investor	23,771	-	82,497	106,268	17.65%
Carlyle	20,933	-	60,921	81,854	13.60%
Access	-	-	84,883	84,883	14.10%
Continuum	669	17,128	37,726	55,523	9.22%
Other	79,958	11,403	7,578	98,939	16.43%
Total	**201,889**	**119,504**	**280,642**	**602,035**	**100.00%**

2. SHARE CLASSES AND SHAREHOLDINGS IN B2 - POST NTL BUYOUT*

Shareholder	Number of shares ('000)				Shareholding
	A	B	C	Total	%
NTL	-	-	-	-	0.00%
IGC	49,290	30,324	84,843	164,457	27.32%
Carlyle	46,452	30,324	63,267	140,043	23.26%
Access	25,519	30,324	87,229	143,072	23.76%
Continuum	669	17,128	37,726	55,523	9.22%
Other	79,958	11,403	7,578	98,939	16.43%
Total	**201,889**	**119,504**	**280,642**	**602,035**	**100.00%**

* Investor, Carlyle and Access buy out NTL

Absolute Changes

Shareholder Preference	A	B	C	Total
NTL	(76,558)	(90,973)	(7,037)	(174,568)
IGC	25,519	30,324	2,346	58,189
Carlyle	25,519	30,324	2,346	58,189
Access	25,519	30,324	2,346	58,189
Continuum	-	-	-	-
	-	-	-	-
Other	-	-	-	-
Total	201,889	119,504	280,642	602,035

Exhibit 10.7

Cap Table IGC – B2 Investment History

All figures in SEK

Share series	Share Class	Investment date (mm/yr)	Total number of Shares	Total Investment	IGC Number of Shares	% of Round	Actual Cost		Adjusted Cost	
							Per share	Total ('000)	Per share	Total ('000)
Common 1st r.	A	Jun-99	34,601,382	204,759,345	4,074,074	11.77%	5.92	24,109	5.54	22,570
Common 2nd r.	A	Dec-99	38,218,800	510,220,981	4,500,000	11.77%	13.35	60,075	5.54	24,930
Common 3rd r.	A	Mar-00	9,224,150	366,484,698	1,086,080	11.77%	39.73	43,151	5.54	6,017
Common convertible	A	Aug-00	119,844,668	991,115,403	14,110,883	11.77%	8.27	116,697	5.54	78,174
Bridge con. A	B	Feb-01	64,495,208	357,303,454	12,683,392	19.67%	5.54	70,266	5.54	70,266
Bridge con. B+C	B	Mar/Apr-01	55,008,792	304,748,706	10,817,828	19.67%	5.54	59,931	5.54	59,931
Bridge con. D, E & F	C	Jun/Aug-01	46,264,798	256,306,982	9,725,606	21.02%	5.54	53,880	5.54	53,880
Pref. C tranche 1	C	Sept-01	140,160,080	776,486,843	29,463,907	21.02%	5.54	162,230	5.54	162,230
Pref. C tranche 2	C	Mar-02	94,217,122	521,962,855	19,805,957	21.02%	5.54	109,725	5.54	109,725
Total			**602,035,000**	**4,289,389,268**	**106,267,727**	**17.65%**	**7.12**	**700,064**	**5.54**	**587,723**

Valuation comments
Pre-money equity valuation September 6:th, 2000, was set at SEK 1,045bn or SEK 5.54/share. 5.54 is the minimum share price as stipulated in the anti-dilution provisions in the shareholders agreement
All the bridge convertibles A-F will be converted into Pref C shares as part of the round.
Ownership percentage above is pro-forma the Mar-02 tranche.

Source: B2 Q2-02 Status Report.

Exhibit 10.8

B2 Customer Base Forecast 2003 – 2009

B2 Forecast	2003	2004	2005	2006	2007	2008	2009
B-ISP	311	400	600	795	994	1,242	1,553
VAS (100mb)	10	33	45	58	78	105	142
TOTAL Broadband	321	433	645	853	1,072	1,348	1,695
Broadband Market Share	16%	17%	17%	17%	18%	20%	23%
Telephony							
- PSTN	29	5	-	-	-	-	-
- IPT	61	191	284	362	398	438	482
TOTAL TLPH	2,064	195	284	362	398	438	482
Enterprise	30	77	101	116	133	153	176
TOTAL SERVICED CONTRACTS	2,415	705	1,030	1,331	1,603	1,939	2,353

Definitions

B-ISP	Broadband - Internet Service Provider
VAS	Value Added Service
PSTN	Public switched telephone network
IPT	Internet Protocol (IP) - Telephony

Exhibit 10.9

P&L

B2 Bredband AB, Consolidated

Profit & Loss

	2001	2002	2003	2004	2005	2006
	Full year	Full year	Full year	Full year	Full year	Full year
MSEK	Actual	Actual	Forecast	Forecast	Forecast	Forecast
Sales	166.9	245.1	441.2	724.8	979.2	1,199.9
COGS	(163.9)	(147.7)	(181.4)	(253.1)	(315.9)	(374.6)
Gross income	**3.0**	**97.4**	**259.8**	**471.7**	**663.3**	**825.3**
G&A	(167.6)	(87.3)	(58.6)	(64.0)	(64.0)	(64.0)
S&M	(96.4)	(68.4)	(63.8)	(57.6)	(58.2)	(55.0)
Technology & installation	(62.1)	(70.7)	(122.7)	(122.3)	(131.8)	(140.6)
Customer care and support	(90.9)	(63.3)	(78.3)	(78.0)	(83.2)	(85.5)
Other operating costs	(45.8)	(48.3)	-	-	-	-
EBITDA	**(459.8)**	**(240.6)**	**(63.5)**	**149.8**	**326.1**	**480.2**
Restructuring cost	(82.4)	-	(10.5)	-	-	-
Depreciation and amortization	(297.6)	(420.3)	(447.9)	(490.0)	(546.8)	(598.1)
EBIT	**(839.8)**	**(660.9)**	**(522.0)**	**(340.2)**	**(220.7)**	**(117.9)**
Fin net	(70.7)	151.1	1.0	(0.1)	(0.1)	-
Fx gain/Loss	(59.3)	(30.9)	-	-	-	-
Items affecting comparability	(0.7)	-	-	-	-	-
Taxes	-	-	-	-	-	-
Net income	**(894.0)**	**(540.8)**	**(520.9)**	**(340.3)**	**(220.8)**	**(117.9)**
EPS	-	-	-	-	-	-

Exhibit 10.10
Balance Sheet

B2 Bredband AB, Consolidated
Balance Sheet

MSEK	2001 Actual	2002 Actual	2003 Forecast	2004 Forecast	2005 Forecast	2006 Forecast
ASSETS						
Cash and cash equivalents	557.0	314.7	-	(0.0)	11.6	135.4
Trade accounts and other receivables	88.3	55.0	47.8	98.2	129.7	154.0
Prepaid expenses and accrued income	61.6	50.0	50.0	50.0	50.0	50.0
Other current assets	2.4	35.0	35.0	35.0	35.0	35.0
Net tangible assets	1,932.2	1,505.0	1,476.4	1,274.4	1,005.4	621.8
Net intangible assets	170.0	136.5	131.4	131.4	131.4	131.4
Net installation & hook-up costs	46.8	46.6	44.1	47.4	50.8	52.1
Total Assets	2,858.3	2,142.8	1,784.6	1,636.5	1,413.9	1,179.7
LIABILITIES						
Current portion of long-term liabilities	12.5	22.8	-	(0.0)	(0.0)	(0.0)
Trade accounts payable	142.5	114.0	98.9	118.4	126.5	123.4
Other current liabilities	131.1	114.8	87.8	87.8	87.8	87.8
Accrued liabilities and deferred revenues	65.7	95.0	95.0	95.0	95.0	95.0
Long-term liabilities	9.9	9.9	9.9	9.9	-	-
Vendor Financing 2)	869.6	659.5	566.0	566.0	566.0	452.9
SHAREHOLDERS EQUITY						
Shareholders' equity 4)	1,780.0	1,126.8	605.9	265.6	44.8	(73.1)
Total liab. & shareholders' equity	3,011.3	2,142.8	1,463.5	1,142.7	920.2	686.0

2) Assumes repayments finalized in 2009

4) Before additional funding

Exhibit 10.11
Comparables

As of Q1-03	Price per share	Change since	Previous Q	Market	Net	EV	Performance					
							Current year			Next year		
Company	This Q	previous Q	Market Cap	cap	Debt		Sales	EBIT	EPS	Sales	EBIT	EPS
	2/27/2003											
T-Online	12.53	-5.3%	16,191	15,335	-3,590	11,745	1,539	-384	-0.3	1,973	-260	-0.2
Terra Networks	8.16	-21.9%	6,510	5,082	-190	4,892	904	-279	-0.8	1,124	-130	-0.4
Wanadoo	6.06	2.1%	8,584	8,763	-2,000	6,763	2,100	-114	-0.1	2,640	59	0.1
Web.de	3.71	-43.7%	245	138	-110	28	31	-15	-0.4	49	-3	-0.1
Freenet	10.5	-24.5%	249	188	-54	134	42	-12	-0.5	53	-4	0.1
Jippii Group	0.37	-8.3%	36	33	5	38	111	2	-0.2	151	11	0.0
Lycos Europe	0.62	-22.5%	275	213	-320		152	N/A	N/A	170	N/A	N/A
Yahoo!	14.82	-17.1%	10,292	8,536	-1,765	6,771	781	178	0.1	956	384	0.2
AOL Time Warner	23.05	-38.6%	165,945	101,812	22,000	123,812	41,800	6,000	1.0	45,717	2,639	1.2

Note: AOL Time Warner EBIT excludes goodwill write-downs of US$45 billion.
Source: Investor AB.

Exhibit 10.12

Bostream P&L & Balance Sheet

Bostream P&L*

MSEK	2001/02 15 mths	2002/03 Actual	2003/04 Actual	2004/05 Forecast*	2005/06 Forecast*	2006/07 Forecast*
Revenue	124.8	222.0	371.7	511.0	722.0	886.0
External costs	(102.4)	(165.4)	(279.0)	(352.1)	(399.6)	(475.0)
Personnel costs	(13.5)	(24.8)	(36.4)	(38.2)	(36.2)	(36.5)
EBITDA	9.0	31.8	56.3	113.0	279.0	368.0
D&A	(1.1)	(4.2)	(9.0)	(21.0)	(30.0)	(36.0)
EBIT	7.9	27.6	47.3	93.0	249.0	332.0
Financials	0.3	1.8	2.1			
EBT	8.2	29.4	49.4			
Appropriations and taxes	(4.1)	(8.4)	(14.1)			
Net income	4.1	20.9	35.3			
EBITDA margin (%)	7.2%	14.3%	15.2%	22.0%	39.0%	41.0%
EBIT margin (%)	6.3%	12.4%	12.7%	18.0%	35.0%	37.0%

Source: Bostream Annual Report 03/04 (Fiscal Year ending 31/03 2003).

Bostream Balance Sheet*

MSEK	2001/02 15 mths	2002/03 Actual	2003/04 Actual	2004/05 Forecast*	2005/06 Forecast*	2006/07 Forecast*
Net Tangible fixed assets	34.9	36.8	38.7	40.6	42.7	44.8
Net Other fixed assets	3.2	3.4	3.6	3.8	4.0	4.2
Net Fixed assets	38.2	40.2	42.3	44.4	46.6	49.0
Inventories	4.3	4.6	4.8	5.0	5.3	5.6
Accounts receivable	78.9	83.0	87.4	91.8	96.4	101.2
Other current assets	11.2	11.8	12.4	13.0	13.7	14.4
Cash and bank	43.0	45.3	47.7	50.1	52.6	55.2
Current assets	137.5	144.7	152.3	159.9	167.9	176.3
Total assets	175.6	184.9	194.6	204.3	214.5	225.3
Equity	10.4	10.9	11.5	12.1	12.7	13.3
Liability to group company	34.4	34.4	34.4	34.4	34.4	34.4
Payables	42.3	44.6	46.9	49.2	51.7	54.3
Other current liabilities	91.9	96.7	101.8	106.9	112.2	117.8
Total current liabilities	165.2	173.9	183.1	192.3	201.9	212.0
Total equity and liabilities	175.6	184.9	194.6	204.3	214.5	225.3

Exhibit 10.13
Media Gallery

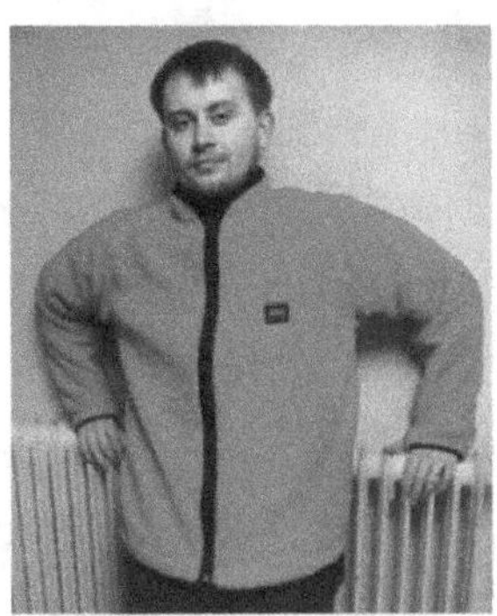

Bredbandsbolaget Founder – Jonas Birgersson
Picture by: Realtid.se

Access Industries – Len Blavatnik
Picture by: timesonline.com

Further Articles on Bredbandsbolaget:

Exit Watch
Private Equity Week Volume: 12 Issue: 23 (2005-05-30) p. 7-7. ISSN: 1099-341X.

Groups Seeking Low-Fee UMTS Licenses As Sweden, Norway Spur Development.
Wall Street Journal Volume: 236 Issue: 33 (2000-08-17) Latour, Alma. ISSN: 0099-9660.

Sveriges IT-guru
Aftonbladet: (2000-01-09) – http://wwwc.aftonbladet.se/nyheter/0001/09/birger.html.

High on ethernet
Tele.Com Volume: 4 Issue: 19 (1999-10-04) pp. 34-35. ISSN: 1086-7821.

SECTION IV Leveraged Buyouts (LBOs)

We like to think of ourselves as industrialists. We buy a company and look at what we can do to make it better. To me, there's much more to investing than buying low and selling high.

—**Henry R. Kravis**, Co-Chairman and Co-CEO, KKR

CASE 11 CHIPS ON THE SIDE (A)
THE BUYOUT OF AVAGO TECHNOLOGIES

SYNOPSIS

During the summer of 2005 Agilent initiates a limited auction to sell off its Semiconductor Products Group. By late July, Agilent has selected the consortium of KKR and Silver Lake Partners as the winning bidder pending confirmatory due diligence. Over the two-week confirmatory diligence period, KKR and Silver Lake continue to question the opportunities at the heart of the investment hypothesis, and evaluate the downside risk. The financing package is firmed up and, given the size of the required equity investment, co-investor interest is solicited.

This case is an opportunity for the reader to step into the shoes of a partner at KKR or Silver Lake as the firms consider this carve-out opportunity. To prepare for the signing of the acquisition agreement and the subsequent transfer of ownership, the deal team is revisiting their investment thesis with respect to upsides and risks.

Case 11 focuses on the operational side of the transaction, while Case 12 deals with the implementation of an appropriate financing and capital structure.

PEDAGOGICAL OBJECTIVE OF THE CASE

The case helps to develop a high-level understanding of the workings of leveraged buyouts by discussing the risk–return relationship in private equity and the interplay of financial and operational risks in the deal structuring process. It follows the decision-making process of an investment committee as it tries to balance and understand the trade-offs of different debt instruments and financing structures within the context of a carve-out, which comes with ample operational risk.

The case emphasizes the PE firms' focus on operational value creation ahead of financial structuring when creating value and returns in a typical large buyout. It also analyzes differences in corporate governance models between PE owners and diversified firms (in particular, publicly listed companies). It presents a concrete example illustrating the potential for PE investors to improve the competitive positioning, operations and culture of portfolio companies. Within the context of a carve-out, the case analyzes the main risks to an operations-heavy buyout transaction, and discusses measures to mitigate these risks.

SUGGESTED ASSIGNMENT QUESTIONS

1. Why did Hewlett-Packard and Agilent sell this business, and why might they have struggled to optimize it?
2. What are the highest impact value-creation levers in this deal? Where's the upside?

3. What are the biggest risks (operational and financial) and how might they be mitigated?
4. Given your perspective on the risk–reward of this deal, how would you finance this transaction?

ADDITIONAL RESOURCES

To make the most of this case study, we suggest the following additional sources to provide context and background information:

- In particular, we recommend the following chapters from *Mastering Private Equity—Transformation via Venture Capital, Minority Investments & Buyouts*
  - Chapter 1 Private Equity Essentials
  - Chapter 4 Buyouts
  - Chapter 9 Deal Structuring
  - Chapter 11 Corporate Governance
  - Chapter 12 Securing Management Teams
  - Chapter 23 Risk Management
- Case website for faculty and lecturers: http://cases.insead.edu/chips-on-the-side/
- Jan Vild and Claudia Zeisberger (2014), "Strategic Buyer versus Private Equity Buyers in an Investment Process." Retrieved from: http://centres.insead.edu/global-private-equity-initiative/research-publications/documents/PE-strategic-buyer-workingdoc.pdf
- You may also refer to the book website for further material:
  www.masteringprivateequity.com

Chips on the Side (A)

The Buyout of Avago Technologies

03/2015-5832

This case was written by Michael Prahl, Senior Research Associate, INSEAD Global Private Equity Initiative (GPEI), and Swati Sawjiany, MBA Class of July 2011, under the supervision of Claudia Zeisberger, Senior Affiliate Professor of Decision Sciences and Entrepreneurship and Family Enterprise, and Vikas A. Aggarwal, Assistant Professor of Entrepreneurship and Family Enterprise, both at INSEAD. It is intended to be used as a basis for class discussion rather than to illustrate either effective or ineffective handling of a particular situation or for any other purpose.

The case is dedicated to Dick Chang, CEO of Avago at the time of the spin-off, in memoriam.

Additional material about INSEAD case studies (e.g., videos, spreadsheets, links) can be accessed at cases.insead.edu.

Chips on the Side (A): The Buyout of Avago Technologies[1]

It was the summer of 2005 when Agilent, a diversified technology company with headquarters in Palo Alto, California, USA, conducted a limited auction to sell off its Semiconductor Products Group (SPG) and Automated Test Group (ATG). By July, Agilent had selected a consortium comprised of Kohlberg Kravis Roberts & Co (KKR) and Silver Lake Partners (SLP) as the winning bid for SPG, pending confirmatory due diligence. KKR and SLP (see Appendix 1 and Exhibits 11.1 and 11.2) had partnered to evaluate the investment opportunity, having conducted initial business, financial and industry due diligence. Over the next few weeks, teams from both firms would begin the process of conducting confirmatory customer, IP, accounting, legal and HR/benefits due diligence of the SPG with the goal of implementing a definitive agreement with Agilent by early August.

Ken Hao, Managing Director at SLP, Adam Clammer, Partner at KKR, and William (Bill) Cornog, Partner at Capstone, KKR's in-house performance improvement group, were on a conference call going through the last presentation they had given to their respective investment committees before the final bid to remind them of the major points while coming up with a refined work plan for the next weeks. Though they all agreed on the main points, each of them had his own set of priorities.

Bill worried how to execute the carve-out on time and on budget, and how to put a hard figure on the cost reductions that the top-down analysis promised: "We were pretty sure that a standalone business could operate with substantially lower SG&A cost as allocated by Agilent, yet we had to piece together a NewCo cost structure bottom up to substantiate this and to establish an operational road-map post signing."

Ken was most concerned about the unrelated portfolio they were going to acquire and how to rationalize it and position it for growth: "This was really not one business but a portfolio of different semiconductor businesses with unrelated products."

Adam was busy hardening the financing package for the deal and soliciting co-investor interest given the size of the required equity investment and perceived risk in the deal: "We had promised a purchase price higher than for any semiconductor deal before, which necessitated a substantial debt package. At the same time the operational risk drove us in the direction of a conservative debt structure."

Above all, the team spent a lot of time trying to comprehend the cyclicality of the industry with a view on understanding what happened during a downturn and the impact on income statement and cash flow.

---

1. The contents may not be regarded in any manner as legal, tax, investment, accounting or other advice or as an offer to sell or a solicitation of an offer to buy an interest in Avago or any other Silver Lake portfolio company or Silver Lake fund (collectively, "Silver Lake") or any other KKR portfolio company or KKR fund (collectively, "KKR"). Neither Silver Lake, KKR, Avago or their affiliates make any representation or warranty, express or implied, as to the accuracy or completeness of the information contained herein.

The case is set at the time when the business was known as the Semiconductor Products Group (SPG) of Agilent. Post buyout it was renamed Avago Technologies. The contents have not been updated to reflect any developments or changes since the transaction.

As in many carve-outs, their work was complicated by the multiple connections between the business to be spun off and the one remaining behind, a lack of fully allocated stand-alone costs and uncertainties on how the business would fare without being under the Agilent umbrella in the market place.

Agilent Technologies

In 2005, Agilent Technologies was a leader in the test and measurement market, focusing on customers in the communications, electronics, life sciences and chemical analysis industries. The firm had emerged as a spin-off of Hewlett-Packard Company (HP), comprising all product lines that were not directly connected with HP's future core businesses of computing, printing and imaging. The new entity had been listed on November 18, 1999 as the largest initial public offering (IPO) in Silicon Valley history up to that time. In 2000, Agilent had launched a sweeping operational transformation to make the company more efficient and cost effective, and by 2004 the firm had largely completed this transformation.

As of 2005, Agilent consisted of four primary businesses, namely Test & Measurement (US$2.9 billion in sales, US$277 million EBIT), Semiconductor Products Group (US$2 billion in sales, US$224 million EBIT), Life Sciences and Chemical Analysis (US$1.3 billion in sales, US$196 million EBIT) and Automated Test (US$0.9 billion in sales, US$11 million EBIT). (For details see Exhibits 11.3-11.5).

The Test and Measurement (T&M) business provided solutions that were predominantly used in the communications industry. In 2004, the business unit had achieved 15% growth in revenue and an 18% increase in overall orders. "Driving T&M's comeback were improved conditions in many of its markets, strong new products, outstanding expense control and the benefits of its restructuring during the past three years."[2]

The Life Sciences and Chemical Analysis (LSCA) business provided application-focused solutions to a range of industries in the chemical and life sciences fields. It had had a consistently strong year, with healthy growth in orders and revenue, a 30% improvement in operating profit, and record orders and revenue in the fourth quarter.

The Automated Test (ATG) business provided test solutions used in the manufacture of semiconductor devices, electronics (primarily printed circuit-board assemblies) and flat panel displays. While revenue had increased by 22% over fiscal 2003, order intake fell 2%, reflecting the softening outlook in the semiconductor and related industries. In 2004, Agilent acquired IBM's flat panel test business, which it believed complemented its existing automated test businesses and offered opportunities for profitable growth.

The Semiconductor Products Group (SPG) business was a leading supplier of semiconductor components, modules and subsystems for consumer and commercial electronics applications. After a strong first half year in 2004, demand from its customer industries slowed significantly, while at the same time the semiconductor industry worked through excess inventory and capacity affecting second-half results

2. Agilent Technologies 2004 corporate report.

in the SPG. Still, for the full year, orders in SPG were up 20%, while revenue had risen by 27%. In the fourth quarter Agilent announced plans to sell SPG's camera module business to Flextronics after it had determined that this business would not achieve acceptable profit levels as part of Agilent.

The Semiconductor Industry

The microelectronics and semiconductor industry was born in 1947 with the invention of the transistor by scientists at Bell Labs. In 2004, global semiconductor sales hit a record of US$213 billion and were expected to grow at 11%–17% per annum. The industry consisted of four major product categories, namely Memory, Microprocessors, Commodity Integrated Circuits and complex 'System on a Chip' products.

The semiconductor industry is one of the most volatile and cyclical industries, with a high/low range of +/- 40% annual growth and no consecutive down years over the last two decades (Exhibit 11.7). Cycles were a result of the long lead times and high fixed-cost investment in bringing a product to market, coupled with uncertain demand cycles in consumer end markets (personal computers, cell phones, automotive and other electronics devices) against a background of accelerating technology cycles. Within the industry there were different sub-cycles depending on the technology, application and end-user industry.

Typically, it can take several years to develop cutting-edge products, to plan and construct fabrication units and put them into operation. Therefore, in favourable market conditions semiconductor manufacturers often begin building new production units or acquire existing manufacturing plants in anticipation of demand growth for semiconductors. After the commencement of commercial operations, fabrication units can increase production volumes rapidly. As a result, large amounts of semiconductor manufacturing capacity typically become available during the same period. In the absence of a proportional growth in demand, this increase in supply often results in semiconductor manufacturing overcapacity, which leads to a sharp decline in prices and significant capacity under-utilization (Exhibit 11.8).

Head-to-head competition for market share between leading semiconductor companies causes cyclicality in price, production and capacity. As industry capacity is 'lumpy', that is, indivisible and involving large fixed costs, firms may choose to add excess capacity for reasons of strategic pre-emption in order to achieve first-mover advantage. However, each firm makes decisions simultaneously and similarly in this investment 'game'. Lacking coordination, firms often add capacity simultaneously, with the result that over-capacity or under-capacity ensues.

Technology changes were an additional significant contributor to the semiconductor industry cycle. The industry has been well known for its rapid technology progress (in accordance with Moore's law) thanks to both product and process innovations. The generally high but uneven pace of technology progress has resulted in shorter product life cycles, a rapid decline in prices, the continuous emergence of new applications and markets, and considerable market uncertainty all adding to the cyclical dynamics of the industry. Overall, inventory levels and book-to-bill ratios are good short-term indicators but provide little visibility on cycles beyond a 12 month time frame.

For the transaction, the question of where the industry was in the cycle was a "big dial" factor, as Ken Hao put it: "We had looked at all the semiconductor deals previously done and, yes, all deals done at the bottom of the cycle did great and the ones at the peak ranged from average to poor. Unfortunately one can't control the cycle. The only thing we knew was that we were just coming out of a downturn and were hoping that the next one would not come too quickly."

Moreover, sellers had become more aware of the relation between point in cycle and purchase price and would no longer underprice assets based on historic numbers from a downturn. So, in Adam's words, the consortium had to pay the highest (in terms of multiple) purchase price for a semiconductor company for the "privilege of buying into a recovery".

The Semiconductor Group (SPG)

The performance of the SPG had generally followed the overall semiconductor industry but had been moderately less cyclical due to a mix across numerous end markets. SPG operates in a medium to highly competitive market, competing against industry heavyweights such as Fairchild Semiconductor (US$1.6 billion in revenues), Vishay Intertechnology (US$2.4 billion), National Semiconductor (US$1.9 billion), Freescale Semiconductor (US$5.7 billion) and Broadcom (US$2.4 billion).

SPG was comprised of six different business units spanning a variety of semiconductor end markets: the ECBU or Core Optoelectronics (45% of SPG revenue), Fibre Optics (15%), Wireless (13%), Imaging Solutions (11%), Enterprise (11%), and Storage (5%). While all BUs had their specifics, the consortium often grouped them into two portfolios with broadly shared characteristics when thinking about them strategically: the first three business units formed the 'Core Portfolio', whereas the latter three made up the 'Tactical Portfolio' (Exhibit 11.8).[3]

The Core Portfolio, specifically the ECBU, was a cost-sensitive, low capex business with a low average sales price model, and most of its operations in Malaysia and Singapore. Although the ECBU operated in a mature industry, it had been able to drive mid-single digit growth (1998-2005E CAGR: 6.6%) and EBIT margins ranging from 19%-34% for the same period. The major concern for the ECBU was that even though it had grown with the industry in the long run, in recent years growth had been slower than the overall market due to a lack of participation in higher growth segments. Overall however the consortium was according to Tony Ling (Director at SLP): "very comfortable with the risk profile of the ECBU as it had a strong range of stable products. Once designed-in in industries such as white goods, automotive or industrial they would have a long life time at steady margins. They would typically only make up a very small part of overall cost to the end products yet be mission critical to its performance."

The Tactical Portfolio was a design-win driven business necessitating large investments in R&D, and operating with a US-based cost structure. While new products would

3. While the split was broadly along BUs some of them had assets in both portfolios notably Wireless and Fiber Optics.

initially generate high profits, the competitiveness of the industry would drive down margins quickly. Short product cycles made it hard to generate sufficient returns on invested capital (ROIC). Overall the tactical portfolio was expected to break even on profitability but remain cash flow negative in 2005. Says Bill Cornog: "The digital products in the Tactical portfolio had a shelf life of 18-24 months. You could move from leader in a product group to laggard in less than 3-4 years. To avoid this, the BUs had to maintain competitive R&D spending, and its associated technology risk, to deliver a steady stream of design wins in the face of intense competition."

Agilent's Management Approach

SPG's product portfolio mix was not highly complementary with that of Agilent's other businesses. SPG operated in the highly volatile and cyclical semiconductor industry, where to compete and achieve profitability required constant innovation, stringent cost optimization, and most importantly the ability to adapt to constantly shifting market trends. Agilent's other businesses, such as T&M and LSCA, operated in slower paced industries and faced different competitive market forces. Its more consistent higher margins allowed it to operate with significantly higher overheads. Consequently, Agilent's organizational culture was that of a measurement company and quite different from that of a semiconductor manufacturer.

Agilent's management viewed SPG as a non-core group, and devoted less senior management focus, expertise and talent to it. Adam Clammer recalled: "After observing and interacting with the management team at SPG throughout the process, we felt that people on the business side would transition well and potentially perform better with a new, more focused owner. It was the staff functions that needed strengthening as they had previously worked in a division of a division of a large company, with little overall responsibility."

Customer and Distribution Considerations

Due to the catalogue nature of the Core Portfolio, the majority of products were sold through distributors (~55%) to a fragmented but stable customer base, reducing the earnings risk due to customer defection. Agilent's strong brand name and customer stickiness in this area acted as major assets. The Tactical Portfolio, on the other hand, had direct sales channels to a concentrated base of customers.

Furthermore, the LED business within the ECBU had been inhibited by Agilent's non-compete agreements with its Lumileds joint venture, restricting the group's ability to pursue faster growing segments. A carve-out or independent sale of the SPG would eliminate these restrictions and allow the strategic buyer to pursue bigger growth opportunities. However, important IP and supply relationship issues would need to be negotiated to enable this.

For specific product lines, SPG's biggest customer was its previous parent, HP. For example, for the ECBU–Motion Control product line, HP represented over 50% of revenue, with the remainder mostly sold through distribution channels. SPG also sold optical encoders for HP's printers. Having its largest customer internal to the company created a significant conflict of interest and transfer pricing issues.

Growth Opportunities for SPG

Organizational restrictions with Agilent had made it more difficult for the ECBU to grow. Agilent had traditionally viewed it as a 'cash cow' and had provided few resources to spur growth. For example, the ECBU only allocated ~5% of its sales to R&D, significantly lower than all other business units and comparables (Exhibits 11.11 and 11.12). Given the fast-moving nature of the industry in which the ECBU operated, underinvestment could have dire consequences for overall market share. Agilent's management viewed SPG as a non-core group taking ECBU cash flows and investing them in other businesses.

Historically, SPG's strategy had been to harvest the slower growth businesses in order to fund higher growth – but often less profitable – businesses. Moreover, Agilent's management discouraged the ECBU management from pursuing revenue that would contribute to operating profits but fell below a specified gross margin, leading to sub-optimal investments and exits from businesses that were cash flow positive and would have had an attractive return on invested capital (ROIC). Despite the limited R&D investments thus far, SPG's management had been successful in driving growth through new product introductions. Historical returns on new product investments were attractive, with typical R&D IRR equalling 84% for products with average life cycles of three years.

According to Ken Hao: "We expected ECBU to continue funding the R&D activities in the Tactical Portfolio, yet were conscious of the fact that ECBU also had to carry the debt package for the transaction. So an improvement in R&D efficiency, concentrating on a few high beta products, was required."

SPG Cost Structure

The Core Portfolio provided SPG with stable, predictable revenues as it functioned as a catalogue business with long product cycles. Its cost structure was Asia-based and mostly flexible (over 85% in variable costs), alleviating cash flow cyclicality. In contrast, SPG's Tactical Portfolio had a US-based structure with higher fixed costs. Coupled with greater volatility in top-line revenues, profits and cash flows fluctuated widely.

Agilent's existing cost allocation policies were designed to cater to the cost structure of a scientific instrument and measurements company. Over time, SPG's cost structure was burdened with an economic model and overhead structure that made it less competitive. Agilent's SGA costs represented over 25%–30% of sales, whereas those of SPG's competitors were 10%–15% of sales. SPG itself had direct SGA costs in line with the competition, yet was assigned an additional 7%–10% corporate cost allocation (see Exhibit 11.11). Other corporate allocations (e.g. R&D) and legacy costs (e.g. Agilent had over a 1000 legacy IT systems) further impacted SPG's profitability and offered opportunities for financial and cost optimization.

From a deal perspective it did not look like a very attractive business, as Adam Clammer recalled: "We effectively inherited a business with very limited profitability [if corporate overheads were fully allocated]. So we spent a lot of time figuring out what the true cost base was like."

Yet while corporate cost allocations seemed to be rich, Agilent did provide a large number of services to its divisions. Bill Cornog's team from Capstone and the Silver Lake Value Creation team had to come up with a robust number for a stand-alone business: "We were tasked to piece together the full SG&A cost structure for NewCo. Benchmarks indicated that SG&A for SPG should be around 12-13% at the bottom of the cycle and 8-9% at the top. So we knew there was a big opportunity to improve the cost structure... the question was by how much."

An encouraging sign was that despite excessive overhead and SGA allocations, SPG's management was well versed in driving costs out. For instance, between 1998 and 2004, management improved average gross margins in its core ECBU division by 20% and EBIT margins by 40% (Exhibit 11.10). Bill added: "In addition, to our top down benchmarking and bottom up build, we solicited quotes from outsourcing vendors such as IBM and Wipro for IT and back office to better understand the real cost of corporate overhead."

Other Transaction Considerations

Carving out SPG from Agilent and setting it up as an independent company was central to KKR and SLP's investment thesis. The proposed carve-out of IT, Real Estate, HR and Legal functions had a number of considerations and risks that needed to be closely managed and mitigated. Detailed Transition Service Agreements (TSA) – where the buyer and/or seller of a business commits for a period of time (and for a fee) to provide certain services to the new buyer – were to be negotiated to be in place for the closing.

"We were under time pressure to become self-sufficient," said Bill. "Each module had a deadline between 3-12 months from closing, with severe penalties typically around $10-15 million for an overrun, plus an escalating service charge afterwards." Among the most challenging projects would be the implementation of a new ERP system as well as the first time set-up of a payroll and HR system, all in less than one year.

In addition to the TSA process, the multiple relationships between SPG and Agilent/HP needed to be managed carefully. One example of where SPG was dependent on ongoing goodwill from the seller was the complex IP patent portfolio. This had an equal chance of becoming an asset (through monetization of dormant patents) or a liability, if it turned out that critical pieces were still owned by the seller. In addition, although SPG would inherit an old and big IP portfolio from HP/Agilent, it contained quite a few change-of-control clauses which needed to be carefully assessed and, if necessary, renegotiated (sometimes with external parties with the help of Agilent).

As Ken explained: "As a notoriously litigious industry, IP in semiconductors is needed on two levels: defensive so that nobody can get between the company and its customers, and offensive to enhance product lines, especially with a view to keeping margins up against low cost competitors." One example was the Storage BU where the extensive IP portfolio created a "virtual" lock on the segment.

Another area to watch out for was the effect of the transition on management and staff. Changes in culture and legacy incentive structure following the buyout might lead to a loss of key managerial, technical/engineering and sales talent. "As part of Agilent, SPG's North American employees were enrolled in defined benefit plans and had several additional corporate benefits. Bonuses for management and key staff were relatively modest and mostly tied to the overall performance of Agilent." Bill outlined the proposed changes: "We planned to switch the company to a defined contribution plan, consistent with industry practice, while eliminating other smaller benefits that were not part of the industry's typical benefits package. While we were also planning to increase bonus targets meaningfully, these would naturally be linked to the performance of SPG which was a more risky proposition given we were creating a new and much smaller entity".

In addition to those changes, SPG's low-cost manufacturing strategy with key operations in Asia prompted the deal team to consider moving headquarters, along with most of the IP, to Singapore. This would enable the new independent company to enjoy low effective tax rates, yet it could also create additional anxiety among employees about the future direction of the company.

Moreover, in the past Agilent had been approached numerous times for the sale of strategic assets in SPG's Tactical Portfolio. This boosted the deal team's confidence in finding a buyer for certain non-core assets. The challenge was in assessing the strategic fit of these assets with SPG and the universe of potential buyers.

Ken described the process the team went through: "Adding the inbound calls to our knowledge of the sector gave us a pretty good picture of who the most promising buyers would be. In addition, we talked to all the BU managers throughout the process about how they fit in SPG. At the end of the day all managers want to 'win', so the question is what do you need to win? And whether SPG can provide the key ingredients or whether there are better platforms out there." One example was the printer business (a major part of the Imaging BU), for which SPG did not have the extensive design libraries required nor access to the latest core technology.

To preserve option value for divesting non-core assets, they needed to make sure that all IP could transfer to a potential buyer and that the business could be pulled off the services platform offered by Agilent and guided by the TSAs without a penalty in the event of sale.

As for an exit from the main business, KKR and SLP evaluated two strategies, namely a strategic sale or an IPO. The team was particularly concerned about exit value considerations. Comparable companies typically traded in a wide range of 15x–32x earnings. In the event of an IPO during a cycle upturn, bankers on the transaction indicated an opportunity for multiples arbitrage. Prior private equity transactions in the sector had benefited from a median EBITDA multiple expansion of almost 150% (Exhibit 11.13). However, the potential to exploit a cyclical upswing and de-lever through an IPO would require a strong growth story with a minimum of mid to high single-digit revenue growth.

The team also had to assess the feasibility of the planned capital structure within the constraints of the proposed covenants, and decide whether the expected returns were adequate for the perceived risk. Before they, however, could address these financial questions they had to be comfortable with the operational base case and its value drivers and risks.

Appendix 1

Background on KKR and Silver Lake Partners

KKR is a leading global alternative assets management firm, which was established in 1976 by founders Henry Kravis and George Roberts, pioneers of the leveraged buyout industry. Some of the firm's pioneering achievements include the first leveraged buyout in excess of US$1 billion (Wometco Enterprises) and the first buyout of a public company by tender offer (Malone & Hyde), both transactions in 1984. As of 2005, the firm had US$19.7 in private equity assets under management (AUM) (Exhibit 11.1). KKR specializes in large, complex buyouts, striving to acquire industry leading companies and working with management to take these businesses to the next level of development. KKR Capstone was created in 2000 and has become a key global resource for strengthening operations in KKR's portfolio companies. The KKR Capstone team works exclusively with the firm's investment professionals and portfolio company management teams, delivering management expertise in areas such as pricing, organizational design, sales force effectiveness and operational efficiency.

Silver Lake Partners was founded in 1999 to focus on large-scale investments in technology and related growth companies. On the back of the strong performance of their maiden fund, the firm had just (in 2004) raised their new $3.6 billion fund, bringing total AUM to $5.9 billion. The firm seeks to invest in market-leading large cap companies that have a distinct competitive advantage with an opportunity to grow revenue and profits, have a strong management team and proprietary technology and business processes. Silver Lake works with management teams to enhance value in its portfolio companies. It established a dedicated Value Creation Team of professionals with extensive operating experience that focuses on business improvement opportunities encompassing both strategic and operational initiatives, enhanced by Silver Lake's sector expertise.

Appendix 2

Short Bios of Key People in the Case
(Companies' websites as of August 2011)

Adam H. Clammer joined KKR in 1995 and currently heads the Technology Group. He has been actively involved with several companies, including Aricent (fka Flextronics Software), Avago Technologies (fka Agilent Semiconductor), Borden, Intermedia Communications, Jazz Pharmaceuticals, MedCath, NuVox, NXP (fka Philips Semiconductor), RELTEC, SunGard Data Systems and TASC. He is currently on the board of directors of Aricent, Avago, Kodak, NXP and TASC and is a member of the Operating Committee of SunGard. Prior to joining KKR, Mr. Clammer was with Morgan Stanley & Co. in Hong Kong and New York in the Mergers and Acquisitions department. He received a B.S. from the University of California and an M.B.A., with High Distinction, Baker Scholar, from Harvard Business School.

William L. Cornog joined KKR Capstone in 2002 and currently serves as Head of KKR Capstone Europe and is a member of KKR's Portfolio Management Committee. He was previously with Williams Communications Group as the Senior Vice President & General Manager of Network Services with P&L responsibility for Wiltel's $1.2 billion network business. Prior to Williams, he was a partner at The Boston Consulting Group. Mr. Cornog has also worked in direct marketing with Age Wave Communications and in marketing and sales positions with SmithKline Beckman. At KKR Capstone, Mr Cornog has been involved with companies across KKR's North American, Asian and European portfolios. He holds a B.A. from Stanford University and an M.B.A. from Harvard Business School.

Ken Hao joined Silver Lake in 2000 and is a Managing Director, Head of Asia, and a member of the Investment and Operating Committees of Silver Lake Partners. He has spent his career as an advisor to and investor in technology companies. Prior to joining Silver Lake, Mr. Hao was a managing director at H&Q. During his ten years at H&Q, he provided strategic advice and venture capital to companies in the semiconductor, computer systems, and software sectors. From 1997 to 1999, Mr. Hao led H&Q's Systems and Semiconductor Investment Banking business. He also led a number of H&Q's investment banking projects in the Asia Pacific region. Mr. Hao currently serves as a director on the boards of Allyes Online Media Holding; Avago Technologies Limited, the successor company to the Semiconductor Products Group of Agilent Technologies; and SMART Modular Technologies (WWH), Inc. He graduated from Harvard University with an A.B. in Economics.

Tony Ling joined Silver Lake in 2005 and is a Director. Prior to joining Silver Lake, Mr Ling worked at Bain Capital where he focused on large-scale leveraged buyouts across a variety of industries, including specifically the technology and industrial sectors. Previously, Mr Ling was a management consultant at Bain & Company where he performed strategic diligence on transactions for private equity clients and strategic development for numerous corporate clients. He currently serves on the board of IPC Systems, Inc. He holds an M.B.A from the Harvard Business School and an A.B. in Economics from Harvard College.

Exhibit 11.1

KKR Assets under Management 1993–2006 (US$ Billions)

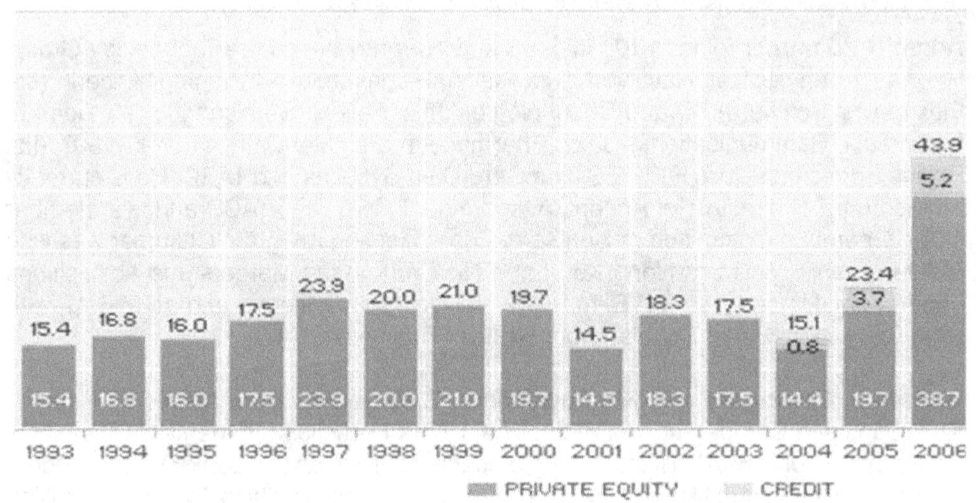

Exhibit 11.2

Silver Lake Partners Invested Capital and Major Transactions 1999–2005

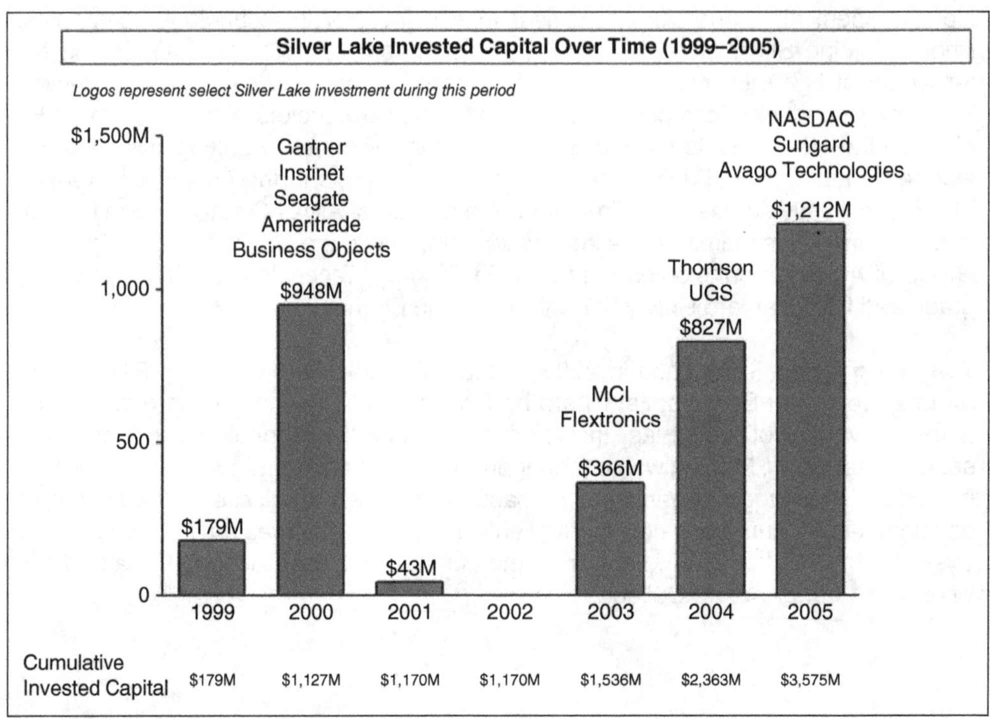

Exhibit 11.3

Agilent Technologies – Business Units

(Agilent Technologies 2004 Corporate Report, emphasis of case author)

BUSINESS UNIT	TEST AND MEASUREMENT	SEMICONDUCTOR PRODUCTS	LIFE SCIENCES AND CHEMICAL ANALYSIS	AUTOMATED TEST
REVENUE 2004	$2.9 billion	$2.0 billion	$1.3 billion	$0.9 billion
EMPLOYEES	11,200	6,800	3,900	2,200
DESCRIPTION	[…] provides standard and customized solutions that are used in the design, development, manufacture, installation, deployment and operation of electronics equipment and communications networks and services.	[…] is a leading supplier of semiconductor components, modules and subsystems for consumer and commercial electronics applications.	[…] provides application-focused solutions that include instruments, software, consumables and services that enable customers to identify, quantify and analyze the physical and biological properties of substances and products.	[…] provides test solutions that are used in the manufacture of semiconductor devices, electronics (primarily printed circuit-board assemblies) and flat panel displays.
MARKETS	[…] markets include the communications test and general purpose test markets.	[…] serves the personal systems and networking markets.	Life science markets (40% of BU) include the pharmaceutical analysis, gene expression and proteomics markets. Chemical analysis markets (60% of BU) include the homeland security and forensics, petrochemical, environmental, and bio-agriculture and food safety markets.	[…] sells to the semiconductor and electronics manufacturing, and flat-panel-display markets.

(Continued)

Exhibit 11.3 (Continued)

PRODUCT AREAS	Communications test products include testing solutions for fibre optic networks; transport networks; broadband and data networks; wireless communications; microwave networks; installation and maintenance solutions; and operations support systems, including monitoring and network management systems. General purpose test solutions include general purpose instruments; modular instruments and test software; digital design products; and high-frequency electronic design tools.	Personal systems products (for use in mobile phones, printers, PC peripherals and consumer electronics) include radio frequency and microwave communications devices, infrared emitters, detectors and transceiver module products; printing application-specific integrated circuits (ASICs); optical image sensors and processors, and optical position sensors; and light emitting diodes (LEDs) and optocoupler products. […] Our networking products include Fibre Channel controller products, fibre optic products and high-speed digital integrated circuit products.	Our seven key product categories include microarrays; microfluidics; gas chromatography; liquid chromatography; mass spectrometry; software and informatics products; and related consumables, reagents and services.	Our automated test business designs, develops and manufactures semiconductor test equipment, electronics manufacturing test equipment (including automated optical inspection products, automated x-ray inspection products, automated incircuit testing products and manufacturing test systems software) and thin-film transistor array test equipment for flat panel displays.

Exhibit 11.4

Agilent Technologies – Business Units
(Agilent Technologies 2004 10K)[4]

	in millions $	Years Ended October 31, 2004	2003	2002	04 over 03 Change	03 over 02 Change
T&M	**Orders**	$2,856	$2,413	$2,549	18%	(5%)
	Product revenue	$2,498	$2,135	$2,219	17%	(4)%
	Services revenue	$405	$394	$393	3%	—
	Total revenue	$2,903	$2,529	$2,612	15%	(3)%
	Income (loss) from operations	$219	$(315)	$(710)	170%	56%
	Operating margin	*8%*	*(12)%*	*(27)%*	*20 ppts*	*15 ppts*
	Return on invested capital ("ROIC")	*8%*	*(9)%*	*(17)%*	*17 ppts*	*8 ppts*
SPG	**Orders**	$1,978	$1,652	$1,568	20%	5%
	Total revenue	$2,021	$1,586	$1,559	27%	0.02
	Income (loss) from operations	$166	$(59)	$(115)	381%	49%
	Operating margin	*8%*	*(4)%*	*(7)%*	*12 ppts*	*3 ppts*
	Return on invested capital ("ROIC")	*17%*	*(2)%*	*(3)%*	*19 ppts*	*1 ppts*
LSCA	**Orders**	$1,332	$1,174	$1,151	13%	2%
	Product revenue	$1,034	$915	$884	13%	0.04
	Services revenue	$299	$271	$249	10%	0.09
	Total revenue	$1,333	$1,186	$1,133	12%	0.05
	Income (loss) from operations	$192	$148	$140	30%	6%
	Operating margin	*14%*	*0.12*	*0.12*	*2 ppts*	–
	Return on invested capital ("ROIC")	*22%*	*0.21*	*0.21*	*1 ppts*	–
ATG	**Orders**	$831	$845	$745	(2%)	13%
	Product revenue	$749	$604	$572	24%	0.06
	Services revenue	$175	$151	$134	16%	0.13
	Total revenue	$924	$755	$706	22%	0.07
	Income (loss) from operations	$66	$(34)	$(70)	294%	51%
	Operating margin	*7%*	*(5)%*	*(10)%*	*12 ppts*	*5 ppts*
	Return on invested capital ("ROIC")	*6%*	*(3)%*	*(6)%*	*9 ppts*	*3 ppts*

4. Reported income (loss) from operations on segment level does not include restructuring, impairment and other costs.

Exhibit 11.5

Agilent Technologies – Consolidated Statement of Operations, Oct 31st 2004[5]

CONSOLIDATED STATEMENT OF OPERATIONS

	Years Ended October 31,	
	2004	**2003**
	(in millions)	
Net Revenue:		
Products	$6,302	$5,240
Services and other	879	816
Total Net Revenue	**7,181**	**6,056**
Cost and expenses (excl. GAAP adjustment):		
Cost of products and services	3,955	3,587
Research and development	914	984
Selling, general and administrative	1,670	1,774
Total costs and expenses	**6,539**	**6,345**
Income (loss) from operations (non GAAP)	**642**	**(289)**
GAAP adjustments (restructuring, impairment, other)	(256)	(436)
Income (loss) from operations (GAAP)	**386**	**(725)**
Other income (expense), net	54	35
Income (loss) from continuing operations before taxes	440	(690)
Provision (benefit) for taxes	91	1,100
Income (loss) from continuing operations	349	(1,790)
(Loss) from sale of discontinued operations	–	–
Income (loss) before cumulative effect of accounting changes	349	(1,790)
Cumulative effect of adopting SFAS No. 142	–	(268)
Net income (loss)	**349**	**(2,058)**

5. Consolidated statement of operations has been adjusted by authors to show income (loss) from operations before GAAP adjustment calculation (from Agilent AR 2004) to provide a bridge to Exhibit 11.4.

Exhibit 11.6

Agilent Technologies – Segment Assets, Capex and Investments, Oct 31st 2004

	Test and Measurement	Automated Test	Scemiconductor Products	Life Sciences and Chemical Analysis	Total Segments
			(in millions)		
As of October 31, 2004:					
Assets	$2,148	$718	$1,434	$725	$5,025
Capital expenditures	$ 43	$ 14	$ 47	$ 14	$ 118
Investments in and advances to equity-method investees	$ 23	$ –	$ 103	$ –	$ 126
As of October 31, 2003:					
Assets	$2,268	$804	$1,420	$680	$5,172
Capital expenditures	$ 85	$ 23	$ 70	$ 27	$ 205
Investments in and advances to equity-method investees	$ 25	$ –	$ 75	$ –	$ 100

Exhibit 11.7

Semiconductor Industry Cycle – Historical Perspective

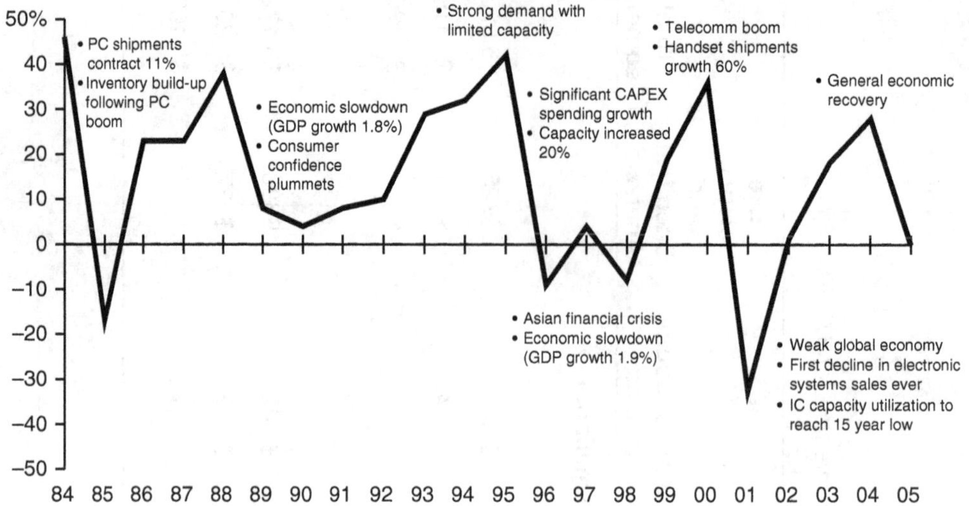

Exhibit 11.8

Semiconductor Industry Cycle – Current Position in 2005

Semiconductor Industry Capacity Utilization[1]

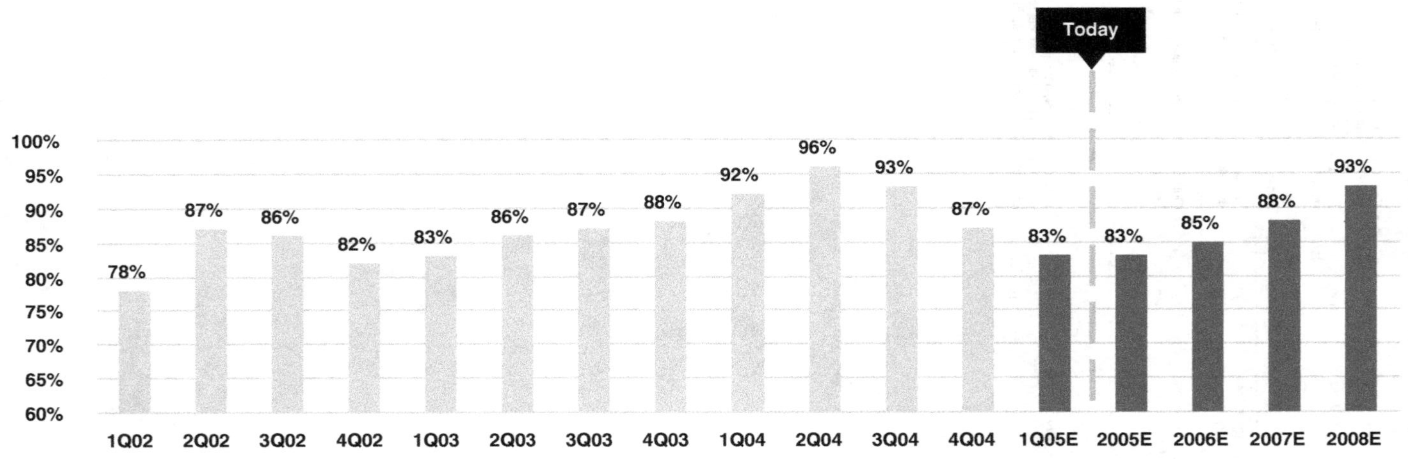
Today
100%
95%
90%
85%
80%
75%
70%
65%
60%
78%
87%
86%
82%
83%
86%
87%
88%
92%
96%
93%
87%
83%
83%
85%
88%
93%
1Q02
2Q02
3Q02
4Q02
1Q03
2Q03
3Q03
4Q03
1Q04
2Q04
3Q04
4Q04
1Q05E
2005E
2006E
2007E
2008E

Inventory Levels at Major OEMs[2]

80
70
60
50
40
30
20
10
0
Dec-99
Mar-00
Jun-00
Sep-00
Dec-00
Mar-01
Jun-01
Sep-01
Dec-01
Mar-02
Jun-02
Sep-02
Dec-02
Mar-03
Jun-03
Sep-03
Dec-03
Mar-04
Jun-04
Sep-04
Dec-04
Average EMS Inventory Days

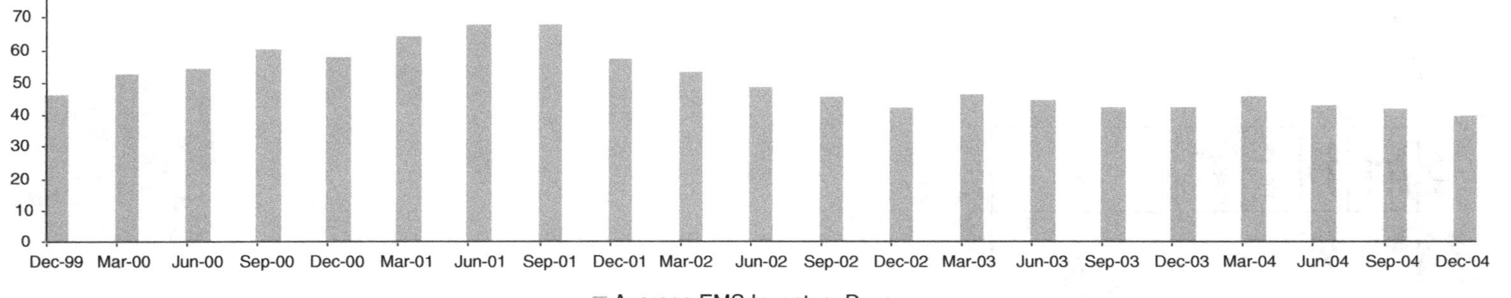

(1) Source: Semiconductor Industry Association, Wall Street Research
(2) Source: Company reports and Lehman Brothers estimates

Exhibit 11.9
SPG Business Units

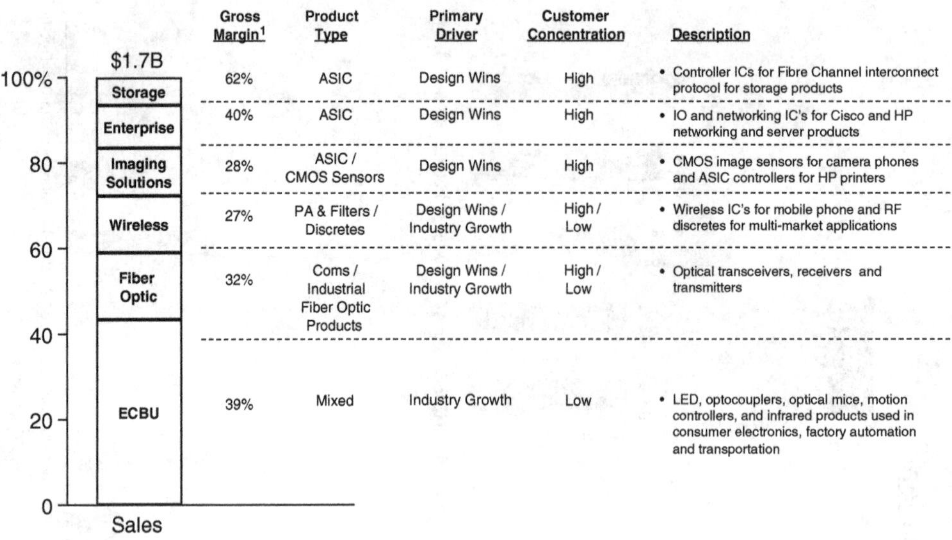

Sales ($1.7B)	Gross Margin[1]	Product Type	Primary Driver	Customer Concentration	Description
Storage	62%	ASIC	Design Wins	High	• Controller ICs for Fibre Channel interconnect protocol for storage products
Enterprise	40%	ASIC	Design Wins	High	• IO and networking IC's for Cisco and HP networking and server products
Imaging Solutions	28%	ASIC / CMOS Sensors	Design Wins	High	• CMOS image sensors for camera phones and ASIC controllers for HP printers
Wireless	27%	PA & Filters / Discretes	Design Wins / Industry Growth	High / Low	• Wireless IC's for mobile phone and RF discretes for multi-market applications
Fiber Optic	32%	Coms / Industrial Fiber Optic Products	Design Wins / Industry Growth	High / Low	• Optical transceivers, receivers and transmitters
ECBU	39%	Mixed	Industry Growth	Low	• LED, optocouplers, optical mice, motion controllers, and infrared products used in consumer electronics, factory automation and transportation

(1) Gross margins with fully allocated corporate allocations (most closely tie to true GM)

Exhibit 11.10

Operational Improvement ECBU Division 1998–2004

	LED			Isolation			Infrared			Motion Control			Average
	1998	2004	Delta	1998	2004	Delta	1998	2004	Delta	1998	2004	Delta	Delta
Revenue	$149.0	$256.1	$107.1	$92.0	$197.1	$105.1	$29.0	$75.4	$46.4	$96.0	$106.4	$10.4	
Direct Gross Profit	(1.0)	79.2	80.2	44.0	124.2	80.2	(2.0)	23.0	25.0	51.0	51.2	0.2	
Direct Gross Margin %	(0.7%)	30.9%	31.6%	47.8%	63.0%	15.2%	(6.9%)	30.5%	37.4%	53.1%	48.1%	(5.0%)	19.8%
Direct EBIT	($38.0)	$71.3	109.3	$30.0	$118.2	88.2	($14.0)	$19.5	33.5	$35.0	$42.6	7.6	
Direct EBIT Margin %	(25.5%)	27.8%	53.3%	32.6%	60.0%	27.4%	(48.3%)	25.9%	74.1%	36.5%	40.0%	3.6%	39.6%

Exhibit 11.11

SPG Business Units – Microeconomics – Last 12 Months (LTM)

	ECBU	Fiber Optics	Wireless	Storage	Enterprise ASICs	Imaging
Total Revenue	**$757.0**	**$247.2**	**$203.9**	**$108.9**	**$169.0**	**$148.1**
COGS Drivers (1)						
Materials & Variances	47.6%	42.5%	29.1%	22.6%	46.5%	64.9%
Mfg Ovarhead (excl. people)	4.9%	10.3%	15.9%	4.9%	3.4%	4.5%
People Cost	2.6%	7.7%	22.8%	1.9%	2.1%	1.7%
SPG Allocations	1.8%	2.3%	2.1%	2.1%	2.0%	1.6%
Corporate Allocations	3.2%	7.0%	8.4%	5.1%	4.1%	4.7%
Total COGS	60.1%	69.8%	78.4%	36.5%	58.1%	77.5%
% COGS Fixed (2)	*19.0%*	*34.0%*	*65.0%*	*30.0%*	*13.0%*	*21.0%*
Gross Margin (1)	**39.9%**	**30.2%**	**21.6%**	**63.5%**	**41.9%**	**22.5%**
R&D (1)						
Total Direct & SPG	4.1%	13.6%	15.7%	29.0%	14.9%	14.2%
Corporate	2.7%	6.1%	5.7%	6.2%	4.9%	4.8%
Total	6.8%	19.8%	21.4%	35.2%	19.8%	19.0%
% R&D Fixed (2)	*75.0%*	*85.0%*	*80.0%*	*88.0%*	*65.0%*	*75.0%*
Sales & Marketing (1)						
Total Direct & SPG	4.2%	8.2%	4.8%	7.3%	2.3%	3.1%
Corporate	1.2%	2.2%	2.4%	1.5%	1.5%	1.5%
Total Sales & Marketing (1)	5.3%	10.5%	7.1%	8.8%	3.8%	4.5%
G&A (1)						
Total Direct & SPG	1.2%	2.7%	2.8%	3.4%	1.9%	1.5%
Corporate	5.0%	7.1%	6.9%	7.4%	6.8%	6.1%
Total G&A (1)	6.2%	9.8%	9.7%	10.9%	8.7%	7.7%
% SG&A Fixed (2)	*80.0%*	*80.0%*	*80.0%*	*80.0%*	*80.0%*	*80.0%*
EBIT (1)	21.6%	(9.9%)	(16.6%)	8.6%	9.6%	(8.7%)
EBIT W/corporate savings (1,3)	27.0%	0.2%	(6.1%)	17.7%	17.4%	(1.0%)
Capex (4,5)	**0.7%**	**1.9%**	**8.3%**	**11.1%**		**4.3%**

Exhibit 11.12

SPG – Operational Statistics vs. Comparables

FY 2004 Operating metrics (%)									
	SPG	Comps						Comp	
	ECBU Unit	AMI	Cypress	Fairchild	IRF	Microsemi	On Semi	Average	Agilent
COGS	57%	53%	52%	72%	59%	65%	68%	61%	57%
R&D	6%	15%	27%	5%	9%	8%	8%	12%	13%
SG&A	10%	14%	16%	11%	15%	15%	12%	14%	25%
Total Cost	72%	81%	94%	88%	82%	88%	87%	87%	95%
EBIT	28%	19%	6%	12%	18%	12%	13%	13%	5%

Exhibit 11.13

SPG Comparable Companies Valuation (at time of transaction)

			Entry Multiples		Exit Multiples					
Target	**Entry Date**	**IPO Date**	**LTM Rev**	**LTM EBITDA**	**LTM Rev**	**LTM EBITDA**	**FTM Rev**	**FTM EBITDA**	**FTM P/E**	**LTM EBITDA Mult. Expansion**
On Semiconductor	5/11/1999	4/27/2000	1.01x	6.1x	2.03x	9.8x	1.76x	7.9x	28.9x	60.1%
Fairchild	1/27/1997	8/3/1999	0.80x	NA	2.05x	9.8x	1.69x	8.5x	20.7x	NA
Integrated Circuit Systems	1/20/1999	5/22/2000	1.44x	6.4x	5.90x	20.6x	4.79x	13.4x	19.1x	221.8%
Intersil	6/3/1999	2/24/2003	1.47x	9.0x	3.93x	20.3x	3.38x	14.0x	58.8x	126.8%
AMI Semiconductor	12/5/2000	9/23/2003	1.37x	4.4x	3.80x	17.4x	3.27x	11.4x	32.7x	292.9%
Ultra Clean Holdings	11/15/2002	3/24/2004	0.34x	NM	1.34x	20.0x	0.53x	4.9x	9.9x	NA
NPTest Communications	6/24/2003	12/10/2003	0.95x	12.5x	1.75x	33.2x	1.62x	29.9x	NM	165.5%
MEMC	11/14/2001	5/15/2003	NA	NA	2.81x [2]	15.2x [2]	2.53x [2]	11.5x [2]	18.1x [2]	NA
ChipPac	8/15/1999	8/8/2000	1.64x	6.4x	2.90x	13.4x	1.93x	6.8x	24.5x	111.0%
Legerity	5/22/2000	NA	2.02x	NA	NA	NA	NA	NA	NA	NA
Zilog [3]	8/21/1997	NA	1.86x	6.5x	NA	NA	NA	NA	NA	NA
		Mean	**1.29x**	**7.3x**	**2.95x**	**17.7x**	**2.39x**	**12.0x**	**26.6x**	**163.0%**
		Median	**1.41x**	**6.4x**	**2.81x**	**17.4x**	**1.93x**	**11.4x**	**22.6x**	**146.1%**

CASE

12 CHIPS ON THE SIDE (B)
THE BUYOUT OF AVAGO TECHNOLOGIES

SYNOPSIS

During the summer of 2005, a consortium of private equity firms (KKR and Silver Lake Partners) is in the process of acquiring the semiconductor division of Agilent. To prepare for the signing of the acquisition agreement and the subsequent transfer of ownership, the deal team is revisiting their investment thesis with respect to upsides and risks. Case 11 focuses on the operational side of the transaction, while Case 12 deals with the implementation of an appropriate financing and capital structure.

PEDAGOGICAL OBJECTIVE OF THE CASE

The case helps to develop a high-level understanding of the workings of leveraged buyouts (LBOs) by discussing the risk–return relationship in private equity and the interplay of financial and operational risks in the deal-structuring process. It follows the decision-making process of an investment committee as it tries to balance and understand the trade-offs of different debt instruments and financing structures within the context of a carve-out, which comes with ample operational risk.

Case B builds on AVAGO (A) and intends to show the interplay between operational and financial considerations in buyout transactions.

Case B can effectively be split into two parts: a discussion of returns versus risk and a debt structuring exercise.

SUGGESTED ASSIGNMENT QUESTIONS

1. In your opinion, does the potential return from the transaction (calculated using the base case) adequately compensate for the operational and financial risks?
2. What are the main drivers for a potential return that is substantially higher than the base case?
3. Given your perspective on the risk–reward of this deal, how would you finance this transaction? Explain why.

ADDITIONAL RESOURCES

To make the most of this case study, we suggest the following additional sources to provide context and background information:

- In particular, we recommend the following chapters from *Mastering Private Equity—Transformation via Venture Capital, Minority Investments & Buyouts*
  - Chapter 1 Private Equity Essentials
  - Chapter 4 Buyouts
  - Chapter 8 Deal Pricing Dynamics
  - Chapter 9 Deal Structuring
  - Chapter 11 Corporate Governance
  - Chapter 12 Securing Management Teams
- Case website for faculty and lecturers: http://cases.insead.edu/chips-on-the-side/
- You may also refer to the book website for further material: www.masteringprivateequity.com
- Werner Ballhaus, Dr Alessandro Pagella and Constantin Vogel (2009), "A Change of Pace for the Semiconductor Industry?" Retrieved from: http://www.pwc.com/en_GX/gx/technology/pdf/change-of-pace-in-the-semiconductor-industry.pdf
- Mimi James and Zane Williams (2012), "Not Enough Comps for Valuation? Try Statistical Modelling." Retrieved from: http://www.mckinsey.com/insights/corporate_finance/not_enough_comps_for_valuation_try_statistical_modeling
- J. Eric Wise (2006), "A Beginner's Guide to Thinking about Covenants." Retrieved from: http://www.kramerlevin.com/media/PublicationDetail.aspx?publication=730

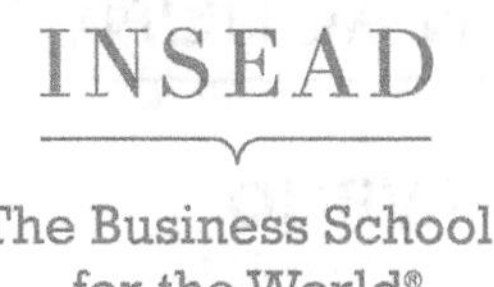

Chips on the Side (B)

The Buyout of Avago Technologies

03/2015-5832

This case was written by Michael Prahl, Senior Research Associate, INSEAD Global Private Equity Initiative (GPEI), under the supervision of Claudia Zeisberger, Senior Affiliate Professor of Decision Sciences and Entrepreneurship and Family Enterprise, and Vikas A. Aggarwal, Assistant Professor of Entrepreneurship and Family Enterprise, both at INSEAD. It is intended to be used as a basis for class discussion rather than to illustrate either effective or ineffective handling of a particular situation, or for any other purpose.

The case is dedicated to Dick Chang, CEO of Avago at the time of the spin-off, in memoriam.

Additional material about INSEAD case studies (e.g., videos, spreadsheets, links) can be accessed at cases.insead.edu.

Chips on the Side (B): The Buyout of Avago Technologies[1]

In parallel to refining the operational case for the business (see Case A), the consortium spent a large amount of time discussing and securing the appropriate financial structure for the new company. While the financing had to be robust enough to absorb the operational risk, it also had to be sizeable enough to maximize equity returns. As Adam Clammer (partner at KKR) recalled: "This was the largest private equity transaction in the semiconductor industry up to this time. To make returns work, we had to push the leverage for the deal. The debt package north of five times EBITDA was ground-breaking for this type of transaction."

The Broad Set-Up

The competitive dynamics of the auction process had led the consortium to offer US$2.759 billion for the equity during the last round of bidding, on the basis of which it was awarded exclusivity, with a roadmap to closing before the end of the summer. The purchase price translated into a roughly 9.6 times EBITDA multiple for the last twelve months (LTM) up to the end of July 2005 (Exhibit 12.1). Based on its analysis, the team was confident that the financial year (ending October) would show a strong finish, bringing full year 2005 EBITDA to US$306.9 million.

The purchase price was calculated on a "cash free/debt free" basis, meaning the consortium had to actually provide some funding for the ongoing business operations (including the transition costs). This new cash in the company was set at US$81.2 million. In addition, a transaction cost of US$130 million for financing and deal fees had to be factored in. The banks had provided a strong indication for a debt package of US$1,725.0 million.

The team came up with a preliminary conservative base case (Exhibit 12.2) as a starting point for discussions with the banks. Thinking around optimizing the portfolio, the consortium had lined up early disposals of two business units (Storage and a large part of Imaging), which would provide US$450 million in cash (after tax) to the balance sheet. These businesses were expected to contribute US$308.4 million in revenue and US$32.1 million in EBITDA to the expected year-end result. In the model, this led to an instant reduction in debt of US$415 million (the remainder being used for other corporate activities and factored into the operational model).

In the low-growth conservative base case, the impact of multiples selection on valuation was enormous. Listed companies (many of them more pure-plays than Avago) traded in a wide range of multiples (Exhibit 12.3). Prior private equity transactions in the

---

1. The contents may not be regarded in any manner as legal, tax, investment, accounting or other advice or as an offer to sell or a solicitation of an offer to buy an interest in Avago or any other Silver Lake portfolio company or Silver Lake fund (collectively, "Silver Lake") or any other KKR portfolio company or KKR fund (collectively, "KKR"). Neither Silver Lake, KKR, Avago or their affiliates make any representation or warranty, express or implied, as to the accuracy or completeness of the information contained herein.

The case is set at the time when the business was known as the Semiconductor Products Group (SPG) of Agilent. Post buyout it was renamed Avago Technologies. The contents have not been updated to reflect any developments or changes since the transaction.

sector had benefited from a median EBITDA multiples expansion of almost 150% (Exhibit 12.4). The consortium planned to highlight the following attributes of the core Optoelectronics/analogue business at the time of its exit (most likely via public markets): moderate growth yet low volatility and high-margin analogue semiconductor business with an Asia-based low-cost, fully fabless[2] operating model.

The Financing Structure

Returning a large portion of the acquisition debt shortly after closing the transaction would obviously reduce the financial risk in the business substantially. Yet neither the exact timing and amount, nor potential subsequent divestures, were known. The deal team had to consider what kinds of instruments were most appropriate to provide the required bridge financing.

The banks were worried that the company would end up with a too aggressively leveraged balance sheet if either the forecasted divestures or the financial results failed to materialise.

Adam Clammer noted:

> *"We were putting the structure together on the back of pro-forma numbers. That meant for us to undertake a lot of analysis to arrive at robust figures. We involved the banks early on for them to get comfortable with the add-backs and saleability of assets."*

In addition, the financing team had to accommodate the operational volatility of the underlying business. Loans typically come with conditions (debt covenants) that oblige the borrower to adhere to certain restrictions (Exhibit 12.5). Debt covenants can severely restrict a company's activities – even forcing it to sell assets or requiring the private equity owners to inject additional equity (with a negative effect on returns) in order to reduce leverage to stay within a debt covenant on gearing. "We were looking for a package that was light on covenants and provided us with sufficient headroom [before breaching covenants]," explained Clammer, "and we put in some extra cushion and set out to control the risks tightly."

On the upside, substantially stronger-than-forecasted results or additional divestures were possible. Financing packages typically severely restrict the ability to pay dividends (resulting, for instance, from the sale of a business unit) to the equity holders until a significantly lower level of leverage has been achieved. And while the company might want to reduce debt and interest payments, debt investors like to receive these payments and impose restrictions or penalties on pre-payment for many debt instruments.

All these considerations had to go into structuring the financing package. There was an abundance of debt instruments to choose from (see Exhibit 12.6 for an overview), each with different costs, structures and terms. Debt instruments were

2. Global Semiconductor Alliance: "Fabless refers to the business methodology of outsourcing the manufacturing of silicon wafers, which has become the preferred business model in the semiconductor industry. Fabless companies focus on the design, development and marketing of their products and form alliances with silicon wafer manufacturers, or foundries."

typically arranged in order of riskiness, expressed through their position in the ranking (seniority) and whether or not they were secured with underlying assets (collateral). In the event of bankruptcy, seniority determines who has first right to the assets. However secured lenders get to claim their collateral first. Seniority also as a rule regulates who gets pre-paid first if the company wants to retire some debt. In accordance with their riskiness, the debt tranches carry different interest rates, the least risky tranches (such as revolving credits and bank term loans) having the lowest rates.

The planned transaction would require a substantial debt package incorporating several different types of debt. While in general everything in the debt markets is freely negotiable, capacity considerations and "market standards" had to be taken into account to provide for a successful placement of the instruments. Specifically, bank loans tend to come with more rigid structures as banks typically guarantee (commit) the debt and worry about being able to distribute it to a wider group of investors. High-yield instruments are more flexible yet significantly more expensive.

The team, working with the banks, had come up with two structures as a starting point for further refinement: Structure 1 emphasized secured, senior and subordinated high-yield notes complemented by a smaller term (bank) loan B. Structure 2 relied on a larger bank loan package with tranches A and B, as well as a big piece of subordinated high-yield notes. Both structures provided the same debt volume (therefore requiring the same amount of equity) yet made different trade-offs between cost and flexibility.

Exhibit 12.1
Purchase Price Summary

Purchase Price Summary	
Enterprise Value	$2,578.8
LTM EBITDA (7/31/05)	$267.7
Purchase Multiple	9.6*x*

Exhibit 12.2
Summary Base Case

			Fiscal Year Ending October 31,					
	2005E	2005PF	2006E	2007E	2008E	2009E	2010E	2011E
Revenue	1,743.4	1,435.0	1,497.0	1,590.6	1,665.0	1,715.3	1,782.3	1,843.6
EBITDA	306.9	274.7	238.0	246.1	259.2	266.9	275.7	282.8
Case	81.2	81.2	81.2	81.2	81.2	81.2	81.2	81.2
Total Debt	1,725.0	1,310.0	1,301.0	1,200.4	1,103.9	975.8	838.1	677.7

Exhibit 12.3
ECBU Comparable Companies Valuations

($ in millions)	Firm Value	Firm Value / Revenue 2005E	Firm Value / Revenue 2006E	Firm Value / EPS 2005E	Firm Value / EPS 2006E	Firm Value / LTM EBITDA	Firm Value / LTM EBITDA-CapEx
Standard Analog							
Epcos (EPC)	1,151	0.8x	0.7x	NM	23.0x	5.6x	66.5x
Fairchild Semi (FCS)	2,079	1.4x	1.3x	45.0x	22.5x	6.1x	12.8x
International Rectifier (INR)	3,029	2.6x	2.3x	20.9x	17.3x	10.0x	17.8x
On Semiconductor (ONNN)	2,361	1.9x	1.8x	21.4x	15.0x	8.8x	11.4x
IXYS (SYXI)	498	1.8x	1.6x	20.8x	16.8x	13.7x	16.4x
Vishay Intertechnology (VSH)	2,277	1.0x	0.9x	27.8x	16.4x	6.9x	14.6x
Median		**1.6x**	**1.5x**	**21.4x**	**17.1x**	**7.9x**	**15.5x**
Mean		**1.6x**	**1.4x**	**27.2x**	**18.5x**	**8.5x**	**23.3x**
High End Analog							
Intersil (ISIL)	2,280	4.1x	3.7x	32.6x	25.6x	19.2x	38.3x
Linear Technologies (LLTC)	10,176	9.4x	8.5x	26.2x	24.3x	16.1x	17.9x
Micrel (MCRL)	951	3.7x	3.2x	35.0x	26.3x	13.1x	23.2x
Maxim (MXIM)	12,336	7.5x	6.4x	25.3x	21.3x	14.4x	18.2x
Power Integrations (POWI)	550	3.8x	3.3x	33.8x	26.7x	17.5x	22.8x
Semtech (SMTC)	1,017	4.3x	3.8x	27.0x	21.7x	13.8x	18.0x
Supertex (SUPX)	153	2.6x	2.0x	34.7x	20.0x	14.0x	16.6x
Median		**4.1x**	**3.7x**	**32.6x**	**24.3x**	**14.4x**	**18.2x**
Mean		**5.1x**	**4.4x**	**30.7x**	**23.7x**	**15.4x**	**22.1x**
Low		**0.8x**	**0.7x**	**20.8x**	**15.0x**	**5.6x**	**11.4x**
Median		**2.6x**	**2.3x**	**27.4x**	**21.7x**	**13.7x**	**17.9x**
Mean		**3.5x**	**3.0x**	**29.2x**	**21.3x**	**12.2x**	**22.7x**
High		**9.4x**	**8.5x**	**45.0x**	**26.7x**	**19.2x**	**66.5x**

Exhibit 12.4

SPG Comparable Companies Valuation (at time of transaction)

			Entry Multiples		Exit Multiples					
Target	**Entry Date**	**IPO Date**	**LTM Rev**	**LTM EBITDA**	**LTM Rev**	**LTM EBITDA**	**FTM Rev**	**FTM EBITDA**	**FTM P/E**	LTM EBITDA **Mult. Expansion**
On Semiconductor	5/11/1999	4/27/2000	1.01x	6.1x	2.03x	9.8x	1.76x	7.9x	28.9x	60.1%
Fairchild	1/27/1997	8/3/1999	0.80x	NA	2.05x	9.8x	1.69x	8.5x	20.7x	NA
Integrated Circuit Systems	1/20/1999	5/22/2000	1.44x	6.4x	5.90x	20.6x	4.79x	13.4x	19.1x	221.8%
Intersil	6/3/1999	2/24/2003	1.47x	9.0x	3.93x	20.3x	3.38x	14.0x	58.8x	126.8%
AMI Semiconductor	12/5/2000	9/23/2003	1.37x	4.4x	3.80x	17.4x	3.27x	11.4x	32.7x	292.9%
Ultra Clean Holdings	11/15/2002	3/24/2004	0.34x	NM	1.34x	20.0x	0.53x	4.9x	9.9x	NA
NPTest Communications	6/24/2003	12/10/2003	0.95x	12.5x	1.75x	33.2x	1.62x	29.9x	NM	165.5%
MEMC	11/14/2001	5/15/2003	NA	NA	2.81x (2)	15.2x (2)	2.53x (2)	11.5x (2)	18.1x (2)	NA
ChipPac	8/15/1999	8/8/2000	1.64x	6.4x	2.90x	13.4x	1.93x	6.8x	24.5x	111.0%
Legerity	5/22/2000	NA	2.02x	NA	NA	NA	NA	NA	NA	NA
Zilog(3)	8/21/1997	NA	1.86x	6.5x	NA	NA	NA	NA	NA	NA
		Mean	**1.29x**	**7.3x**	**2.95x**	**17.7x**	**2.39x**	**12.0x**	**26.6x**	**163.0%**
		Median	**1.41x**	**6.4x**	**2.81x**	**17.4x**	**1.93x**	**11.4x**	**22.6x**	**146.1%**

Exhibit 12.5

An Overview of Financial Covenants

There are many types of covenants, each one seeking to reduce a different risk for the lender. Most relevant for a discussion on financial structuring are financial covenants.

Financial covenants can be broadly divided into two categories: maintenance covenants and incurrence covenants. Each covenant is typically formulated as a ratio of underlying cash flow/ EBITDA to debt or interest, and contains not only the ratio itself but specifies how exactly it should be calculated to minimise accounting leeway for the borrower. With maintenance covenants, the criteria set forth in the covenants must be met on a regular basis (e.g. quarterly). With incurrence covenants, the criteria must be met at the time of a pre-specified event, such as the firm incurring additional debt or paying a dividend to its equity holders.

Credit agreements in most buyouts will have some maintenance covenants, while high-yield instruments typically only contain incurrence covenants. While there are certain market standards (changing over time) regarding the application of covenants, individual covenant and default packages can and will be individually negotiated. A trend over the last decade has been the emergence of covenant-lite loans representing a convergence of the loan and bond markets. The main attractions for sponsors are the absence of maintenance covenants and the ability to incur additional debt (in the case of stronger performance).

Frequently used maintenance covenants are total leverage, interest cover and debt service cover. The leverage covenant imposes restrictions on how much debt the company can raise and typically involves calculating the ratio of net debt to EBITDA. The interest and debt service covers show how well the company is able to pay its interest or service its overall debt. It is usually the calculation of EBITDA divided by the cash cost of paying interest or cash interest plus mandatory debt repayments.

While a breach of a debt covenant would typically allow lenders to demand immediate repayment, the borrower is, at that point in time, often in no position to access funds for such a repayment. Instead, a borrower will try first to negotiate a covenant reset or amendment to create more breathing space (headroom), usually by paying lenders higher interest rates or a one-off fee. If the renegotiation of terms fails, then lenders can seize control of the company, resulting in a full or partial loss on the equity.

Exhibit 12.6
Overview of Debt in LBOs

Debt Type	Revolver	Term Loan A	Term Loan B	Senior Notes	Subordinated Notes	Mezzanine
Interest Rate:	Lowest	Low	Higher	Higher	Higher	Highest
Floating/Fixed?	Floating			Fixed		
Cash Pay?	Yes					Cash / PIK
Tenor:	3–5 years	4–6 years	4–8 years	7–10 years	8–10 years	8–12 years
Amortization:	None	Straight Line	Minimal	Bullet		
Prepayment?	Yes			No		
Investors:	Conservative Banks			HFs, Merchant Banks, Mezzanine Funds		
Seniority	Senior Secured			Senior Unsecured	Senior Subordinated	Equity
Secured?	Yes			Sometimes	No	
Call Protection?	No	Sometimes		Yes		
Covenants:	Maintenance			Incurrence		

Source: http://breakingintowallstreet.com

Exhibit 12.7

Proposed Debt Structures

Debt Structure Summary

Structure 1 – Hybrid Debt Structure

$mm	Rate	Close	Maturity	Key Covenants	Callable
New Revolver	L + 250	–	2011		yes
New Term Loan	L + 250	475.0	2012		yes
Delayed Draw Term Loan	L + 250	250.0	2012		yes
Total Bank Debt		**725.0**		Secured Debt/EBITDA of 4:1 (Maintenance)	
Sr Notes	10.125%	500.0	12/1/13		Callable after Dec 09 at 105
Sr Floaters	L + 550	250.0	6/1/13		Callable after Dec 08 at 101
Total Senior Debt		**1,475.0**			
Sr Sub Notes	11.875%	250.0	12/1/15		Callable after Dec 10 at 106
Total Debt		**1,725.0**		Total Debt/EBITDA of 4.75:1 (Incurrence)	
				Interest Coverage Ratio 2:1 (Incurrence)	

Structure 2 – Bank Loan Structure

$mm	Rate	Close	Maturity	Key Covenants	Callable
New Revolver	L + 250	–	2011		yes
New Term Loan A	L + 250	150.0	2011		Option to repay A or B with
New Term Loan B	L + 250	800.0	2012		proceeds from disposals
Delayed Draw Term Loan	L + 250	250.0	2012		yes
Total Bank Debt		**1,200.0**		Secured Debt/EBITDA of 4:1 (Maintenance)	
				Total Debt/EBITDA of 6:1 (Maintenance)	
				Interest Coverage Ratio 2:1 (Maintenance)	
Sr Sub Notes	10.50%	525.0	12/1/15		Callable after Dec 9 at 105
Total Debt		**1,725.0**		Total Debt/EBITDA of 4.75:1 (Incurrence)	
				Interest Coverage Ratio 2:1 (Incurrence)	

Exhibit 12.8

Summary Base Case with Two Capital Structures

	Base Case/Hybrid Debt Structure Fiscal Year Ending October 31,						Base Case/Bank Loan Structure Fiscal Year Ending October 31,					
	2006E	2007E	2008E	2009E	2010E	2011E	2006E	2007E	2008E	2009E	2010E	2011E
Revenue	1,497.0	1,590.6	1,665.0	1,715.3	1,782.3	1,843.6	1,497.0	1,590.6	1,665.0	1,715.3	1,782.3	1,843.6
growth in %	*4.3%*	*6.3%*	*4.7%*	*3.0%*	*3.9%*	*3.4%*	*4.3%*	*6.3%*	*4.7%*	*3.0%*	*3.9%*	*3.4%*
EBITDA	**238.0**	**246.1**	**259.2**	**266.9**	**275.7**	**282.8**	**238.0**	**246.1**	**259.2**	**266.9**	**275.7**	**282.8**
% of revenue	*15.9%*	*15.5%*	*15.6%*	*15.6%*	*15.5%*	*15.3%*	*15.9%*	*15.5%*	*15.6%*	*15.6%*	*15.5%*	*15.3%*
Interest Expense, Net	**(135.7)**	**(119.5)**	**(113.5)**	**(105.6)**	**(94.4)**	**(79.4)**	**(122.6)**	**(103.6)**	**(96.7)**	**(87.0)**	**(75.9)**	**(63.6)**
One time expenses	(100.0)	–	–	–	–	–	(100.0)	–	–	–	–	–
Proceeds from Asset Sales, after-tax	450.0	–	–	–	–	–	450.0	–	–	–	–	–
Other changes to CF*	(28.3)	(26.0)	(49.2)	(32.9)	(36.6)	(38.9)	(28.3)	(26.3)	(50.9)	(34.8)	(38.5)	(40.5)
CF before financing	**424.0**	**100.6**	**96.5**	**128.3**	**144.7**	**164.5**	**437.1**	**116.2**	**111.6**	**145.0**	**161.3**	**178.7**
Mandatory Debt Repayments	**(7.3)**	**(7.3)**	**(2.5)**	**(2.5)**	**(0.0)**	**–**	**(18.0)**	**(25.5)**	**(40.5)**	**(10.5)**	**(10.5)**	**(2.5)**
Beginning Cash Balance	81.2	81.2	81.2	81.2	81.2	81.2	81.2	81.2	81.2	81.2	81.2	81.2
Minimum Cash Balance	(81.2)	(81.2)	(81.2)	(81.2)	(81.2)	(81.2)	(81.2)	(81.2)	(81.2)	(81.2)	(81.2)	(81.2)
Cash for Optional Repayments	**416.7**	**93.4**	**94.0**	**125.8**	**144.7**	**164.5**	**419.1**	**90.7**	**71.1**	**134.5**	**150.8**	**176.2**
Revolver (Repayments)/ Drawdown	–	–	–	–	–	–	–	–	–	–	–	–
New Term Loan A Repayments							–	(90.7)	(6.8)	–	–	–
New Term Loan B Repayments	(416.7)	(48.8)	–	–	–	–	(419.1)	–	(64.3)	(134.5)	(142.1)	–
Delayed Draw Term Loan Repayments	–	(44.6)	(94.0)	(101.4)	–	–	–	–	–	–	(8.7)	(176.2)
Senior Notes Repayments	–	–	–	–	(144.7)	(164.5)	–	–	–	–	–	–
Senior FRN Repayments	–	–	–	(24.4)	–	–	–	–	–	–	–	–
Senior Sub Repayments	–	–	–	–	–	–	–	–	–	–	–	–

(Continued)

	2005E	2006E	2007E	2008E	2009E	2010E	2011E	2005E	2006E	2007E	2008E	2009E	2010E	2011E
Total Bank Debt		**301.0**	**200.4**	**103.9**	**0.0**	**–**	**–**		**762.9**	**646.7**	**535.1**	**390.1**	**228.8**	**50.1**
Total Debt		**1,301.0**	**1,200.4**	**1,103.9**	**975.8**	**838.1**	**677.7**		**1,287.9**	**1,171.7**	**1,060.1**	**915.1**	**753.8**	**575.1**
Bank Debt / EBITDA		*1.3x*	*0.8x*	*0.4x*	*0.0x*	*–*	*–*		*3.2x*	*2.6x*	*2.1x*	*1.5x*	*0.8x*	*0.2x*
Total Debt / EBITDA		*5.5x*	*4.9x*	*4.3x*	*3.7x*	*3.0x*	*2.4x*		*5.4x*	*4.8x*	*4.1x*	*3.4x*	*2.7x*	*2.0x*
EBITDA / Total Interest Expense		*1.7x*	*2.0x*	*2.2x*	*2.5x*	*2.8x*	*3.5x*		*2.1x*	*2.5x*	*2.6x*	*3.0x*	*3.5x*	*4.3x*
(EBITDA – CapEx) / Total Interest Expense		*1.6x*	*1.9x*	*1.9x*	*2.2x*	*2.6x*	*3.1x*		*1.9x*	*2.3x*	*2.2x*	*2.7x*	*3.2x*	*3.9x*
LTM EBITDA Multiple					9.6x	9.6x	9.6x					9.6x	9.6x	9.6x
Enterprise Value					$2,562	$2,647	$2,715					$2,562	$2,647	$2,715
Gross Multiple of Money					**1.57x**	**1.77x**	**1.99x**					**1.62x**	**1.85x**	**2.09x**
Gross IRR					*11.9%*	*12.1%*	*12.1%*					*12.9%*	*13.1%*	*13.0%*
**e.g. Tax, CapEx, Change in WC, etc.*														

Exhibit 12.9

Summary Downside Case with Two Capital Structures

	Downside Case/Hybrid Debt Structure Fiscal Year Ending October 31,						Downside Case/Bank Loan Structure Fiscal Year Ending October 31,					
	2006E	**2007E**	**2008E**	**2009E**	**2010E**	**2011E**	**2006E**	**2007E**	**2008E**	**2009E**	**2010E**	**2011E**
Revenue	1,497.0	1,347.3	1,279.9	1,407.9	1,548.7	1,672.6	1,497.0	1,347.3	1,279.9	1,407.9	1,548.7	1,672.6
growth in %	*4.3%*	*–10.0%*	*–5.0%*	*10.0%*	*10.0%*	*8.0%*	*4.3%*	*–10.0%*	*–5.0%*	*10.0%*	*10.0%*	*8.0%*
EBITDA	**238.0**	**134.3**	**129.8**	**161.0**	**191.1**	**221.1**	**238.0**	**134.3**	**129.8**	**161.0**	**191.1**	**221.1**
% of revenue	*15.9%*	*10.0%*	*10.1%*	*11.4%*	*12.3%*	*13.2%*	*15.9%*	*10.0%*	*10.1%*	*11.4%*	*12.3%*	*13.2%*
Interest Expense, Net	**(135.7)**	**(122.8)**	**(124.4)**	**(125.4)**	**(125.4)**	**(122.7)**	**(122.6)**	**(106.8)**	**(107.6)**	**(107.2)**	**(106.2)**	**(102.1)**
One time expenses	(100.0)	–	–	–	–	–	(100.0)	–	–	–	–	–
Proceeds from Asset Sales, after-tax	450.0	–	–	–	–	–	450.0	–	–	–	–	–
Other changes to CF*	(28.3)	(12.3)	(38.2)	(34.4)	(36.6)	(36.9)	(28.3)	(12.3)	(38.2)	(34.4)	(36.6)	(36.9)
CF before financing	**424.0**	**(0.7)**	**(32.9)**	**1.2**	**29.1**	**61.6**	**437.1**	**15.3**	**(16.0)**	**19.4**	**48.4**	**82.1**
Mandatory Debt Repayments	**(7.3)**	**(7.3)**	**(7.3)**	**(7.3)**	**(7.3)**	**(7.3)**	**(18.0)**	**(25.5)**	**(40.5)**	**(55.5)**	**(40.5)**	**(33.0)**
Beginning Cash Balance	81.2	81.2	81.2	81.2	81.2	81.2	81.2	81.2	81.2	81.2	81.2	81.2
Minimum Cash Balance	(81.2)	(81.2)	(81.2)	(81.2)	(81.2)	(81.2)	(81.2)	(81.2)	(81.2)	(81.2)	(81.2)	(81.2)
Cash for Optional Repayments	**416.7**	**(8.0)**	**(40.1)**	**(6.0)**	**21.9**	**54.3**	**419.1**	**(10.2)**	**(56.5)**	**(36.1)**	**7.9**	**49.1**
Revolver (Repayments)/ Drawdown	–	8.0	40.1	6.0	(21.9)	(32.3)	–	10.2	56.5	36.1	(7.9)	(49.1)
New Term Loan A Repayments							–	–	–	–	–	–
New Term Loan B Repayments	(416.7)	–	–	–	–	(22.0)	(419.1)	–	–	–	–	–
Delayed Draw Term Loan Repayments	–	–	–	–	–	–	–	–	–	–	–	–
Senior Notes Repayments	–	–	–	–	–	–	–	–	–	–	–	–
Senior FRN Repayments	–	–	–	–	–	–	–	–	–	–	–	–
Senior Sub Repayments	–	–	–	–	–	–	–	–	–	–	–	–

(Continued)

	2005E (left)	2006E	2007E	2008E	2009E	2010E	2011E	2005E (right)	2006E	2007E	2008E	2009E	2010E	2011E
Total Bank Debt		**301.0**	**293.8**	**286.5**	**279.3**	**272.0**	**242.7**		**762.9**	**737.4**	**696.9**	**641.4**	**600.9**	**567.9**
Total Debt		**1,301.0**	**1,301.7**	**1,334.6**	**1,333.4**	**1,304.3**	**1,242.7**		**1,287.9**	**1,272.6**	**1,288.6**	**1,269.2**	**1,220.9**	**1,138.8**
Bank Debt/EBITDA		*1.3x*	*2.2x*	*2.2x*	*1.7x*	*1.4x*	*1.1x*		*3.2x*	*5.5x*	*5.4x*	*4.0x*	*3.1x*	*2.6x*
Total Debt/EBITDA		*5.5x*	*9.7x*	*10.3x*	*8.3x*	*6.8x*	*5.6x*		*5.4x*	*9.5x*	*9.9x*	*7.9x*	*6.4x*	*5.2x*
EBITDA/Total Interest Expense		*1.7x*	*1.1x*	*1.0x*	*1.3x*	*1.5x*	*1.8x*		*2.1x*	*1.3x*	*1.3x*	*1.5x*	*1.8x*	*2.1x*
(EBITDA – CapEx)/Total Interest Expense		*1.6x*	*0.9x*	*0.7x*	*1.1x*	*1.3x*	*1.5x*		*1.9x*	*1.1x*	*0.9x*	*1.3x*	*1.6x*	*1.9x*
	2005E	**2006E**	**2007E**	**2008E**	**2009E**	**2010E**	**2011E**	**2005E**	**2006E**	**2007E**	**2008E**	**2009E**	**2010E**	**2011E**
LTM EBITDA Multiple					9.6x	9.6x	9.6x					9.6x	9.6x	9.6x
Enterprise Value					$1,545	$1,835	$2,123					$1,545	$1,835	$2,123
Gross Multiple of Money					**0.28x**	**0.57x**	**0.90x**					**0.34x**	**0.65x**	**1.00x**
Gross IRR					*–27.6%*	*–10.5%*	*–1.7%*					*–23.9%*	*–8.2%*	*0.0%*
**e.g. Tax, CapEx, Change in WC, etc.*														

CASE

13 GOING PLACES
THE BUYOUT OF AMADEUS GLOBAL TRAVEL DISTRIBUTION

SYNOPSIS

In 2004, BC Partners, an established private equity firm focused on buyouts in Europe and the US, is considering an investment in Amadeus, a major IT player in the global airlines and travel industry. In a very competitive auction setting, BC Partners needs to evaluate two distinct business strategies as to their risk–return profile and impact on financing structure.

PEDAGOGICAL OBJECTIVE OF THE CASE

The case asks students to evaluate different strategic options for an investment in a target company and to consider how they impact the bidding structure and drive returns later on. It sets the scene to discuss how private equity firms position themselves in a competitive mergers and acquisition process and ensure deal flow.

SUGGESTED ASSIGNMENT QUESTIONS

With only two days until the investment committee meeting, the team must come up with credible answers to the following questions:

1. What characteristics make this an attractive leveraged buyout?
2. What are the specific risks and benefits of each of the two strategies?
3. Which strategy should they propose and why?
4. How can BC Partners differentiate themselves from other bidders?
5. Auction dynamic: how should they position themselves to win the deal?

ADDITIONAL RESOURCES

To make the most of this case study, we suggest below additional sources to provide context and background information:

- In particular, we recommend the following chapters from *Mastering Private Equity—Transformation via Venture Capital, Minority Investments & Buyouts*
    - Chapter 1 Private Equity Essentials
    - Chapter 6 Deal Sourcing & Due Diligence
    - Chapter 8 Deal Pricing Dynamics
    - Chapter 9 Deal Structuring
    - Chapter 10 Transaction Documentation
- You may also refer to the book website for further material:
  www.masteringprivateequity.com

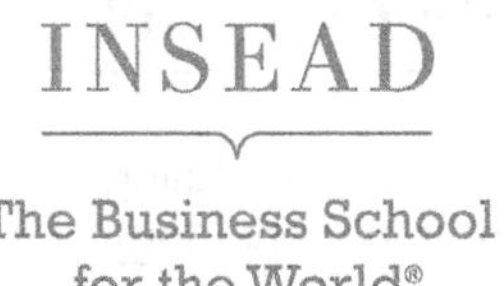

Going Places

The Buyout of Amadeus Global Travel Distribution

05/2015-6106

This case was written by Nikhil Malik (a member of the Amadeus deal team with BC Partners) and Michael Prahl, Adjunct Professor of Entrepreneurship & Family Enterprise and Executive Director of INSEAD's Global Private Equity Initiative (GPEI). It is intended to be used as a basis for class discussion rather than to illustrate either effective or ineffective handling of a management situation, or for any other purpose.

The information in the case is derived from publicly available sources.

It originated from a class project by Bahar Obdan, Amrita Priya, Abhishek Shankar Ram, Alexander Tomines Sarmiento and David Schultheis (MBA class of December 2014), under the supervision of Professor Claudia Zeisberger, Affiliate Professor of Entrepreneurship and Family Enterprise at INSEAD.

Additional material about INSEAD case studies (e.g., videos, spreadsheets, links) can be accessed at cases.insead.edu.

In October 2004, BC Partners, a European private equity fund, was contemplating bidding for Amadeus Global Travel Distribution, S.A. – a major information technology player in the global airlines and travel industry. Amadeus had three lines of business:

1. A global distribution system (GDS): a computerized system that enabled airlines and other travel service providers to distribute flights to a large selection of travel agents and ticket offices, and provided information about schedules, seat availability and fares;
2. Airline IT solutions: complementary services mainly in reservation and sales management (147 airlines outsourced this function to Amadeus in 2004), inventory management and departure control systems;
3. E-commerce: a booking engine provided to online merchant sites to allow them to connect to the GDS.

Amadeus also owned minority stakes in a number of online travel agencies. In June 2004, it acquired a majority stake (55%) in Opodo, Europe's largest online travel agency.

Listed on the Madrid, Paris and Frankfurt Stock Exchanges, it was one of four major global industry players, and regarded as co-leader thanks to the quality of its technology and its vast database of airlines and travel agencies.

The company's share price, however, did not seem to reflect its solid market position or financial standing. Floated at €6 per share by the four founding airlines on the Madrid stock exchange in October 1999, the stock had traded up to a maximum of €16 in the early months of 2000, but had then followed the general downward trend in the European exchanges and the IT sector, stabilizing around the €5 – €5.5 level.

The day before the interest of financial investors became public (13th August 2004), shares were trading at €4.92. Once rumours of a possible public-to-private transaction reached the market, they traded up to €6.38. Whatever the final bid for the company, a premium over the current price had likely to be paid (see Exhibit 13.1 for recent bid premia).

In view of this valuation, BC Partners saw an interesting investment opportunity, particularly given Amadeus' attractive growth track record, strong management team, close-to-zero debt and consistent cash-flow generation – operating cash flow was expected to reach more than €400 million in 2004. In many respects Amadeus appeared to be an ideal candidate for a leveraged buyout (LBO).

The Target: Amadeus

The global travel distribution company was founded by Air France, Iberia, SAS and Lufthansa in 1987. From the outset, it had delivered a robust financial performance, benefitting from the sustained growth in air travel worldwide – a trend that analysts expected to continue. Averaging a growth rate of 6.7% over the last four years (2000–04), EBITDA margins had improved by 2.7% during the period.

Over the preceding years, a series of crises had hit the global travel industry, including the wars in Iraq and Afghanistan, the 9/11 terrorist attacks, and the avian flu epidemic in 2003, sending air traffic volumes into a tailspin, but the company managed to sustain its impressive growth. Its leading market position was also protected by high barriers to entry (mainly the difficulty of replicating the technology and the network effect).

In 2004, Amadeus held a leading competitive position in the global GDS market with a 29% share. Its market share ranged from over 50% in Western Europe (94% in Spain, 80% in France and Scandinavia, and 75% in Germany) to slightly less than 10% in North America, where its three major competitors were based.

Its leadership in the GDS and airline IT solutions space was attributed to:

- Continuous investment in technology since 1988, which put it well ahead of the competition in terms of technical architecture and the efficiency of its IT systems. Among its rivals, Amadeus had the clearest path to integrating more robust and flexible open-source operating systems (as opposed to closed-source "legacy" IT systems).
- Outsourcing contracts signed with major airlines for Airline IT Solutions, such as the highly acclaimed migration of Qantas' inventory management, a critical airline system, in October 2004. Notwithstanding, its Airline IT Solutions business was still in its infancy. In 2004, the majority of clients had only recently been acquired and it was still in the pilot phase.
- A major advantage of the Amadeus business model was its scalability. The company's cost and capital base were relatively fixed, which meant that additional booking volume meant wider margins and faster cash generation.
- Founder and CEO, Jose Antonio Tazon, and the members of the Executive Committee, were regarded as pioneers in the industry. Most had been with Amadeus from the start (average tenure was 15 years).

Pre-Acquisition Challenges

Several challenges were identified by the BC Partners deal team:

- Given the complexity of the business, it was vital to have a top management succession plan and ensure that successful managers stayed with the company.
- Keeping the four airline owners 'onside' was equally important, as they were likely to remain minority investors with rights that protected them strategically, such as to veto the company falling into the hands of a competitor.
- The business model had to adapt to new trends; a new revenue stream had to be established based on the sale of broader IT solutions to airlines, hotels and other travel operators. The management team had heavily invested in this area, convinced of the growth opportunities it presented.
- The emergence of low-cost carriers trying to avoid the GDS (by creating their own online booking engines) was undermining the market, taking business from legacy carriers and selling tickets direct to travellers (bypassing the travel agent). Internet booking sites were taking sales volumes from traditional brick-and-mortar agencies and airline offices, the main outlets for Amadeus' information. The threat of disintermediation created uncertainty, especially with respect to price developments. Similarly, online ticket sales by traditional airlines were a cause for concern as they bypassed the GDS and lowered margins (travel agent commissions were eliminated).
- The impending deregulation of Europe's GDS industry left a question mark about the ability to maintain the existing networks, notably the discrimination between suppliers (e.g. airlines) and customers (e.g. travel agencies and booking offices). It also gave the American GDS's a chance to penetrate the European market. The US market had undergone deregulation in the past, providing clues as to what the impact might be.

The Suitor: BC Partners

A pan-European buyout investor, BC Partners was founded in 1986 as Baring Capital Investors by a group of four Europeans. It had maintained the same strategy and approach since its first fund began investing, focusing on buyouts of larger businesses exhibiting defensive growth characteristics, in Europe and (selectively) elsewhere.

With its last fund of €4.3 billion raised in 2001, BC Partners was in the process of raising over €5 billion for its next fund. Consequently, reputation and public perceptions of any investments to be made were more important than usual. It was looking to add Amadeus to a high-profile portfolio that included, amongst others, the Italian cheese maker Galbani, French frozen foods retailer Picard, and UK care homes provider General Healthcare Group.

The Process

BC Partners had been contacted several months earlier by Air France, one of the founders/owners of Amadeus (See Exhibit 13.1), informing them of the upcoming auction for the three main shareholder stakes in the company.

Rumour had it that Apax, Permira, Carlyle, Cinven, PAI, CVC (Citigroup Venture Capital)/Worldspan, CVC Europe, Blackstone and a couple of smaller players were all considering participating in the auction. Given the prospect of a highly contested bidding process, BC Partners needed to stand out from the crowd.

With the deal a top priority due to its profile and size, BC Partners had so far focused on building good relationships with the three shareholder airlines. It had also engaged a number of advisors, including former members of Amadeus senior management, who provided insight into the current management's strategic views and business proposition. In their view, the airlines and management were not just seeking a financial sponsor but a partner that would proactively support their strategy for Amadeus, while allowing them to preserve certain governance rights.

Once BC Partners' initial research had revealed the strengths of the Amadeus business model, the opportunity to acquire the firm was very attractive despite the challenges that lay in wait for the new owner. The private equity firm now had to weigh its options. In pursuing Amadeus, what strategy should it employ to unlock value?

The Strategic Options for Amadeus

Based on a first analysis, two approaches seemed feasible and could lead to significant value creation:

1. BC Partners could continue developing Amadeus as the leading travel distribution company, growing sales across different regions by pushing its GDS services.
2. Alternatively, BC Partners could try to modify the underlying business model by repositioning Amadeus as an IT solutions company.

Option A: A travel distribution company focused on geographical expansion

Under this strategy, the company would focus on the reservations platform offering, and grow by geographically expanding into new markets. Additionally it would focus on the e-commerce platforms for travel agency customers.

In 2005, Amadeus had near-monopoly status in Europe, where its market share exceeded 50% in Western Europe overall, and was as high as 80% in certain countries. In North America, however, it had a small presence and a mere 10% market share in the face of stiff competition from Sabre, Worldspan and Galileo.

Amadeus could increase its market share in North America by leveraging its superior technology and higher service level. But dislodging the incumbents in the largest and most competitive market in the world would be a huge challenge. In Asia, the company's presence was limited, but there was strong potential since air travel was growing rapidly. The International Air Transport Association (IATA) expected the Asia Pacific market to grow by 8% and the Middle East market by 7.5% over the medium term. Amadeus could with limited effort take advantage of these growth markets by increasing its network with airlines here (see Exhibit 13.2).

Another focus area in this strategy would be the e-commerce business, a high growth segment. Amadeus had already made acquisitions in this space, and with pan-European online travel agency Opodo, it was set to become one of the top three online travel agencies in Europe. In the first half of 2005, airlines' e-commerce bookings grew by 67%, yet despite this growth, Opodo and similar acquisitions were mostly losing money in 2004. The risk was that online travel agents and airlines could use the internet to bypass Amadeus and apply pressure on its pricing.

The team estimated that under this strategy (excluding growth initiatives in the online travel space) the business would continue to grow about 1% below the historical average, and profit margins would grow at about 0.2% p.a. for three years and remain flat in years four and five. This strategy would allow for a reduction of the ongoing investment in the business from the current €151 million (in 2004) to 90% the following year, and a stable proportion of revenues thereafter. Exit multiples would likely be similar to the entry.

Option B: Develop the IT Solutions division and position Amadeus as a fully-fledged IT supplier to travel providers

Although commonly perceived as a travel business with strong expertise in information technology, Amadeus considered itself to be the "leader in information technology, serving the marketing, sales and distribution needs of the global travel and tourism industry." Its IT Solutions division provided sales and registration services, inventory management, route planning management and customer management systems, as well as passenger departure control solutions (check-in processes). The customer management system had been designed with low-cost carriers in mind, and was expected to give Amadeus a competitive edge over stand-alone low-cost carrier systems. The IT Solutions business division Altéa Plan was currently used by a small number of airlines including British Airways, TACA, TAROM, and Qantas.

Going forward, BC Partners could consider leveraging Amadeus' software and IT capabilities to reposition Amadeus as a full-IT service provider. Promoting the IT Solutions portfolio to airlines would bring new customers and increase revenues from existing ones. This strategy would also create a captive base of airline customers, by reducing the risk of them leaving the system and giving Amadeus almost complete control of their IT systems. In addition, the markets perceived IT companies as attractive thanks to their healthy margins, low exposure to business cycles, non-labour-intensive nature and highly scalable business models.

The team estimated that this scenario would require significantly more investment in the early years (+33% more Capex in Y1 and Y2, and a steady proportion of revenues afterwards) but could result in significantly higher growth of +2%, +3%, +4% and +5% over historical average in Y2-Y5. With IT services being a higher margin business, EBITDA as a percentage of sales should grow by 0.6% annually in Y2-Y5. Based on other IT company comparables (see Exhibit 13.7), it was fair to assume a moderate increase in exit multiple.

However, shifting the business model might entail significant risks. How would customers react to a change in business model? Would Lufthansa, Iberia and Air France be supportive of the strategic change in focus? Would it allow competitors to move into the market or strengthen their existing market position? Would management support the strategy and be able to execute it? What if technology problems were to arise from Amadeus and disrupt the business of the major airlines?

With Amadeus set to be one of the largest European buyouts ever, the auction reverberated throughout the finance community, with several banks reaching out. Indications for debt were in line with recent large buyout transactions (see Exhibit 13.8), but the final debt structure would depend on the operating case pursued by the company. Even by simply refinancing and leveraging the deal there could be significant value creation.

Exhibit 13.1
Premiums (bid price vs. share price one month before offer)

	1998–2004 (%)	2002–2004 – transactions above € 100m (%)
France	12.3	21.0
Germany	9.9	16.3
UK	19.5	13.3
Italy	14.6	15.4
Spain	7.5	18.2
Northern Europe	17.0	16.6
Benelux	20.9	7.7
Total Europe	**16.6**	**16.1**

Source: Mergermarket.com

Exhibit 13.2
Ownership Structure of Amadeus pre-LBO

Ownership Structure of Amadeus	Class "A" Shares	% of Class "A" Shares	% of Total Votes
Société Air France	137,847,654	23.36%	43.21%
Iberia Líneas Aéreas de España, S.A.	107,826,173	18.28%	33.80%
Lufthansa Commercial Holding, GmbH	29,826,173	5.05%	9.34%
Other	314,500,000	53.31%	13.65%
TOTAL	**590,000,000**	**100%**	**100%**

Exhibit 13.3
Amadeus Sales Breakdown by Region (2004)

Revenues (In EUR millions)	2004	%
Europe	1371.9	66.71%
United States	169.7	8.25%
Rest of the World	514.9	25.03%
Total	**2056.6**	**100.0%**

Exhibit 13.4

Amadeus Consolidated Statements of Income (31 July, 2005)

CONSOLIDATED STATEMENTS OF INCOME	July 31 2005	December 31 2004
Revenue	1,406,285	2,056,680
Cost of Sales	1,104,382	1,620,379
Gross Profit	301,903	436,301
SG&A Expenses	59,349	92,887
Operating Income	242,554	343,414
Other Income (Expense)		
Interest expense, net	(3,354)	(6,045)
Exchange gains (losses), net	1,901	(4,109)
Other income (expenses), net	1,691	397
Income Before Income Taxes	242,792	333,657
Income Tax	90,317	129,018
Income After Tax	152,475	204,639
Equity income (losses) from associates	12,562	(8,279)
Minority interests	7,359	11,672
Net income	172,396	208,032
Basic earnings per class "A" share, in EURs	0.30	0.36
Basic earnings per class "B" share, in EURs	0.00	0.00
Diluted earnings per class "A" share, in EURs	0.30	0.36
Diluted earnings per class "B" share, in EURs	0.00	0.00

Exhibit 13.5

Amadeus Consolidated Balance Sheet (July 31, 2005)

ASSETS	July 31 2005	December 31 2004
Current Assets		
Cash and cash equivalents	192,467	104,669
Accounts receivable, net	300,567	245,228
Accounts receivables – affiliates, net	73,341	58,921
Loans receivable and advances – affiliates	–	1,190
Taxes receivable	57,489	41,611
Prepayments and other current assets	73,957	77,456
Total current assets	697,821	529,075
Tangible Assets		
Land and buildings	129,451	130,142
Data processing hardware and software	508,518	465,097
Other tangible assets	145,527	138,616
	783,496	733,855
Less accumulated depreciation	472,080	446,321
Net tangible assets	311,416	287,534
Intangible Assets		
Patents, trademarks and licenses	101,422	79,903
Purchased technology	83,459	72,282
Software development projects	415,923	371,859
Purchased contracts	325,153	274,748
Goodwill	450,413	453,383
Other intangible assets	2,476	9,137
	1,378,846	1,261,312
Less accumulated amortization	513,283	604,103
Net intangible assets	865,563	657,209
Deferred income taxes	107,410	108,779
Loans receivable – affiliates	1,955	1,015
Investments in associates	17,726	27,588
Other long-term investments, net	58,171	63,839
Total other non-current assets	185,262	201,221
Total non-current assets	1,362,241	1,145,964
Total Assets	2,060,062	1,675,039

(*Continued*)

Exhibit 13.5 (Continued)

LIABILITIES AND SHAREHOLDERS EQUITY	July 31 2005	December 31 2004
Current Liabilities		
Accounts payable, net	427,877	316,768
Accounts payable – affiliate, net	43,121	27,032
Dividends payable	43	34
Debt payable within one year	13,483	8,562
Current obligations under finance leases	24,196	9,996
Income taxes payable	38,752	32,651
Other current liabilities	134,996	127,863
Total current liabilities	682,468	522,906
Long-Term Liabilities		
Long-term debt	2,304	2,538
Obligations under finance leases	101,840	96,003
Deferred income taxes payable	87,464	74,528
Other long-term liabilities	46,359	37,303
Total long-term liabilities	237,967	210,372
Shareholders' Equity		
Share capital	23,044	23,044
Additional paid-in capital	380,358	365,219
Treasury shares and other similar equity instruments	(107,923)	(109,499)
Retained earnings and other reserves	846,905	681,517
Cumulative translation adjustments	(20,518)	(28,557)
Subtotal shareholders' equity	1,121,866	931,724
Minority interests	17,761	10,037
Total shareholders' equity	1,139,627	941,761
Total Liabilities and Shareholders' Equity	2,060,062	1,675,039

Exhibit 13.6

Amadeus Consolidated Statements of Cash Flows (July 31, 2005)

CONSOLIDATED STATEMENTS OF CASH FLOWS	July 31 2005	December 31 2004
Cash Flows from Operating Activities		
Operating income	242,554	343,414
Adjustments for:		
Depreciation and amortization	130,542	205,991
Employee stock compensation expense	13,575	–
Operating income before changes in working capital net of amounts acquired	386,671	549,405
Accounts receivable	(34,032)	4,334
Taxes receivable	(23,906)	(5,810)
Other current assets	7,883	8,053
Accounts payable	73,840	(24,855)
Other current liabilities	(2,052)	(10,397)
Other long-term liabilities	2,368	(5,127)
Cash provided from operating activities	410,772	515,603
Taxes paid	(69,838)	(105,621)
Net cash provided from operating activities	340,934	409,982
Cash Flows from Investing Activities		
Additions to tangible assets	(50,403)	(77,011)
Additions to intangible assets	(54,586)	(73,830)
Investment in subsidiaries and associates, net of cash acquired	(146,106)	(55,884)
Proceeds from sales of investment in associates	2,506	–
Interest received	3,022	4,631
Sundry investments and deposits	(4,315)	(4,257)
Loans to third parties	(795)	(4,367)
Loans to affiliates	–	(585)
Cash proceeds collected/(paid) – derivative agreements	(7,703)	3,889
Disposal of sundry investments	9,048	3,663
Dividends received	2,838	7,828
Proceeds obtained from disposal of fixed assets	2,722	3,598
Net cash used in investing activities	(243,772)	(192,325)

CONSOLIDATED STATEMENTS OF CASH FLOWS	July 31 2005	December 31 2004
Cash Flows from Financing Activities		
Proceeds from borrowings	60,647	32,864
Repayments of borrowing	(56,204)	(106,076)
Interest paid	(6,674)	(12,533)
Redemption of Class "B" shares	–	(485)
Acquisition of Treasury shares	(29)	(63,086)
Disposals of Treasury shares	1,604	39,215
Dividends paid	–	(35,000)
Payment of finance lease liabilities	(9,651)	(10,419)
Net cash used in financing activities	(10,307)	(155,520)
Effect of Exchange Rate Changes of Cash and Cash Equivalents	943	431
Net Increase/(Decrease) in Cash and Cash Equivalents	87,798	62,568
Cash and Cash Equivalents at Beginning of Period	104,669	42,101
Cash and Cash Equivalents at End of Period	192,467	104,669

Exhibit 13.7
Publicly Traded Comparables

Travel Agents and Other Similar Comps

Trading statistics	**AV/Sales**			**AV/EBITDA**			**AV/EBITA**			**Adj. P/E Ratio**			**PEG**	
Company name	12/2004E	12/1005E	12/2006E	12/2004E	12/2005E	12/2006E	12/2004E	12/2005E	12/2006E	12/2004E	12/2005E	12/2006E	12/2004E	12/2005E
On-line Travel														
E Brokers	1.1	1.0	1.0	11.1	6.8	5.9	NM	NM	NM	NM	NM	NM	NA	NA
Ctrip	16.7	12.5	10.1	38.2	27.0	20.9	40.6	28.2	21.6	47.5	35.2	27.8	1.4	1.1
LASTMINUTE	1.1	0.9	NA	10.1	5.9	4.0	18.6	8.3	5.2	22.2	9.8	7.5	1.3	0.6
PRICELINE	0.9	0.8	0.8	19.7	15.4	13.1	25.7	19.2	15.9	23.3	17.7	15.9	1.6	1.2
ORBITZ	1.9	1.7	NA	13.6	8.3	NA	20.4	10.5	NA	27.9	18.8	NA	1.4	0.9
Mean	**4.3**	**3.4**	**4.0**	**18.5**	**12.7**	**11.0**	**26.3**	**16.6**	**14.2**	**30.2**	**20.4**	**17.1**	**1.4**	**1.0**
Median	**1.1**	**1.0**	**1.0**	**13.6**	**8.3**	**9.5**	**23.1**	**14.9**	**15.9**	**25.6**	**18.3**	**15.9**	**1.4**	**1.0**
Diversified / Travel Comparables														
CENDANT	1.2	1.1	1.0	7.0	6.4	5.8	NA	NA	NA	11.7	10.7	NA	0.8	0.8
IAC / INTERACTIVE	1.8	1.5	NA	8.9	7.1	NA	10.3	8.1	NA	10.5	10.9	13.9	NA	NA
Mean	**1.5**	**1.3**	**1.0**	**8.0**	**6.8**	**5.8**	**10.3**	**8.1**		**11.1**	**10.8**	**13.9**	**0.8**	**0.8**
Median	**1.5**	**1.3**	**1.0**	**8.0**	**6.8**	**5.8**	**10.3**	**8.1**		**11.1**	**10.8**	**13.9**	**0.8**	**0.8**
Internet Software and Services														
Amazon	2.2	1.8	1.5	24.7	19.6	15.5	28.3	23.4	20.1	34.9	25.4	24.4	1.1	0.8
Ebay	18.9	14.2	11.1	45.9	33.9	25.2	54.6	39.3	29.1	79.9	59.9	46.1	2.2	1.6
Yahoo	15.8	12.1	9.9	40.4	29.2	22.6	60.1	39.2	31.3	105.9	74.4	59.3	3.2	2.3
Mean	**12.3**	**9.4**	**7.5**	**37.0**	**27.6**	**21.1**	**47.7**	**34.0**	**26.8**	**73.6**	**53.2**	**43.3**	**2.2**	**1.6**
Median	**15.8**	**12.1**	**9.9**	**40.4**	**29.2**	**22.6**	**54.6**	**39.2**	**29.1**	**79.6**	**59.9**	**46.1**	**2.2**	**1.6**

IT Services

Trading statistics			AV/Sales			AV/EBITDA			AV/EBITA			Adj. P/E Ratio		
Company name	Equity value (€MM)	Aggregate Value (€MM)	12/2004E	12/1005E	12/2006E	12/2004E	12/2005E	12/2006E	12/2004E	12/2005E	12/2006E	12/2004E	12/2005E	12/2006E
North American Universe														
Accenture	19,609	18,147	1.76	1.55	1.44	11.8	10.5	10	13.7	12	10.8	21.3	19.4	17.8
EDS	8,656	8,806	0.57	0.6	0.59	5.5	5	4.6	11	8.5	7.6	16.2	12.1	10.1
CSC	7,857	9,229	0.88	0.78	0.72	6.7	6	5.4	13.8	12.1	11.2	20	17.9	16.1
ACS	5,947	6,171	1.83	1.59	NA	9.2	7.9	NA	12.3	10.6		19.4	16.5	NA
Amdocs	4,238	3,668	3.13	2.69	2.48	13.4	11.3	10.4	17.3	14.4	13.1	18.3	15.5	14.4
CGI	2,206	2,391	1.17	0.95	0.89	7.6	6.1	5.6	11.3	9.4	8.4	16.5	14	12.4
Bearing Point	1,285	1,464	0.56	0.54	0.49	9.9	6.9	5.1	15.9	9.7	6.5	32.5	17.1	10.5
Mean			**1.41**	**1.24**	**1.10**	**9.2**	**7.7**	**6.9**	**13.6**	**11.0**	**9.6**	**20.6**	**16.1**	**13.6**
Median			**1.17**	**0.95**	**0.805**	**9.2**	**6.9**	**5.5**	**13.7**	**10.6**	**9.6**	**19.4**	**16.5**	**13.4**
European Universe														
Atos Origin	3,396	4,122	0.79	0.78	0.75	8.5	7.4	7.1	11.4	10.4	10.2	16.8	14.1	13.1
Capgemini	3,317	3,221	0.51	0.48	0.48	15.7	8.3	6.5	NM	14.7	10.1	NM	24.2	15.9
LogicaCMG	2,053	2,334	0.98	0.95	0.89	12.9	9.6	8.2	17.3	12.1	10.1	16.7	13.7	13.7
Tietoenator	1,973	2,031	1.33	1.25	1.17	8.5	8	7.4	12	11	10.1	15.9	14.7	13.5
Indra	1,812	1,988	2.03	1.85	1.7	15.6	14.3	12.8	18.2	16.3	14.6	19.8	20.3	18.4
Mean			**1.13**	**1.06**	**1.00**	**12.2**	**9.5**	**8.4**	**14.7**	**12.9**	**11.0**	**17.3**	**17.4**	**14.9**
Median			**0.98**	**0.95**	**0.89**	**12.9**	**8.3**	**7.4**	**14.7**	**12.1**	**10.1**	**16.8**	**14.7**	**13.7**
Total Mean			**1.3**	**1.2**	**1.0**	**10.3**	**8.3**	**7.3**	**14.0**	**11.6**	**10.1**	**19.5**	**166**	**14.1**
Total Median			**1.1**	**1.0**	**0.9**	**9.6**	**8.0**	**7.1**	**13.7**	**11.5**	**10.1**	**18.3**	**16.0**	**13.7**

1. Market data as of December 02, 2004

2. Excluding Goodwill Amortisation and Extraordinary items

Exhibit 13.8

Selected Recent European LBOs with Leverage >6x

Figures in EUR m	Yellow Brick Road	Seat Pagine	Elis	Grohe	Picard Surgeles
Sales	370	1522	770	896	712
EBITDA	150	623	161	186	107
Margin	40.5%	40.9%	20.9%	20.8%	15.0%
Capex	6.8	42	51	45	22
EBITDA-Capex	143.2	581	110	141	85
EBITDA-Capex margin	38.7%	38.2%	14.3%	15.7%	11.9%
Historic Sales Growth	5.7% (01-03)	3.4% (01-03)	10.1% (00-02)	7.1% (92-03)	8.8% (02-04)
Projected Sales Growth	4.7% (03-08)	5.4% (03-07)	6.2% (02-07)	2.8% (03-08)	8.2% (04-07)
Historic EBITDA Margin Improvement	880 (01-03)	580 (01-03)	0 (00-02)	200 (00-03)	30 (02-04)
Projected EBITDA Margin Improvement	40 (03-08)	450 (03-07)	230 (02-07)	70 (03-08)	30 (04-07)
Senior Debt	725 4.8x	2850 4.6x	768 4.5x	800 4.3x	569 5.3x
Subordinated Debt	275 1.8x	1150 1.8x	290 1.7x	335 1.8x	85 0.8x
TOTAL DEBT	1000 6.7x	4000 6.4x	1058 6.2x	1135 6.1x	654 6.1x
EBITDA/Cash Interest Y1	2.47x	2.09x	2.10x	2.30x	n/d

SECTION V
Turnarounds and Distressed Investing

Turnaround or growth, it's getting your people focused on the goal that is still the job of leadership.

—**Anne M. Mulcahy**, Former Chair and CEO of Xerox

CASE

14 CRISIS AT THE MILL WEAVING AN INDIAN TURNAROUND*

SYNOPSIS

Emerging markets are challenging and require special expertise; India in particular is known to be a tricky business environment for even the most experienced managers, even in good times. The case follows two senior executives, Sankar and Nikhil from Alvarez & Marsal's (A&M) India practice, as they deal with an urgent request from one of their US private equity clients, Sapphire Capital.

The situation is critical, with allegations from a past employee claiming irregular activities by senior management at the root of the company's financial difficulties. The company in question is a leading woollen textile manufacturer and exporter with operations in north India. The A&M team needs to act quickly, yet must tread carefully and investigate discretely in the event that the accusations prove to be unfounded.

PEDAGOGICAL OBJECTIVE OF THE CASE

During good times (almost) anyone can lead; it is the tricky times that separate the wheat from the chaff. This case provides the opportunity for managers and professionals to try their hands at a demanding turnaround situation, with financial distress exacerbated by allegations of fraud. Add the setting in India to the mix and one might describe the situation as a perfect storm.

The case provides a challenging setting for readers to improve their understanding of cash flow management and the various business drivers, but with a focus on the short-term needs of the business. An additional complexity comes from the emerging markets setting and malpractice accusations.

SUGGESTED ASSIGNMENT QUESTIONS

Put yourself in the shoes of Sankar and Nikhil, the senior executives at A&M's India office and develop a plan of action for the interim managers in the role of finance and operations.

1. Where do you see the opportunities to improve the performance of the firm?
2. How would you handle the sensitivities around the accusations of malpractice by (former) senior management?
3. Finally, what would be the key ingredients to make this a successful turnaround?

*Winner of the 2015 EFMD Case Writing Competition in the category "Indian Management Issues & Opportunities."

Using the cash flow templates included in the case, please address the following questions:

4. Does the company have sufficient cash to operate? Determine this by modeling the cash flow from November 2010 to March 2011.
5. What could be done in advance (in November 2010) to improve the situation? Analyze the situation and offer suggestions. Students should grapple with the situation and offer options rather than targeting a perfect answer.

ADDITIONAL RESOURCES

To make the most of this case study, we suggest the following additional sources to provide context and information:

- In particular, we recommend the following chapters from *Mastering Private Equity—Transformation via Venture Capital, Minority Investments & Buyouts*
  - Chapter 1 Private Equity Essentials
  - Chapter 5 Alternative Strategies
  - Chapter 9 Deal Structuring
- Case website for faculty and lecturers: http://cases.insead.edu/alvarez-marsal/
- You may also refer to the book website for further material:
  www.masteringprivateequity.com

Crisis at the Mill: Weaving an Indian Turnaround

Alvarez & Marsal

Winner
"Indian Management Issues and Opportunities" category
EFMD Case Writing Competition 2015

06/2016-6069

This case was written by Sankar Krishnan and Nikhil Shah from Alvarez & Marsal under the guidance of Anne-Marie Carrick, Research Associate, and Claudia Zeisberger, Affiliate Professor of Decision Sciences and Entrepreneurship & Family business, both at INSEAD. It is intended to be used as a basis for class discussion rather than to illustrate either effective or ineffective handling of an administrative situation.

Additional material about INSEAD case studies (e.g., videos, spreadsheets, links) can be accessed at cases.insead.edu.

Phone call, November 2010:

To: Sankar Krishnan, Managing Director at the global professional services firm Alvarez & Marsal (A&M)

From: Steve Cohen, Managing Director of Alvarez & Marsal's North American Commercial Restructuring practice

Steve Cohen: Sankar, I've just received some worrying news from Sapphire Capital (SC). You know the firm? It's one of our large US-based distress private equity fund clients. We have advised them on several engagements. One of their Indian portfolio companies has some serious issues. It seems the top management may have been involved in some irregular activities and the company is in a crisis. That's all the information I have at the moment, but they seem very nervous.

Sankar Krishnan: Yes, I know SC. This sounds serious. We need to organize a call with the fund and with Nikhil to discuss what steps we should take next. Nikhil is on vacation with his family, but from the sound of it we can't wait. Let's speak tomorrow at 8.30am. I'll call Nikhil if you can organize getting the SC people together?

Allegations...

When Sankar Krishnan and Nikhil Shah, Senior Director at A&M, called Steve Cohen the next day, they found that the fund's entire leadership team, including the chairman, investment committee members, general counsel and CFO were part of the discussion. They explained that the situation was indeed grave. A&M's team was quickly brought up to date with events.

The portfolio company in question was a leading woollen textile manufacturer and exporter, WoolEx Mills, with operations based in Northern India. The company had been growing, with a turnover of INR 8,000 million but a bottom line in the red. However, it had been profitable at the operating level. Its products were sold not only in India but worldwide through distribution channel partners and retail stores.

The situation had been brought to Sapphire Capital's attention a few weeks earlier when a former employee had contacted them. He informed the fund that he had witnessed irregular activities during his time at the company, allegedly involving the senior management. However, the employee had since been fired for underperforming.

This meant the fund would have to tread carefully and investigate discretely – particularly if the accusations proved to be unfounded. The fund was in a tricky position as they owned almost the entire portfolio company, if the allegations were upheld it would call into question Sapphire Capital's credibility and ability to manage its investments. There was no time to waste.

The fund's first step was to hire a corporate investigations firm to run a preliminary check into the claims. The detectives met covertly with ex-employees, clients and suppliers before they presented Sapphire Capital with their final report. They concluded that there was indeed substance to the accusations, but to gain definitive proof inside access to the company's operations was required. For this, the fund called upon the help of A&M.

The Groundwork

Sankar and his team quickly evaluated the alternatives for handling the situation. The top five members of WoolEx Mills' senior management team were reportedly involved in irregular activities that had led to shareholder losses. The A&M team would need to proceed with caution as it was unclear who was trustworthy at WoolEx Mills. Even a minor leak to the press of the investigation would be catastrophic – evidence could be destroyed that was crucial for the forensic investigation they had to carry out. The A&M team was almost working in the dark as they were not even given access to the investigator's report – all they knew was there had been some irregularities that needed further examination.

Over the following week, the team, led by Sankar, spoke daily with Sapphire Capital's investment committee and general counsel for three hours. They drew up a plan of action for the intervention and eventual takeover of the company's operations by the A&M team. Each step of the plan's execution was discussed in minute detail to ensure that it was carried out as smoothly as possible. Sankar assembled two teams: an interim management team to take over management; and a forensic team to conduct investigations made up of members from A&M's New York and Chicago offices.

Action...

Just seven days later, WoolEx Mills' CEO and CFO were invited to Sapphire Capital's Mumbai offices for what they believed was a regular board meeting. It was of utmost importance that they not find anything suspicious about the fund's request for a meeting. The heads of manufacturing, sourcing and sales departments were also asked to participate via video conference – the two latter executives were suspected of being in collusion with the CEO and CFO. They were due to attend the meeting at a Reliance Web World office, a facility that provided video conference services in the city of Amritsar, where the company's headquarters and manufacturing plant were located. Unknown to these executives, Sankar and Nikhil, along with the other A&M team members, were sitting in the room adjacent, observing the video conference.

The video conference began as planned. The chairman rose from his chair in the meeting room and announced the suspension of the CEO and CFO forthwith. The two senior executives were visibly stunned – they had not been expecting this coup.

Back in Amritsar, the A&M team burst into the conference room from the office next door and informed the senior executives of the allegations against them. They were served with a suspension order from the board, with a final decision to be taken pending further investigation. All suspended parties were asked to hand over their mobile phones and laptops. The three executives in the conference room were separated and interviewed individually by an assigned A&M team member – Sankar, Nikhil and Al Lakhani, who led the forensics team. They were informed of the board's decision to bar them from the company's offices until further notice. Next they were given an opportunity to provide their own version of events. One of them almost broke down in tears. They all denied the charges levelled against them.

The Takeover

Following these dramatic events, the A&M team headed to the WoolEx Mills' campus where both its headquarters and manufacturing plant were located. The chairman of the board had informed the company's HR & administrative heads of the imminent replacement of the top management team, asking them to ensure that the security guards co-operate fully with the incoming A&M team. Despite these precautions, the experienced A&M team brought their own security guards in case of any trouble.

Upon arrival, the A&M team took full possession of all personal computers, servers and other electronic devices that would be key for their forensic investigation into the alleged irregularities. All these items were locked up, with three guards in place to ensure their safekeeping. The chairman of the board then sent a company-wide communication explaining the change of management; describing the new management team; and requesting the co-operation of all employees during the investigation.

The new management team consisted of Sankar as the CEO, Nikhil as CFO, Nikhil Khanna, another A&M Senior Director, as Head of Manufacturing & Sourcing, and Neil Agarwal, a person affiliated with the fund, as Head of Sales.

New Day, New Team

The following day, the new team called a meeting with WoolEx Mills' top 25 employees, with the chairman of the board participating by phone. Sankar informed them of the change of regime and expressed his intention to work alongside them to ensure that the business ran smoothly. He also made it clear that there was now an 'open door' policy – all employees could come forward and disclose information that might be of help for the new management to "clean up" the company. Such information, he assured them, would be treated confidentially.

Meanwhile the forensics team set to work. They began with the electronic data analysis, interviewed key people, and carried out a forensic accounting review of the books.

The interim management team also began looking at how to restructure operations. They considered what the different roles and responsibilities would be for each department's key personnel – what issues they faced in their respective functions – with the express goal of turning the situation and the company around as fast as possible.

The Challenges Ahead

The challenges the interim management team faced were daunting. They included a workforce of more than 2,200 employees, mounting costs of raw materials, old plant equipment that was responsible for manufacturing efficiencies declining to 50% of optimal levels, rising accounts receivable and inventory levels, a tired brand, and unclear procurement processes – plus not really knowing what the real impact had been of the previous management's irregularities. It was paramount for the team to maintain customer confidence while resolving these issues.

The new CEO had to ensure that all stakeholders ("good" employees, customers, vendors, lenders and the owners) were aligned with the turnaround, while any unethical employees were replaced – all to be undertaken without disrupting the business.

The Textile Company

Production Process

WoolEx Mills imported raw materials (called "tops") typically from Australia or South Africa. Tops came from fine quality wool, combed and weeded to free it from any defects, and then sent to the dye-house where it was treated to obtain the required colour and shade, and dried. Dyed tops were sent to the spinning unit for conversion to yarns. The desired fineness of the finished fabric depended on the fineness and quality achieved in the spinning unit. Spinning was a critical part of the process as it established the flexibility and elasticity of the fabric.

These yarns then moved on to the weaving unit, where a number of power looms wove them into a fabric based on designs that were pre-fed into the looms. The fabric from the weaving unit then went to the finishing section, where the fabric achieved its desired finish and texture. After this last process, the fabric underwent several quality checks before it was sent to the finished goods warehouse.

Creating a fine woollen fabric involved tight controls on quality at all stages. Mandatory to the production of a high-quality fabric was state-of-the-art machinery maintained at the highest standards, and a close control of the manufacturing process with inspections at all stages. Unlike many price-conscious consumers in India, the company's direct customers were major distributors and large retailers who carried out rigorous quality checks on incoming shipments. Its export customers imposed even more stringent quality standards.

The textile and apparel industry operated on a two-season basis, with the design departments beginning work well in advance on new designs for the forthcoming season. Prototypes were developed and sent to all the major distributors for their input in the hope of obtaining orders. Once orders were confirmed, they were integrated into production plans that were generated in a pre-determined production cycle.

Raw Material

Wool was one of the company's key raw materials. India boasted the third largest sheep population in the world. However, the average yield per sheep was approximately 0.9kg compared to the global average of over 2.4kg. From this yield, 85% of Indian wool was of a coarser grade and thus unsuitable for the organized fabric manufacturing industry (Exhibit 14.1 gives an overview of the industry). Fine quality wool production in India was insufficient to meet the organized woollen industry's needs and thus depended

largely on raw material imports. Most of the fabric grade wool in India was imported from Australia, New Zealand and South Africa.

Dyes were the other key raw material. The production team from A&M believed that savings of 5–10% could be achieved if they changed vendors. One of the allegations against the management was that they took kick-backs from vendors, so replacing them would get rid of "bad" vendors.

A number of trials were carried out in the dye-house, with a goal to institutionalize new dyes. The introduction of new systems or suppliers was made more complicated by the background of irregularities in the existing sourcing practices.

Sales

Even though the company's brand was well known throughout India, WoolEx Mills did not command premium prices. It was widely believed that its products were of inferior quality to its competitors. Its major customers in India were the large multi-brand distributors who sold its products to multi-brand retailers. As a result, the company required few showrooms. Exports accounted for approximately 20% of its revenues, with leading names in the fashion industry from the USA, Europe and Japan among its customers.

Operations

Sankar and Nikhil discovered there were some serious quality issues that needed to be addressed urgently. This came to light one morning in March 2011 when the head of sales received an email from the company's main export customer in Japan complaining about the quality of the latest shipment. The Japanese customer was threatening to ask for a credit note of approximately 40% of the value of the invoice. On questioning the head of quality, Sankar and Nikhil realized that this case was not unusual. In the past, the company had received credit notes for quality issues from other export customers, but a credit note for 40% of the invoice value was unheard of. The issue of quality thus became another priority for the A&M team.

The company's quality issues could be attributed to two main things. 1) WoolEx Mills was not up-to speed with the technological advances in the industry and was using outdated, old equipment. 2) The company's manufacturing processes were not designed to produce the high-quality fabrics that were now being demanded in the industry.

Financial Position of the Company

Nikhil Shah, the new CFO, discovered several issues in the company's finances. The accounts receivable were high and outdated on a month-by-month basis. Customers paid invoices with an average of 130 days delay, leading to cash flow issues. In addition, some of the discounts given were not recorded in the firm's books, and no credit notes were issued. The budgeting process was not carried out in a detailed manner. There were several loopholes in the costing process and the Management Information System (MIS) was being maintained manually.

The price of the high-quality fine wool imports from Australia and South Africa that the company so heavily relied upon had increased from September 2010 to March 2011 by over 65%. This severely constrained profitability and cash flows. Raw material purchases were generally made through advanced payments and accounted for 50% of the selling price. Other major purchase items included dyes, chemicals and consumables that accounted for 10% of sales.

Nikhil soon realized that the company did not follow any scientific inventory management or ordering practices. One example was the coal for firing a steam boiler that was stocked unnecessarily six months in advance, thus blocking working capital. There was a need to define ordering procedures for critical purchases. Large domestic customers were contributing to higher sales outstanding. Irregularities in sales practices with some customers contributed to high outstanding receivables. These, together with irregular payables management, were damaging the company's liquidity.

Given all the above issues, reducing the high working capital through cash flow forecasting was the primary focus for the CFO, as well as strengthening the checks and controls within the finance function.

Capital Expenditure Plan

The company used old and outdated equipment. About two thirds of the looms in operation broke down frequently. Poor maintenance also contributed to losses in manufacturing efficiencies and contributed to the quality issue. There was an urgent need to upgrade these looms with superior technology, but the capital expenditure required had regularly been postponed.

Critical testing equipment was also amiss in the quality lab. The design function had antiquated looms for the manufacture of prototype fabrics for new designs. Some immediate requirements in the dye-house and finishing section had been overlooked in the capital expenditure plans. Even though an ERP package was installed in the company, it was not used to its full potential. The plant's structures required immediate repairs – the poor state of infrastructure became clear when the entire plant was flooded after a heavy day of rain during the monsoon.

Setting the Stage for Turnaround

The situation was critical, the issues were multifaceted, and there was a pressing need to improve performance. Following the team's initial investigations, they cited three main areas that had to be addressed: improvement of the working capital and liquidity position; enhancement of manufacturing efficiency; and cutting rejection rates – all aimed at improving efficiency and quality together with general cost reduction.

Exhibit 14.1
Industry Background

The Indian woollen textiles sector is relatively small compared to the country's cotton, man-made fibre textiles and clothing industry. It is estimated to be worth approximately Rs. 100 bn. The industry is dominated by a large number of "unorganized" players on a small scale. These are small knitting units, power loom units, carpet manufacturers and dyeing houses. The remainder of the industry is made up of the "organized" sector – large integrated textile mills, combing units and spinning units.

There are only a handful of large integrated woollen textile mills in India. These mills manufacture mostly finished fabric that is sold to the domestic and export markets. Some of the mills also sell apparel and garments. A few have gained a reputation as quality manufacturers of woollen textiles and their products are exported worldwide. The woollen fabric industry is dominated by one large player that controls more than 65% of the market. Historically the market has grown at a rate of 9% in the last two years, and is expected to sustain these growth rates.

Due to the small number of players in the organized segment in India and the specialized nature of equipment required for manufacturing woollen fabrics, the industry is dependent on imported machinery and equipment. Most of the looms and other equipment are imported from European countries, USA, and Japan.

Appendix 1
Income Statement

(in INR millions)	**FY09 Mar-09**	**FY10 Mar-10**	**Month of Nov-10**	**FY to date Nov-10**
Income				
Sales and job work	1,597.3	1,598.8	99.0	1,222.7
Other income	16.4	35.1	10.9	26.8
Total Income	**1,613.6**	**1,633.9**	**109.9**	**1,249.5**
Expenditure				
Cost of Goods Sold	(596.3)	(625.2)	(21.2)	(504.1)
Employee Cost	(249.6)	(236.2)	(22.2)	(173.8)
Other Expenses	(540.9)	(527.9)	(52.4)	(386.5)
Total Expenditure	(1,386.9)	(1,389.3)	(95.8)	(1,064.4)
EBITDA	**226.8**	**244.7**	**14.1**	**185.1**
as % of Income	*14.1%*	*15.0%*	*12.8%*	*14.8%*
Depreciation	(131.5)	(135.8)	(11.3)	(91.6)
Finance Charges	(60.4)	(50.4)	(3.7)	(31.6)
Profit Before Tax	34.8	58.4	(0.9)	61.8
Provision for tax	(6.6)	(10.2)	–	(11.1)
Profit After Tax	**28.2**	**48.2**	**(0.9)**	**50.7**
as % of Income	*1.7%*	*3.0%*	*(0.9%)*	*4.1%*

Appendix 2
Balance Sheet

(in INR millions)	FY09 Mar-09	FY10 Mar-10	As on Nov-10
LIABILITIES			
Shareholder's Funds			
Share Capital	1,356.7	1,356.7	1,356.7
Reserves and Surplus	560.7	609.0	670.8
Loan Funds			
Secured Loans	395.7	272.3	223.6
TOTAL LIABILITIES	**2,313.2**	**2,237.9**	**2,251.1**
ASSETS			
Fixed Assets			
Gross Block	2,120.0	2,168.7	2,172.1
(less) Acc Depreciation	648.7	784.5	875.8
Net Block	1,471.3	1,384.2	1,296.2
Capital WIP	8.1	6.4	63.7
Fixed Assets	**1,479.5**	**1,390.6**	**1,359.9**
Investments	0.0	0.0	0.0
Current Assets			
Inventories	513.0	478.6	666.0
Sundry debtors	579.9	651.4	663.8
Cash and bank balances	55.4	52.4	53.2
Loans and advances	31.6	46.3	77.7
Other current assets	0.3	1.8	–
Current Assets	1,180.2	1,230.6	1,460.7
Less: Current Liabilities and Provisions			
Current liabilities	318.8	366.1	544.8
Provisions	27.7	17.1	24.7
Current Liabilities and Provisions	346.6	383.2	569.5
Net Current Assets	**833.7**	**847.3**	**891.2**
TOTAL ASSETS	**2,313.2**	**2,237.9**	**2,251.1**

Appendix 3
Cash Flow Statement

	(in INR millions)	FY09 Mar-09	FY10 Mar-10	Month of Nov-10	FY to date Nov-10
A	Cash Flow from Operating Activities				
	Net Income (Loss)	34.8	58.4	(0.9)	61.8
	Adjustments				
	Depreciation & Amortisation of Fixed Assets	131.5	135.8	11.3	91.4
	Loss / (Gain) on sale of fixed assets	(0.2)	(0.0)	–	–
	Interest expense	55.7	47.4	–	–
	Interest income	(5.5)	(15.2)	–	–
	Direct Taxes / FBT paid	(6.3)	(19.0)	–	–
	Accounts Receivables-Net	(100.5)	(73.9)	124.0	(12.4)
	Inventories	(154.7)	34.5	(84.4)	(187.4)
	Advance & Deposits	–	–	4.7	(26.5)
	Current Liabilities & Provisions	16.3	34.2	2.4	186.3
	Total Adjustments	(63.6)	143.8	57.9	51.4
	Cash Flow from Operating Activities	**(28.8)**	**202.2**	**57.0**	**113.2**
B	Cash Flow from Investing Activities				
	Capital Expenditure	(103.1)	(46.9)	(2.6)	(64.0)
	Proceeds from Sale of Fixed Assets	0.3	0.0	0.0	0.2
	Interest income received	5.7	13.7	–	–
	Net Cash used by Investing Activities	**(97.1)**	**(33.2)**	**(2.6)**	**(63.8)**
C	Cash Flow from Financing Activities				
	Borrowings/(payments) of Term Loan	133.8	(10.2)	(9.0)	(39.7)
	Borrowings/(payments) of Working Capital Loan	46.4	(112.4)	(47.5)	(9.0)
	Borrowings/(payments) of Vehicle Loan	1.0	(0.9)	–	–
	Interest paid	(52.8)	(48.6)	–	–
	Net change in unsecured Deposits	–	–	–	–
	Net Cash provided by Financing activities	**128.3**	**(172.0)**	**(56.5)**	**(48.6)**
	Net change in cash & cash equivalents	2.4	(3.0)	(2.0)	0.8
	Beginning cash & cash equivalents	53.0	55.4	55.3	52.4
	Ending cash & cash equivalents	**55.4**	**52.4**	**53.2**	**53.2**

Appendix 4

Ageing schedule of receivables as on 30-Nov-10

(in INR millions)	Total Outstanding	<= 60 Days	61–90 Days	91–120 Days	> 120 Days
A. **Domestic:**					
Area					
Pb/Ch/Hr/Hp/Jk	79.0	34.7	21.3	7.4	15.6
Delhi	28.9	14.2	3.4	4.9	6.4
U.P. West	30.6	6.5	6.5	3.3	14.4
Rajasthan	10.7	6.1	2.5	0.9	1.2
Maharashtra	33.2	14.8	8.9	6.7	2.6
Gujrat	25.0	3.7	2.2	2.6	16.5
A.P.	79.6	8.4	16.3	33.4	21.5
M.P.	11.5	6.8	1.3	2.3	1.1
Tamilnadu	5.4	1.1	1.5	0.5	2.3
Karnatka	15.5	7.3	4.4	2.1	1.8
U.P. - Allahabad	2.4	1.9	0.1	0.1	0.3
U.P. - East	19.3	9.1	7.4	1.5	1.3
North East	13.1	2.8	2.5	2.4	5.4
Bihar	27.4	12.8	8.4	2.8	3.4
Orissa	5.6	2.1	1.1	0.8	1.5
West Bengal	7.0	3.9	1.7	0.4	1.0
Nepal	58.4	36.0	11.4	0.4	10.7
U.P. Central	48.5	26.0	9.9	7.4	5.2
Convertors etc.	8.1	1.2	2.2	0.2	4.5
Sub Total	**509.4**	**199.4**	**113.0**	**80.3**	**116.6**
B. Govt. / Institutional	96.2	48.5	22.0	14.2	11.5
C. Export	46.0	30.9	14.1	0.4	0.5
D. Job Spinning	6.5	6.4	0.1	0.0	0.0
E. Garments	5.8	3.5	–	–	2.2
TOTAL	**663.8**	**288.8**	**149.1**	**95.0**	**130.9**

Appendix 5

Inventory schedule as on 30-Nov-10

(in INR '000s)

S.No.	Particulars	Unit	Qty.	Value
1	**Raw Materials**			
	Wool	Kgs.	248,382	135,689
	Polyester	Kgs.	216,433	32,482
	Purchased Yarn	Kgs.	36,043	11,012
	Waste	Kgs.	31,701	918
	Dyes & Chemicals			6,573
				186,673
2	**Work-in-process**			
	Dyeing Dept.	Kgs.	19,525	9,595
	Spinning Dept.	Kgs.	102,314	41,007
	Yarn stores	Kgs.	104,861	43,200
	Weaving Dept.	Kgs.	65,159	41,585
	Fnshng Dept.	Mtrs.	126,585	30,568
				165,955
3	**Finished Goods**			
	Cloth	Mtrs.	933,511	243,844
	Blankets	Nos	7,010	3,850
	Garments	Nos	8,476	10,999
				258,692
4	**Stores & Spares**			54,661
	Total			**665,982**

Appendix 6

Capital Expenditure Plan

(in INR '000s)	**Planned Capex (Budget)**	**Advance to suppliers as on Nov-10**	**Expenditure**				
			Up to Oct'10	**Nov'10**	**Total**	**Against Capex Plan 2009–10**	**Grand Total**
Spares	28,162.1	1,766.3	7,024.4	15.0	8,805.7	121.0	8,926.7
New Machines	67,224.4	4,808.1	3,337.7	25.0	8,170.8	36,621.5	44,792.3
Others							
Building & Roads Repair	23,025.6	2,098.4	10,454.5	1,483.5	14,036.4	617.1	14,653.5
Misc.	3,075.0	1,633.4	–	–	1,633.4	–	1,633.4
Contingency	6,432.9	688.8	3,252.5	907.6	4,848.9	–	4,848.9
Total	**127,920.0**	**10,995.0**	**24,069.1**	**2,431.1**	**37,495.2**	**37,359.7**	**74,854.8**

Appendix 7

Credit and Payment terms

Credit terms for all sales:

Category	Credit terms
Fabric Sales	
Domestic Customers	– 3 months from the date of sale
Government Institutions	– 3 months from the date of sale
Exports	– 3 months from the date of sale
Others	
Job work	– All cash sale
Other Liquidation	– All cash sale
Other Income	– No other major source of income

Payment terms for all purchases:

Category	Payment terms	Additional information
Raw materials		
Imported Wool tops	– Letter of Credit; Payment to the bank generally 2 months from date of purchase	– All RM purchases can be considered to be imported
Importer Polyester	– Letter of Credit; Payment to the bank generally 2 months from date of purchase	
Other domestic purchases	– Letter of Credit; Payment to the bank generally 2 months from date of purchase	
Finance charges for LC	– INR 6.25 Mn / month for supporting the facility	
Stores and Dyes		
Local purchases	– 2 months from date of purchase	– All stores and dye purchases are local purchases
Power and Fuel		
Power	– Daily settlement of power bought from exchange	– Power constitutes 62% of the total power and fuel expense
	– End of month settlement of power sourced from government grids	– Coal and fuel contribute to 24% and 14% respectively
Coal	– 1 week from the date of purchase	– Orders placed in the 1st of the month and deliveries made in the 2nd week of the month
Furnace Oil	– 1 week from the date of purchase	– Orders placed in the 1st of the month and deliveries made in the 2nd week of the month
Marketing		
Agencies for marketing campaigns	– 1 month from the date of consumption	– Media expenses form 40% of total marketing expense
Logistics / Freight	– 1 month from date of incurring the expenditure	– Selling commission is ~50% of total marketing expenditure – Freight is ~10% of total marketing expenditure
All other overheads		
Development expenditure and other overheads	– 1 month from the date of incurring the expenditure	
Others		
All other daily miscellaneous expenses	– Daily settlement	

CASE

15 VENDEX KBB

FIRST HUNDRED DAYS IN CRISIS

SYNOPSIS

The case describes the dilemma that Vendex KBB faces at the end of 2004. A consortium of private equity investors had bought out the Dutch diversified holding company earlier that year. However, Vendex KBB has developed poorly, in particular its flagship business: the V&D department stores has reached a crisis point. The PE team needs to recruit a new CEO to turn the company around. They persuade retail veteran Tony DeNunzio to take the job; with a clear mandate to turn the company around and add value for all stakeholders, not just the PE investor. His mission is tricky: not only is he dealing with an iconic brand in the Netherlands, but he is also up against the reputation PE firms have acquired in recent years—barbarians at the gate and locusts to name but a few. The case ends with Tony about to embark on his first 100 days.

PEDAGOGICAL OBJECTIVE OF THE CASE

The case demonstrates how good leadership in a crisis, together with a clear turnaround plan, can save an ailing company. It underscores the importance of the first 100 days after taking over as CEO. Difficult decisions need to be taken to ensure a viable future for the company, without immediate payoff. Communication with all stakeholders is key. The case can be used to illustrate that turning around a company under private ownership with a strong financial focus is easier than in a publicly listed firm; it also shows that PE takeovers can be less about "milking the cow" and more about adding value for all stakeholders, not just investors.

SUGGESTED ASSIGNMENT QUESTIONS

Students should be asked to develop a 100-day plan and step into Tony DeNunzio's shoes.

1. What is the situation at hand and what went wrong in the prior years?
2. Identify the main stakeholders and how Tony should communicate with them.
3. What should his message be to his employees on his first day in the office?
4. How should he set his priorities?
5. Develop his 100-day plan.

ADDITIONAL RESOURCES

To make the most of this case study, we suggest the following additional sources to provide context and background information:

- In particular, we recommend the following chapters from *Mastering Private Equity—Transformation via Venture Capital, Minority Investments & Buyouts*
  - Chapter 1 Private Equity Essentials
  - Chapter 5 Alternative Strategies
  - Chapter 12 Securing Management Teams
  - Chapter 13 Operational Value Creation
- Case website for faculty and lecturers: http://cases.insead.edu/vendexkbb-maxeda/
- You may also refer to the book website for further material:
  www.masteringprivateequity.com

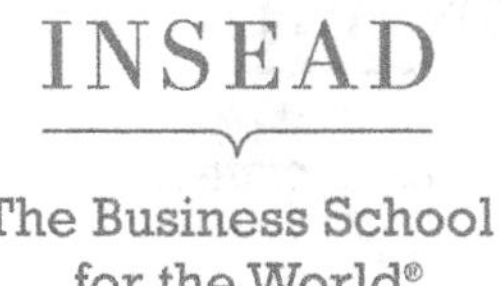

Vendex KBB

First Hundred Days in Crisis

03/2014-5886

This case was written by Joost de Haas, Adjunct Professor of Entrepreneurship and Family Business, and Anne-Marie Carrick-Cagna, Research Associate, both at INSEAD. It is intended to be used as a basis for class discussion rather than to illustrate either effective or ineffective handling of an administrative situation. We also thank the former and current Maxeda management for their time and input into preparing this case study and the accompanying teaching note and films.

We gratefully acknowledge the support of the Entrepreneurship Teaching Innovation Fund, created by alumni Timothy Bovard and Andy Phillipps at INSEAD.

Additional material about INSEAD case studies (e.g., videos, spreadsheets, links) can be accessed at cases.insead.edu.

"In the first place, this isn't true, it is totally untrue. And finally, it doesn't matter to you a bloody thing!"

Anton Dreesmann, CEO of Vendex International

June 1st 2005

It was Tony DeNunzio's first day at the Dutch conglomerate Vendex KBB – a company he knew little about until he was approached to take over as CEO. After some persuasion from the group's private equity owners, Tony finally agreed to take on the challenging role on the understanding that the appointment would be for three years and after the first 18 months he would work part time. After all, he was based in the UK and had no intention of moving to The Netherlands on a permanent basis.

The search for a suitable person to take the helm of the ailing Dutch holding company had been long and difficult. Tony had been head-hunted by a consortium of private equity firms that had acquired the struggling Dutch giant a year before, in June 2004. The company was a mishmash of different businesses under the Vendex KBB umbrella. Although there were clearly some jewels in the Vendex KBB crown, the V&D department store chain in particular was in serious trouble, with reported operating losses of €58 million for fiscal year 2005. The other formats in the group were keeping V&D afloat. More than 14,000 jobs were on the line at V&D alone. EBITDA had dropped, sales were declining, and investors were becoming increasingly nervous as they watched the group's equity value slide.

When private equity firms KKR and AlpInvest had acquired Vendex KBB, they believed that the business had been purchased at the lowest point of the economic cycle from a consumer confidence perspective. However, despite a short uplift around the buy-out date, consumer confidence and spending had declined once more.

Their controversial takeover had generated much negative press for the group. It was the first large public-to-private transaction in the Netherlands and the media was rife with talk of barbarians taking over the country's heritage. V&D, de Bijenkorf and HEMA were after all household names.

Tony was intrigued by what he referred to as the "stamp collection" of businesses. There was obviously potential, with little competition in the Dutch retail sector, yet some of the formats were old fashioned and had clearly been mismanaged. The consortium had reacted swiftly by appointing Ronald van der Mark, an experienced finance expert, as CFO on day one.

The employees had inevitably been wary of the private consortium taking over, with rumours of "cows being milked before exit". Tony had to convince them that what they intended to do was grow the units and thus add value before any part of the company would be sold off. He needed to act quickly: they were expecting change and would be more receptive to it early on.

A Colourful History

Vendex KBB was created following the merger of two Dutch retail companies, Vendex and Koninklijke Bijenkorf Beheer (KBB) in 1999.

Vendex International

The origins of Vendex International dated back to 1887, from the merger of two family businesses – the Dreesmanns who were German immigrants and the Dutch Vroom family. Both ran small drapery shops in Amsterdam. The newly-formed business, Vroom en Dreesmann, many years later would be known simply as V&D. The company was handed down from generation to generation and by 1971 had grown into a chain of department stores throughout the country. They were run independently rather than as one cohesive company.

The arrival of Anton Dreesmann, who took charge in 1971 after his elder brother died in a car accident, hailed a new era. He embarked on what observers saw as a "spending spree" on acquisitions – the company was thriving financially and his vision was to grow it into a large conglomerate. He gave the company an overhaul, introducing standardized operating procedures and expanding into new sectors including food retail, fashion, banking, hardware retail, jewellery, mail-order services and employment services. These acquisitions were financed for the most part by debt.

In the late 1970s, the Dutch government's review of the corporate tax structure saddled large companies such as V&D with significantly higher tax bills. In response, Anton went on another spending spree, this time outside his native country. He acquired companies in the US, Brazil, France, Belgium and Saudi Arabia. Throughout the 1980s, he organised the company's businesses into separate operating divisions managed by one holding company – Vendex International NV as it was known from 1985.[1] The original department stores retained the name V&D and represented just 15% of total turnover. Anton remained at the helm since the Dreesmann family retained the majority of the shares. Revenues and profitability continued to increase until the late 1980s.

But at the end of the decade the company was facing serious financial challenges. By concentrating on international expansion it had failed to adapt to changes in the domestic market. A slowdown in the Dutch economy led to a decline in sales. The heavy debt and high interest rates also contributed to significant losses in certain sectors. In addition, Anton suffered a series of strokes, which left him with no choice but to step down. He named Arie Van der Zwan as his replacement, but the appointment was short-lived. Van der Zwan's decision to take drastic action involving huge lay-offs angered Dreesmann, who fired Van der Zwan from his sick bed. Despite his ill health, he returned to run the company.

Two years later, Jan Michiel Hessels, a former McKinsey consultant, replaced Dreesmann with a mandate from the former chairman to revitalise the company through "divesting unprofitable, non-core businesses; restructuring the retail department store division by concentrating on improved profitability and domestic acquisitions; and reducing corporate debt."[2] Hessels embarked on a disposal programme, resulting in net profit almost doubling over the next five years. In 1995, Vendex International listed on the Amsterdam stock exchange. By this time the V&D department stores represented 40% of the retail sector in the Netherlands.

1. The retail trading division comprised food stores, department stores, specialty fashion, hard goods and home furnishings. The business services division was made up of maintenance services, employment agencies and other miscellaneous services.
2. Source: www.fundinguniverse.com.

Koninklijke Bijenkorf Beheer (KBB)

Koninklijke Bijenkorf Beheer (KBB) was a haberdashery store founded in 1870 by Simon Philip Goudsmit in Amsterdam. Its range of goods gradually grew. After his death in 1889 his widow expanded the business further with the help of a cousin, until her son Arthur Isaac was old enough to take over. A period of expansion followed with the purchase of a number of adjacent buildings and the construction of a new shop in 1909.

In 1926, the founders opened the first Hollandsche Eenheidsprijzen Maatschappij Amsterdam[3] (HEMA) store. Its target was "everyone" and items were sold at set prices of 10, 25 and 50 cents. The shop became synonymous with simplicity and quality. Known as a 'variety store' rather than a department store, it was an instant success. In 1927, the first HEMA shops outside Amsterdam were opened.

From 1958, the pace of new branch openings increased, followed by expansion to other European countries including Belgium, Germany and Luxemburg. HEMA introduced one of the first franchise systems in the Netherlands. Together with the department stores, HEMA remained one the most successful parts of the KBB holding.

After the Second World War, the company grew into a national chain with branches throughout the Netherlands. Variety and department stores remained the group's only activity until the mid-1980s, when it diversified into clothing and DIY retailing. As a result, a conscious effort was made to decentralise operational management. However, by the 1990s, despite further acquisitions, stagnating sales led to outlets closing down and falling profits.

Vendex KBB Is Born

In 1997, Vendex began negotiations with the unlisted KBB for a possible merger between the two Dutch retail giants. The process, however, was complex and faced scrutiny from the Dutch competition authorities as well as KBB's shareholders who claimed Vendex's bid was too low. A hostile battle ensued when a counter offer was made by the unlisted WE International. In response, Vendex increased its offer for KBB in October 1998 and eventually completed the deal in 1999.

The merged company, Vendex KBB, was the largest non-food retail business in the Netherlands, with a diverse portfolio including department stores, electrical goods, fashion, DIY, sports, toys, optical and jewellery (Exhibit 15.1). It held 11% of the Dutch market, with further room for expansion.[4]

The merger was considered beneficial for both parties given the potential for increased purchasing power and cost savings in IT, real estate management and services, among others. The new company boosted its holdings by acquiring further

3. Literally translated as "unique pricing" - meaning uniform pricing that is all articles have the same price or a limited range of prices.

4. If a combined entity has a higher market share than 20%, the Dutch competition authorities may conclude that the merger will lead to a dominant player. However, a company is allowed to grow its market share above 20% organically.

businesses, including an electronics retailer in 2000 and a DIY retailer, Brico, in 2002, in a deal worth US$440.8 million. In an effort to focus on its core business, Vendex KBB sold its troubled FAO Schwarz toy stores in 2002.[5]

The Stamps Don't Stick!

> *"There was a big disconnect between the head office and the formats. The head office didn't know what was going on and was 'flying blind'. Formats with average performance were under the illusion that they were top performers (HEMA) as they were only benchmarking within the group. Head office had lost the business units' respect and, rightly so, weren't being taken seriously."*
>
> Ronald van der Mark, CFO Maxeda

While Vendex KBB appeared to be well positioned to compete in the non-food retailing sector, a host of challenges emerged in the early years of the new millennium. Market conditions were less favourable, with consumer confidence falling to its lowest levels since 1983. Price wars ensued as consumer spending flattened out. This, together with heightened competition from specialist retailers, left Vendex KBB's major department store operations (V&D and de Bijenkorf) struggling to stay profitable. As van der Mark observed:

> *"In my opinion, department stores have one of the most complex and capital-intensive business models in retailing. Furthermore, at that time consumers were moving towards specialist retailers with a better offer and service."*

By 2003, company shareholders demanded action and recommended that management either take Vendex KBB private or split up the company. The share price was structurally low, resulting in an activist shareholder in the US, K Capital, demanding that management address the 'serious devaluation' and sell the company.[6] Vendex KBB was unable to refinance bridge funding and heavy financial losses ensued. There was low cash generation despite the strong brands in the group (Exhibits 15.2 and 15.3).

The two firms had been enemies until the merger, with very different corporate cultures, and in fact they were still competing against each other rather than working together. There was no communication between the units and the synergies that had been envisaged were not pursued. Each part of the holding company worked independently, with no shared information or best practices – it was a collection of dysfunctional fiefdoms.

V&D – Part of Dutch Heritage

> *"At a retail conference in 2004, there was a panel discussion where they discussed if V&D would be closed within or after one year following the buyout – not **if** V&D would be closed. That was considered a given"*
>
> Ronald van der Mark, CFO, Maxeda

5. http://www.referenceforbusiness.com/history2/85/Koninklijke-Vendex-KBB-N-V-Royal-Vendex-KBB-N-V.html.
6. http://www.prnewswire.com/news-releases/k-capital-sends-letter-to-koninklijke-vendex-kbb-nv-holdings-vndx-na-70894892.html or just Google "Vendex KBB K Capital.

A major problem for the Vendex KBB holding was the once-thriving V&D department stores. The flagship business and pride of the Vroom and Dreesmann families was now in serious financial trouble. By 2004 it was losing almost €60 million per year. The offer memorandum for the 2006 PIK stated:

> *"Our V&D business unit has been experiencing significant losses and may continue to be unprofitable. V&D, one of our department store business units, reported an operating loss of €45 million (before restructuring costs of €80 million, offset by a release of provisions of €6 million) in Fiscal 2003. In Fiscal 2003, we designed a comprehensive phased restructuring plan for V&D that has begun to be implemented. In Fiscal 2004, V&D reported an operating loss of €44 million (including a €10 million one-time charge of depreciation costs). In Fiscal 2005, V&D reported an operating loss of €58 million (including an exceptional charge of €8 million related to an inventory revaluation following the implementation of SAP and reorganization charges).*
>
> *The first phase of the restructuring plan has already resulted in annualized cost savings of over €50 million. While a significant portion of the cash outflows relating to the restructuring plan have occurred between Fiscal 2003 and Fiscal 2005, we expect to incur additional cash outflows over the coming years as part of the continuous implementation of the measures under the V&D restructuring plan, and for which provisions have been made. In addition, we cannot assure you that the operating profits of V&D will improve or that we will be successful in re-establishing historic levels of profitability. If the operating profits of V&D fail to improve, our financial condition and results of operations could be materially adversely affected."*

In addition, the chain was consistently listed as the worst place to work, having never shaken off the hierarchal regime that dated back to Dreesmanns' reign. In V&D regional stores, for example, the managing director still had his own bathroom. This mentality was rife throughout the company, with elevators and a dining area reserved exclusively for top management at headquarters.

Some effort had been made to revamp the chain. A famous Dutch designer had been hired to change the physical look of the stores, but this yielded no concrete results. Underinvestment meant that an enormous amount of maintenance was required for the old-fashioned stores.

Poor space allocation, low display density

Unimaginative category lead shop floor merchandising

Out of Stock

Factors that had contributed to V&D's difficulties included a promotion-driven purchasing strategy and outdated supply chain management. These were compounded by the poor product offering, together with incoherent positioning within and among product categories. There had been relatively no new merchandise brought into the stores for years. Ed Hamming had made some progress during his time as V&D's CEO, introducing own-label brands, but the "A" brands were unwilling to set up in V&D as they felt it would have a negative impact given the poor state of stores. Despite attempts to revitalise V&D, they had failed to get to the core of the problem. Rogier Rijnja, former HR Director, explained:

> *"The people who worked at V&D were proud of the company's rich history and labels, but over the years this had translated into conservatism. The many attempts to restructure the stores had led to further scepticism when they failed. Therefore any new attempts would lead to a negative reaction."*

La Place

"By 2004, V&D was a great food business with a jumble sale attached. The non-food part of the store was an area that people were forced to walk through to get to the popular La Place restaurant."

Cheryl Potter, investor, Permira

V&D's most recent "redeemer" was its in-house restaurant *La Place.* Thanks to its high-quality food made with fresh ingredients, these made a good profit, managed to keep footfall high and thus "saved" V&D. They were modern, elegant restaurants with simple, fresh food that was healthy, and bread baked on the premises. La Place first opened in September 1987, and by 2004 was the second largest food outlet in the Netherlands after McDonald's.

Other Formats in the Vendex KBB Portfolio

In spite of its problems, in 2004 Vendex KBB was still the leading non-food retailer in the Netherlands. It was active in six other countries: Belgium, Luxemburg, Denmark, Germany, France and Spain. For the year 2003/04, the holding generated net turnover of approximately €4.5 billion, with over 43,000 employees and almost 1,800 stores. The group's retail chains had been divided into six business units according to the markets in which they were active. The HEMA, V&D and de Bijenkorf formats were all independent business units responsible for their own reporting and results. The remaining formats were part of the DIY, fashion consumer and electronics business units (Exhibits 15.4a and b).

Time to sell

"Vendex defined non-food retail in the Netherlands at the time."

Todd Fisher, KKR

Ed Hamming, CEO of Vendex KBB, recognised the severity of the situation, claiming in a September 2003 *Financial Times* article: "If we do not quickly put our house in order our credibility will suffer." Rumours began to circulate about a possible takeover of Vendex KBB as earnings continued to falter by the end of 2003, forcing Vendex KBB to sell formats to generate cash. In 2002, it sold six in one transaction to CVC: Hans Anders, Perry Sport, Prenatal, Kijkshop, Siebel and Scapino.

In 2003, Marcel Smits, Vendex KBB's CFO at the time, launched a limited auction. The company had already been on the private equity firm KKR's radar for some time, as Todd Fisher, KKR investor, explained:

> *"I met Marcel in Amsterdam in September 2001, having first cold-called him. Vendex KBB had been on our radar screen as a potential company to acquire – it was listed and traded cheaply. Marcel was ready for change and a dialogue was opened between us – although nothing was official at that stage."*

Todd and a team from KKR researched the company in more detail over the next two years using public sources and visiting the stores in the Netherlands to get a clear understanding of how they operated.

> *"I also wanted to figure out if V&D really was the poisoned pill that everyone claimed it to be. I finally met with Ed Hamming, the CEO, in 2002 and formally approached Vendex KBB with regards to an acquisition. It wasn't, however, the right time."*

But that wasn't the end of the story. Towards the end of 2003, Floris Maljers took over as chairman, which meant that the situation had changed (Exhibit 15.5), as Todd Fisher acknowledged:

> *"He was a businessman with vast experience. Maljers recognised the potential in a deal and was more willing to take risks. At KKR we saw this as an opportune moment – I took Henry Kravis with me to meet him and we subsequently made an offer."*

As Vendex KBB was a listed company, Smits opened up the bidding to two other firms but KKR was well positioned as they were already one step ahead of the other bidders. KKR won the bid in what was at the time the second largest retail buyout in Europe. The price paid for the shares was €1,376 million, with an enterprise value of €2,517 million (Exhibit 15.6). For KKR it was the largest cheque they had signed since the Nabisco deal in 1989.[7] However, as one equity partner (Change Capital) pulled out at the last minute, KKR together with the other partner, AlpInvest, syndicated part of the equity to Cinven and Permira on 5th August 2004 (Exhibits 15.7 and 15.8). For KKR it was a classic transaction, as Todd explained:

1. *Good fundamental "bones"* – Vendex KBB had the potential to be world class. The store locations were good with well-known and unique brands (Exhibit 15.9).
2. *Benign market conditions* – competition in the Netherlands was far less stiff than in the UK or US. If V&D had operated in the UK, Todd was adamant it wouldn't have survived. However, in the Netherlands it was still a strong brand and KKR believed they could make a difference to the company's operations.
3. *Right time in the economic cycle* – the economy seemed to be improving after a couple of years of strong decline. (Exhibit 15.10)

---

7. The most famous transaction engineered by KKR was the purchase of RJR Nabisco Inc. for $30.6bn in 1989 that held the record for the largest LBO until 2006. The deal was also the subject of the well-known book *Barbarians at the Gate*.

4. *Fundamentally under-managed* – a great opportunity for operational improvements.
5. *V&D could thrive if properly managed* – this went against the market's belief that the chain was a black hole – "Observers believed we had made an error with V&D."

The First 100 Days

The private equity consortium took over officially on 5th July 2004, the same day Ronald van der Mark took over as CFO. Smits decided to resign once the buyout went through, as Todd Fisher explained:

> *"When Marcel Smits announced he was resigning, I was shocked as we had a good relationship. It also meant that we were under pressure to get a good CFO* ***and*** *CEO. We were lucky to get Ronald van der Mark. Erik Thyssen, one of the other investors, knew him and introduced him to me. He was the ideal person."*

From the beginning, the consortium made it clear they were going to restructure, bringing value to the units but with the intention of eventually selling them. Despite their reassurances, there was still fear among the units that they would destroy the businesses, according to Rogier Rijnja, former director of HR: "What they didn't realise is they would grow them, thus adding value before any unit would be sold." A Permira investor, Cheryl Potter, commented: "The group was run as a portfolio and not actively managed. There was no rationale for combining different formats; a break-up was evident."

A 'capstone team' (part of KKR's internal operations group) went into the company and began work immediately, with all the managers discussing what they could do to drive value. The private equity consortium gave a presentation to the top 25 managers outlining the governance model, strategy and vision for the future, as Fisher explained:

> *"We wanted to take advantage immediately to start change as soon as we came on board, as people expect change and are open to it."*

Changing Management

> *"The top priority for us as the new owners was to get a new leader in place. There were few candidates in the Netherlands, so we opened the search to the UK."*
>
> Erik Thyssen, AlpInvest

At the time of the buyout, Vendex KBB was led by Ed Hamming, former head of the V&D chain. Although Hamming was named an 'outperformer' in 2003 as he beat the performance of the small cap market index, he was voted 'worst CEO of the year' in 2004 by MKB Nederland, a Dutch organisation representing smaller and mid-sized companies. There were clearly issues with regards to top management. After the buy-out, an assessment by Egon Zehnder of the top 50 managers reinforced this belief – the results were poor and there were few outperformers among the team.

The first board meeting confirmed the consortium's suspicions. It lasted from 8.30 in the morning to midnight and carried on the next day, due to all the units having different reporting systems. Ronald van der Mark made the following diagnosis:

"I arrived on day one to find a head office that wasn't adding value to the formats and that weren't working together... in the early days winning employees over was the biggest challenge. They had experienced so many failed strategies over the previous years that they were just waiting for the next failure. The lack of controls in place meant it was also hard to establish the true financial position of the company. Before we could realistically start any reforms, we had to gain control by introducing accurate, usable reporting, improved controls over working capital, and clear key performance indicators (KPIs)."[8]

Within a few months, Van der Mark had aligned all the reporting systems, making board meetings less long and painful. However, there was still the issue of finding a suitable CEO who could drive the change needed in the company. It was clear that Ed Hamming was not the person for the job.

Change – Tony DeNunzio

After considerable searching, the consortium approached Tony DeNunzio. With his vast experience in the retail world, he was perfect for the task (Exhibit 15.11). However, Tony needed some persuading. He finally agreed on condition that he would be CEO for three years and go part time after 18 months. Cheryl Potter admitted:

"This wasn't ideal for us but we were convinced he was the only person with the calibre to sort out the business. We needed someone who had run large businesses with different types of goods."

Day 1

Tony began on 1 June 2005. He knew it would be a challenge given all the different stakeholders to deal with. Works councils in the Netherlands were relatively powerful and would need to be handled in a transparent way. Having looked into the company before accepting the job, he had found strong brands and good market positions despite the economy and declining sales. The company seemed to have suffered from a poor vision and strategic direction. This had ultimately led to a lack of pride among the workforce and no teamwork, so synergies were nonexistent. As Tony saw it, there was a huge potential for improvement. He now had to decide what to do on day one and during his first 100 days.

8. Maxeda Mag – the Story 2004-2011.

Exhibit 15.1

Complete List of Formats at the Time Vendex KBB Was Created – 2000

Name	Activity
V&D	Middle market offer with wide range for women aged 30 to 60 and their families. Is the largest department store in the NL.
De Bijenkorf	De Bijenkorf has 12 department stores in the Netherlands, with flagship stores in Amsterdam, Rotterdam and The Hague.
HEMA	Unique format with an outstanding brand. Clearly a Dutch institute. Wide range of everyday products (apparel, hard goods and food) sold almost exclusively under own brand at attractive prices.
Dixons	PC, phones and portable electronics.
Dixtone	Phone and communications shops.
Dynabyte	PC, phones and portable electronics.
It's	Domestic appliances, audio, video, TV and computers.
Van Boxtel	20 shops which sell hearing equipment.
Modern Electronics	Domestic appliances, audio, video, TV and computers.
Kijkshop	Showcase stores which offer a wide range of everyday products.
Hans Anders	Opticians and hearing aid specialist in the Netherlands.
Het Huis Opticiens	A national optician chain with 110 stores throughout the Netherlands.
Perry	Has the largest collection of premium brands in sportswear.
Scapino	With over 200 stores, it is the largest supplier of shoes, fashion, sports and leisure goods.
Siebel Juweliers	Wide collection of watches, jewellery and wedding/relationship rings. From classic to modern and gold jewellery with diamonds to trendy silver jewellery combined with the latest fashion colours.
Schaap en Citroen	In 2010 is still one of the most famous jewellers in the country and represents as no other contemporary fashion jewellery, watches and luxury accessories.
Lucardi Juweliers	A national chain with 91 branches and is part of KIN Netherlands BV.
Juwel Exchange	Shop in Rotterdam where customers can sell their own jewellery.
Het Huis Juweliers	Franchise for jewellers outside big cities; 8 stores.
M&S Mode	International chain providing women over 35 with casual fashion in relaxed, classic and stylish looks. The size range (38 to 54) is offered at the same price.
Hunkemöller	Hunkemöller, established in 1886, is a Dutch brand. One of the largest lingerie specialists in Europe and a market leader in the Benelux countries.

Exhibit 15.1 (Continued)

Name	Activity
Prenetal	Prenatal is the largest Dutch chain of baby stores. Besides clothes for expectant mothers, babies and toddlers, has an assortment of items used during pregnancy and in the first year thereafter.
Claudia Strater	High-end format and casual apparel.
America Today	Targets those young peole who are aware of popular brands and contemporary fashion.
Praxis	DIY extensive range of home improvement products and garden centres. Number 2 in NL.
Formido	DIY franchise organisation – extensive range of home improvement products and garden centres.
FAO Schwartz	For nearly 150 years, it has enchanted children and adults alike with its unequalled collection of toys and other fine children's products.

Source: company data

Exhibit 15.2
Share Price

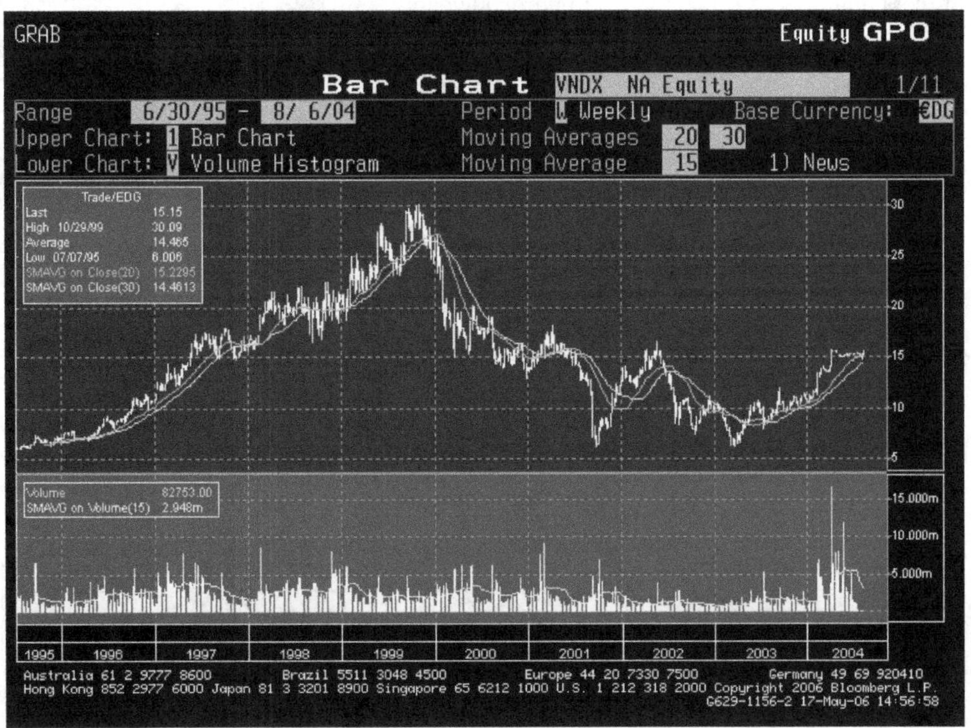

Exhibit 15.3
Formats

1995	2000	End of 2006
Total 33	**Total 27**	**Total 10**
V&D	V&D	V&D
Edah	de Bijenkorf	de Bijenkorf
Konmar	HEMA	HEMA
Basismarkt	Dixons	Praxis
Dagmarkt	Dixtone	Formido
Battard	Dynabyte	Brico
Echo	It's	Claudia Sträter
Eda	Van Boxtel	Hunkermöller
Pet's Place	Modern Electronics	M&S Mode
America Today	Kijkshop	Schaap en Citroen
Claudia Sträter	Hans Anders	
Hunkermöller	Het Huis Opticiens	
Kien	Perry	
Kreymborg	Scapino	
Perry Sport	Siebel Juweliers	
Schaap en Citroen	Schaap en Citroen	
Luigi Lucardi	Lucardi Juweliers	
Siebel	Het Huis Juweliers	
Royal Gold	Juwel Exchange	
Rovato	M&S Mode	
Kijkshop	Hunkermöller	
Best-sellers	Prénatal	
Dixons	Claudia Sträter	
Electro-Jacobs	America Today	
Guco	Praxis	
Heijmans	Formido	
Valkenberg	FAO Schwarz	
Klick		
Vedior		
Abilis		
Bakker Continental		
Markgraaf		
F.A.A.		

Source: Maxeda

Exhibita 15.4a

Consolidated Financial Statements

Please note these are available on a separate Excel spreadsheet, please see https://cases.insead.edu/vendexkbb-maxeda/

Exhibit 15.4b

Vendex KBB: Divisional Breakdown of Sales and EBITA
(in millions € unless otherwise stated)

	2002/03A	2003/04A
Sales		
HEMA	911	918
V&D	855	812
Bijenkorf	389	398
Department stores	2,155	2,129
DIY	1,063	1,220
Fashion	456	457
Consumer Electronics	815	803
Speciality stores	2,134	2,280
Other act/holding	38	42
Discontinued	350	0
Total	4,887	4,451
EBIT(A)		
HEMA	37	39
V&D	–11	–39
Bijenkorf	2	2
Department stores	28	2
DIY	78	82
Fashion	46	35
Consumer Electronics	25	17
Speciality stores	149	134
Other act/holding	–31	–19
Discontinued	162	–3
Results on internal rent	40	36
Total	348	150
Goodwill amortisation	7	14
Result on disposal of property	11	5
Exceptionals	–48	–80
EBIT	304	xx
Retail EBITA – margin		
HEMA	4.1%	4.2%
V&D	–1.3%	–4.8%
Bijenkorf	0.5%	0.5%
Department stores	1.3%	0.1%
DIY	7.3%	6.7%
Fashion	10.1%	7.7%
Consumer Electronics	4.1%	2.8%
Speciality stores	7.0%	5.9%

Source: company data – Credit Suisse, First Boston

Exhibit 15.5
Profile of Floris Maljers

Mr Floris A. Maljers, KBE served as President, Chief Executive Officer and Chairman of the Board of Management of Unilever N.V. Mr Maljers serves as Chairman of Roompot and Recreatie Group. Mr Maljers serves as Chairman of the supervisory board of Amsterdam Concertgebouw N.V. He serves as Chairman of the supervisory board of the Rotterdam School of Management, Erasmus University. He served as Chairman of Supervisory Board of Royal Vendex KBB N.V. since 2003. Mr Maljers served as Chairman of KLM Royal Dutch Airlines since 2000. He served as Chairman of Supervisory Board at Maxeda B.V. since 2003. He serves as a Director of Koninklijke Vendex KBB. He serves as Director of Rand Europe. He serves as a Member of the supervisory board of Vendex N.V. He served as a Non-Executive Director of BP PLC since December 1998. He served as a Director of Air France, a subsidiary of Air France-KLM since 2004. Mr Maljers served as a Director of Amoco Corporation since 1994. He served as a Member of Supervisory Board of Royal Vendex KBB N.V. since 1997 and Koninklijke Philips Electronics NV. Mr Maljers served as a Member of the Supervisory Board of KLM Royal Dutch Airlines since 1999 and Member of the Supervisory Board of SHV Holdings NV until May 25, 2005. He served as an Independent Director of Air France-KLM since June 24, 2004. He served as Member of Supervisory Board of Maxeda B.V. He serves as a Member of the Preferred Stock Committee of DSM. Mr Maljers holds M.A. in Economics, from Universiteit van Amsterdam.

Exhibit 15.6

External Valuations Vendex KBB

	DIY	HEMA	Apparel	Bijenkorf	V&D	Consumer Electronics	Corporate	Total	Real Estate[2]	Vendex Group
Firm Value (€ millions)										
SNS Securities	802	401	417	131	0	153	(142)	**1,762**	629	**2,391**
CSFB	616	295	279	107	(88)	145	(77)	**1,277**	693	**1,970**
Deutsche Bank	779	418	642	128	73	230	(160)	**2,110**	620	**2,730**
Fortis	754	396	450	204	176	137	0	**2,117**	770	**2,887**
Petercam	824	513	656	109	0	165	(180)	**2,087**	615	**2,702**
Rabo Bank[1]	690	482	414	190	342	97	35	**2,250**	0	**2,250**
Average	**755**	**405**	**489**	**136**	**32**	**166**	**(112)**	**1,871**	**665**	**2,536**
Firm Value/EBITDA FY04										
SNS Securities	7.6x	6.1x	7.7x	7.1x	–	6.6x	–	**6.4x**	–	**7.1x**
CSFB	5.9	4.5	5.2	5.8	–	6.3	–	**4.6**	–	**5.8**
Deutsche Bank	7.4	6.3	11.9	6.9	3.5	10.0	–	**7.6**	–	**8.1**
Fortis	7.2	6.0	8.3	11.0	8.5	5.9	–	**7.6**	–	**8.5**
Petercam	7.8	7.8	12.1	5.9	–	7.1	–	**7.5**	–	**8.0**
Rabo Bank	6.6	7.3	7.7	10.3	16.4	4.2	–	**8.1**	–	**6.6**
Average	**7.2x**	**6.1x**	**9.1x**	**7.3x**	**1.5x**	**7.2x**	–	**6.8x**	–	**7.5x**

Note: Multiples based on FY04 EBITDA of €277 million

(1) Rabo Bank valuations for Real Estate are embedded in the valuations of HEMA, Bijenkorf, and V&D and hence have been excluded from calculations of averages

(2) Cushman & Wakefield have valued the real estate assets at € 803m

Exhibit 15.7
The Deal Structure

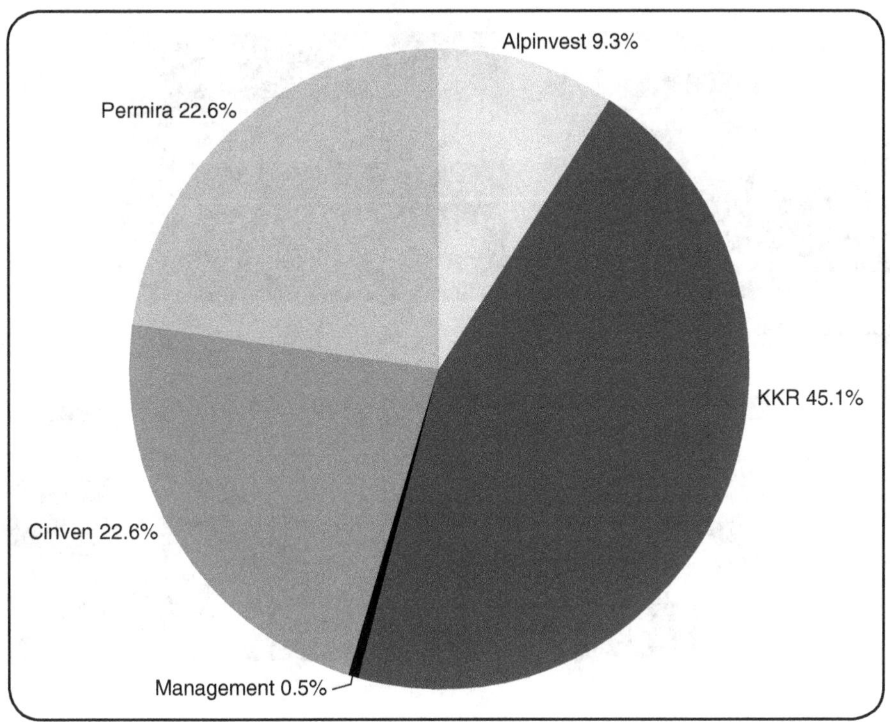

	In €Min
Equity	970
Debt	945
Mortgage Loan	600
Total	2515

Exhibit 15.8
The Investors

KKR – founded in 1976 and led by Henry Kravis and George Roberts, KKR is a leading global alternative asset manager with approximately €60 billion in assets under management for 2011.

Cinven – European firm founded in 1977. Since then it has completed transactions valued in excess of €60 billion. Cinven focuses on European-based companies that require an equity investment of €100 million or more.

Permira Funds – have made over 190 private equity investments since 1985 and have returned €16 billion to their investors over the past decade.

AlpInvest – founded in 1999. With over €32.3 billion of assets under management, it is one of the world's leading private equity investment managers. In January 2011, the Carlyle Group, together with the management of AlpInvest, bought the company from APG and PGGM, two major Dutch pension funds.

Source: Maxeda Mag, The Story 2004–2011

Exhibit 15.9

Formats June 2004

Claudia Sträter

V&D

De Bijenkorf

HEMA

M&S Mode

Hunkemöller

La Place

Brico

Formido

Praxis

Plan-It

Schaap en Citroen

Dynabyte

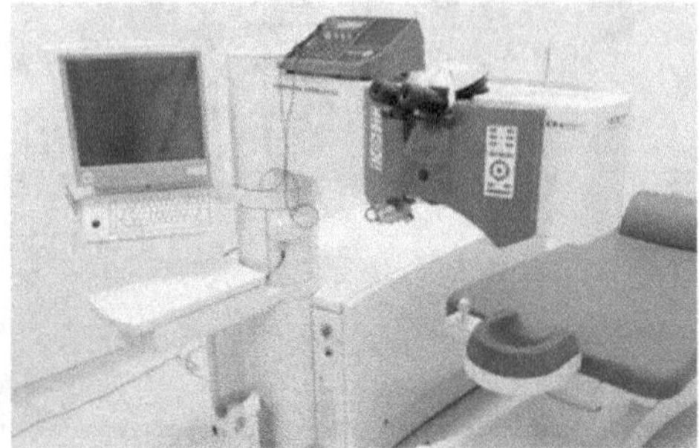

Vision Clinics

Dixons

Exhibit 15.10
Consumer Confidence

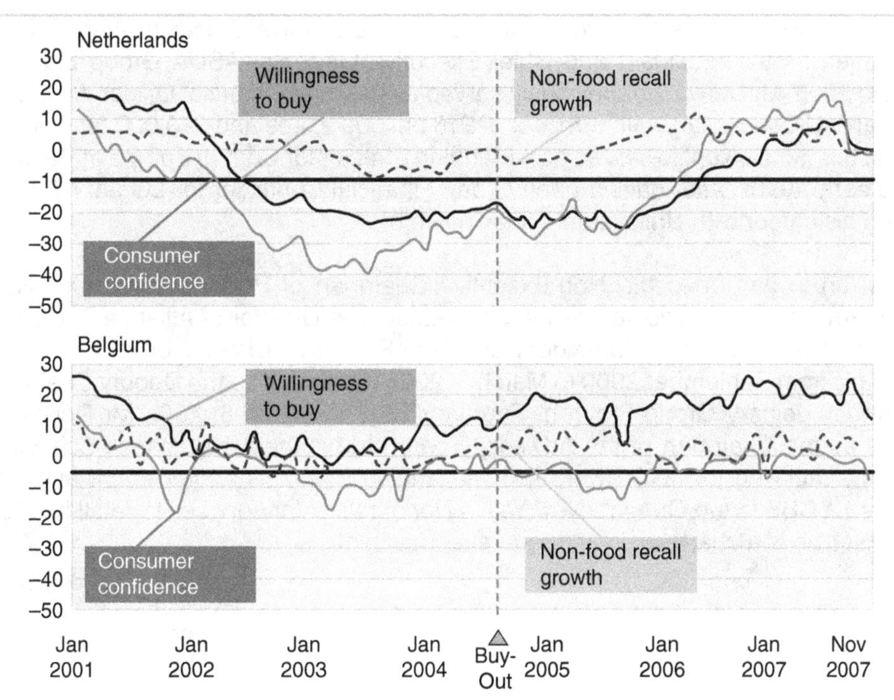

Source: Eurostat

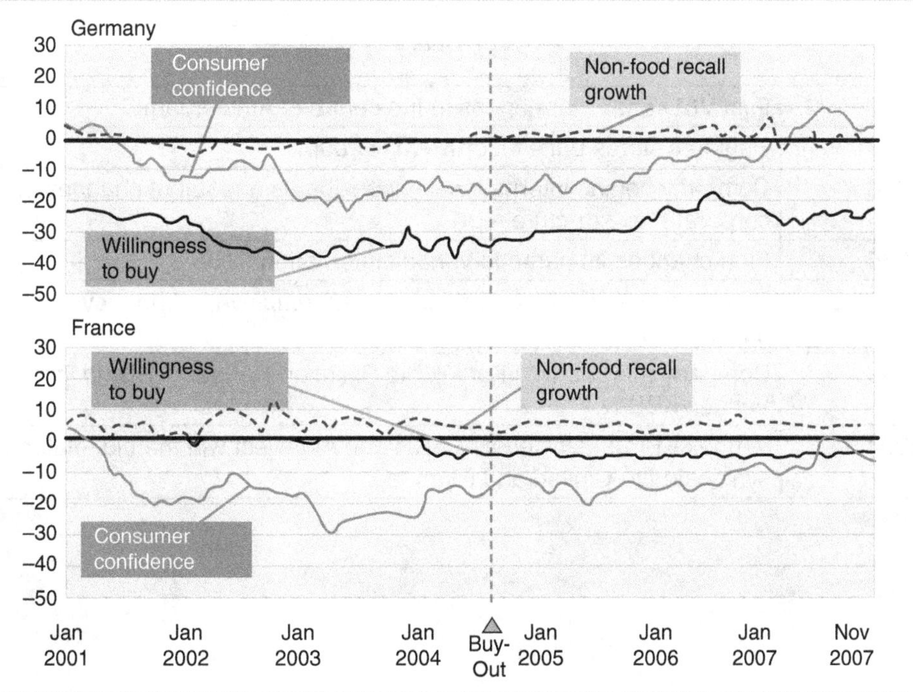

Source: Eurostat

Exhibit 15.11

Profile of Tony DeNunzio

Mr Tony DeNunzio was the President and Chief Executive Officer of Asda Stores. He served as the President and Chief Executive Officer of ASDA Group Ltd from 2002 to 2005. Mr DeNunzio previously served as its Chief Financial Officer. Asda was Walmart's UK subsidiary with turnover of £15 bn, 300 stores and 120,000 employees. Prior to this, Mr DeNunzio served as a Planning Director for Central Europe at PepsiCo in the early 1990s, after having been Group Financial Controller for L'Oreal (UK). He started his career with Unilever in a financial role.

Mr DeNunzio has been the Non-Executive Chairman of Pets at Home Ltd. since March 2010. Mr DeNunzio serves as a Non-Executive Director of Alliance Boots Ltd. He served as a Senior Independent and Non-Executive Director of MFI Furniture Group plc from September 2000 to March 6, 2007. He served as the Deputy Chairman of Howden Joinery Group Plc from February 2005 to March 6, 2007. Mr DeNunzio serves as the Chairman of the Advisory Board of Manchester Business School. In 2004, he received the IGD award for Outstanding Business Achievement and was awarded a CBE in the Queen's New Year's Honours List for services to retail in 2005. Mr DeNunzio is a chartered management accountant.

Annex

Key Dates

1887	First V&D retail store opens in the centre of Amsterdam
1973	Regional stores unite to form V&D Group
1978	Company begins international expansion as a result of changes in corporate tax structure
1985	Firm changes its name to Vendex International NV
1998	Vendex spins off its food and temporary employment agency businesses
1999	Company merges with Koninklijke Bijenkorf Beheer (KBB) to form Vendex KBB N.V.
2004	Vendex KBB is delisted and KKR and AlpInvest win the bid – later syndicated to Cinven and Permira

CASE

16 TURNING AN ELEPHANT INTO A CHEETAH
THE TURNAROUND OF INDIAN RAILWAYS

SYNOPSIS

The case describes the transformation of Indian Railways (IR), the world's largest employer with over 1.4 million employees, from near-bankruptcy to a profitable and viable business. We follow Sudhir Kumar, Officer on Special Duty to the Minister of Railways, as he deals with the various constituencies and stakeholders in the quest for a successful and sustainable turnaround of this government-run institution, often referred to as the "lifeline of the nation."

Despite growing domestic demand for transportation, IR is losing market share in the freight sector, which together with a mismatched pricing system oriented towards political rather than economic goals, is dragging IR towards bankruptcy. While various policy recommendations have been made over the years, virtually none of the proposed reforms had been put into practice until Lalu Yadav Prasad took over as Union Minister of Railways in 2004. Given his ambitions to run for office again in 2009, he is determined to be the hero who turns IR around. He selects Sudhir Kumar, who has a strong background in public sector management, to help him achieve this task.

PEDAGOGICAL OBJECTIVE OF THE CASE

The case highlights the importance of managing the various stakeholders in a turnaround process, in particular in organizations with a wide power distribution. To deliver the desired results in a highly political environment, a smart negotiation strategy is needed, combined with a clear and consistent communication strategy.

SUGGESTED ASSIGNMENT QUESTIONS

1. Why was the typical top-down solution proposed by the international group of experts not a viable option within IR? What was amiss?
2. List the stakeholders involved in this case and explain their motivation.
3. To what extent was it vital that Sudhir Kumar was from India and familiar with the company's history and the local customs?
4. Negotiate with your assigned partner the planned changes to the axle load.

ADDITIONAL RESOURCES

To make the most of this case study, we suggest the following additional sources to provide context and background information:

- In particular, we recommend the following chapters from *Mastering Private Equity—Transformation via Venture Capital, Minority Investments & Buyouts*
  - Chapter 1 Private Equity Essentials
  - Chapter 5 Alternative Strategies
  - Chapter 13 Operational Value Creation
- You may also refer to the book website for further material:
  www.masteringprivateequity.com

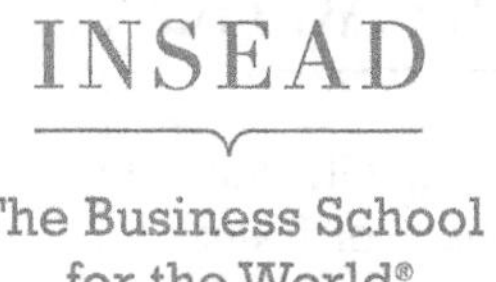

Turning an Elephant into a Cheetah[1]

The Turnaround of Indian Railways

09/2009-5623

This case was written by Claudia Gehlen, Research Associate, under the direction of Claudia Zeisberger and Horacio Falcao, Affiliate Professors of Decision Sciences at INSEAD. It is intended to be used as a basis for class discussion rather than to illustrate either effective or ineffective handling of an administrative situation.

The authors gratefully acknowledge the assistance of Sudhir Kumar, Officer on Special Duty to the Minister of Railways.

1. Presenting the interim railway budget to Parliament on 13 February 2009, the Minister of Railways, Lalu Prasad, stated: "Hathi ko cheetah bana diya" ("I have turned an elephant into a cheetah").

In his spartan room facing the Minister's office, Sudhir Kumar was diligently studying endless lists of statistics on passengers, freight and on-time arrivals of trains. As Officer on Special Duty to the Minister of Railways, Kumar had recently been assigned to the task of turning the ailing giant around. The newly appointed Minister of Railways, Lalu Prasad, had decided to bring in Kumar, after he had done a tremendous job for Lalu in the state of Bihar as sales tax commissioner. However, his previous successful assignment had hardly prepared him for this daunting task, nor did he specifically want the portfolio.

A complete newcomer to the world of railways, Kumar was quite overwhelmed by the complexity of this 150-year-old institution and the numerous challenges it was facing. His mission was to save one of the world's largest state-owned enterprises by staging a dramatic turnaround. After all, the Indian Railways' fate and performance were intrinsically linked to the national economy. While he could sense that resistance to change permeated all management levels, he was determined to trigger a fundamental shift in mindset. More importantly, however, he had to walk a tightrope in order to balance conflicting commercial and social objectives, as well as to reconcile vested interests with the overarching goal.

Indian Railways

As the lifeline of the nation, Indian Railways (IR) had always been a source of national pride among Indians, even during British colonial rule. Throughout its history, the railway system had spurred India's national and regional development, linking remote areas to major hubs and acting as a unifying force. In 1853, the first train service was formally inaugurated and much of the initial railroad construction was led by private firms, such as the East India Company. After India's independence in 1947, 42 railroad companies and their separate rail systems were consolidated into a state-owned enterprise. This gave rise to one of the world's largest railway networks covering over 63,000 kilometres (See Exhibit 16.1).

The railways transported not only commuters and tourists but also migrant labourers in search of work and pilgrims travelling to various sanctuaries. Passenger trains were the only affordable means of transport for the majority of Indian travellers (See Exhibit 16.2). Freight trains carried vital commodities, such as coal, steel, cement, grain and fertilizer to factories, shops and farmers. Every day, IR operated some 13,000 trains ferrying about 17 million passengers and 2 million tonnes of cargo between 7,000 railway stations. At election times, it moved voting machines, politicians, officials, guards and voters, playing a pivotal role in preserving the world's largest democracy. IR was India's largest employer with 1.4 million employees and 1.1 million pensioners. It provided indirect employment to over 7 million people.

Given its vital role in the nation's economy, Indian Railways operated as a government department. The Ministry of Railways was headed by the Union Minister for Railways, assisted by two Ministers of State for Railways. It was administered by the Railway Board comprising a chairman and six members heading functional departments (See Exhibit 16.3). The Chairman of the Board reported to the Minister of Railways and the board oversaw a number of directorates and geographical zones led by general managers. After rising through the ranks of the institution, board members generally occupied their posts for a year or two before they retired. They brought sound experience and deep insight to the highest level of decision making.

With a fleet of 200,000 wagons, 40,000 coaches and 8,000 locomotives, Indian Railways plied long-distance routes and operated suburban networks in major cities. Under a single umbrella organisation, it financed, built, owned and managed most of its assets. Due to import substitution of technology-related products, IR manufactured the bulk of its rolling stock and heavy engineering components through its wholly-owned subsidiaries. Workshops provided regular maintenance, upgrading and renewal for bridges dating from the colonial era and century-old tracks. Indian Railways also owned considerable stretches of land, as well as hotels, schools, hospitals and staff housing.

While the number of rail accidents continued to fall, Indian Railways considered an accident-free record as unrealistic, given the size of its operations. It strove to minimise the rate and frequency of accidents primarily caused by human error due to outdated communication, safety and signalling equipment. During the period 2001-2004, train collisions, derailments, fires and level-crossing accidents caused 1,038 fatalities and 2,282 people were injured (See Exhibit 16.4). Regularly affected by natural disasters, such as floods, cyclones and landslides, IR's easily accessible and unguarded assets were also the target of vandalism, terrorist attacks and bomb blasts.

Railways in India have traditionally been a favourite outlet for protesters, who resort to burning down stations, pulling up tracks and paralysing services as a way of attracting attention. Kumar explained: "The railways are a soft target and it gets you immediate publicity." These acts of sabotage, which from 2001 to 2004 caused 42 train accidents, not only took a heavy toll on railway property but frequently resulted in the cancellation of trains and huge losses of revenue. For example, when the Gujjar tribe clashed with police in the state of Rajasthan, services were disrupted for 17 days with more than 1,000 trains diverted, cancelled or short-terminated. Since passenger and freight trains generally shared the same tracks and infrastructure, freight services were severely disrupted. In the light of this, Kumar wanted to push ahead with plans to build dedicated freight corridors that would prevent the entire system from being paralysed.

The Looming Crisis in 2001

Following the boom in road transport in the early 1980s, Indian Railways was steadily losing market share in the freight sector. In the 1990s, the liberalisation of the Indian economy and higher GDP growth accelerated demand for transport. In response to changing market requirements, IR struggled to boost its carrying capacity and to modernise its assets, unable to keep pace with the country's growth rate (See Exhibit 16.5). Its traffic share continued to decline as it faced increased competition from road in the freight segment and from airlines, luxury buses and personal vehicles in the passenger segment.

Passenger trains represented about 70% of train runs but accounted for less than 35% of total revenue, while freight trains made up 30% of all trains, contributing 65% to the overall revenue (See Exhibit 16.6). The implicit political directive of maintaining affordable second-class passenger fares led IR to offset rising operational costs by increasing freight rates. This policy led to the cross-subsidising of second-class travel and transport of essential commodities by overcharging freight and premium class passengers (See Exhibits 16.7a and b). As a result, premium customers increasingly switched to budget airlines and market share in the freight segment continued to decline.

While freight volume grew slowly during the 1990s, staff and fuel costs increased faster than labour productivity as a direct result of inflation (See Exhibit 16.8). Central government was not in a position to provide additional budgetary support to the Ministry of Railways. To make matters worse, the scarce resources available tended to be used to serve the political ambitions of respective railway ministers, and were often invested in unviable projects such as uneconomic lines. Consequently, not only did IR failed to adequately finance the replacement of its ageing assets, but the growing backlog of track renewals represented a real safety hazard.

By 2001, the organisation had defaulted on dividend payments to the government of India and was clearly heading towards bankruptcy (See Exhibit 16.9). The operating ratio had deteriorated to 98% and the cash balance had shrunk to the bare minimum. By 2002, IR had 73 pensioners for every 100 employees, and staff salaries and pensions represented over 40% of overall costs (See Exhibit 16.10). In comparison, staff costs at China Railways, which had shed non-core businesses, accounted for about 15%. Despite making improvements in the following years, IR's financial condition remained precarious and traffic growth continued to trail GDP growth.

Recommendations of the Expert Group

Indian Railways displayed all the shortcomings of a large bureaucracy – operational inefficiency, lack of customer focus and accountability, low employee productivity and a burden of social obligations. In 1999, a group of experts consisting of highly experienced policymakers and private sector experts was convened to halt the decline in performance. The Expert Committee was chaired by Dr. Rakesh Mohan, who had served as Economic Adviser to the government of India and as director of several banks. Attributing IR's woes to the inherent dilemma of having to reconcile political and commercial objectives, the Committee drew up a drastic reform package (See Exhibit 16.11).

The main recommendations of the reform package focused on a 25% reduction of IR's 1.5 million workforce over five years and an annual increase in second-class fares by 8% to 10% over five years, with the explicit aim of eliminating hidden subsidies. In addition, IR would be corporatised and non-core services, such as health care, education, production and maintenance of trains would be divested. Social and commercial obligations would be separated, involving the unions early on with a view to avoiding acrimony. Calling for a separate regulator, the report also suggested turning top management into an Executive Board that would relinquish its conflicting responsibilities as manager, policymaker and regulator.

Freight and passenger growth rates were to be boosted by adding rolling stock and introducing information technology. New technology was crucial to reducing the gap of nearly 20 years of neglect. Government financing would be high in the initial seven years and returns would be guaranteed after 15 years. The outcome would be the complete modernisation of the system and a quantum leap in speed and quality of service.

The report triggered vehement reactions. Labour unions staged demonstrations, staff morale dipped and there was a general unease about the reform of top management.

In response to the recommendations, the board issued a paper including proposals to privatise non-core activities, to reduce staff size through natural attrition, to rationalise fares and to consider loans from various sources. It stopped short of suggesting the unbundling of the monolithic management structure. However, little progress was made in implementing the reforms until Lalu Prasad took over as Union Minister of Railways in 2004.

Lalu Prasad

Born into a poor family, Lalu hailed from the lowly Yadav caste. His home state of Bihar stood out as India's most impoverished and lawless state. Lalu began work as a cowherd before becoming politically active as a student at Patna University and embarking on a 40-year career in politics. Throughout his rise to power he maintained his image as a villager, which gave him great political influence vis-à-vis the masses. From 1980 to 1989, he served as a member of the Bihar Legislative Assembly and as Chief Minister of Bihar from 1990 to 1997.

Despite his humble origins, he failed to improve his people's plight. Rather, he became notorious for dubious practices and embroiled in a major corruption scandal. After the corruption allegations forced him to resign, Lalu single-handedly appointed his wife as his successor. Indeed, politicians were repeatedly cited in high-profile criminal cases:

> *"Indians are used to news about politicians being involved in crime – a recent study suggests that nearly a quarter of the country's MPs are facing criminal charges ranging from murder to extortion and even rape."*[2]

His unpopular rule in Bihar led to Lalu's image being tarnished at the time of his nomination as Minister of Railways. A populist and colourful leader, Lalu sternly opposed most of the Expert Group's recommendations. In his announcements, he unequivocally stated his priorities, promising to reduce passenger fares across all classes and to generate employment for the poor. Instead of privatising the organisation, he planned to build three new production units to manufacture engines, wheels and coaches in his constituency of Bihar. His mantra "reforms with a human face" met with public disbelief and contempt in the media.

As Minister of Railways he liked to refer to his modest background and to challenge his staff with his rustic imagery. He would ask his managers why a cowherd like him could produce a profitable herd of 500 from a few cows, while Indian Railways, with its impressive rolling stock, was running at a loss. His answer would invariably be: "If you do not milk the cow fully, it falls sick." Lalu wanted to prove his detractors wrong by bringing the railways back on track. His ambitions were clear, as he planned to run again in the 2009 Bihar elections and Indian Railways was an ideal constituency-building portfolio. However, one of his smartest moves was to nominate Sudhir Kumar as his advisor.

2. "Watershed year for Indian law", BBC, 5 January 2007.

Sudhir Kumar

Sudhir Kumar came from Haryana and had a strong business background. Of his family, he liked to say: "If there is money lying around, we can smell it." His father was a clothing wholesaler and his brothers and sisters all made a fortune in business. Kumar was an alumnus of the Delhi School of Economics and held a degree in business management. Nevertheless, he took pride in having renounced the lofty rewards of free enterprise to work for the government instead. Since his father had told him to go and serve the people, it was a calling he regarded as nobler than working for personal gain.

Among thousands of aspirants, Kumar was chosen as one of a select few to join the Indian Administrative Service, an elite group of civil servants. Administrators were sent out all over India to solve the most intractable problems and were moved from one assignment to the next.

One of his major assignments was as sales tax commissioner when the state of Bihar was broken up into two smaller states in 2000. As Bihar was losing more than half of its sales tax revenue to the new state, Kumar's task was to restore the revenues of Bihar to pre-partition levels within five to seven years. Instead of the planned seven years, it took Kumar only 30 months to succeed. He ingeniously closed loopholes in the tax code, made arrangements with tax cheats and collected taxes with unprecedented intensity.

When Kumar entered the Railways Ministry in 2004, he started by reading all the files he could get hold of in order to build his knowledge and understanding of the industry. He approached this gigantic task with great humility and developed a deep passion that proved contagious and invigorating. His business acumen would serve him well in transforming the Minister's down-to-earth ideas into economically sound initiatives.

The Complexity of the Turnaround

Kumar knew that textbook recipes would not work. The "World Bank approach", as he called the conventional policies prescribing retrenchment, privatisation and tariff hikes, did not take the political mandate into account. His challenge was to maintain the dual nature of Indian Railways as a public utility service and a commercial organisation. Political imperatives precluded standard remedies because Lalu discarded any measure that could burden poor customers or railway employees. Selling underperforming assets, laying off employees or increasing fares were not an option. Kumar commented wryly: "I had to serve an omelette to the nation without breaking any eggs."

Kumar decided to analyse and scrutinise every possible aspect of the organisation with the aim of earmarking niches for improvement. He then screened potential initiatives from two angles; on the one hand their commercial viability and on the other hand their political desirability. He intuitively felt that less than originally expected was political and that more could be done on the commercial front.

Fixed costs dominated, whereas variable costs were relatively low. Although he could not retrench or divest, and thus had little control over operating expenses, he could distribute them more widely. In comparison to the Chinese and American railroads, the Indian Railways' assets seemed to be severely underutilised. While China Railways was an equally large state-owned enterprise and boasted a similar number of passenger kilometres, it transported four times more freight than Indian Railways.

Making Indian trains faster, heavier and longer would reduce unit costs and increase asset productivity because there was no need for additional crew, engine or tracks. Freight returns could thus be improved by a combination of measures, such as increasing axle loads (heavier), adding extra wagons (longer) or reducing wagon turnaround time (faster). Better loading and unloading facilities, as well as round-the-clock work at major terminals, could substantially reduce the time between successive loadings. With loading and unloading requiring a full day or more, the engine lost precious time commuting back and forth. If freight customers invested in their terminals, the engine could stand by and the wagons could be released much more quickly. In addition, train inspections, that generally took about 16 hours, could be shortened and their frequency diminished.

These revenue-generating measures sounded simple and straightforward but hitherto had not been implemented. The structure and processes of the organisation were so complex that each intervention required intensive negotiation across departments, zones and divisions. Employees still had a monopoly mindset, although Indian Railways no longer enjoyed a natural monopoly in the business of transportation. On the contrary, there was fierce competition from roads, air travel, oil pipelines and even coastal shipping. By 2004, the road transport sector had captured 70% of market share in the road and rail industry. IR's shrinking market share was even more unsettling given the poor road conditions and administrative hurdles facing truck transportation. Unlike trains, they had to clear customs and pay taxes at the borders between India's 28 states and seven union territories.

Kumar felt the need to challenge traditional perceptions. Freight and parcel tariffs were not determined by market conditions and elasticity of demand and non-price factors were not given any consideration. The freight tariff policy was based on the principle that low-value commodities, such as iron ore and other minerals, were charged less than finished products. For the majority of its freight customers (63%), IR transported these raw materials door to door, from the pithead to the factory. In this segment it had a clear competitive advantage and enhanced pricing power by providing a door-to-door service. Moreover, global demand for raw materials was experiencing a boom and prices were steadily increasing.

In comparison, tariffs for high-value finished products like steel and cement were much higher, although Indian Railways ensured their transportation only from station to station. Furthermore, in this segment it was facing stiff competition from the road sector. As IR steadily raised charges for steel and cement, it was gradually pricing itself out of the market. For example, when in the 1990s steel manufacturers resorted to trucking, IR's share of their business declined from 67% in 1991 to 36% in 2004.

Freight rates for station-to-station products had to be reduced, while the rates for door-to-door commodities could be increased. This implied a thorough revision of freight tariffs, which were based on an obsolete tariff schedule dating back to 1958. Out of 4,000 different commodities classified in 500 pages, a mere eight commodities accounted for 85% of total freight traffic. In addition, due to the lack of transparency in the tariff structure, goods clerks wielded enormous discretionary powers, leading to tariff evasion and customer harassment.

Kumar intended to introduce dynamic and differential pricing. For example, iron ore was mined in the central plateau regions of India, where bad road conditions and the bulky nature of the commodity made trucking unviable. In this segment, Indian Railways could easily raise freight rates. A surcharge could be levied during the peak season and for loading on congested routes, whereas discounts could be offered for loading in the empty flow direction and during the lean season. Demand typically plunged during the monsoon season from July to October because tracks and mines were flooded. Slowing construction activity dampened demand for steel and cement and coal transport declined as hydroelectric power plants came into being.

The Main Issues

Kumar identified three high-priority interventions, which met his criteria of low cost, short gestation and rapid payback. More importantly, he considered them as potentially low risk and high return.

Axle Load and Safety

During his first months in office, the Minister received complaints about the overloading of trains. In response, he decided to personally visit a railway station in Bihar and conduct a spot inspection of the freight. When he observed the overloading, Lalu requested that every train be weighed at one of the country's electronic weighbridges. He was furious to find out that the overloading of wagons of iron ore and coal was rife. All the while, corrupt employees and conniving customers had engaged in this fraudulent practice, yet Indian Railways had not generated any income from the additional freight.

The spot inspections immediately brought the axle load issue to the top of his agenda. Lalu asked for weighbridges to be installed at all originating points. His aim was to officially boost volumes and revenues, and at the same time reduce illegal overloading. However, any potential increase in axle load raised the safety alarm, and within IR safety issues were "political hot potatoes". A thorough assessment of risks and their mitigation would be required.

Unions and the Parcel Service

Indian Railways carried parcels from station to station but demand for parcel booking was low on passenger trains that frequently stopped and travelled short distances. The organisation was incurring heavy losses in the parcel services and losing market share to road traffic. Since Indian Railways did not transport parcels at a discount, Kumar investigated why earnings were so low and how unutilised capacity could be tapped into.

He unilaterally decided to open up the parcel service to wholesale leasing through competitive bidding in order to reduce losses in that segment. Although the parcel operation touched the sensitive area of employment, Kumar did not anticipate strong resistance to his plans and did not consult the unions. While the smaller unions seemed to accept the outsourcing of the parcel business, the big unions decided otherwise and staged disruptive demonstrations at major train stations.

Customers' Side Tracks

Since the 1960s, the main railway lines had been upgraded to electric traction, whereas the feeder branch lines, usually the first and last mile on the same route, had not been electrified. It was a daily routine that a train started from a diesel track territory and had to pass through an electrified territory or vice versa. On the traction change points, which Kumar called "graveyards of trains", the diesel locomotive had then to be detached and replaced by an electric locomotive.

Organizing the locomotive, the driver, the crew and taking care of other operational requirements caused delays of 10 to 15 hours at the traction change points. This was the equivalent of a day of revenue lost. In his efforts to reduce the turnaround time, Kumar viewed these traction points as a major stumbling block. In the past, IR had tried to force the customers who owned the branch lines leading to their factories to migrate to electric traction. If the customers were willing to invest, IR provided the connectivity to their premises. However, without clear incentives the customers refused to bear the cost of electrification since they had the option of shifting to other modes of transport.

Kumar had to deliver fast results. How should he prioritise the three initiatives? Who exactly were the main stakeholders in each case and how should Kumar deal with them?

Bibliography

Bankruptcy to Billions: How the Indian Railways were Transformed by Sudhir Kumar and Shagun Mehrotra, Oxford University Press, 2009.

Exhibit 16.1

Network of Indian Railways

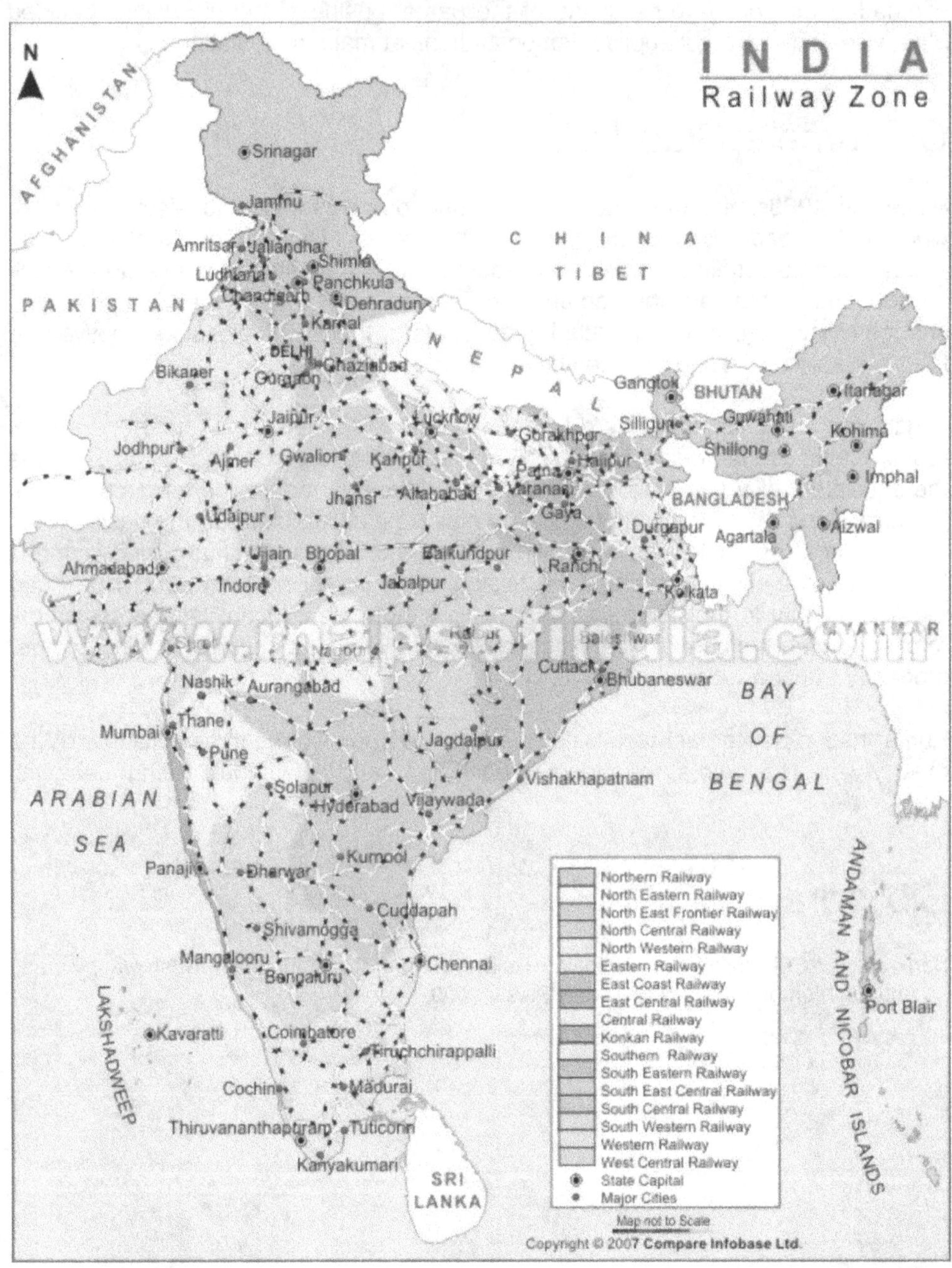

Source: Ministry of Railways

Exhibit 16.2

Indian Railways – The Nation's Lifeline

Source: Chennai Television

Exhibit 16.3

Organisation Structure of Indian Railways

Minister of Railways

Minister of State for Railways-MSR(1)

Minister of State for Railways-MSR(2)

Railway Board

Chairman Railway Board

Member Electrical

Member Staff

Member Engineering

Member Mechanical

Member Traffic

Financial Commissioner

Director-General Rly. Health Services

Director-General RPF

Secretary

Estt. Matters

Admn. Matters

Zonal Railways

Production Units

Other Units

Public Sector Undertakings/ Corporations, etc.

Zonal Railways	Production Units	Other Units	Public Sector Undertakings/ Corporations, etc.
General Managers	**General Managers**	**General Managers**	IRCON
Central	Chittaranjan Locomotive Works	NF Railway (Construction)	RITES
Eastern	Diesel Locomotive Works	Metro Railway, Kolkata	CRIS
East Central	Integral Coach Factory	Central Organization for Railway Electrification	CONCOR
East Coast	Rail Coach Factory	**Director-General**	IRFC
Northern	Rail Wheel Factory	Railway Staff College	KRC
North Central	**CAO (R)***	**Director-General & Ex. Officio General Manager**	IRCTC
North Eastern	Diesel Loco Modernization Works	RDSO	RCIL
Northeast Frontier	Central Organization for Modernization of Workshops		MRVC
North Western			RVNL
Southern			
South Central			
South Eastern			
South East Central			
South Western			
Western			
West Central			

Source: Ministry of Railways, 2006-b

Exhibit 16.4

Casualties in Train Accidents

	Killed				Injured			
Year	Passengers	Rly. Staff	Others	Total	Passengers	Rly. Staff	Others	Total
2001–2002	144	14	168	326	595	38	175	808
2002–2003	157	29	232	418	658	41	283	982
2003–2004	135	4	155	294	302	31	159	492

Source: Ministry of Railways, safety performance

Exhibit 16.5

Indian Economy's Annual Growth Rates of Real GDP at Factor Cost

Year ending March	Annual Growth Rate of GDP percentage
1996	7.3
1997	7.8
1998	4.8
1999	6.5
2000	6.1
2001	4.4
2002	5.2
2003	3.8
2004	8.5

Source: Economic Survey 2006–2007, Government of India and Ministry of Finance, Budget Papers 2007

Exhibit 16.6

Passenger and Freight Revenue

						Rs crores
Year ending March	Freight revenue			Passenger revenue		
	Actual	Increase	% increase	Actual	Increase	% increase
1996	15,290	1,620	11.85	6,113	654	11.98
1997	16,668	1,378	9.01	6,616	503	8.23
1998	19,866	3,198	19.19	7,554	938	14.18
1999	19,960	94	0.47	8,527	973	12.88
2000	22,341	2,381	11.93	9,556	1,029	12.07
2001	23,305	964	4.31	10,483	927	9.70
2002	24,845	1,540	6.61	11,196	713	6.80
2003	26,505	1,660	6.68	12,575	1,379	12.32
2004	27,618	1,113	4.20	13,298	723	5.75

Source: ASARC Working Paper 2008/06, "Financial Turnaround of the Indian Railways"

Crore: equivalent to 10,000,000 rupees (Rs)

Exhibit 16.7a

Analysis of Freight Earnings

Year ending March	Net tonne Kms million*	Earnings Rs in crores	Percentage of avg annual growth over previous years		Rate per net tonne per km in paise**
			volume	earnings	
1996	270,489	15,290	8.38	13.9	55.35
1997	277,567	16,668	2.62	9.0	55.89
1998	284,249	19,866	2.41	19.18	68.93
1999	281,513	19,960	–0.01	0.005	69.89
2000	305,201	22,341	8.41	11.92	71.27
2001	312,371	23,305	2.34	4.31	74.60
2002	333,228	24,845	6.68	6.61	74.56
2003	353,194	26,505	5.99	6.68	75.04
2004	381,241	27,618	7.94	4.20	72.44

Source: Statistical Summary, Indian Railways

*Net tonne kilometres: the measure of the net weight of freight carried on a train (not including the weight of the wagons) multiplied by the number of kilometres travelled.

**Paise: Indian currency unit equivalent to 1 US cent

Exhibit 16.7b

Analysis of Passenger Earnings

Year ending March	Passenger earning in Rs Crore	No. of Passenger in millions	Passenger kms in millions	Average rate per passenger kms in paise**
1996	6,113	4,018	341,999	17.87
1997	6,616	4,153	357,013	18.53
1998	7,554	4,398	379,897	19.88
1999	8,527	4,411	403,666	21.11
2000	9,556	4,585	430,666	22.19
2001	10,483	4,833	457,022	22.94
2002	11,196	5,246	494,914	22.62
2003	12,575	5,126	516,500	24.35
2004	13,298	5,293	542,896	24.50

Source: Statistical Summary, Indian Railways

Exhibit 16.8

Overall Performance of Indian Railways, 1988–2004

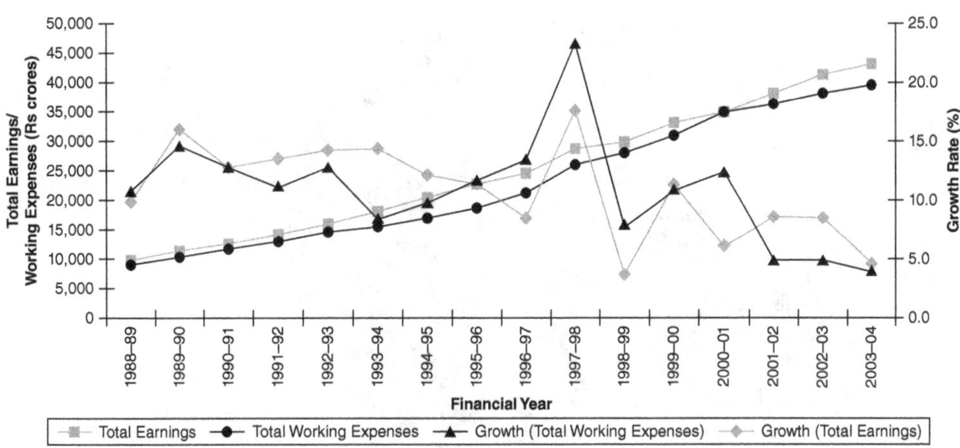

Source: Railway Budget (2006)

Exhibit 16.9

Financial Performance Indicators of Indian Railways (year ending March)

	1996	1997	1998	1999	2000	2001	2002	2003	2004
Surplus/deficit Rs crores	2,870	2,117	1,535	1,399	846	**763**	1,000	1,115	1,091
Operating ratio	82.45	86.22	90.92	93.34	93.31	**98.3**	96.02	92.3	92.1
Net revenue to capital %	14.92	11.73	8.94	5.81	6.88	**2.5**	4.96	7.5	8
Total dividend payment Rs crores	1,264	1,507	1,489	1,742	1,890	**308**	1,337	2,715	3,087
Number of staff '000	1,587	1,584	1,579	1,578	1,577	**1,545**	1,511	1,472	1,442
Systems length (Km)	62,915	62,725	62,495	62,809	62,759	**63,028**	63,140	63,122	63,122
Freight revenue Rs crores	15,290	16,668	19,866	19,960	22,341	**23,305**	24,845	26,505	27,618
Freight volume million tonnes	391	409	429	421	456	**474**	493	519	557
Passenger revenue Rs crores	6,113	6,616	7,554	8,527	9,556	**10,483**	11,196	12,575	13,298
Passenger volume (million)	4,018	4,153	4,398	4,411	4,585	**4,833**	5,246	5,126	5,293
Total revenue Rs crores	22,813	24,801	29,134	30,234	33,856	**36,011**	39,358	41,856	43,961
Total wages Rs crores	9,363	10,514	14,141	15,611	16,289	**18,841**	19,214	19,915	20,929

Source: ASARC Working Paper, June 2008, "Financial Turnaround of the Indian Railways"

Exhibit 16.10
Cost Structure

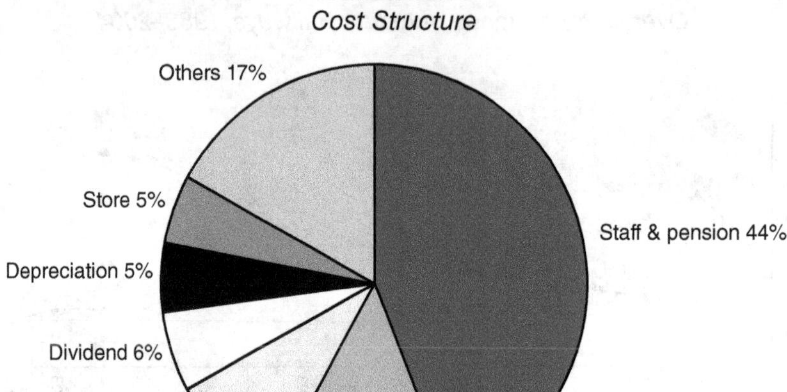

Source: Ministry of Railways, Deutsche Bank

Exhibit 16.11

Main Recommendations of the World Bank and the Expert Group

India's Transport Sector: The Challenges Ahead, World Bank, 2002	**Report of the Expert Group on Indian Railways, 2001**
Separation of policy, regulation and business functions.	Separation of roles into policy, regulatory and management functions.
IR to be corporatised as a business entity and operated on commercial lines.	Corporatisation of Indian Railways.
Non-core activities to be managed separately with the objective of eventual divestiture.	Non-core business should be spun off – IR should engage itself only with its core-activity related to rail-based logistics and passenger transport.
	IR to consider management of its freight terminals and railway goods sheds by outside agencies.
Enterprise functions to become lines of business.	Restructure railways to become a business oriented customer-driven institution, the main components being freight, passenger, suburban, shared and fixed infrastructure. The business units to function on commercial lines.
Adoption of commercial accounting format.	IR's accounts to be recast into company format.
Legislation to be suitably amended to facilitate changes.	
Clear differentiation between social obligations and commercial imperatives.	Differentiation between social obligations and performance imperatives: government to provide subsidy for social projects and to fund operating losses.
Leverage benefits arising from leasing of equipment.	IR should attract private investments in financing and leasing of rolling stock.
	Downsize staff strength.

Source: Asian Development Bank

SECTION VI
Private Equity in Emerging Markets

In growth markets, the private equity model is very different from the rest [of the world]. In the West, private equity is about financial leverage, about driving operational efficiency. In our part of the world, it is about growth capital, and about helping businesses transform themselves; creating opportunity where opportunity wasn't previously available.

—**Arif Naqvi,** Founder and Group Chief Executive, The Abraaj Group

CASE

17 RICE FROM AFRICA FOR AFRICA
RICE FARMING IN TANZANIA AND INVESTING IN AGRICULTURE

SYNOPSIS

A specialist agribusiness investor is evaluating an equity investment in rice farming and processing in Tanzania, Africa. Duxton Asset Management has a business strategy of investing in and operating agricultural assets, many of which are in developing or even frontier markets. The case discusses the complexities of investing in an atypical multi-dimensional asset and allows for an exploration of the fast-growing space of impact investing.

This case touches upon several relevant aspects of alternative private equity (PE) strategies:

- Agriculture has been an underinvested asset class for some time. It is currently not well understood by mainstream investors yet is becoming increasingly important in the context of a growing world population facing resource constraints. In addition, direct investments into farmlands require specialized knowledge and expertise.
- Farmland investments are intricately connected to environmental, social and corporate governance (ESG) issues, which the case highlights through references to SRI (socially responsible investment) and Duxton's approach to ESG. One of Duxton's strengths lies in its responsible and proactive management of ESG risks.
- The destination here is Tanzania, a frontier market for private capital investments. Local dynamics are promising and rewards can be high, yet many challenges exist. Few investors have the ability to spot and manage operating assets in this part of the world. Foreign investors are intrigued but not completely convinced of Africa's potential to compensate for the risks involved.

PEDAGOGICAL OBJECTIVE OF THE CASE

The case illustrates an investment in an atypical multidimensional asset class—an agribusiness/farmland investment in frontier markets—and adds the dimension of responsible investing. Readers have the opportunity to examine the potential risks and rewards of a farmland investment with strong ESG impact and potential in an emerging market. The PE investor needs to decide on its next action, as he is faced with a change in circumstances on the financing side. Before making the decision, he needs to explore alternatives and assess the implications on the business and operating strategy.

SUGGESTED ASSIGNMENT QUESTIONS

1. Describe Duxton's investment strategy within the PE context. Can it be defined as impact investing?

2. What are the highest impact value-creation levers and biggest risks in this deal? In your opinion, does the potential return from the transaction adequately compensate for the risks?
3. What should Duxton do now that their funding partner has unexpectedly backed out with respect to this project?
4. Evaluate Duxton's new strategy and how it compares to its historical strategy in light of the decision it is facing.

ADDITIONAL RESOURCES

This case does not require prior knowledge of PE but students will find it helpful to have a basic context of asset classes, valuation concepts and business models in asset management/PE. To make the most of this case study, we suggest below additional sources to provide context and background material/reading:

- In particular, we recommend the following chapters from *Mastering Private Equity—Transformation via Venture Capital, Minority Investments & Buyouts*
  - Chapter 1 Private Equity Essentials
  - Chapter 5 Alternative Strategies
  - Chapter 14 Responsible Investment
- You may also refer to the book website for further material:
  www.masteringprivateequity.com

Rice from Africa for Africa

Duxton Asset Management and its Investment in Tanzanian Rice Farming

03/2015-6007

This case was written by Anindita Sharma, under the supervision of Michael Prahl, Executive Director, INSEAD Global Private Equity Initiative, and Claudia Zeisberger, Senior Affiliate Professor of Decision Sciences and Entrepreneurship and Family Enterprise at INSEAD. It is intended to be used as a basis for class discussion rather than to illustrate either effective or ineffective handling of an administrative situation.

Funding for this case study was provided by INSEAD's Global Private Equity Initiative (GPEI).

Additional material about INSEAD case studies (e.g., videos, spreadsheets, links) can be accessed at cases.insead.edu.

"We have abundant land, a long-standing tradition of growing rice, and with just 3% of Africa's water resources currently being used, plenty of water."

Dr Aliou Diagne, AfricaRice

Desmond (Des) Sheehy, co-founder and CIO of Duxton Asset Management, sat back and thought about the phone call he had just had with one of his key investors. There had been a setback. The discussions over an imminent investment in a sustainable rice farm in Tanzania had taken an unexpected turn. Their key investor would not be making the investment of $12.46 million, or 97% of the $12.84 million that had been agreed upon.

Duxton Asset Management was located in a beautifully converted shop house in the Duxton Hill neighbourhood of Singapore, thousands of miles from Ruaha River valley in Mbeya, south-western Tanzania, where the farm stood. It was May 2012, more than a year after the deal had first come to the team's attention.

Des thought of the endless discussions, memos, due diligence and research work done by his investment team – John Simpson and Alex Lepori – who had travelled the 5,000 miles from Singapore to Tanzania many times that year. Duxton's strict due diligence standards had made the process particularly trying. The sellers, too, had spent considerable time, effort and funds on the process. Des had been excited about adding the farm to Duxton's portfolio. The project had sound financial potential and the team was confident of their unique ability to manage the risks in this investment. Now, however, they needed to make some quick decisions.

Background and History of Duxton AM

Having graduated in engineering from University College, Cork, Ireland, Des Sheehy had spent nine years working on large infrastructure projects in Europe and Asia before getting an MBA from INSEAD and joining the International Finance Corporation. As senior investment officer he was responsible for the origination, execution and supervision of investments throughout Asia.

Des had been at the IFC for more than six years when he met Ed Peter from Deutsche Bank in Singapore. Ed ran Deutsche Bank's asset management business in Asia Pacific, Middle East and North Africa. He asked Des to build an illiquid asset portfolio, which included farmland and other agricultural investments. Des started this work in 2005. By 2009, he was a managing director heading "Complex Asset Investments" within the bank's asset management division.

When an opportunity presented itself in 2009, Des and Ed along with their team (Exhibit 17.1), including Stephen Duerden (CFO) and Chong Kuan Yew (head of investments) spun off the portfolio into an independent business and co-founded Duxton Asset Management, a Singapore-based MAS-registered asset manager.[1] Deutsche Bank continued to maintain a 19.9% stake in this business.

1. A fund or asset manager regulated by the Monetary Authority of Singapore under the Securities and Futures Act.

Duxton was appointed by Deutsche Bank as the delegated fund manager for DWS Vietnam and DWS GALOF funds,[2] and a $40 million portfolio of wine funds. Over the next few years, Duxton's mandate expanded and it added new funds:

- In 2010, Duxton started DALT (Duxton Agricultural Land Trust), a hybrid mutual open-end fund with bi-annual redemption.
- In the same year, Duxton won a €150 million segregated institutional mandate from a large pension fund in Europe. Duxton was to manage a non-discretionary mandate by investing in agricultural production related assets.
- In 2011, Duxton launched two new funds: DALF (Duxton Agricultural Land Fund), and DACE (Duxton Agricultural Commodities and Equities Fund). DALF, a Cayman closed fund, would invest in a global portfolio of agricultural farmland, and DACE, a daily liquidity fund, would invest in global agricultural related securities.

In 2012 Deutsche Bank decided to restructure its asset management business and sold its minority stake in Duxton to the team.

Duxton's Investment Philosophy

By 2011 Duxton's investment philosophy had evolved considerably. The focus was on building a diversified portfolio of private equity investments with minimum leverage. It employed two broad investment styles –

- Management Buy Out/Buy In: Duxton would identify a good management team and help it acquire the asset where it worked, or other assets. Duxton would have a controlling interest for providing the capital, incentivizing management through co-investments and an equity participation programme.
- Permission investing: Duxton would identify projects to execute with partners that would provide the bulk of the capital while it would contribute a combination of both capital and its expertise in growing businesses. In such structures, Duxton would be a minority investor with strong influence.

By 2012 Duxton had invested in farmland on four continents and across a variety of produce including cereals, dairy and meat. The team believed that a well-diversified portfolio would have lower downside risk and be able to withstand the variability in agriculture.

With holdings across continents, Duxton began to delineate its approach between developed and frontier markets, recognizing that optimal farming methods had to reflect the underlying market dynamics and could not be blindly replicated across geographies:

- Developed market investments benefited from consolidation and scale, whereas farms in developing markets with historical smallholder[3] farming practices could not be consolidated easily. In developing markets it made economic sense for investments to vertically integrate through the value chain, covering not just primary production but also processing.

2. DWS Vietnam Fund was started in 2006, a closed-end fund that invested in listed Vietnamese securities and unlisted Vietnamese assets. DWS GALOF Fund (DWS Global Agricultural Land and Opportunities Fund) was launched in 2007, a closed-end fund with a mandate to invest in unlisted agricultural assets.
3. Marginal and sub-marginal farm households that own or/and cultivate less than 2 hectares of land.

- Developed country farming practices were capital-intensive with sparse populations and large holdings. Developing markets were labour-intensive. They required a longer term approach of building trust-based relationships and collaborative working practices with neighbouring communities.
- Finally, while direct agricultural investments had high environmental, social and governance risks in both markets, in developing markets the issues would often be more sensitive from a political and social standpoint. Conversely, the ability to positively impact a developing country was higher.

Overall, even though frontier or developing market deals could be smaller in scale, the potential returns from these markets were expected to be much higher. Duxton actively pursued frontier market deals for their portfolio.

Benefits and Risks of Farmland Investments

Farmland investments[4] are highly specialized, with unique features vis-à-vis other investments. Between 1926 and 2009, farm real estate had a high average annualized return of 10.3%, second only to small cap equities. It also had a low standard deviation of 8.3%, making its volatility profile far lower than that of equities and even long-term corporate or government bonds.

The notion of low volatility may seem counterintuitive, as agricultural commodity markets are known to be cyclical and volatile. However, the smoothness in farmland returns derives from the rent earned on the land, a common source of returns to the landowner and a hedge against the cyclical nature of its produce markets.

Farmland investments also provide the benefit of diversification. Between 1997 and 2011 these investments had a low correlation to most major asset classes and a slight negative correlation to the US bond index. Farmland investments also have hedging properties, generally keeping pace with inflation.

Additionally, with growing concerns about world food security, farmland investments were expected to provide attractive financial returns as land became scarce and produce more valuable in the face of strong demand. Capital invested in this sector would help improve efficiency by spreading best farming practices globally, and improving world food security in the process (see Exhibit 17.2).

Agribusiness, in particular farmland investments, face a number of risks, including liquidity risks, macro risks, currency risks, business and operational risks, and ESG risks.

- Farmland investments are illiquid. Transactions require long lead times. This makes these investments suitable only for portfolios that can take longer time horizons.
- Farmland investments carry numerous macro risks, such as the risk of political turmoil, price controls and trade restrictions. In the case of farmland investments in frontier locations, these can be even more significant as the value of farmland is directly linked to political turmoil in a country.

4. Investors can gain exposure to the agriculture industry through soft commodities, listed equities, or farmland. The most common way is through commodity futures and over-the-counter (OTC) derivatives, followed by listed companies (usually processing, logistics, and fertilizer companies). In contrast, Duxton invests directly in farming enterprises.

- With most agricultural commodities priced in USD, most farmland investment tends to be implicitly long, which provides a hedge in countries with a depreciating currency while creating margin pressure in a currency appreciation setting.
- Any farmland investment carries all the other risks of an operational business such as adverse market conditions and poor farm or financial management. Yields can vary significantly depending on weather, the management and operational effectiveness of the asset. As an example, in Kapunga during the 2011/12 season the lowest yield was 2.6 MT/ha and the highest was 8.2 MT/ha. Due to this high performance variability and the inherent operational leverage, Duxton preferred to have low financial leverage on farmland assets.
- Finally, farmland investments touch on a spectrum of ESG (environmental, social and governance) concerns. Common problems include land-grabbing from smallholders, hostility to foreign ownership of farmland or to the export of a food crop. Any displacement of a community or people due to a farm's activities can create hostility, as can the perception that a farm is using more than its fair share of resources. Farmlands can spark environmental concerns about water usage and management, encroachment on national parks, pollution through farm activities, and displacement of natural resources.

Farmland investments were estimated to be between 0.5% and 3% of large institutional investors' invested AUM.[5] A separate study commissioned by OECD[6] indicated that farmland investments by private investment funds were highest in Australia/New Zealand, followed by South America, North America, Europe and Africa.

Duxton and Socially Responsible Investing (SRI)

Socially responsible investing (SRI) had gained momentum since the 1990s along with greater public awareness of global issues. By 2010, more than US$3 trillion of professionally managed assets in the US used SRI strategies. In Europe, such assets had grown 87% from €2.7 trillion in 2007 to €5 trillion in 2009. By 2012, SRI had become an important aspect for almost all institutional investors.

In the early days, funds implemented SRI through the use of "exclusion" screens, which were used by investors to screen out assets tied to alcohol or tobacco, or companies that had been sued or convicted of environmental damage. Over time, funds added "inclusion" screens to add exposure to companies with desirable ESG practices. Exclusion and inclusion screens continue to be the most common approach to managing responsible investments.

Screening (exclusion or inclusion) is a passive form of SRI. More active SRI can take the form of shareholder activism, and community or social investments where social outcomes are expected with or without a financial return. One specific sub-category –

5. June 2012 estimate by Grain.org/Publications.

6. HighQuest Partners, United States (2010), "Private Financial Sector Investment in Farmland and Agricultural Infrastructure", OECD Food, Agriculture and Fisheries Papers, No. 33, OECD Publishing http://dx.doi.org/10.1787/5km7nzpjlr8v-en.

impact investing[7] – refers to an investment that has an explicit and measurable agenda for positive impact over and above financial returns. Impact investing can be fairly hands-on as it resembles traditional venture funding, with typically a substantial degree of influence for the investor.

Duxton took ESG seriously but did not call itself an impact investor. Unlike an impact investor it did not set any explicit non-financial impact objectives. Duxton chose to engage with such issues responsibly and head-on rather than avoiding or underplaying their importance. As such, Duxton would be viewed as a 'responsible investor'.

> *Our experience suggests that in developed countries with transparent pricing we can identify good production-only assets. In the emerging markets, however, this can be more difficult. As a result we have begun to assess assets with some value-add that also play a big role in the local community. This can help us to leverage smallholder production and mitigate political risk, as well as adding significant value to an investment.* (Des Sheehy)

Africa as an Investment Destination

Historically, most of the funding Africa received was tied to a developmental agenda. Foreign investors perceived Africa to be "high maintenance" rather than an attractive destination for financial investments, in contrast to Asia's success in attracting foreign funds.

In the 1990s, as many African nations emerged from war and conflict, some such as Nigeria started privatization campaigns. At the same time, growth in emerging economies and the resulting boom in demand for resources started working in Africa's favour. The continent is immensely resource rich, with substantial oil reserves, 40% of the world's gold, and 80-90% of the world's chromium and platinum reserves.[8]

In a second fundamental shift, Africa's trading patterns benefited from the emerging South-South trade. Between 1990 and 2008, Europe's share of Africa's trade fell from 51% to 28%, while inter-Africa trade increased from 14% to 28%. In addition, new partnerships were forged with Asia and Latin America through bilateral arrangements with China, India, Brazil and countries in the Middle East.

These shifts in turn created socio-economic momentum, in the form of urbanization, an expanding labour force, and a growing middle class.

- The percentage of Africans living in urban areas increased from 28% in 1990 to 40% in 2008, and was expected to reach 50% by 2030. Urbanization is a main driver of productivity, aggregating demand and supplying labour to an expanding economy.
- Africa has a young population, with 500 million working-age Africans contributing to its economy. It is expected to have 1.2 billion working-age people by 2050; one in every four workers in the world will be from Africa, one in eight from China.

---

7. Other forms of impact financing have evolved in recent years. Social investment or impact bonds (SIBs) started around 2010, promising to provide investors a return if the social objectives of the underlying investment are met. Soon after, investors started providing unfunded guarantees to investee companies to help them obtain banking facilities. Most recently, crowd funding has become a popular way of investing in ventures that have more than just a profit motive.
8. McKinsey Quarterly, June 2010, "What is Driving Africa's Growth?"

- The global resource boom and increased trade activity have led to the creation of a large middle class in Africa. In 2000, only 59 million African households earned more than US$5,000[9] per year. In 2012, the number was estimated to be 128 million.

Accordingly, investors had developed a strong interest in Africa. Foreign direct investment (FDI) in Africa had grown substantially, from $9 billion in 2000 to $62 billion by 2008, and was expected to reach $150 billion by 2015. A 2011 survey of private equity investors[10] showed that 57% of investors in private equity in Sub-Saharan Africa expected annual returns of at least 16%.

Africa also holds a special place in agriculture and food security. It has almost 60% of the world's uncultivated arable land. Surprisingly, while the 'green revolution'[11] has increased productivity elsewhere, its effect has lagged in Africa due to poor infrastructure. This implied that food productivity gains were still possible in Africa because efficient production techniques were not widely used.

Duxton had first invested in Africa in 2009. By 2012 it was a seasoned investor managing one of the largest fund-structured agribusiness portfolios with direct investments of US$30.1 million between the DRC, Tanzania and Zambia. Duxton had hands-on experience of managing assets on the continent and understood the upside potential of the right assets.

The Kapunga Rice Project Limited (KRPL)

The Kapunga Rice Farm asset came to Duxton's attention through one of its team members who knew the owners of the asset. KRPL was one of only three large-scale rice farms in Tanzania. The site had originally been identified in the 1980s to create large commercial rice farms, which were built using funds from the African Development Fund and the Nigeria Trust Fund.[12] After completion, the asset had been handed over to the government but had quickly fallen into disrepair. The current owners had bought the asset from the government in 2006. At that time the asset was commercially non-viable, with little or no marketable production. They had turned around the asset, and now, with the farm at an inflexion point, were looking for help with the further expansion of operations (see Exhibit 17.4 on KRPL location and key features).

The current owner ('sponsor') was one of the largest soft commodities traders in Africa and the Middle East, with almost 40 years of reputable trading experience. They were one of the leading fertilizer, seed and cereal importers in Africa, and an integral partner of food aid supplies for the UN, World Food Programme and Red Cross. Their expertise was in developing agricultural production projects and in trading commodities, but not in operating farms. Notably, they had made a successful exit from an agricultural production project in Zambia, which was regarded by the

9. An income of US$5000 or more implies that this group is able to divert income to discretionary purchases after paying for food and shelter.
10. Emerging Markets Private Equity Association (EMPEA) - Coller 2011 survey.
11. A series of R&D and technology transfers around the world between the 1940s and 60s which helped increase agricultural output significantly.
12. Loans made to the Government of Tanzania.

World Bank as one of the more successful cases in which a production asset had been privatized, turned around by the investor, and sold on to a secondary investor with expertise in managing ongoing operations of a developed project.

Farm management was coordinated by the Verus farming group, headed by Justin Vermaak, a pioneer of precision farming in Africa and more recently of commercial bio-cropping and environmentally sustainable agriculture. Justin and his team were considered to be one of the best in Africa for such turnaround projects. Justin was a co-owner of the asset and would assume a lead role in the negotiations with Duxton.

Duxton's Initial (Top Down) Assessment of KRPL

Duxton used both a top-down and a bottom-up analysis for all its investments including KRPL. The top-down approach was used to identify and pre-select attractive opportunities, and only if the top-down analysis looked promising would a rigorous bottom-up process follow.

As a first step, Duxton typically looked at demand patterns for the asset's produce, either strong international demand or (as in the case of KRPL) exceptionally strong local demand. The business case for supplying high-quality rice within Tanzania seemed convincing at first glance:

- Tanzania's real GDP had grown at an annualized 7% between 2003 and 20.[13] The resulting income growth had driven up domestic consumption of goods and services. Culturally, maize was the staple in Tanzania, but people aspired to consume rice as their income levels went up.
- As opposed to Asia, where greater concentration of protein in the diet was leading to slower growth in staple demand, Sub-Saharan Africa was at an earlier stage of the growth curve with staple demand increasing. Local demand for rice was expected to triple by 2020 due to rising urbanization, incomes and population.
- The government, in line with EAC (East African Countries) tariffs, imposed a 75% import tax on foreign rice. This was meant to manage currency reserves and encourage the production of domestic rice. Despite this, in Tanzania the domestic supply met only 90% of domestic demand in 2010, with the remaining 10% met through imported rice. In addition an overall deficit of more than 450,000MT per annum existed in the region.

Second, Duxton believed that when a region had produced a commodity for over 50 years, it was likely that:

- the location was suitable (subject to climate change)
- some infrastructure to support that industry was in place
- it was possible to tap into an existing local skill base

KRPL checked all three boxes. The Mbeya region was the third-largest producer of rice in Tanzania with 12% of total domestic rice production. Rice was the second most

13. OECD 2012.

important crop in the region after maize, with over 100,000 smallholders producing it. Mbeya rice was the most coveted variety in Tanzania. Mbeya had a certain level of existing infrastructure to support the area's rice ambitions. In fact, the government of Tanzania had identified Mbeya rice as a priority crop/region in its 'National Rice Development Strategy' which aimed to double rice production by 2018.[14] The local communities had the skill set needed for rice farming, and could provide labour and tenant farmers.

KRPL Business Highlights and Plans

Duxton made a deeper assessment of KRPL before presenting it to their investment committee for approval to start a formal due diligence process.

Of KRPL's total land area of 7,980 ha, 4,400 ha was considered cultivable for rice. All of this area could be irrigated using feeder canals from the Ruaha River. The remaining land could be used for other crops such as soya, barley, bamboo, etc. At the time that the farm came to Duxton's attention, 3,500 ha were irrigated, of which 3,200 ha were cultivated (530 plots of 6 ha each). In the 2011/12 season, the average rice yield was 5.23 MT/ha, up from 2.5 MT/ha in 2009/10.

KRPL's produce was sold at the farm gate and in the local markets. The farm had also obtained an export license which allowed them to export up to 3,000 MT per year of rice to Zambia and DRC. Yet despite the premium paid (over the local price) in these markets, the farm was not using the export license at the time due to strong local demand.

The farm had a well-developed infrastructure, silo capacity, fully-fledged workshops, an administration building, a rice mill, and dryer & packing plant, all of which had been upgraded. It had a silo capacity for 10,000 MT and milling capacity for 21,000 MT per year. The processing features were attractive to Duxton – value-added activities improved agricultural returns significantly above pure production.

Tenant Programme:[15] Kapunga had a successful tenant programme under which 75-78 tenants leased 1,227 ha of rice paddy. Tenant leaseholders were provided with seed and fertilizer, while Kapunga would subsequently harvest and mill the crop. The tenant and Kapunga would agree on a rental fee (generally $150/ha). The first 3.4 MT/ha of rice harvested would go to Kapunga to cover costs. Leaseholders in this scheme typically came from a professional background and included the local district commissioner, local doctors and the regional surgeon. A key advantage of the programme was that it provided the project with significant downside protection through the political capital and good relations it forged, along with the rental returns. It also provided an annual hedge against the cost of production and operational risk. If the farm's own operations became too costly or ineffective, the entire farm could be leased out under the programme as large-scale commercial farms were not always viable in developing countries.

14. Gates Foundation, July 2012,"Developing the Rice Industry in Africa – Tanzania Assessment".

15. The tenants were part of the long term strategy of the farm. When the farm yielded less than 6MT/Ha, it would make financial sense to lease land to the tenants as the profit margins were about the same. Upon exceeding 6MT/Ha of rice, it would become more profitable for the farm to produce instead of the leaseholders. At such point, management would move the tenants to the to-be-developed areas of the farm where they would develop the land in a cost effective manner.

Management's Five-year Business Plan

To increase productivity and output, management planned to:

- Increase planted land to 4,400 ha from the current 3,200 ha.
- Increase average yields by process efficiencies and through the hiring of a rice expert. They hoped to achieve a yield of 6 MT/ha by 2014/15 and 8 MT in the long run.
- Use 720 ha of land to grow barley and legumes in the off season.

To implement this plan the farm would require:

- Land levelling – by using precision levelling, the farm would be able to maximize its available water resources through optimal irrigation and drainage.
- Investment in equipment, which would allow the farm to scale up its production further.
- Aerial seeding and spraying, which would increase efficiency of seed spraying while reducing the risk of loss from ground spraying, or of poor operational implementation.

The estimated cost to implement this plan was US$ 7.58 million, to be spent over the five-year period as shown below.

New Capex ***(All figures in USD)***		2011/12	2012/13	2013/14	2014/15	2015/16
New Machinery						
Heavy Tractor (Motor Vehicles)		275,000				
Medium Tractor (Motor Vehicles)			200,000	200,000	200,000	
Harvesting Unit (Plant & Machinery)		300,000	300,000	300,000		
Harvestor Support (Plant & Machinery)						275,000
Pick-Ups (Motor Vehicles)		102,000				
Cropsprayer (Plant & Machinery)		185,000				
Implements (Plant & Machinery)		195,000			150,000	
Grader (Plant & Machinery)		350,000				
Milling & Storage						
Polisher (Plant & Machinery)		96,000				
Colour Sorter (Plant & Machinery)		120,000				
Silo Extension (Building)			660,000			
Dryer Upgrade (Plant & Machinery)				300,000		
Briquetting Machine (Plant & Machinery)			120,000			
Land Works						
Cut and Fill (Basic Farm Area)		270,000	270,000	270,000	270,000	0
Transformation (Expansion Area)		0	0	840,000	840,000	0
Contingency	500,000	133,536	109,340	134,735	102,991	19,399
TOTAL CAPEX (incl. contingency)		**2,026,536**	**1,659,340**	**2,044,735**	**1,562,991**	**294,399**

Key Risks for the Deal

- **Weaknesses in the Tanzanian rice sector:** The sector faced structural and operational constraints that potentially threatened its growth ambitions. There was a significant lack of knowledge of improved seeds, and little effort had been made to disseminate improved seed varieties to farmers. Kapunga mitigated this risk by encouraging research on its farm with the International Rice Research Institute and through the procurement of varieties from other regions.
- **Smallholder and community relations:** Kapunga had a successful tenant leasing model, but did not have one for the smallholders in the community. Historically, some tension between the farm and the local community had existed. Yet the tenants of the farm had excellent relations with the farm's management and provided strong credibility with the local community and smallholders. Duxton could build on this as they had run successful smallholder programmes in other projects and were planning to do so in Kapunga.
- **Procurement:** The procurement of input, machinery and spare parts was challenging in Africa. Parts that could not be found or replaced in time could lead to delays in planting or harvesting operations (e.g. spare parts for aerial seeding equipment or harvesters). Kapunga used several strategies to mitigate this risk. It had a standardised fleet and sourced only from manufacturers with proven supply lines into Eastern and Southern Africa. It also used a procurement expert who specialized in sourcing and importing in Sub-Saharan Africa. Management also kept a significant inventory of essential parts and supplies on the farm to deal with any contingencies.
- **Competition for labour:** Some of Kapunga's machinery and equipment required skilled operators who were difficult to find in Tanzania. A mining boom and increased investment activity had intensified competition for skilled labour. Kapunga was aware of this risk and farm management worked hard to incentivize trained staff by providing accommodation, competitive wages and benefits for families, including schooling and healthcare. Kapunga management planned to reduce over-reliance on skilled operators by increasing the scale of machinery and transferring operations from the ground to the air.
- **Availability and use of water:** Rice is very water-intensive but the farm's topography and its location in a flood plain made it best suited to rice production. Water management on the farm was critical, especially with the risk of drought every 4-5 years. Management felt that if used intelligently, water should not be an issue for the original 3,500 ha of land. Scaling the farm up to 4,400 ha of irrigated land, however, could make water management more of a challenge.
- **ESG issues:** Sensitive lands were not cleared for production. The land designated for extension by the company was already in use by the farm's tenants. Furthermore, in the original environmental impact assessment (EIA) performed for the farm, it was suggested that 450 ha within the farm be left as a conservation area for the birdlife and mammals (see Exhibit 17.5 on KRPL's SRI initiatives).
- **Sponsor and related party transactions:** Under the farm's off-take contract with the sponsor, the sponsor guaranteed to buy 100% of the off-take at a specified minimum price in return for a guarantee fee of about US$1-2 per tonne. The guarantee helped the farm raise low-cost input financing from banks by back-stopping a minimum guaranteed revenue level. The farm was not required to sell to the sponsor if market prices were better. In fact, the farm currently did not sell through the sponsor because there was a premium of US$80-90 per tonne at the farm gate. There was an agreement for any rice exports to go through the sponsor. A tender procedure was in place for the purchase of all inputs from the sponsor.

Any and all contractual arrangements between the sponsor and the farm were on an arm's-length basis and presented no transfer pricing risk or the risk that the farm was captive to the sponsor. To further mitigate risks, Duxton negotiated a board-level veto clause for any related party transactions.

- **Exit:** Although Kapunga was a desirable asset, the liquidity of the asset and the exit for the investor remained a risk. The sponsor had, however, demonstrated an ability to turn around and exit a similar farm in neighbouring Zambia by selling it to a regional business. The farm, once fully scaled, could be an attractive value-chain play for agribusinesses looking to scale and grow. The outlook for African agribusiness was positive, and increased investor demand was anticipated. A sale to another investor was not inconceivable. There was some scarcity value as well, because following the collapse of the commercial farming industry in Zimbabwe, farms in East Africa had become increasingly sought after.

Proposed Deal Structure

Duxton had negotiated an entry price of US$19 million,[16] which was at a significant discount to indicative prices using comparables, DCF-based valuation, or to a previous independent valuation.

A total investment of US$12.84 million was envisioned, which would include:

- A subscription amount of up to US$7.58 million to support the management's five-year business plan
- A US$5.2 million investment for secondary shares in the property. It was structured such that the secondary shares could be bought after an initial investment of US$ 3 million.

These would give the investor a shareholding of up to a maximum of 48.3% of the holding company.

Duxton calculated a base case IRR of 26.8% using a seven-year holding period. Several upside and downside scenarios were evaluated. A single-factor upside and downside case are described below.

- Faster rice yield development (upside) – Kapunga's rice yields could exceed the base case assumptions if a rice agronomist could be hired to help get to full potential. Duxton calculated an IRR of 29.7% under this scenario (cf. 26.8% in their base case). The model was very sensitive to yields and the rate at which they would be achieved.
- Temporary removal of rice tariffs (downside) – There was the risk of the government temporarily removing import taxes. Duxton believed that such a measure was unlikely and would be short-lived if implemented. KRPL could protect itself by storing its milled rice until prices returned to normal or by exporting its produce to neighbouring countries. Duxton modelled a conservative 34% decrease in local rice prices for two years assuming the tariffs would be reinstated thereafter. The IRR under this scenario would shrink to 21.7% (cf. 26.8% in the base case).

16. For good practice, the team was requesting internal approval to invest up to $21 million.

Final Assessment and Approval

After more than a year of research and due diligence, the Investment Committee (IC) approved the investment of US$12.84 million, of which 97% would be from the LP and the remaining 3% split between two Duxton mandates.

The sponsor, too, welcomed the decision. Justin Vermaak and the other partners were supportive throughout the due diligence process and professional during the negotiations, which concluded satisfactorily for all parties. With their IC approval, the investment team instructed the lawyers in Tanzania to draft the final legal documents and prepare the closing mechanisms in order to fund the investment.

A Change in Circumstances

Des Sheehy sat back and pondered the call from the key investor, who was now withdrawing from the deal late in the process. The reasons were multiple, but none had to do with the asset itself. The investor had a new focus on developed market farmlands, and their ESG criteria had a renewed focus on exclusion factors which made farmland investments a challenge (managing such risks was key to the asset class).

As the team contemplated the prospect of their 97% funding partner backing out, different possibilities were considered. John suggested:

> *We have the option to try and find other investors who could take up some or all of this asset, but a process to identify and onboard a suitable partner would take time. Additional time would be needed for the new investors' internal investment processes. We should ideally lock in our due diligence and assessment of the farm or the due diligence will be seen as outdated in 6-12 months' time and we will lose momentum.*

On the other end of the spectrum Alex Lepori suggested:

> *There is the also the option to walk away from this investment and revisit it at a later point when the prospects look better. However, by doing so we would pass up on an opportunity we are excited about, and future conditions may not be quite as attractive. There could also be credibility issues with the sponsors the next time around.*

Des felt there could be a third option:

> *If we believe the opportunity is truly convincing, we can consider funding from funds that we have discretion over. Our funds will not be able to take up the entire US$12.84 million, but would be able to absorb some part of the investment. This option would give us an entry into the asset. We would certainly get a better understanding of the risks involved. It would also give potential investors comfort that we accepted the investment conditions and operational risk. However, by doing so we could run the risk that the amount invested does not make a material difference to the sponsor and the farm's operation.*

Duxton would be able to invest only $2 million immediately, which would buy them a secondary shareholding and less than 10% ownership. They were fairly confident that they could raise another $3 million from investors but needed a few months to arrange it. There were more questions on the team's mind:

- How would an investment of that size affect KRPL's growth and investment plans?
- What would it mean for Duxton's ability to manage and influence KRPL?
- How would this work with Duxton's broader investment and business strategy?
- What type of additional risks would a small investment entail compared to a more significant investment?

A Meeting in Istanbul Airport

While Duxton was debating its strategy internally, KRPL's sponsors were waiting for an answer. They had confidence in Duxton's ability to help grow the farm's operations and had hoped for the parties to collaborate. This was obviously a big setback to the sponsor's plans. Justin Vermaak was frequently on the phone with Duxton, concerned about the next steps.

Des and John arranged a meeting with Justin. They would fly from Singapore to Istanbul on their way to the Gulf, Justin would fly from Tanzania to Istanbul, and they would get together in the airport lounge. It was the quickest way to arrange a face-to-face meeting.

As Des and John flew to Istanbul, the key question remained unanswered: What would they say to Justin?

Exhibit 17.1
Bios

Duxton Asset Management – Principals

Ed Peter (CEO) is the co-founder of Duxton Asset Management. Prior to joining Duxton, Ed was Head of Deutsche Asset Management for Asia-Pacific and the Middle-East and member of the Global Operating Committee for Deutsche Asset Management. Ed joined Deutsche Bank in 1999, having since served as Head of Asian & Australian Equities, Head of Global Emerging Markets Equities and as Head of Equities and branch manager for Deutsche Bank Switzerland, after 13 years of experience at UBS Warburg and Credit Suisse in Geneva.

Desmond Sheehy (Managing Director and CIO) is the co-founder of Duxton Asset Management. Prior to joining Duxton, Desmond worked for DeAM Asia from 2005–2009, where he was the Head of the Complex Asset Investments Team. In addition to providing fiduciary oversight and managing the day-to-day running of the funds, Desmond's roles included sourcing and evaluating new opportunities for investment, planning, structuring, financing and conducting due diligence. Previously, Desmond worked at the International Finance Corporation as a Senior Investment Officer both in Washington DC and Hong Kong where he was responsible for the origination, execution and supervision of investments throughout Asia. Before joining the International Finance Corporation, Desmond spent nine years as an engineer working throughout Europe and Asia on large infrastructure projects. Desmond holds an MBA from INSEAD (1998) and a BE (1988) from UCC in Ireland.

Stephen Duerden (CFO/COO) has 20 years of experience in the Investment Management industry. Prior to joining Duxton, Stephen spent over 15 years at DeAM, in various roles in which he was exposed to a broad range of financial products and services. Stephen is a member of Duxton's Investment Committee charged with evaluating investment/divestment opportunities and the fiduciary oversight of its mandates. Stephen's previous role at DeAM was COO of the Complex Asset Investments Team before which he was COO of DeAM Singapore. As COO of the Complex Asset Investment, Stephen provided operational oversight of all Complex Asset businesses and fiduciary oversight as Director of Complex Asset Cayman based funds. Stephen holds a B.Comm. (Accounting Finance and Systems with merit) from the UNSW and a Grad. Dip. in Applied Finance and Investments from FINSIA. Stephen is a Fellow of FINSIA and is a CPA.

Kuan-Yew Chong (Director) joined Duxton in May 2009. Kuan-Yew's career in finance spans over 16 years. Prior to joining Duxton, Kuan-Yew was in DeAM Asia's Complex Asset Investments Team, where he spearheaded DWS Vietnam's unlisted equities team. Kuan-Yew was responsible for deal origination, negotiation, structuring, due diligence and closing of numerous private-equity investments as well as monitoring of all investments for the DWS Vietnam Fund. Additionally, Kuan-Yew was also responsible for investments into agricultural farmland in Zambia and Tanzania for the DWS GALOF fund. Prior to Deutsche, he was an Associate Director of the Direct Investment team at AIG Investments in Malaysia where he was involved in equity investments in a broad array of sectors including natural resources and Agribusiness. Prior to that, he was an equity research analyst with NatWest Markets and Credit Lyonnais Securities Asia. He holds a BCom in Accounting and Quantitative Methods from the University of Melbourne, Australia.

Duxton Asset Management – Kapunga Rice Project Deal Team

John Y Simpson (Vice-President/Head Africa) joined Duxton in 2010 and works as part of the private equity investment team. His work includes the origination and evaluation of investments in African markets, projects which have important social and environmental aspects, often featuring smallholder cultivation schemes and challenging operational environments. John sits on the board of investments in Zambia, DRC and Tanzania. John also takes responsibility for co-coordinating Duxton's ESG/SRI strategy and processes. John has deep emerging markets experience in countries such as Tanzania, India, Serbia and Afghanistan having worked as an advisor for the United Nations Assistance Mission in Afghanistan ("UNAMA"), and consulting the Sheriff of Mumbai on economic development issues. John worked for the Institute for War and Peace Reporting in Serbia, where he introduced economic & business analyses into the organization's news output and wrote regular reports on the region's economic development. John holds a MSc in 'Population and Economic Development' from the London School of Economics and a BSc in 'Economics and Business' from University College London.

Alex Lepori (Vice-President) has 10 years of experience in principal and third-party funds investing in emerging markets across a number of sectors. Prior to joining Duxton, Alex was based out of London and worked for several of RREEF's real estate private equity funds with total assets under management of over USD 10 billion. During his time at RREEF, Alex participated in as well as closed a number of transactions involving either the acquisition of portfolios of established commercial real estate assets in Western Europe or the development of new retail and residential assets in joint ventures with local partners in Central and Eastern Europe. Before joining RREEF in 2005, Alex spent 5 years with the International Finance Corporation in Washington DC providing both greenfield and expansion project financing for a number of private-sector mobile telecommunications networks in developing countries. During his time at IFC, Alex worked on transactions in Zambia, Cameroon, Yemen, Colombia, Honduras, El Salvador, Dominican Republic and Romania and helped close on deals involving over USD 200 million of structured loan and equity financing. Alex holds a BSEng in Electrical Engineering and a BSEcon in Finance (First Class Honours) from the University of Pennsylvania as well as a MBA in Finance from the Wharton School.

Kapunga Rice Project & Vendor's representative

Justin Vermaak (CEO Verus Farms & Co-Shareholder in Kapunga Rice Project Limited) spent 11 years in the South African Special Forces with 1 Reconnaissance Regiment based in Durban. In this period he accrued a wide variety of skills including specialist demolitions, weapons expertise, signals, covert warfare and parachuting. He deployed on active service on a regular basis in Africa during the conflicts rooted in the fight between communism and capitalism, being awarded several medals for his service and bravery including the prestigious Honoris Crux. During this time he developed a deep understanding of Africa, its people and how to thrive in the African hinterland – preparing him well for his career in the African agricultural sector. On retirement from the army, he started a business with the aspirations of being a farmer.

Verus Farms was founded in 1990 with a few chickens, pigs and a small dairy. The first 6 months were disastrous due to a collapse in chicken prices and the vagaries of animal mortality – despite careful planning and budgets calculated to within 1% of actual costs a-la military style. It became clear very quickly to Justin that to succeed in farming the sales price and control of costs was as important as good husbandry and capital. By 1993 Justin had innovated a system where pigs and chickens were sold at a pre-set price and raised against a strict cost budget from inputs purchased through set price contracts with input suppliers – all calculated on a new device called a personal computer. This thinking led to a low cost farming model that had capacity to supply not only South Africa, but its regional neighbours. When the South African state controlled price boards ceased to operate in 1994, Verus was the only company in the market that was positioned to offer a truly stable supply chain product. Justin saw the opportunity and entered into bigger contracts to supply other companies with maize and soya on fixed contracts. Within 3 years the program had been so successful that it expanded nationally to all the major corporate agribusiness and the range of crops grew to include maize, soya, wheat and sunflower. Huge strides were taken by Justin's farmers to make production cheaper through the introduction of precision farming technology, allowing them to compete on a global platform.

The dynamic built and led Verus to setup an input division, collective bargaining for farmers further drive down costs and increase revenues from pooled marketing, with Verus becoming a founding member of SAFEX AMD. This allowed hedging of prices and risk management for famers. Verus traded 6% of the national crop and was the 5th biggest Agribusiness in South Africa. By 2003 Verus had rolled out similar programmes in Namibia, Botswana, Zambia, Brazil, Panama and Romania.

Justin's strong personal drive to expand into Africa has led him to invest in the Zambian cereal sector, rice in Tanzania as well as managing a large portfolio of development assets across the continent growing sugar, cereals and biofuel crops.

Exhibit 17.2

World Food Security

The price of any good, commodity or service is a combined outcome of the forces of demand and supply in its market. Increasing demand for food comes from a fast-growing world population which is also dynamically changing its consumption patterns with increasing incomes in emerging economies. While a billion people are still perennially hungry, and another billion remain undernourished, on average developing economies are moving from a low-protein to high-protein diet as their people earn more, and consumers in developed economies like the US and UK continue to waste one in every three calories that they buy.

By March 2012, the world population had exceeded 7 billion, representing 5% of all the people in the world that have ever lived. In the last decade alone, humanity has added an unprecedented billion new members, and it is expected that population will get to 9.2 billion by the year 2050.

The fundamental concern with this scenario is that the supply of food will be stretched to keep up with such explosive growth in demand. The first and foremost constraint is the availability of additional arable land. For the first time in the history of man, our population is growing geometrically while the land available to support our calorific needs is growing arithmetically.

A second level of problem can be seen through the basic economic construct of marginal productivity of the new land. The most productive land has already been used and what is still available is less productive, more difficult to till, with less access to water resources, and ultimately only able to produce less per acre than the land currently in use.

In an additional twist, the dynamics in the oil and petrochemicals market have created a current and anticipated demand for biofuels, which means that in the future food crops must compete with biofuels for space and other resources.

Climate change adds yet another dimension to the food problem, by introducing new weather patterns, unprecedented increases in natural disasters, and a new level of variability in output. Finally, the supply of available water is drying up. The International Food Policy Research Institute (IFPRI) forecasts that 4.8 billion people (more than half the world's population) and about half of global grain production will be at risk due to water stress by 2050 if status quo, business-as-usual behaviour is followed.

Perhaps as a precursor to what the future could be, in 2008 total global food supply stood at 18% of the world's requirements, or just enough to feed the planet for 68 days. These fundamental global shifts lead us to consider the possibilities that expensive world food prices are here to stay, and that yields must increase if we are to maintain a sustainable world which supports our growth and still allows for biodiversity.

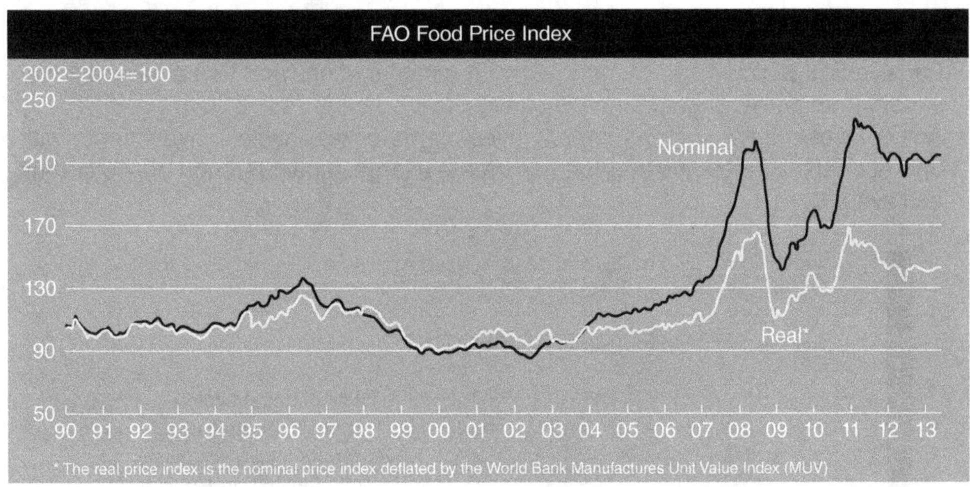

The FAO Food Price Index is a measure of the monthly change in international prices of a basket of food commodities. It consists of the average of five commodity group price indices (representing 55 quotations), weighted with the average export shares of each of the groups for 2002–2004.

Exhibit 17.3

SRI and Impact Investments

Impact and Return Expectations

- When we differentiate SRI/ESG/non-profit investments on the basis of returns expected, we see that the traditional model of giving has been via grants with no financial returns expected.
- Impact investments are designed to create financial and non-financial returns, although it is not uncommon for investors to relax their hurdle requirements in view of the social benefits of a project.
- Responsible investments combine traditional market investments with strong ESG components. These investments require and investors expect a market rate of return.

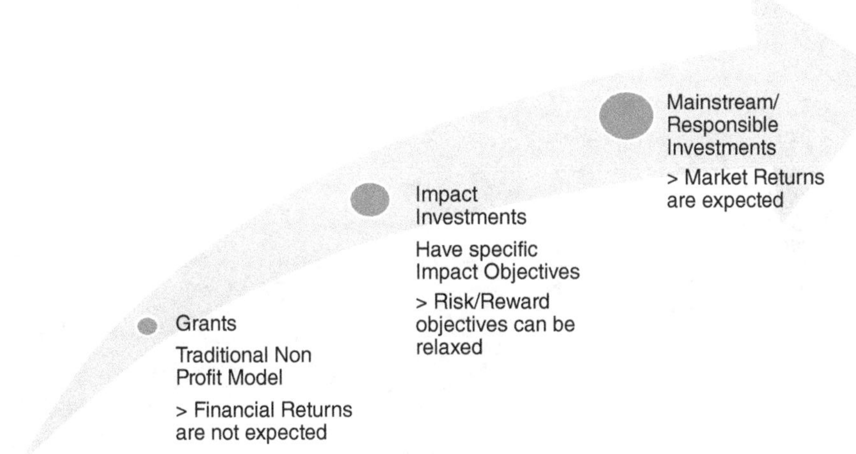

SRI Impact and Level of Resources Required

- Passive SRI policies can be handled with minimal effort, and these have a lower impact than active engagement with investees.
- Active investments, such as impact investments or responsible investments with operational guidance and support can create a large impact through the outcomes achieved.

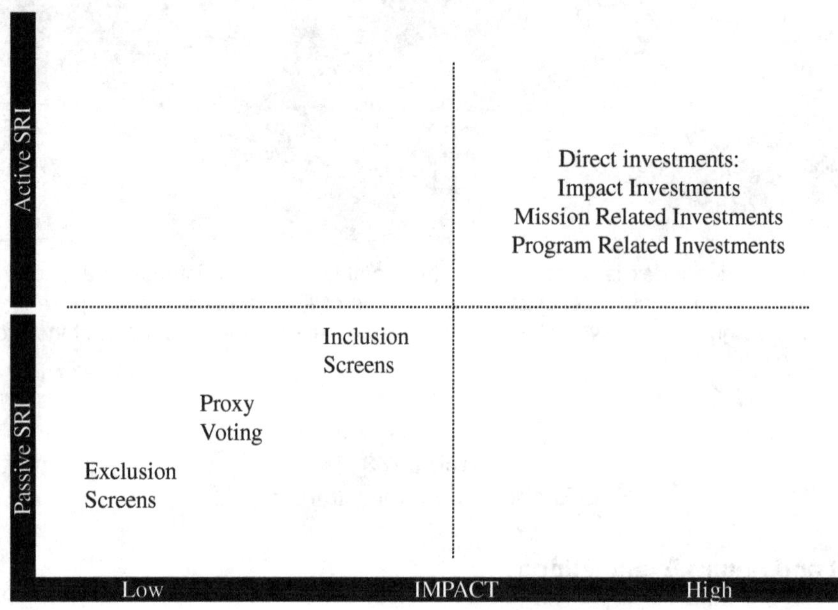

Exhibit 17.4

Kapunga Rice Project Limited: Map and Highlights

Main Geographical Features

- Kapunga's total area is 7,890 ha. Its current productive area is broken down into 530 paddies of 6 ha each, totalling about 3,200 ha, that is fed from a 12km feeder canal.
- Electricity and water is available in the workshops, mill and administration building. Electricity is provided by a dedicated transmission line from the national electricity grid which runs 12km alongside the feeder canal.
- The roads within the farm are negotiable through all seasons.
- A wireless communication network provides a cost-effective means of communication.
- The estate has extremely well developed infrastructure, a silo capacity of 10,000 MT, fully fledged workshops, an administration building, a rice mill, dryer and packing plant – all upgraded during the latest round of improvements.
- The estate further comprises of a housing section that can accommodate over 56 families. This is in addition to its community service centre, schools and clinic.

Exhibit 17.5
KRPL SRI Credentials

A Summary of SRI Initiatives

External Development Initiatives[17]	Farm Level Initiatives	Local Community Outreach
EVD Private Sector Investment Programme	Provision of services to tenant farmers	Road grading
World Food Programme Supplier	Health and education	Canal maintenance for smallholders
Black Coucal research	Direct and indirect employment	
Sustainable agriculture expertise	Efficient water usage	
IRRI Seed programme	450ha nature reserve	
	Environmental protection rules	

Collaboration with Dutch Ministry of Foreign Affairs: In 2010, Kapunga was selected by the Dutch Ministry of Foreign Affairs to be involved in its Private Sector Investment Programme (PSI). As part of the programme, Kapunga is provided with a grant to train smallholder farmers in agricultural processes.

World Food Programme supplier: The sponsor, one of the main suppliers to the World Food Programme (WFP) in Sub-Saharan Africa, has invested in systems that allow fast delivery of bulk orders to WFP depots in case of an emergency. This makes the sponsor a preferred partner of the WFP.

Sustainable agriculture expertise: Justin Vermaak, a respected expert in environmentally-friendly farming techniques in Africa, runs a number of projects that spearhead biofuel crop research, including high-yielding Jatropha seeds for use on non-arable land. Furthermore, Verus Group has won a number of awards in South Africa for the design of sustainable farming systems and initiatives. The company is currently involved in the development and financing of commercial wind power generation modules for farms in South Africa. On farm, Verus have implemented strict environmental impact restrictions. No mineral oils are used, waste is minimised, recycling encouraged and burning banned. Management has also gazetted 450 ha of the farm as a wildlife preservation area to allow native bird species to breed.

Cooperation with the IRRI research programme: The International Rice Research Institute (IRRI) has a base and seed nursery at Kapunga where it stations some of its research scientists. IRRI uses the base to research local seed varieties and conducts tests on fertilisation, seed purification, yield enhancement and disease resistance.

Black Coucal research programme – Max Planck Institute, Germany: The bird life around the Kapunga farm is rich and diverse, with a plethora of scientifically important species. Each year since 2001, the Max Planck Institute for Ornithology (Germany) has been sending a team to Kapunga to study the Black Coucal cuckoo. The Max Planck team has been able to establish a full-time base at the farm, including a permanent laboratory and accommodation space.

Farm level development initiatives: Medical and school facilities on the farm provide health and education services for children of labourers and local management staff as well as for some of the children from the surrounding community.

17. In July 2012, the farm was visited by Richard Rogers, head of the Agricultural Programmes for the Gates Foundation. Kapunga has been chosen as the East African Gates Foundation site from which improved cultivation and growing techniques will be introduced to regional farmers.

Exhibit 17.6

VALUATION & IRR

Base case

Base Case: Assume upfront share purchase 25% up front, becoming 45% on exit, funding 100% of CAPEX

Holding year	0	1	2	3	4	5	6	7
Financial Year	2010/11	2011/12	2012/13	2013/14	2014/15	2015/16	2016/17	2017/18
Tulip Ownership	*44.9%*	*44.9%*	*44.9%*	*44.9%*	*44.9%*	*44.9%*	*44.9%*	*44.9%*
Tulip Equity Flows								
Purchase of Shares	(5,250,000)							
New Shares	(7,588,000)							
Closing Costs	0							
FCFE (Dividends)		1,948,322	1,617,881	2,839,881	4,084,547	5,056,871	4,791,837	5,156,076
Return of Capital (NAV)		0	0	0	0	0	0	19,232,441
Total Tulip Equity Flows	(12,838,000)	**1,948,322**	**1,617,881**	**2,839,881**	**4,084,547**	**5,056,871**	**4,791,837**	**24,388,517**

IRR = 26.80%
Exit Multiple = 3.48x

Upside (Faster yield development)

Base Case: Assume upfront share purchase 25% up front, becoming 45% on exit, funding 100% of CAPEX

Holding year	0	1	2	3	4	5	6	7
Financial Year	2010/11	2011/12	2012/13	2013/14	2014/15	2015/16	2016/17	2017/18
Tulip Ownership	*44.9%*	*44.9%*	*44.9%*	*44.9%*	*44.9%*	*44.9%*	*44.9%*	*44.9%*
Tulip Equity Flows								
Purchase of Shares	(5,250,000)							
New Shares	(7,588,000)							
Closing Costs	0							
FCFE (Dividends)		2,362,192	2,260,934	3,568,634	4,979,771	4,699,721	4,900,691	5,159,464
Return of Capital (NAV)		0	0	0	0	0	0	19,232,441
Total Tulip Equity Flows	(12,838,000)	**2,362,192**	**2,260,934**	**3,568,634**	**4,979,771**	**4,699,721**	**4,900,691**	**24,391,905**

IRR = 26.66%
Exit Multiple = 3.67x

Downside (temporary removal of rice tariffs)

Base Case: Assume upfront share purchase 25% up front, becoming 45% on exit, funding 100% of CAPEX

Holding year	0	1	2	3	4	5	6	7
Financial Year	2010/11	2011/12	2012/13	2013/14	2014/15	2015/16	2016/17	2017/18
Tulip Ownership	*44.9%*	*44.9%*	*44.9%*	*44.9%*	*44.9%*	*44.9%*	*44.9%*	*44.9%*
Tulip Equity Flows								
Purchase of Shares	(5,250,000)							
New Shares	(7,588,000)							
Closing Costs	0							
FCFE (Dividends)		1,948,322	240,395	885,543	3,201,404	4,620,807	4,773,800	4,180,574
Return of Capital (NAV)		0	0	0	0	0	0	19,217,658
Total Tulip Equity Flows	(12,838,000)	**1,948,322**	**240,395**	**885,543**	**3,201,404**	**4,620,807**	**4,773,800**	**23,398,232**

IRR = 21.69%
Exit Multiple = 3.04x

Sensitivity Analysis

ENTRY vs EXIT VALUATION — Method 1

EXIT VALUATION			ENTRY VALUATION							
			44.9%	**45.3%**	**45.7%**	**46.1%**	**46.5%**	**46.9%**	**47.4%**	**% Ownership**
			21,000,000	**20,475,000**	**19,950,000**	**19,425,000**	**18,900,000**	**18,375,000**	**17,850,000**	**Entry Valuation**
			0.0%	**–2.5%**	**–5.0%**	**–7.5%**	**–10.0%**	**–12.5%**	**–15.0%**	**% Change in Entry Valuation**
3.3x	36,403,215	–15.00%	25.6%	26.1%	26.6%	27.2%	27.7%	28.3%	28.8%	
3.5x	38,544,580	–10.00%	26.0%	26.5%	27.0%	27.6%	28.1%	28.7%	29.2%	
3.7x	40,685,946	–5.00%	26.4%	26.9%	27.4%	27.9%	28.5%	29.0%	29.6%	
3.9x	42,827,311	0.00%	26.8%	27.3%	27.8%	28.3%	28.9%	29.4%	30.0%	
4.1x	44,968,677	5.00%	27.2%	27.7%	28.2%	28.7%	29.2%	29.8%	30.4%	
4.3x	47,110,043	10.00%	27.5%	28.0%	28.5%	29.1%	29.6%	30.2%	30.7%	
4.5x	49,251,408	15.00%	27.9%	28.4%	28.9%	29.4%	30.0%	30.5%	31.1%	
Implied Exit P/E Ratio	Exit Valuation (USD)	% Change in Exit Value								
Method	*1*									

ENTRY vs EXIT VALUATION — Method 2

EXIT VALUATION			ENTRY VALUATION							
			44.9%	**45.3%**	**45.7%**	**46.1%**	**46.5%**	**46.9%**	**47.4%**	**% Ownership**
			21,000,000	**20,475,000**	**19,950,000**	**19,425,000**	**18,900,000**	**18,375,000**	**17,850,000**	**Entry Valuation**
			0.0%	**–2.5%**	**–5.0%**	**–7.5%**	**–10.0%**	**–12.5%**	**–15.0%**	**% Change in Entry Valuation**
4.4x	47,783,677	–15.00%	27.7%	28.2%	28.7%	29.2%	29.7%	30.3%	30.8%	
4.6x	50,594,481	–10.00%	28.1%	28.6%	29.1%	29.6%	30.2%	30.7%	31.3%	
4.9x	53,405,286	–5.00%	28.6%	29.1%	29.6%	30.1%	30.6%	31.2%	31.8%	
5.1x	56,216,090	0.00%	29.0%	29.5%	30.0%	30.5%	31.1%	31.6%	32.2%	
5.4x	59,026,895	5.00%	29.5%	30.0%	30.5%	31.0%	31.5%	32.1%	32.6%	
5.7x	61,837,689	10.00%	29.9%	30.4%	30.9%	31.4%	31.9%	32.5%	33.1%	
5.9x	64,648,504	15.00%	30.3%	30.8%	31.3%	31.8%	32.4%	32.9%	33.5%	
Implied Exit P/E Ratio	Exit Valuation (USD)	% Change in Exit Value								
Method	*2*									

ENTRY vs EXIT VALUATION — Method 3

EXIT VALUATION			ENTRY VALUATION							
			44.9%	**45.3%**	**45.7%**	**46.1%**	**46.5%**	**46.9%**	**47.4%**	**% Ownership**
			21,000,000	**20,475,000**	**19,950,000**	**19,425,000**	**18,900,000**	**18,375,000**	**17,850,000**	**Entry Valuation**
			0.0%	**–2.5%**	**–5.0%**	**–7.5%**	**–10.0%**	**–12.5%**	**–15.0%**	**% Change in Entry Valuation**
8.5x	92,854,502	–15.00%	34.0%	34.5%	35.0%	35.5%	36.1%	36.6%	37.2%	
9.0x	98,316,531	–10.00%	34.6%	35.1%	35.6%	36.2%	36.7%	37.2%	37.8%	
9.5x	103,778,561	–5.00%	35.3%	35.8%	36.3%	36.8%	37.3%	37.9%	38.4%	
10.0x	109,240,590	0.00%	35.9%	36.4%	36.9%	37.4%	37.9%	38.5%	39.0%	
10.5x	114,702,620	5.00%	36.5%	36.9%	37.5%	38.0%	38.5%	39.1%	39.6%	
11.0x	120,164,649	10.00%	37.0%	37.5%	38.0%	38.5%	39.1%	39.6%	40.2%	
11.5x	125,626,679	15.00%	37.6%	38.1%	38.6%	39.1%	39.6%	40.2%	40.7%	
Implied Exit P/E Ratio	Exit Valuation (USD)	% Change in Exit Value								
Method	*3*									

OUTPUT PRICES vs YIELDS									
	YIELDS								
OUTPUT PRICES	**−10.0%**	**−7.5%**	**−5.0%**	**−2.5%**	0.0%	**2.5%**	**5.0%**	**7.5%**	**10.0%**
−10.0%	21.5%	22.1%	22.7%	23.3%	23.9%	24.4%	25.0%	25.6%	26.1%
−7.5%	22.2%	22.8%	23.4%	24.0%	24.6%	25.2%	25.8%	26.4%	26.9%
−5.0%	22.9%	23.5%	24.1%	24.7%	25.3%	25.9%	26.5%	27.1%	27.7%
−2.5%	23.6%	24.2%	24.8%	25.5%	26.1%	26.7%	27.3%	27.9%	28.5%
0.0%	24.3%	24.9%	25.5%	26.2%	26.8%	27.4%	28.1%	28.7%	29.3%
2.5%	24.9%	25.6%	26.2%	26.9%	27.5%	28.2%	28.8%	29.5%	30.1%
5.0%	25.6%	26.3%	26.9%	27.6%	28.3%	28.9%	29.6%	30.2%	30.9%
7.5%	26.2%	26.9%	27.6%	28.3%	29.0%	29.6%	30.3%	31.0%	31.6%
10.0%	26.9%	27.6%	28.3%	29.0%	29.7%	30.4%	31.1%	31.7%	32.4%

OUTPUT PRICES vs DIRECT COSTS									
	OUTPUT PRICES								
DIRECT COSTS	**−10.0%**	**−7.5%**	**−5.0%**	**−2.5%**	0.0%	**2.5%**	**5.0%**	**7.5%**	**10.0%**
10.0%	22.4%	23.2%	23.9%	24.7%	25.4%	26.1%	26.9%	27.6%	28.3%
7.5%	22.8%	23.5%	24.3%	25.0%	25.8%	26.5%	27.2%	27.9%	28.7%
5.0%	23.1%	23.9%	24.6%	25.4%	26.1%	26.8%	27.6%	28.3%	29.0%
2.5%	23.5%	24.3%	25.0%	25.7%	26.5%	27.2%	27.9%	28.6%	29.3%
0.0%	23.9%	24.6%	25.3%	26.1%	26.8%	27.5%	28.3%	29.0%	29.7%
−2.5%	24.2%	25.0%	25.7%	26.4%	27.1%	27.9%	28.6%	29.3%	30.0%
−5.0%	24.6%	25.3%	26.0%	26.8%	27.5%	28.2%	28.9%	29.7%	30.4%
−7.5%	24.9%	25.7%	26.4%	27.1%	27.8%	28.6%	29.3%	30.0%	30.7%
−10.0%	25.3%	26.0%	26.7%	27.5%	28.2%	28.9%	29.6%	30.4%	31.1%

CAPEX vs EXIT YEAR									
	CAPEX								
EXIT YEAR	**15.0%**	**12.5%**	**10.0%**	**7.5%**	0.0%	**−2.5%**	**−5.0%**	**−7.5%**	**−10.0%**
5	24.9%	25.0%	25.1%	25.2%	25.5%	25.6%	25.7%	25.8%	25.9%
6	25.7%	25.8%	25.9%	26.0%	26.2%	26.3%	26.4%	26.5%	26.6%
7	26.3%	26.4%	26.4%	26.5%	26.8%	26.9%	27.0%	27.1%	27.2%
8	26.7%	26.8%	26.9%	27.0%	27.2%	27.3%	27.4%	27.5%	27.6%
9	27.0%	27.1%	27.2%	27.3%	27.5%	27.6%	27.7%	27.8%	27.8%
10	27.3%	27.4%	27.4%	27.5%	27.8%	27.8%	27.9%	28.0%	28.1%

Exhibit 17.7

KRPL Investment at a Glance

Deal & Valuation: Pre-money Valuation: US$ 19m Deal size: US$ 12.84m – US$ 5.25m for 25% of sponsor's stake – US$7.59m CAPEX/new shares S'holding Pre-money: 100% Sponsor Post-: 51.7% Sponsor 48.3% Duxton Investors	**Returns:** IRR: 26.8% (7-year hold) Cash Multiple: 3.5x **IRR Sensitivities:** Removal of rice tariff: 21.7% Faster Yield development: 29.7%
Farm: Total area: 7,890ha Farmed now (irrigated): 3,200ha Farmed post-expansion (irrigated): 4,400ha Off-season Barley/Legumes: 720ha Lease length: 99 years from 1995 Expiry: 82 years in 2094 Roads: over 70km (graded) Irrigation canals: 27km primary, 80km secondary Grid / generator power access, farm-wide Wi-Fi Water Rights: 4.8cumecs – renewable every 4y	**Mill:** Fully refurbished – Buhler (German) Capacity: 25,000MT (35,000MT after CAPEX) Current utilisation:15,000MT 175kwh power required – grid + generator **Mill-out Ratios:** Milled Rice: 64% → 67% Bran: 4.8% → 4.5% Husk: 30.8% → 28.5%
Rice Market: Tanzania consumption: 1M MT/year Tanzania production: 900,000MT/year Tanzania imports: 100,000MT/year World Price: US$ 500/MT TZ Price: US$ 1,200/MT (75pc tariff) DRC Price: US$ 1,600/MT Average yield TZ: 1.5MT/ha	**Yields:** Yield average (2012): 5.23MT/ha Top 10pc yields: 7.6MT/ha Lowest 10pc yields: 2.6MT/ha Highest yield achieved: 8.16 MT/ha **Rice varieties:** Saro 5, Kapunga Star, Faye Dumi – mix of aromatic and non-aromatic
Financing: Debt: No long-term debt Short-term financing for Production and CMA: US$ 3m and 7m StanChart facilities **Sales & Marketing:** Bulk sold farm gate in 50kg bags Premium paid as bulk availability Customers incl. army/hospitals/traders Potential to go into smaller retail bags Brand – "Rice from Africa for Africa"	**Key-Ratios:** **Margins:** Gross: 55% → 67% EBITDA: 30% → 58% **Profitability:** ROA: 2% → 10% ROE: 2% → 15% **Growth:** Net Sales: 18% Net Income: 42%
Outgrower Programme: 75 individual tenants (locals) on 1,227ha of land Allows farm to scale-up quickly Enhances local relations/political capital Inputs and services financed by farm in return for guaranteed paddy for the mill & share of crop	**Management & Shareholders:** Mgmt: Verus – SA & local – proven experience S'holders:–large agri commodity trading company
SRI/ESG features: Gates Foundation – outgrower excellence site Netherlands MoFA – outgrower programme World Food Programme – S'holders supply to IRRI – variety research programme hosted farm Black Coucal/reserve – 450ha. wildlife reserve Road Grading – provided for free to community School & Medical for employees and outgrowers	**Due diligence completed:** Financial ✓ Legal ✓ Agronomic ✓ Outgrower Programme ✓ Water/Irrigation ✓ Tax/Structuring advice ✓ Background checks on Sponsors ✓ Farm security procedures ✓ Chemical/fertiliser safety ✓

CASE

18 PRIVATE EQUITY IN FRONTIER MARKETS
CREATING A FUND IN GEORGIA

SYNOPSIS

In 2013, George Bachiashvili is tasked by the then prime minister of Georgia to start an investment fund to invest private capital in the country, spur foreign investment and stimulate long-term economic growth. With little precedent, George has to decide on a range of key parameters for the new fund—from its mission, to its investment strategy as well as its structure and required resources.

PEDAGOGICAL OBJECTIVE OF THE CASE

The case highlights the challenges of setting up an institutional-quality private equity firm under greenfield conditions. Readers are asked to develop a coherent framework for the fund, taking the specific constraints and opportunities of the setting into account. Therefore, two main topics lend themselves for exploration: (a) private equity in emerging and, in particular, frontier markets and (b) setting up a first-time fund.

SUGGESTED ASSIGNMENT QUESTIONS

1. What would you suggest to be the mission of the fund? What should the relation between strategic and financial goals be?
2. What type of additional investors would you target for the fund? (Consider global or regional, pension funds, fund of funds, sovereign wealth funds, high net worth individuals, family offices, development finance institutions.)
3. What investment strategy would you recommend for the fund? Given the resources available, how should George construct his team?
4. What private equity fund structure would best enable George to fulfill the fund's strategic and financial objectives, satisfy the needs of the limited partner base, and execute his investment strategy?

ADDITIONAL RESOURCES

To make the most of this case study, we suggest the following additional sources to provide context and background information:

- In particular, we recommend the following chapters from *Mastering Private Equity—Transformation via Venture Capital, Minority Investments & Buyouts*
  - Chapter 16 Fund Formation
  - Chapter 17 Fundraising
  - Chapter 21 LP Direct Investment
- You may also refer to the book website for further material:
  www.masteringprivateequity.com

Private Equity in Frontier Markets

Creating a Fund in Georgia

09/2016-6215

This case was written by Bernardo Bluhm Alves, INSEAD MBA July 2015, under the supervision of Bowen White, Associate Director of the INSEAD Global Private Equity Initiative (GPEI), Michael Prahl, Distinguished Fellow of the GPEI, and Anne-Marie Carrick, Research Associate at INSEAD. It is intended to be used as a basis for class discussion rather than to illustrate either effective or ineffective handling of an administrative situation.

Funding for this case was provided by the Georgian Co-Investment Fund.

The authors gratefully acknowledge the help of George Bachiashvili, Founder & CEO, Thea Jokhadze, MD Finance, Risk and Investor Relations, Sopho Khelashvili, Senior Risk Analyst, Ilia Kekelidze, Senior Financial Analyst and Nikoloz Khatiashvili, Senior Investment Analyst.

Additional material about INSEAD case studies (e.g., videos, spreadsheets, links) can be accessed at cases.insead.edu.

February 2013

George Bachiashvili, deputy CEO of the Partnership Fund,[1] was excited yet daunted by the task he had been assigned. Bidzina Ivanishvili, Prime Minister of Georgia and one of the country's wealthiest people, had given him a mandate to create an investment vehicle funded entirely with private capital for investment in Georgia. The goal was to spur foreign investment and stimulate long-term economic growth. Having no precedent for such a vehicle in Georgia, best practices would have to be identified and incorporated from other sources to get it off the ground.

While Georgia clearly needed capital, it was not on the radar of most international investors. However, the US$1 billion anchor investment pledged by the Prime Minister with no strings attached gave it some serious chips in the game. Even so, "frontier markets" were among the most challenging contexts in which to raise private funding with capital deployment often hindered by an unstable political environment, weak institutions and corruption. Until 2012, Georgia had suffered from a lack of inward capital flows and investment, despite a strong track record of liberal reforms following independence from the Soviet Union in 1991.

Returning to his office, George reflected on the task at hand (Exhibit 18.1 George Bachiashvili's bio). He was responsible for a new investment vehicle which, if successful, could transform the Georgian economy.

Background

Social and Political Environment

Georgia lies to the east of the Black Sea bordered by Turkey and Armenia to the south, Azerbaijan to the southeast and Russia to the north. It is located on the Transport Corridor Europe-Caucasus-Asia (TRACECA), the shortest route connecting central Asia to Europe. It had a population of 3.7 million in 2013.[2] The official language was Georgian, but Russian was widely spoken; most Georgians were comfortable conducting business meetings in Russian. English was also an established business language in Georgia unlike some other ex-Soviet countries.

In April 1991, Georgia had declared independence from the Soviet Union shortly before the communist regime collapsed. After the political upheaval that followed,

1. This was a government-sponsored fund created to foster private investment in the Georgian economy.
2. National Statistics Office of Georgia.

Eduard Shevardnadze, the Soviet regime's representative in Georgia during the 1970s and early 1980s, steered the country towards economic improvements. However, his government was widely considered inefficient, corrupt, nepotistic and excessively bureaucratic.

After the 'Rose Revolution' of November 2003, Georgia pursued a pro-Western foreign policy. The peaceful uprising forced Shevardnadze to cede power following an election that was widely considered to have been rigged. An interim government was assembled in January 2004 and Mikheil Saakashvili was elected president with 96% of the popular vote. Saakashvili had been Justice Minister in the Shevardnadze's government.[3] Constitutional amendments were rushed through parliament to strengthen the powers of the president, to dismiss parliament and create the office of Prime Minister.

The new president faced many problems, including over 230,000 internally displaced people that put an enormous strain on the economy. In the separatist areas of Abkhazia and South Ossetia, overseen by Russian and United Nations peacekeepers, peace remained fragile. Relations deteriorated when semi-separatist Ajarian leader Aslan Abashidze rejected Saakashvili's demands for the right of the Tbilisi government to run in Ajaria. Both sides mobilised forces in preparation for a military confrontation. Saakashvili's ultimatum, together with street demonstrations, forced Abashidze to resign and flee.

Under pressure to deliver on his promised reforms, Saakashvili's popularity began to wane in the face of high unemployment, continued corruption and the unresolved dispute over Abkhazia. In 2007, anti-government protests in Georgia spurred changes in the labour laws, reduced combined social and income tax rates (from 32% to 25% in 2008 and to 20% in 2009). It loosened the license and permits required for business. Saakashvili called parliamentary and presidential elections in January 2008, which he won. Russia's continued political, economic and military support for the separatist governments in Abkhazia and South Ossetia meant that relations remained fraught. In August 2008 a crisis erupted over South Ossetia that led to war. [4]

In October 2012, following free and fair parliamentary elections, Georgia experienced its first peaceful and constitutional transfer of power through elections, with Saakashvili conceding defeat to Bidzina Ivanishvili, leader of the opposition coalition that was called the Georgian Dream.

The Business Environment

Following its independence from the Soviet Union in 1991, Georgia's economy was "opened up". From 1990 to 1994, the size of its economy shrank by 72% as the new state wrestled with internal political instability, a drop in trade with other ex-Soviet countries, and civil unrest in the regions of Abkhazia and South Ossetia.[5] Prices and

---

3. European Stability Initiative. (n.d.). Retrieved April 21, 2016, from http://www.esiweb.org/index.php?lang=en.
4. An international diplomatic crisis erupted when Russia announced that it would no longer respect the Commonwealth of Independent States' economic sanctions on Abkhazia in 1996, and established direct relations with the separatist authorities in Abkhazia and South Ossetia. The crisis was linked to the push for Georgia to be readied for NATO Membership and, indirectly, a unilateral declaration of independence by Kosovo.
5. Source: (2009) *The World Bank in Georgia 1993-2007.* Independent Evaluation Group, World Bank, Washington, D.C.

government revenues also took a hit during the period: consumer prices increased more than 89,000 times during the same timeframe and tax revenues fell from 22.1% of GDP in the first year of independence to 3% in 1994.[6] After reaching an all-time low, the economy experienced a phase of expansion and grew by 30% between 1995 and 1998. However, growth was again derailed in 1998 by the Russian financial crisis. With its weak institutions and misguided policy, Georgia struggled to break the mould and advance to new heights. The investment climate suffered as a result of onerous taxation, widespread corruption and weak regulatory frameworks.

By 2003, following the Rose Revolution, Georgia's economy saw a gradual growth trajectory, spurred mainly by government spending.[7] Saakashvili's objective was to create a low-regulation, low-tax business environment, small and efficient government, and free market policies. The government rolled out a series of reforms to reduce red tape and fight corruption. Initial steps were taken to overhaul Soviet-style legislation that governed the labour market. The Economic Liberty Act imposed fiscal constraints[8] designed to reinforce economic stability and simplify the tax regime to encourage business creation.[9]

By 2013, the impact of these reforms was evident. GDP increased fourfold to approximately US$16 billion from 1999 to 2013, while inflation was below 10%.[10] In 2006 and 2008, the World Bank named Georgia the world's top reformer. In 2010, the World Bank's Ease of Doing Business survey pronounced Georgia one of the friendliest investor destinations in the world – ranked 11th.[11] The same year, Transparency International rated Georgia first for the relative reduction in the level of corruption. These accolades were underpinned by activity on the ground – new ventures increased from approximately 3,200 in 2004 to almost 15,000 in 2012.[12] It was widely acknowledged that Georgia was ahead of its post-Soviet peers as a good place for business (Exhibit 18.2).

Investment Environment

> *"Growth would benefit from regional expansion, including greater access to European, Russian and other neighbouring markets that would attract large-scale investments. Georgia's location and favourable investment climate should support the transition from a strategic transit corridor to a logistics platform for*

---

6. Inflation Source: (2009) *The World Bank in Georgia 1993-2007.* Independent Evaluation Group, World Bank, Washington, D.C. Tax revenue source: Wang, J. (1999) *The Georgian Hyperinflation and Stabilization.* International Monetary Fund.
7. Much of this economic growth was derived from a major but one-time investment in the Baku-Tbilisi-Ceyhan oil pipeline.
8. This law prohibited the government from moving away from its fiscally conservative policies. It mandated that the budget deficit stay below 3% of GDP, total public debt below 60% of GDP, and budgetary expenditures below 30% of GDP. The law also banned the possibility of the introduction of new state taxes or increases in existing taxes, (with a very few exceptions) except when approved in a nationwide referendum.
9. As an example, due to the elimination of existing licensing requirements, time to start a new business decreased from 25 days in 2003 to 2 days in 2013.
10. World Bank, in Local Current Unit.
11. According to the World Bank, Georgia's public debt remained sustainable. Total public sector debt fell from 38.7% of GDP in 2010 to 32.2% in 2013 due to continued fiscal consolidation efforts. About 80% of public debt in 2013 was external and was dominated by bilateral and multilateral debt. Further, the Georgian fiscal and monetary policy was focused on low fiscal deficits, low inflation, and a free floating exchange rate.
12. World Bank.

the wider region. This requires further improvements to transport infrastructure, investing in logistics facilities and industries adding value to goods transiting through the country."

Source: Strategy for Georgia 2013, European Bank for Reconstruction & Development

Despite the strides made in structural reforms and economic development, the investment environment failed to improve. Investor interest was dampened by the 2008 conflict over South Ossetia with Russia. The risk appetite of global investors declined during the global financial crisis and hit Georgia hard. There was a sharp drop in inbound foreign direct investment (FDI), from US$1,564 million in 2008 to US$658 million in 2009. By 2013 it had partially recovered to US$942 (Exhibits 18.3, 18.4, 18.5 and 18.6).

Deflation, unemployment and minimal foreign exchange reserves were additional challenges to contend with. Although the National Bank of Georgia (NBG) adopted an inflation target of 5%, prices fell in 2012 by 1% and were on track to decrease in 2013. As of 2009, the rate of unemployment hovered between 15% and 17%. According to the NBG, official foreign exchange reserves were US$3.1 billion in October 2013.

These challenges were typified, and compounded, by Georgia's currency, the lari. Although a fully convertible currency, with trading volumes comparable to its peers in the region as a percentage of GDP, the small absolute size of the lari market posed problems for large transactions. Lari-dollar and lari-euro markets amounted to US$27.9 billion and €9.9 billion, respectively in 2012. Large transactions could easily affect the exchange rate.[13] In addition, there were no liquid forwards or futures instruments to hedge the lari risk.

Most of Georgia's companies were small – given its relatively recent transition to a market economy (1991) – and only 20 had EBITDA above US$40 million, built mainly on the remnants of Soviet era assets that had been privatised.[14] By 2013, the service sector accounted for 57% of GDP. Agriculture was the country's largest employer – accounting for 53% of the workforce or two million people (see Exhibit 18.7).

Georgia's Stock Exchange (GSE), established in 1999, provided limited liquidity for companies to raise capital. Only a handful of the 133 securities admitted to the Georgian stock exchange represented actively traded shares in listed companies. By late 2013, the GSE had a total market capitalisation of just under US$1 billion – approximately 6% of 2012 GDP – and only a few securities on the stock exchange had daily turnover that exceeded US$1,000.[15] However, the largest Georgian bank was listed in the premium segment of the London Stock Exchange with market cap of €498.1 as of year-end 2013.[16]

---

13. Excluding activity conducted directly by the National Bank of Georgia (Source: National Bank of Georgia). The lari had been stable over the last three years; ranging from 1.69 to 1.65 to the US$, due in part to illiquidity in the forex market (Source: World Bank database).
14. Case interviews.
15. (2014) *Georgia: Private Sector Financing and the Role of Risk-bearing Instruments, November 2013.* European Investment Bank.
16. Bank of Georgia was listed on 24 Nov 2006.

Setting up a New Investment Vehicle

George began the task of setting up a new private equity fund by organising it into three phases. First he needed to identify the right Limited Partner (LP) base. Next, to select a fund structure that would be most attractive to these LPs. Finally he needed a compelling investment strategy. While Ivanishvili's anchor investment came with no strings attached, it raised the question of how investors would react to the Prime Minister's involvement. He had pledged not to interfere with how the fund was run; it was understood that his participation was meant to help provide political cover for investment activity within Georgia. Potential investors would need to be both comfortable with some degree of engagement yet assured that there would be no "meddling" in the fund's management. It was not clear whether they would be interested in a purely economic capacity, or simply seeking to connect more closely with the Prime Minister.

Potential LPs – Regional or Global

Capital investment in Georgia came from a variety of sources that were managed by different structures (Exhibit 18.8). The list of potential participants for PE fundraising was significantly larger. Ivanishvili's anchor investment had given George a great start for attracting other LPs' interest. He now had to focus his efforts on the best investors – from pension funds to high net worth individuals and investment banks.

Should he focus on regional or global investors? With the US$1 billion commitment, George should be able to attract large global investors in the PE asset class. If he succeeded, this would shine a spotlight on Georgia and stimulate further capital inflow into the economy, but he was aware that large LPs in North America and Western Europe might not see Georgia as a compelling growth story but as a risky environment.

Attracting regional investors was another challenge. Although investors in Eastern Europe and the Caucuses were accustomed to deploying capital in countries like Georgia, they were typically not active participants in private equity funds. Furthermore, the number of regional investors with sufficient capital to commit to an investment of this size was limited.

Which LP?

In addition to the regional vs. global LP issue, George needed to decide what type of LPs he should focus on.

Institutional Investors: These accounted for more than two thirds of the total capital allocated to private equity[17] and included pension and superannuation funds, sovereign wealth funds, insurance companies and banks. However, institutional investors' PE programmes typically accounted for less than 8% of their total assets under management (AUM). They often employed a highly structured approach in allocating

17. Preqin 2013 Private Equity & Venture Capital Report.

capital to private equity, building a fund that focused on creating a diversified portfolio of brand-name managers. They had explicit target returns and cash-flow requirements based on defined future liabilities. The due diligence process for institutional investors was extensive and required significant engagement from the fundraising entity to address standardized due diligence questionnaires. Given the often public nature of the institutional beneficiaries, LPs might be required to report potentially sensitive information with regards to their fund investments, without which their capacity to invest in specific sectors could be restricted.

Endowments & Foundations: These invested funds on behalf of non-profit organisations with less rigid mandates than institutional investors. As of 2013, they accounted for roughly 20% of total private equity AUM. Processes were similar to institutional LPs but less constrained by defined future liabilities, investment restrictions and regulations. Endowments allocated more aggressively to this asset class, with approximately 12% of their assets in PE as of 2013.

Family Offices: These represented 5% of the PE industry's total AUM. On average they allocated 20-30% of their overall portfolios to PE. They also undertook high levels of direct investment in private deals, often in the same sector as a family-owned business. Their due diligence process for assessing allocation opportunities to PE funds was less structured than that of institutional investors. Investment decision-making was often based on one family member's personal preference.

Corporate Investors: This group represented 2% of total global private equity AUM as of 2013, with a larger portion in emerging markets. Their allocation to PE funds differed from institutional and other financial sector LPs: in addition to financial returns they might be keen to gain access to new markets and additional deal flow for co-investment or future mergers and acquisitions (M&A) activity.

DFIs: Development Finance Institutions (DFIs) could be interested in the general development of Georgia or the Caucasus region. Some private investors might wish to invest for the first or second time in the region with a trusted local partner. This would enable them to gain more regional experience before making a larger commitment. Other DFIs might be interested purely in financial returns for their diversified global portfolios.

Funds of Funds: Private equity funds of funds acted as intermediaries between traditional LPs and PE managers. They raised capital for investment in PE funds' portfolios and, in turn, allocated capital to PE fund managers in that portfolio. Due to the diversification benefits of this model, they often allocated capital to riskier funds. Funds of funds also created tailored portfolios that focused on specific geographies or strategies.

Structural Options

Once he had decided which type of LP to focus on, George had to select an appropriate fund structure for the investment opportunity. In a "frontier market" with no established best practice, limited regulatory guidance on PE investing, and where processes and structures (such as limited liability partnership structure for funds' limited partners) and tax transparency were still to be established, the simplest route would be to domicile a fund abroad in a more established jurisdiction. That way, George could take advantage of existing double taxation and bilateral investment treaties to funnel and secure the capital for investment in fund opportunities.

However, there was still the question of which fund structure to opt for, which was key to the mechanics of investing capital and financing his day-to-day activities – building an investment team, making payroll and establishing relationships for future fundraising. While he knew the fund's specific terms and conditions would be set in stone through negotiations with individual LPs, George narrowed his options to five well-established fund models.

Closed-end Funds

A limited partnership would enable a closed-end structure, the dominant PE fund model. With a limited partnership, investors committed a defined amount of capital to a blind investment pool for a period ranging from 8 to 12 years, managed by a general partner (GP) who was responsible for all investment decisions. It was called a "blind pool" as LPs had no discretion over the specific investments made from the fund.[18] Closed-end funds had a pre-defined investment period with an average of five years. During this time GPs called capital from LPs to finance investments. Management fees were drawn from committed capital during a predefined investment period and on invested capital for the remainder of the fund's term, which financed day-to-day operating expenses. Investors realised a return when the fund exited its investments and distributed the invested capital and any capital appreciation. GPs earned an incentive fee – or carried interest – that was defined as a percentage of the excess return generated on investment.

Evergreen Funds or Permanent Capital Private Equity Vehicles

These vehicles had no defined fund life, which allowed for continuous new investments and distributions. Funding could be raised at any time by issuances to new investors or by investors rolling-over existing commitments. Distributions were made to fund investors via the proceeds from dividends, divestments or capital provided by incoming investors. This structure eliminated artificial time constraints for the fund manager to improve portfolio companies' operations and saved time which would otherwise be spent on fundraising activities. However, the open-ended nature of these vehicles removed the discipline of exits required in a closed-end fund model and created issues of intermittent valuation for the calculation of carried interest and management fees, and between existing and new investors. They also implied longer lock-ups of investor capital.

Pledge Funds

Pledge funds were pools of "soft" commitments from investors to the totality of the fund's committed capital. Participants could choose to partake in investments on a

18. Individual LPs can include terms that negate their participation in deals in specific sectors, but LPs in this structure typically participate in nearly all fund investments and face stiff penalties for defaulting on capital calls.

deal-by-deal basis. A vehicle would be created for each investment or portfolio of investments to cater to the different investors. Fund managers were required to finance day-to-day activity without the benefit of management fees on committed capital, and typically drew management fees and carried interest on invested capital. Carried interest was calculated on a deal-by-deal basis. The decision-making process, however, could hinder the ability to execute fast on an investment opportunity. Managing different groups of investors across different investments could potentially become complex.

Co-investment Fund

A co-investment fund focused on direct investment in companies alongside a lead PE investor on virtually the same terms. Co-investment rights were often granted to LPs in a closed-end fund and could provide additional exposure to an attractive investment opportunity. Co-investment also allowed lead PE funds to draw additional capital directly from LPs to execute large deals. Existing LPs and PE fund managers typically had a list of accredited co-investment partners. The GPs invited trusted investors to co-invest with them based on their ability to add value – to foster their relationship and bridge the gap between what they could invest in and the deal size. LPs typically participated in co-investment opportunities on a one-off basis, paying no, or reduced, management fees nor carried interest. In a co-investment fund structure, however, management fees and carried interest – while typically reduced – were required.

Search Funds

Search funds were mainly used to buy a single company that would be run by the fund manager. In the initial stage, the manager raised funds to cover the expenses involved in searching for an enterprise to acquire. This could take up to two years, with the risk that no suitable business might be found during this time. If a suitable target was identified, he/she called for additional capital from investors to finance the acquisition, and would then take on an operational role as CEO or other strategic management position. As there was a single target company, search funds were usually backed by a limited number of investors. Depending on the target company size, the amount of capital required might not be large. If no suitable company was found and acquired, expenses were considered sunk costs.

Investment Strategy

The final phase for George was to decide on the investment strategy. He had a crucial decision to make on the fund's mandate based on the goals of the capital providers and the investment opportunities in Georgia. What deals would he be able to access? What growth strategies could he execute given the human resources and opportunities available? Ivanishvili's desire for his capital to stimulate a resurgence of private foreign investment in George augured well for success, but the strategy had to be defined.

Given the fund's scale, George was concerned that it could distort funding of other sectors and potentially tip smaller Georgian businesses into bankruptcy for want of funding. Moreover, by investing in heavily regulated industries he might be accused of benefiting from political connections. He thus had to tread carefully when looking at industries with many small players or industries where the government played an extensive role (e.g. government tenders and contracts) (Exhibit 18.9).

George also needed to determine an average deal size, the target number of investment projects and whether the fund would focus on control or minority stakes. These considerations would define the size of the fund's targets.[19] The number of projects would be key to deciding the size of the team.

To invest in a frontier market, investors needed to trust the team's capability to create deal flow and to affect changes at the operational level. George was keen to find a way to mitigate the investment risk. It was crucial to know what professional expertise the fund would need internally, for example a partner with some specific know-how. Many PE firms employed professionals uniquely from a finance background. While there was a talent pool of financial professionals in Georgia – like himself, many of them had studied abroad – managerial and technical professionals with a deeper understanding of business to propel growth were in short supply. These skills were particularly sought after for greenfield projects.

The Challenge

Time was short and George had some tough decisions make and solutions to find before presenting his plan to Ivanishvili. The task was daunting with the vast number of opportunities to be considered. Which options could best bring long-term benefits to the economy and the region? A poorly conceived strategy or investment execution could blemish the investment track record in the Caucasus for the foreseeable future. George had just a few days to prepare for the meeting with his anchor investor.

Exhibit 18.1

Bio: George Bachiashvili

Born in Moscow to a Georgian family of medical doctors, at the age of 7, George moved to Georgia with his family. After graduating from Caucasus University in 2005, George Bachiashvili started his career at Bank of Georgia. From there, he was hired to work at Dhabi Group, where he coordinated M&A transactions for Georgia, including the establishment of KOR Bank Georgia, and later the acquisition of Standard Bank Georgia (today, the merged bank is called KOR Standard Bank) and a Millennium brand hotel development project (to be commissioned in June 2016). George left to pursue an MBA at INSEAD in 2009. A year later, right after graduation, he started working at Booz & Company in Moscow. Shortly after, he assumed the position of CFO at Unicor Management Company, which owned and operated large-scale pharmaceutical, real estate, banking and agricultural assets in Russia. Unicor was owned by the Georgian billionaire Bidzina Ivanishvili. In late 2011, Ivanishvili announced that he would run for the office of prime minister and decided to sell all his Russian assets. George was part of the team responsible for this task. After successful divestments, in October 2012 he was invited to assume the position of Deputy CEO at the Partnership Fund, where he served until September 2013.

19. Smaller companies would probably require more advice and could potentially be more time consuming as management tended to be less professional and many best governance practices were still not implemented.

Exhibit 18.2

Worldwide Governance Indicators (WGI)

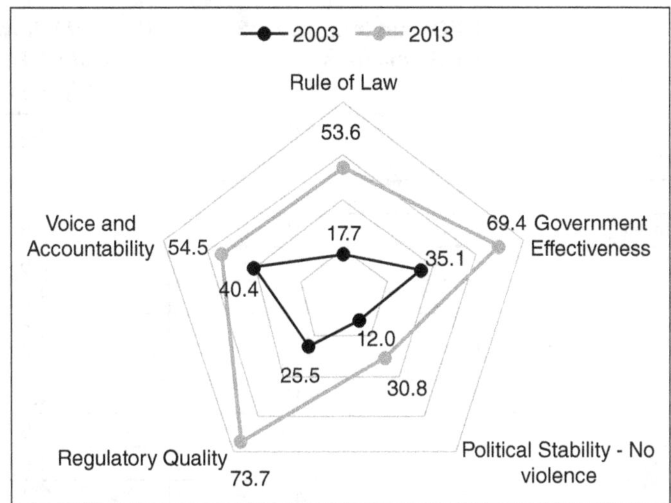

Percentile ranking among 214 countries in this study. It ranges from 0 (lowest) to 100 (highest) rank.

Source: World Bank

Exhibit 18.3

Georgia's Investment Climate

A 2003 paper written by the IMF's Clinton R. Shiells summarized the situation:

"The investment climate depends on a wide array of factors including burdensome taxation, widespread corruption and poor governance, weak legal and regulatory frameworks (including property rights violations) accompanied in many instances by pervasive state involvement in the economy, and the need to follow through with (or in some instances to initiate) structural reform programs. Underlying the weak investment climate is the need to build institutions appropriate to a market economy."

A 2014 statement from the U.S. State Department summarised the improvement in the country's fortunes:

"Companies in past years reported occasional issues arising from a lack of judicial independence, lack of intellectual property rights enforcement, lack of effective anti-trust policies, selective enforcement of economic laws, and difficulties resolving disputes over property rights. Georgia's Georgian Dream government has pledged to address these issues. Despite these remaining challenges, Georgia stands far ahead of its post-Soviet peers as a good place to do business."

Exhibit 18.4

Foreign Direct Investment (FDI) in Eastern Europe and Caucasus

Countries	FDI, net inflows 2013 US$ millions	FDI, net inflows 2013 as % of GDP
Albania	1,254	9.7
Armenia	370	3.5
Azerbaijan	2,619	3.6
Belarus	2,246	3.1
Bosnia and Herzegovina	315	1.8
Bulgaria	1,888	3.5
Georgia	942	5.9
Hungary	–4,112	–3.1
Kazakhstan	9,739	4.2
Kosovo	343	4.9
Kyrgyz Republic	758	10.3
Macedonia, FYR	413	3.8
Moldova	249	3.1
Montenegro	446	10.1
Romania	4,108	2.2
Russian Federation	69,219	3.3
Serbia	1,974	4.3
Tajikistan	–54	-0.6
Turkey	12,457	1.5
Turkmenistan	3,061	7.5
Ukraine	4,509	2.5
Uzbekistan	1,077	1.9

Source: World Bank

Exhibit 18.5

FDI in Georgia (US$ millions)

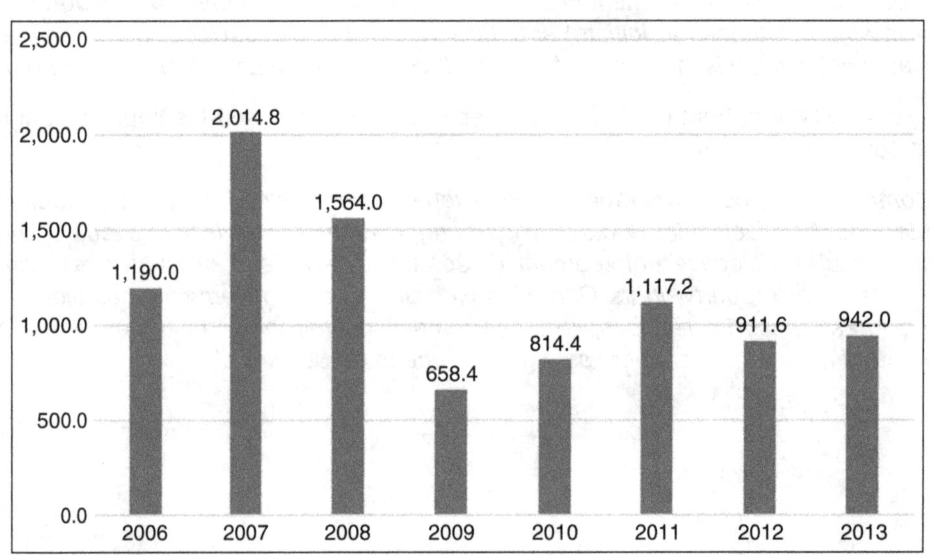

Source: National Statistics Office of Georgia (GEOSTAT)

Exhibit 18.6
Major Investors in Georgia in 2013 (US$ millions)

	2006	2007	2008	2009	2010	2011	2012	2013
Total	**1,190**	**2,015**	**1,564**	**658**	**814**	**1,117**	**912**	**942**
of which:								
Netherlands	19	299	136	33	73	242	35	153
Luxembourg	0	9	6	9	7	43	42	143
China	5	7	–2	–2	–8	10	36	90
Azerbaijan	78	41	24	30	58	138	59	82
United Arab Emirates	0	131	307	163	56	–52	24	62
United Kingdom	187	145	149	72	59	55	94	55
International Organizations	9	14	24	31	45	95	63	55
United States	183	84	168	–10	136	28	20	45
Czech Republic	15	228	35	46	24	47	8	44
Malta	–	–	–	–	17	6	32	43
Other countries	695	1,055	719	287	348	506	497	171

Source: National Statistics Office of Georgia (GEOSTAT)

Exhibit 18.7
GDP Breakdown in Georgia

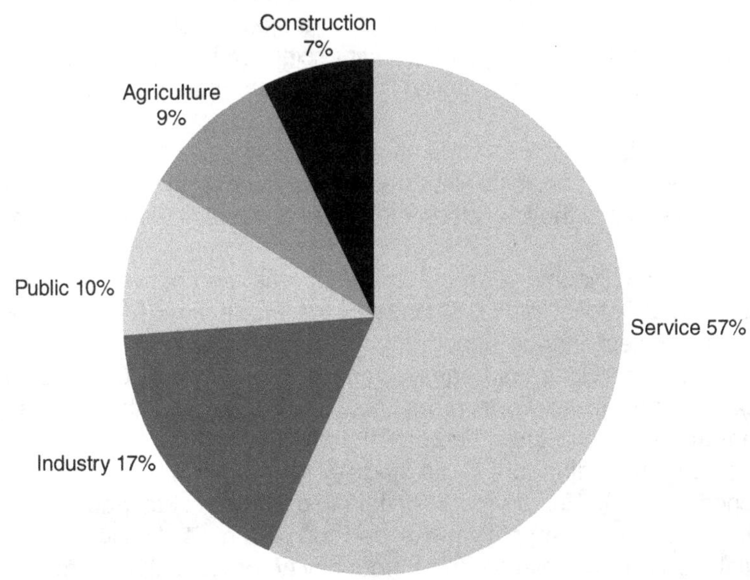

Source: World Bank

Exhibit 18.8
Active Investment in Georgia

Foreign Direct Investment[20]

Since the fall of the Soviet Union, foreign direct investment (FDI) had been the dominant source of investment capital. Yet, despite a liberal investment environment with minimal capital controls, a low and equal approach to foreign and domestic investors regarding taxation and relatively low corruption, FDI fell by 30% following the war in South Ossetia in 2008. The total FDI in 2008 and 2009 dropped to US$2.2 million from US$3.2 million in 2006 and 2007, the two years preceding the war.

Attracting FDI was a priority according to the Ministry of Economy of Georgia:

> *"Attraction of FDI is one of the main priorities for Georgia. Liberal investment environment and equal approach to local and foreign investors makes the country as an attractive destination for FDI. Stable economic development, liberal and free market oriented economic policy [...] reduced tax rates [...] dramatically simplified administrative procedures, preferential trade regimes with foreign countries, advantageous geographic location, well developed and integrated transport infrastructure, educated, skilled and competitive workforce presents a solid ground for successful business in Georgia."*

Development Finance Institutions

There were four Development Finance Institutions (DFI) active in Georgia in 2013. The European Bank for Reconstruction and Development (EBRD) had been investing in Georgia since 1998.[21] It invested in around 110 projects totalling US$831 million, with 19% of its capital invested in energy, 49% in financial services, 21% in industry, commerce and agriculture combined and finally, 11% in infrastructure projects, excluding energy.

KfW, a German DFI, had been operating in Georgia since 1993, initially investing in the energy sector.[22] Later on, it also invested in clean drinking water, sewage treatment and waste removal and in the financial sector, creating the first Georgian microfinance bank.

The International Finance Corporation (IFC) was also active in Georgia both as an investor and facilitator of trade.[23] Since 1995, the IFC provided a total of about US$1 billion in long-term project finance, supporting around 50 projects in the financial, agriculture, manufacturing, services, and energy sectors. In addition, IFC had supported import and export trade flows worth more than US$250 million through its trade finance program and implemented a number of advisory projects focused on private sector development. According to IFC, its strategy for the country was to "increase access to finance for MSMEs, promote sustainable private sector-driven growth through increased trade and competitiveness, develop Georgia's significant renewable energy potential, support improvements in productivity for agricultural processing and food safety, and foster the development of public-private partnerships."

20. National Statistics Office of Georgia.
21. EBRD website.
22. KfW website.
23. *IFC in Georgia,* webpage in www.ifc.org.

The Asian Development Bank (ADB) has been supporting Georgia since 2007, primarily assisting with the development of public infrastructure and services.[24] The sovereign assistance of ADB to Georgia amounted to more than US$1 billion in approved loans.

Other DFIs without a local presence also invested in Georgia from time to time, such as the FMO, DEG, European Investment Bank, Proparco, Black Sea Trade and Development Bank. Most of their investments were in agriculture, financial services and infrastructure.

Georgian Government-backed Fund

To expand financing options available to domestic firms, in 2011, the Georgian government created the JSC Partnership Fund (PF). The PF consolidated ownership of Georgia's largest state-owned enterprises (SOEs)[25] and financed its investment activity through dividend proceeds from these SOEs, customized earmarks of regular budget appropriation and PF's exits from prior investments. The PF's management team was overseen by the supervisory board chaired by the Prime Minister of Georgia.

PF's investment activity included overseeing a portfolio of active and planned projects in various sectors with a total value of over US$1 billion. The fund could only invest in Georgia by providing equity and quasi-equity financing to viable projects at their initial stage of development and could only take minority stakes in projects. PF's target sectors were agribusiness, energy, infrastructure, logistics, manufacturing, real estate and hospitality.

The fund's main objective was to promote investments in Georgia by attracting FDI. Private investors could invest directly in projects that PF initiated, funding them either partially or in their entirety. Further, PF's mid to-long-term involvement in projects on pre-determined conditions was meant to give additional management and financial stability to its investments and partners and decrease the country risk for foreign investors.

Strategic Investors

As of 2013, several strategic investors operated in Georgia with a particular focus on heavy industry, real estate, hospitality and construction. The largest players are Adjara Group, one of the country's largest hospitality groups; GMT Group, a private investor with three real estate companies and a dairy processing plant in its Georgian portfolio; the Silk Road Group, one of the leading hospitality groups, telecom operator and a leading oil and fuel transport and trading operator; Energo-Pro Georgia, a Czech group that has been operating in the country since 2007 and one of the largest independent energy players; Georgian Industrial Group, the largest industrial holding in Georgia with a portfolio that includes coal mining, energy generation (hydro, natural gas and coal fired power plants), natural gas, retail and real estate; Georgian American Alloys, based in the US a global manufacturer and distributor of ferroalloy, silicomanganese and ferrosilicon; RMG Gold and RMG Copper, the leading mining companies in Georgia; Integrated healthcare and insurance provider Georgian Healthcare Group; Magticom, Geocell and Beeline, the largest telecom service providers; and two leading UK listed banks – Bank of Georgia and TBC Bank.

24. ADB website.

25. The PF managed SOEs operating in the transportation, energy, and infrastructure sectors with combined, 2012 turnover of over US$750 million. PF's portfolio of SOEs was comprised of: Georgian Railway (100% stake), Georgian Oil and Gas Corporation (100%), Georgian State Electrosystem (100%), Electricity System Commercial Operator (100%) and Telasi (24.5%).

Financial Investors

Only a handful of financial investors had successfully deployed capital in Georgia in 2013. In 2006, the closed-end Georgian Regional Development Fund (GRDF) started operating in Georgia with US$30 million of subscribed capital. It was funded solely by the Millennium Challenge Corporation[26] and managed by the US-based Small Enterprise Assistance Fund (SEAF).[27] Its strategy was to provide long-term risk capital and assistance to SMEs in the agriculture and tourism industries in order to foster economic growth in Georgia. GRDF was established with a 10-year lifespan divided equally in investment and divestment period and would invest up to US$3 million through concessionary debt and equity instruments in a single investment. The fund successfully deployed capital in companies whose activities ranged from concrete production, anchovy fishing, regional hotels, hazelnut production and processing, poultry breeding, and telecommunications infrastructure.[28] As of 2013, the fund remained actively invested in several portfolio companies.

Liberty Consumer was created in 2006 and was funded primarily by Bank of Georgia and its long-term investors, as well as retail funding raised at the initial public offering (IPO) on the Georgian Stock Exchange. By 2013, the shares were trading at 65% of the IPO price and investors were unlikely to recoup their losses. Some of the reasons for its failure are believed to have been the strategy to invest in many small companies and only a few larger ones. Minimum scale to support professional management is a serious consideration in Georgia, given the country's small size.

In 2008, the Caucasus Energy & Infrastructure (CEI), an energy fund[29] structured as a joint stock company organized in compliance with Georgian legislation, raised US$50 million via an IPO on the Georgian Stock Exchange.[30] Roughly 90% of the capital raised was from foreign investment funds.[31] CEI holds a mandate to invest in Transcaucasian companies engaged in the production, transmission and distribution of gas and electricity. CEI deployed capital in a hydro power plant project and real estate holdings. Throughout 2013, the company traded at 40% to 70% discount to its IPO price.[32]

Finally, there was also the SEAF Caucasus Growth Fund, which was mostly funded by IFC and managed by the Small Enterprise Assistance Funds (SEAF). It was a US$40 million PE fund that targeted consumer and business services, agribusiness, distribution, energy, and retail SMEs in Georgia, Azerbaijan and Armenia. It started operating in March 2012. Its general objective was to promote transparent private sector development, domestic growth and economic independence and stability.

---

26. The Millenium Challenge Corporation is an entity established by the Georgian government to implement the US-funded US$295 million Millennium Challenge Account (MCA) aid program. Source: (2007) *MCG Launches Investment Fund to Foster Tourism, Agribusiness.* Retrieved from: http://www.civil.ge/eng/article.php?id=14535.
27. SEAF is a global investment management firm based in Washington DC, US providing risk capital to SMEs in emerging markets. It has been active in Eastern Europe, Latin America and Asia since 1989.
28. *Georgia Regional Development Fund.* Retrieved from: http://seaf.com/what-we-do/our-locations-investment-vehicles/central-eastern-europe/georgia-regional-development-fund/.
29. (2010) Retrieved from: http://www.cei.ge/en/media/press_center/728/.
30. One month after the listing, CEI established a global depository receipts programme and appointed Bank of New York Mellon as its depository bank.
31. (2014) *Final Report, Regulatory Impact Assessment, Georgian Law on Securities Market.* USAID.
32. Retrieved from: http://www.cei.ge/en/investors/share_price.

Exhibit 18.9

Possible Investment Opportunities

Energy

The Georgian energy market offered many investment opportunities. The graph below presents Georgia's actual and projected annual energy balances between 2008 and 2020.

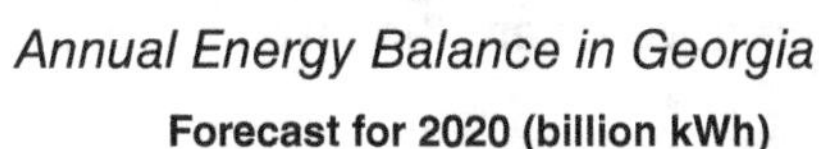

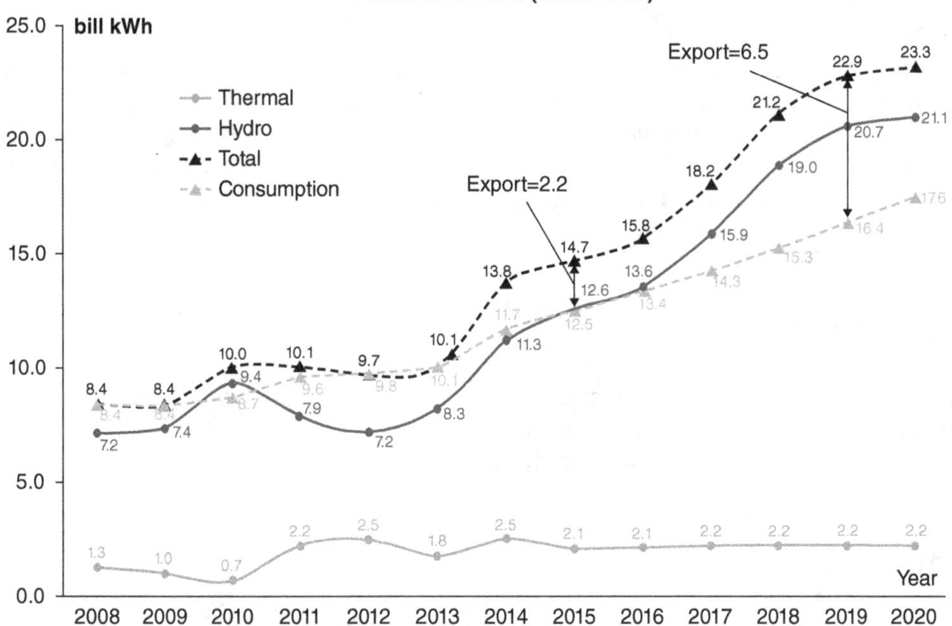

Source: Georgian State Electrosystem Annual Report 2013

Hydro

Georgia had one of the largest untapped hydro resources per capita in the world, with a potential to produce up to 33 TWh per annum from Hydro Power Plants (HPP), three times more than current production.[33] From 2008, Georgia began to deregulate its energy market. Renewable projects were then based on Build-Own-Operate (BOO) principle.

Since 2005, electricity generation increased 1.5 times, reaching 10.1 TWh in 2013, of which hydropower accounted for approximately 78%. Georgia endeavoured to develop a regional power market and served as a transmission hub as well as a seasonal exporter of environmentally clean hydro power.

33. Georgian Investment Agency.

Georgia was also surrounded by countries with higher generation costs, such as Armenia, Bulgaria, Romania and Israel.

Thermal[34]

Thermal power was more expensive than hydro power and was used during wintertime peaks when hydro production was low. The government would pay a reserve tariff to leave thermal plants available throughout the year. When the thermal plants received a notice from the government they would need to start producing energy within 24 hours.

In 2013, only natural gas thermal power plants were operating in Georgia with natural gas imported from Azerbaijan. Georgia had the potential to develop geothermal water or local coal based generation capacity. According to recent hydro-geological studies, the Georgian geothermal water reserves reached 250 million m^3 per year. In 2013, there were more than 250 natural and artificial water channels where the average temperature of geothermal waters ranges from 30° C to 110° C, while the total debit is 160,000 m^3 per day and night.

Biomass

Georgia's climate favoured forest and agricultural development with therefore a huge potential for biomass energy generation, yet there were none under development by 2013. Forests accounted for 40% of the country's total territory.

Solar

Solar radiation in Georgia is high: between 1,250-1,800 KWh/m^2 annually, with 250-280 sunny days a year in most regions. Georgia's total solar energy potential is estimated at 108 MW. There were no solar projects under development in 2013.

Wind[35]

Georgia had an estimated achievable potential wind power of up to 4 TWh. There were no ongoing wind projects in 2013.

Agriculture[36]

In 2013, the agricultural sector was dominated by small subsistence farmers (average farm size of 1.55 ha). Due to high historical fragmentation of land and lack of investment, productivity of farmers was almost three times lower than the world average.[37]

34. Georgian National Investment Agency – Invest in Georgia.
35. *Ibid.*
36. *Ibid.*
37. Band of Georgia, FAOStat.

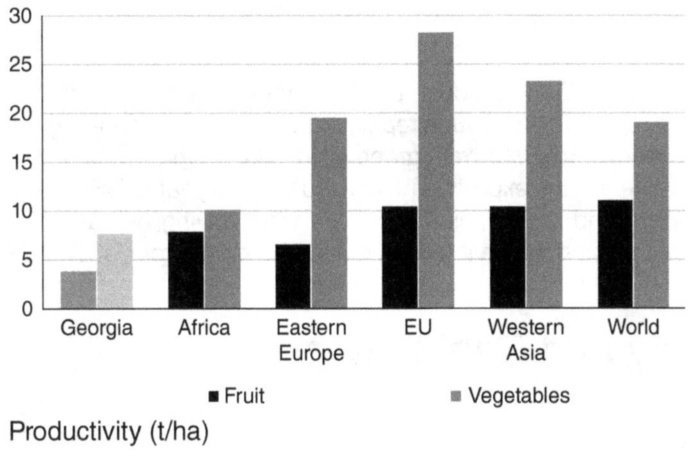

Productivity (t/ha)

The Government provided cheap and long-term funding that resulted in a 20%[38] increase in sown areas. By 2017, the Georgian government planned to create irrigation systems on up to 278,000 ha of agricultural land, an increase of 11 times that of 2013. Production of annual and perennial crops grew as livestock numbers increased with it the production of meat, milk and eggs.

Agriculture accounted for approximately 9% of the Georgian GDP, 1.5% of FDI and 17.5% of total trade volume in 2013. Georgia was a net importer of agricultural and food products with a trade deficit of US$406 million in 2013 (see chart below). If productivity increased, CIS and EU markets could become export markets as they imported large volumes of fruit and vegetables.

Source: Georgian National Investment Agency

38. State Agricultural Fund – US$0.6 billion of subsidized loans; grants that covered the cost of 75% of irrigation systems, infrastructure and logistics.

Wine[39]

Georgia had the potential to produce ten times more volume (500 million litres) in the future than produced in 2013 through replanting vineyards and applying modern farming techniques to improve yield. Current grape yields were approximately a third the global average. The value of wine exports had doubled year on year to US$141 million in 2013. Increased tourism and local consumer tastes were driving demand for bottled wine, domestic consumption doubled in 2013[40] to US$46 million from US$22 million in 2012.

Hospitality and Real Estate

Hospitality

Visitors to Georgia had been increasing over a decade by 30% annually, with 5.5 million in 2013. According to the Georgian National Tourism Administration, the majority of visitors came from Turkey 35%, Armenia 21%, Azerbaijan 21% and Russia 11%. The country had more than 12,000 historical and cultural monuments, eight national parks and different climates that catered for sun beach, winter sports, four seasons, spa and gambling resorts.

There were approximately 16,000 hotel rooms in 2013, most on the lower quality side. However, there was clear demand for good quality midscale local hotels as eastern Georgia was generating high average daily rates (ADR) and occupancy rates mainly due to proximity to Tbilisi. Some international brands were already present, representing 1,250 rooms, with an aggressive move into the country planned – over 2,500 rooms within the next five years. The main opportunities were in the mid- and budget segments.

The government was investing in infrastructure to promote tourism in key tourist destinations. There were three established ski resorts with 76kms of ski runs and 22 cableways, and an additional resort under development.

Number of International Arrivals in Georgia (in Millions)

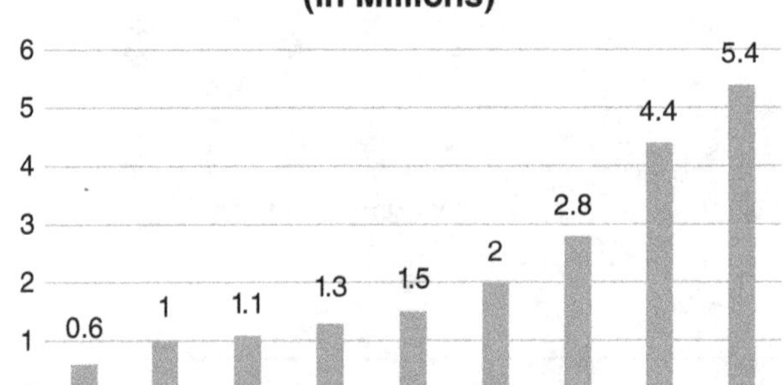

Source: Georgian National Investment Agency

39. Source: Bank of Georgia Wine Report.
40. Bank of Georgia conservatively expects 270,000 wine and food tourists to arrive in Georgia annually by 2019, up from 110,000 in 2013.

Office[41]

Total office stock in large cities amounted to 1 million m², with 85% in the capital. It was underdeveloped with the only business centres present in Tbilisi. Prime rent rate in Tbilisi was approximately US$21/m² comparable to most Central and Eastern Europe (CE) capitals. The prime office yield in Tbilisi (12%) was significantly higher than the CEE average.[42]

Retail[43]

The majority of retail stock in Georgia (80%) was concentrated in Tbilisi, with 890,000 m². Allocation was broken down to 28% street retail, 29% shopping centres and the remainder bazaars and open markets. The most expensive street retail rent rates stood at approximately US$60/m² with average rates on secondary retail streets at US$35-40/m². Shopping centre retail space supply in the capital accounted for 151,000 m². Prices achieved in modern shopping centres ranged from US$24-38/m². Another large shopping centre (70,000 m²) was under construction, due to open at the beginning of 2015.

Manufacturing

Georgia had competitive labour and energy costs[44] and was well positioned to trade goods between Asia and Europe. There were preferential/free trade agreements and two free trade zones where businesses were free of all taxes, except for personal income tax.

Western China had received approximately US$50 billion of investments in manufacturing and infrastructure – Georgia could play a role in connecting this region to Europe. Georgia had three international airports, two ports, two oil terminals, one deep-sea port and 2,100 km of rail and 1,500 km of road, respectively. Transit goods were not subject to taxes.[45]

Manufacturing, mining and quarrying accounted for 11.5% of GDP in 2013.[46] The sector was mainly driven by metals (ferroalloys, copper ores, bars and rods and other), non-metallic mineral products (cyanides, cyanide oxides and complex cyanides, cement, glassware and other) and chemicals (fertilizers, pharmaceuticals, beauty, perfumes, make-up preparations among others) industries[47]. There were manganese and copper ores mines. They produced ferroalloys mainly for export (approximately US$230 million). Producers and exporters of gold and copper (RMG Copper, formerly Madneuli), ferroalloys (Georgian Manganese) and ammonium nitrate fertilizers (Rustavi Azot) accounted for around 50% of the sector.[48]

---

41. Collier International – Georgia Office Market Report 2014.
43. Collier International – Georgia Real Estate Market Report 2014.
44. The Georgian National Investment Agency stated that in the manufacturing sector, the current monthly wage is around US$400, including both blue and white collar workers.
45. Georgian National Investment Agency.
46. National Statistics Office of Georgia.
47. Georgian National Investment Agency.
48. Georgian Economy: Setting New Targets, Bank of Georgia Research.

Apparel was the fastest growing industry in manufacturing, with more than 200 apparel manufacturing companies (Georgian and foreign investors) – 93% were microenterprises. Approximately 95% of apparel produced by investor companies was exported to Turkey and/or to the EU markets.[49] Recently, several Georgian companies had started producing apparel for export.

Over the last decade, increased building activity boosted the construction material industry. Real estate and infrastructure were one of the fastest-growing business sectors in Georgia. There were also several large hydropower projects under development.

Source: Georgian National Investment Agency

Financial Services[50]

Georgian Financial Institutions Institutions (# of companies by function)

Type	2013	2012	2011	2010	2009
Banks	21	19	19	19	19
Microfinance institutions	67	62	62	49	38
Non-bank deposit institutions	17	18	18	18	18
Exchange Bureaus	1,089	1,029	1,500	1,624	1,352
Insurance Companies	14	15	15	16	14
Pension Funds	5	6	7	6	6
Stock Exchanges	1	1	1	1	1

Source: National Bank of Georgia and European Development Bank

The financial sector was dominated by 20 commercial banks, with other players representing only 5% of assets. Financial intermediation remained low compared to OECD countries as total bank assets were under 60% of GDP. The banking sector was concentrated, with the two largest players holding 59.5% of the total banking assets in 2013.[51] The microfinance and credit union sectors served niche customers. The leasing segment was constrained by a lack of access to funds. Risk capital was almost non-existent in Georgia.

49. Georgian National Investment Agency.
50. National Bank of Georgia and European Development Bank.
51. Bank of Georgia Investor Presentation, page 8, *Peer group's market share in total assets.*

CASE

19 ASIAN PRIVATE EQUITY A FAMILY OFFICE'S QUEST FOR RETURN

SYNOPSIS

A European multi-family office is weighing whether and how to invest in Asian private equity. The case moves from a discussion of the historical and current state of Asian PE to the outlook and risks associated with such an investment. It also starts a discussion of returns in Asian PE and whether they adequately compensate for the risks identified earlier.

PEDAGOGICAL OBJECTIVE OF THE CASE

The case gives an overview of the Asian PE landscape with respect to development, size and growth prospects. It helps to understand PE as an asset class from the investors' perspective and explains the at times contentious relationship between limited partners and general partners. The case discusses the opportunities as well as the risk–return considerations within the PE context. In particular, it highlights both similarities and differences between PE in Asia and developed market funds; return expectations are discussed. The case can further be used as a launch pad for implementation questions, from identifying and accessing top-performing funds to overall portfolio construction and a discussion of the respective advantages and disadvantages of investing in PE via a direct or indirect strategy.

SUGGESTED ASSIGNMENT QUESTIONS

1. Where do you see the future potential for PE in Asia (or other emerging markets)? To what extent is the present environment for PE different from the mid-1990s?
2. What would be a reasonable target return for PE in Asia? Think about PE-specific and Asia-specific risks and how investors expect to be compensated for them.
3. In your opinion, which PE strategy will be the most successful in delivering high risk-adjusted returns in developing markets and why?

ADDITIONAL RESOURCES

To make the most of this case study, we suggest the following additional sources to provide context and background information:

- In particular, we recommend the following chapters from *Mastering Private Equity—Transformation via Venture Capital, Minority Investments & Buyouts*
  - Chapter 1 Private Equity Essentials
  - Chapter 3 Growth Equity
  - Chapter 14 Responsible Investment
  - Chapter 17 Fundraising
  - Chapter 18 LP Portfolio Management
  - Chapter 19 Performance Reporting
- You may also refer to the book website for further material:
  www.masteringprivateequity.com

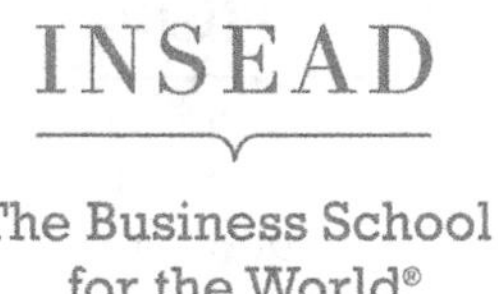

Asian Private Equity (A)

The Quest for Return

04/2013-5712

This case was written by Michael Prahl, Visiting Senior Research Associate, under the direction of Claudia Zeisberger, Affiliate Professor of Decision Sciences and Academic Co-Director of the Global Private Equity Initiative (GPEI) at INSEAD. It is intended to be used as a basis for class discussion rather than to illustrate either effective or ineffective handling of an administrative situation.

Additional material about INSEAD case studies (e.g., videos, spreadsheets, links) can be accessed at cases.insead.edu.

Georg Bergmann[1] was looking out of the window of the nineteenth century villa which his company, a multi-family office, occupied in a prestigious but low-key suburb of Zurich. He had just finished reading an article on Hong Kong becoming the world's largest centre for IPOs in 2009, comfortably overtaking New York, with Shanghai a close third.[2] It was just the type of news to remind him of the discussions and decisions ahead of him.

He was getting ready for a meeting of the shareholder committee where he would present his recommendations with respect to an investment approach in Asian private equity. This required careful preparation as any positive decision would involve a long-term commitment and significant resources from the firm that could otherwise be deployed elsewhere.

A Multi-family Office's Approach to Private Equity

Bergmann was the Senior Investment Director in charge of alternative assets (Alternatives)[3] for one of the largest European multi-family offices, managing more than €6 billion on behalf of several families. The original source of capital had come from the sale of one very large family business more than 25 years ago, after which the family decided to establish a platform for family interaction and continued involvement in common projects.

Over time the assets grew, as did the professional team involved, and in the 1990s the founders chose to open the office services to other families. However, the decision process remained comparatively lean and the investment approach in general tended to be entrepreneurial and risk taking, at least within the parameters of a family office where capital preservation is usually the foremost objective.

Having started with investments in stocks and bonds, frequently in line with historic family interests, the company had evolved into a true diversified asset manager. Almost 15 years earlier, its first investments had been made in the alternative space, initially in US venture capital (VC), followed by US and European private equity (PE). Then, a few years back, hedge funds were added to the mix. Overall allocation to Alternatives had grown to more than 25% of assets under management (AUM), the bulk of it in private equity.

Bergmann had driven and overseen this move into Alternatives, which had contributed meaningfully to the firm's capital formation. He was not interested in chasing early trends yet he prided himself on being able to identify the point at which they turned into profitable mainstream. This had worked out with venture capital in

1. Name of protagonist and some details have been changed to avoid their identity and that of the family office to be determined.
2. As of early December US$26.81 billion had been raised through initial public offerings in Hong Kong, US$17.11 billion on NY Stock Exchange and US$14 billion in Shanghai. Source: Wall Street Journal, 8 Dec 2009.
3. While often broadly defined as everything else but traditional investments (stocks, bond, and cash) its most important strategies include private equity, hedge funds and real estate.

the US in the 90s, hedge funds after the demise of LTCM,[4] and European buyouts in the early 2000s.

While the bulk of the portfolio allocation was given to larger, well-established investors, his firm had habitually supported or even seeded smaller funds with new investment strategies in order to gain an early read on emerging trends. Some of those early investments went on to become very successful, giving him strong personal relationships with many senior investment people in those firms. Besides providing insight into the inner workings of these firms, he found it useful for broad market intelligence as well as a valuable source of ideas for other asset classes.

In recent years it had become clear to him and the other senior managers that the firm was underexposed to the growing Asian markets.[5] The firm had allocated some money to fund managers focusing broadly on Asian large-cap stocks as well as the booming commodities markets mainly in Australia, and had benefitted from both investment categories. Yet the Asian segment of the portfolio ignored the large private sector, smaller more entrepreneurial companies, and emerging Asia in general.

In fact, the firm was seriously investigating how to expand in Asia in late 2007 when the first warning signs in the US of what was to become a full-blown global financial crisis made the team concentrate on their existing portfolio, postponing all new strategic initiatives. The focus switched to preserving capital rather than growing it. However, the year 2009 had ended on a more optimistic note and with a substantial portion of the firm's assets currently in cash or near cash it was time to revisit the investment strategy.

Asia seemed to have avoided the worst of the financial crisis and looked set to continue its long-term growth. In addition to its steadily growing middle class and consumption story, and a young population in emerging Asia, most countries were also in a better fiscal position than the West, a complete reversal of the situation after the Asian financial crisis just over a decade earlier. So the shareholders had agreed during their last meeting to substantially increase the allocation to Asia. As part of this broader Asia strategy they had tasked Bergmann to come up with a proposal as to whether to invest in Asian Private Equity, and if so, how.

Bergmann was aware of the many risks of doing business in Asia, ranging from cultural barriers to underdeveloped institutions. Adding the intrinsic risks of private equity as an illiquid and sometimes non-transparent asset class, the first question in his mind was whether Asian private equity had already gone beyond the point at which it made sense per se for an investment by his firm. The second question was what role Asian private equity should play in a global investment strategy that sought geographic diversification. Thirdly, provided he and his shareholders could get comfortable with the above questions, how should they go about developing and implementing an investment strategy?

He decided to revisit the material prepared for him by his team with the help of outside consultants.

---

4. Long-Term Capital Management (LTCM) was a major U.S. hedge fund run by an all-star team of traders and academics (among them two winners of the noble price for economics) that failed spectacularly in the late 1990s, leading to a bailout by other financial institutions under the supervision of the Federal Reserve.

5. Throughout the case, 'Asia' refers to the area commonly known as Asia Pacific (which tends to include Australia/ New Zealand in the South and India in the West). Not all data sources apply the same definition.

A History of Asian Private Equity

The Early Days[6]

Private equity as an asset class had been present in Asia for decades, yet financing had usually been provided either by wealthy families or by commercial banks in unique (sometimes workout-type) situations, and thus lacked the institutional quality of fund-based private equity investments in the Western world.

Institutional private equity arrived in Asia in the early 90s, following the explosive growth of the industry in the US. With record returns generated from the surge in US equity markets, institutional investors were on the lookout for new opportunities. Asia (and emerging markets in general) seemed like fertile ground for the tried and tested private equity business model and attracted early institutional investors looking for portfolio diversification and the opportunity to earn exceptional returns.

This development was part of a broader trend of foreign direct investment which in Asia saw a compound annual growth rate of 19% between 1992 and 1998. Meanwhile, only a relatively small number of large firms had access to bank financing. Therefore the demand side for private equity looked very strong. The framework for investing was considered to be attractive not only from a macroeconomic growth perspective but also from a more receptive attitude towards the private sector in general. So the supply side followed, with about 500 Asian funds (excluding Japan) raising more than $50 billion in new capital between 1992 and 1999, almost all of them for the first time.

Yet the performance of most of these funds turned out to be poor both in absolute and relative terms. The main reasons cited were low standards of corporate governance both for information prior to an investment decision and then to monitor performance, weakness of the legal system in enforcing contracts and protecting all classes of investors, lack of exit prospects and, on the investor side, the general inexperience and poor quality of fund managers (not surprising, given that few individuals had relevant previous experience). The Asian financial crisis exacerbated the problem by bringing huge macroeconomic contradictions to light, leading to a rerating of emerging market risk, wild currency swings, and reducing the opportunity for divestment to a trickle. In fact, divestures in 1998 and 1999 averaged about $2.5 billion per year, a small portion of the $35 billion invested between 1992 and 1999.

After the Asian Crisis

The end of the 1990s saw growth in two pockets of the industry, namely distressed debt investing (post-Asian financial crisis) and the global technology boom. Distressed assets in Indonesia, Korea and Japan were prime targets for investors and subsequently generated good returns. For instance, Goldman Sachs tripled the $500 million it invested in Kookmin Bank in 1999, while Ripplewood's buyout, restructuring and flotation of Long Term Credit Bank in Tokyo (since renamed Shinsei) – leading to a more than six times return – has become a legend in Japanese finance.

6. Section draws on "Private Equity Investing in Emerging markets" by Roger Leeds and Judie Sutherland in Journal of Applied Corporate Finance Vol. 15 No 4, Spring 2003.

Beyond that, most of the investments during this period were directed towards early-stage venture investments, mostly in South East Asia. However, the lack of industry maturity resulted in poor quality deals being executed in the region. The technology crash of 2000/01 resulted in the flight of capital to more conservative investments in old-economy companies. The poor performance of mainstream private equity (excluding distressed investing) led to a number of early institutional investors withdrawing from the market.

The Seeds of Greatness

After 2001 most deals in Asia were expansion capital or mid-sized buyouts. This period saw the entry of large international investors. A number of good quality domestic investors also blossomed. It was truly a transition point for Asian private equity as these early investors educated the business community on the values of PE investments, lobbied various governments for regulatory reforms, and worked hard to demonstrate returns on their investments. Countries such as China, India and Vietnam opened up to international private equity. Today, these represent the lion's share of the PE capital flowing into the region.

Ironically, the poor fundraising of the early 2000s (Asian funds excluding Japan had their worst fundraising in 2002 since 1993),[7] coupled with strong market conditions over the years prior to the global financial crisis of 2008, enabled many Asian funds, especially of 2002/2003 vintage, to report internal rates of return (IRR) – or compound returns accounting for inflation and currency fluctuations – of at least 20-30%. The numbers are similar to those seen in the US or Europe.

Asian Private Equity Today

The general growth of Asian economies and the strong returns on deals from the early 2000s resulted in renewed interest in Asian private equity and a massive inflow of capital. Over the last 15 years, Asian private equity funds under management increased ninefold from US$30 billion in 1994 to about US$283 billion in 2009. About 60% of that money was added during the last five years alone (see Exhibit 19.1).

Following several strong years of investing, fundraising peaked in 2008 with over US$50 billion of capital raised, while the pace of investment remained strong with US$44 billion invested in transactions across Asia Pacific. However, with the advent of the global financial crisis, sentiment changed towards the end of the year and 2009 saw a more sober mood, with fundraising and investment dropping by 55% and 57% respectively (see Exhibit 19.2).

This coincided with a global meltdown in private equity activity worldwide, starting in the second half of 2008. Developed markets' private equity was massively impacted by the drying up of credit as leveraged buyouts relied on large amounts of cheap debt. Only one deal in 2009, the take-private of IMS Health Inc. for $5.2 billion, could be in any way compared to the mega deals of the previous era. Despite the strong drop in activity, Asia nevertheless increased its share of global private equity investment to

7. Asia Private Equity Review, 2002 Year-End Review.

around 13-14% from a historic range of 5-7% (see Exhibit 19.3). Paradoxically, Asian private equity (excluding venture capital) as a portion of GDP and M&A activity was now almost on par with Western economies. However, this was less a reflection of tremendous growth in Asia than of a steep decline in private equity penetration in Europe and the US (see Exhibit 19.4).

Between 2006 and 2009 the majority of funds invested went to China, Japan, India, Australia and South Korea (see Exhibit 19.5), the largest economies in Asia Pacific, which accordingly received the largest share of investment. Over time, more money started flowing into developing rather than developed Asia. This shift was exacerbated to a certain extent by the typically higher portion of buy-out deals in developed Asia that dried up during the financial turmoil due to their reliance on debt.

The type of deal by geography reflected the specific developmental situation in which each country found itself at this point (see Exhibit 19.6). Most transactions in India and China in 2008 were growth capital deals, while most deals in the developed economies were buyouts or (in the case of Japan) turnarounds. Also, countries with large and open stock markets had a significant number of private investments in public equity (PIPEs) and occasional public to private (PtP) transactions. The overall emphasis on growth deals in Asia was reflected in the relatively small average deal size, which oscillated around $50 million in recent years (see Exhibit 19.7).

Perhaps the single most critical driver of private equity in Asia was the recent track record of successful exits by not only domestic but also foreign investors. The environment improved and exit opportunities developed. While investment activity was still weak, 2009 showed a marked recovery of exits (the third highest divestment amount since 2004). This was very much a result of resurgent capital markets in the second half of 2009, which were the preferred exit route for private equity portfolio companies with a share of more than 45% of exits (see Exhibit 19.8). Besides the high share of Japanese divestments (more than half of it from the sale of Sanyo Electric), landmark exits in India and China particularly reassured investors about liquidity and availability of exits in these markets.

Asian Private Equity Growth Drivers

Bergmann had recently returned from a long business trip to Asia where he had visited a large number of investment managers and investors. There was a noticeable difference in the optimism that he had found in Asia compared to Europe. Most experts had pointed out the strong growth prospects of the region and how this was creating a broad set of investment opportunities. Furthermore, some had mentioned an improvement in management quality and sophistication, which in turn had led to a more favourable attitude to private equity.

Macroeconomic Growth

Macroeconomic growth is an important factor driving private equity investments/exits as it shapes the context in which companies and businesses operate. The growth in economies provides a boost to companies operating in the region by driving both top-line and bottom-line growth, hence creating wealth for investors. In the case of Asia, growth has been exponential and provides a tremendous impetus for private equity activity.

Asia is home to three of the world's largest economies – Japan, China and India – and more than half the world's population. The rise in income levels (especially on a PPP basis), improved life expectancy, high savings rate, and a continued low-cost structure in the region had turned Asia into the powerhouse of the global economic engine. Much of emerging Asia was diversifying beyond its historical export and manufacturing model, developing into strong consumer markets with a supplemental services industry. Not surprisingly, Asia had one of the highest growth rates in the world. China, already the third largest economy behind the US and Japan, was expected to become the world's number two by 2010/11 (see Exhibit 19.9).

Broad Set of Investment Opportunities

Investment opportunities in Asia fell into two broad categories: a resource pool to cater to global markets (export driven industries) and a large underserved domestic market (media, retail and lifestyle, infrastructure-related business), especially in China and India.

Economic growth combined with the privatisation of the economy in countries such as China and India had generated an increasing number of flourishing private companies. These had tremendous prospects given the cost advantage and the growing consumer market of these countries. These growing, viable and more stable private equity companies were good targets for PE investments. Japan and Australia, on the other hand, offered more developed and stable markets to invest in with less risk.

As Asian private equity matured, the nature and size of the deals done continued to evolve. While the mid-90s were a period for small-size early-stage investments, the proportion of expansion and buyout deals continued to increase. In 2009, control deals accounted for 45% of all investments in value.[8]

Higher Quality Management and Increased Awareness of Private Equity

The role of strong and cohesive management teams in generating private equity returns should never be underestimated. After the Asian financial crisis of 1998, a new class of firms had emerged with a more professional style of management. These created renewed confidence in the region thanks to increased entrepreneurship, the emergence of "good" local managers, the adoption of US/Europe standards and skills, and methods brought by western managers. With these, corporate governance standards improved, providing a safer environment for investing.

8. Asian Private Equity Review, 2009 Year-End Review.

The new generation of managers in Asia were also a lot more comfortable with private equity as an asset class and the notion of using PE for the creation of value and wealth for themselves and their owners. The track record of recent investments and exits also went a long way towards assuring management teams that private equity was not 'vulture' investing but, rather, a useful mechanism for building businesses.

Asian Private Equity Risks

Re-reading the data, Bergmann noticed that the industry had come a long way. Yet some of the current optimism seemed eerily similar to that which had prevailed in the mid-90s. As an experienced investor he couldn't fail to notice the generally upbeat tone of the report. He wondered how to think about risk in the region and whether there were specific factors making private equity investing in Asia more difficult.

To an outsider, Asia might seem like one large homogenous region; in fact it is a complex geography with individual country markets that differ not just in economic status but also in terms of business culture and regulatory regimes. How attractive a country is for private equity investment will therefore be determined not only by core economic factors such as market size and growth prospects but equally by its legal and social framework.

Taken as a whole, Asia already offered an environment as favourable to VC/PE activities as that prevailing in Western Europe (see Exhibit 19.10). However, Bergmann knew from experience the need to differentiate between developed and developing Asia and for the latter focus on the emerging market risks that could have a strong impact on private equity-invested companies and the investment managers themselves. Such risks included political and macroeconomic stability, policies on investments in specific sectors by foreign investors, policies on capital gains tax, legal enforcement issues or questionable business practices. A lot of these risks were typical of developing economies; eventually Asian markets might, as one practitioner put it, "all evolve towards similar developed market models as the economies keep pace."[9]

Yet Bergmann had also noticed a certain casualness – even among investment managers – about the specifics of private equity investing. Most of the investing experience in Asia had been built up or at least influenced by capital market investing. Many of the PE managers came from investment banking backgrounds, unlike in Europe and the US where a more diversified mix of former bankers, consultants and industry people formed the talent pool for PE. There was even a term for the type of investing most popular in emerging Asia: growth investments were often called "pre-IPO investments." Bergmann wondered whether Asia's PE managers always understood the inherit riskiness of private equity investing, and whether this led to suboptimal investment structures. A typical deal in developing Asia would be a $30-50 million minority deal, with the intention of exiting through an IPO.

He had also seen a recent poll among investors in emerging markets (see Exhibit 19.11), including (but not exclusive to) emerging Asia about reasons to not continue investing with their General Partner (GP) relations. While the top-ranked cause of poor returns was one shared globally, some of the other reasons pointed to a generally lower

9. Vibhav Panandiker, MD JPMorgan Capital Partners at INSEAD's PE conference in Singapore, Dec 2009.

transparency and maturity of the local GP community. As one Limited Partner (LP) put it, "I wish [Asian] GPs (...) would strengthen the core team capabilities and improve their internal investment process, portfolio monitoring, value creation, report quality, succession planning and carry allocation, instead of enriching a few partners or asking LPs to trust them."[10]

Given the risks and attractions of Asian private equity, Bergmann wondered what returns investors should expect from their PE investments in Asia? And should they be benchmarked against private equity in other geographies or against other asset classes in Asia?

Asian Private Equity Returns

Measuring returns in private equity is a notoriously difficult business due to the absence of an efficient and transparent market for this asset class. Investments in private equity are long-term, illiquid, non-transparent, and the underlying company investments are not priced by a market. Therefore the PE industry does not have time series of market prices as a measure for performance, nor does it have proper indices.

There are publicly listed PE funds, yet they are few, and the transparency of the underlying private investments – although better – remains an issue. There has also been a trend in recent years for PE firms to list their management vehicles (i.e., the GP), allowing the interested investor to gauge multiple funds' performance over time. Overall, however, the vast majority of funds and assets under management remain private. There is a market for second-hand interests and unfunded commitments in private equity LPs (secondaries) but it is a comparatively small market, with lumpy transactions typically used to provide the original investor with liquidity or help rebalance the portfolio.

Most of the reporting to LPs is based on IRRs which has several problems, including the fact that valuations for active investments are made by GPs themselves – hence irregular and inconsistent between different fund managers. Furthermore, the typical life cycle of PE investing leads to (reported) negative returns in the early years and investment gains in outlying years as the portfolio of companies matures (J-curve). This is a bigger issue for Asian private equity with its comparatively short history as an asset class and few managers who have even fully exited their first fund (and hence raised their third or fourth one).

According to a representative survey by Coller Capital (a secondaries specialist) and EMPEA[11] (see Exhibit 19.12), institutional investors expect a risk premium over developed market buyouts of between 6% and 7.3%. Long-term developed market buyout IRRs have historically been in the range of 12-16% (net after fees), meaning Asian developing markets IRRs should be in the 18-23% range.

How has Asian private equity performed against these (high) expectations? According to data from Cambridge Associates (see Exhibit 19.13), it returned 4.65% p.a. over the last ten years. The performance is better for the five-year period but worse for the shorter periods when the effect of the recent financial crisis weighs heavily on

10. Kelvin Chan, Senior VP, Partners Group.

11. Emerging Markets Private Equity Association.

the results. The quarter ending 30 June 2009 shows a strong rebound in line with economies in Asia but is meaningless from a long-term perspective.

A comparison with emerging markets stock market performance (MSCI Emerging Markets, where Asia constitutes the highest proportion) leads to the question of whether private equity is indeed an attractive asset class in Asia or just a generous compensation scheme for PE managers free-riding on the Asian economies' (and stock markets') robust performance.

On the other hand, Bergmann had also seen some excellent return data (see Exhibit 19.14): Asian GPs had managed to not only exit individual portfolio companies at attractive returns but to complement some of the home runs with other solid exits and a low number of lost deals leading to strong fund performances. Perhaps the average performance data was not telling the full story.

Looking beyond the hype and the doomsayers, Bergmann was still unsure whether Asian private equity had reached the point of maturity he was searching for. There could be no doubt that the industry was professionalising and the environment was improving, yet there were concerns about too much money flowing into the industry backing mediocre managers. There were clearly numerous risks that had not been fully taken into account by many participants in the market, nor were investors properly compensated for assuming them. Nevertheless, much of the global economic future lay in Asia, especially in its private sector. Could a serious investment firm really forego exposure to this strong growth trend?

Exhibit 19.1

Asian Private Equity Pool – Aggregate (in US$ bn)

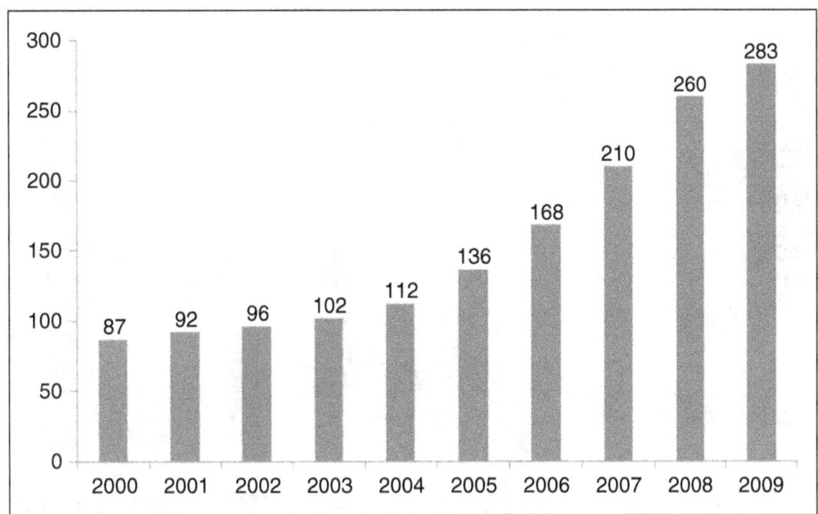

Source: Asia Private Equity Review

Exhibit 19.2

Asian Private Equity Capital raised & invested (in US$ bn)

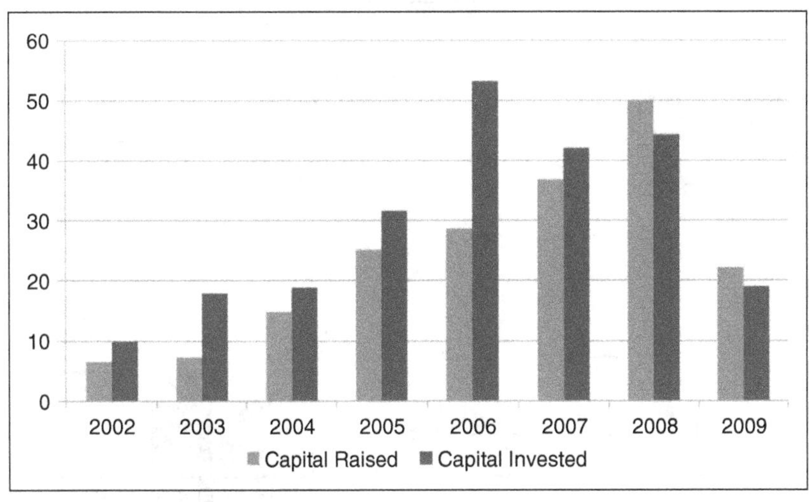

Source: Asia Private Equity Review

Exhibit 19.3

Asian Private Equity Share of Global Private Equity Invested (in %)

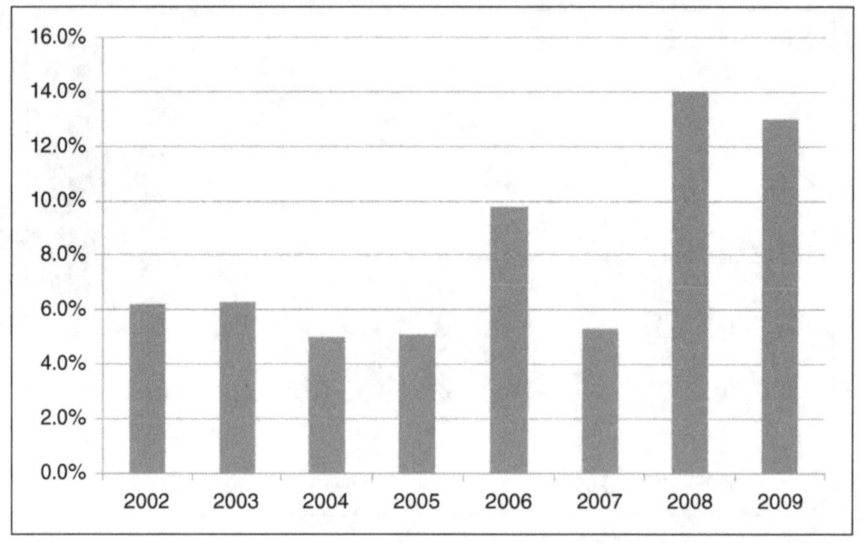

Source: Asia Private Equity Review, 2009 Year-End Review, Venture Economics

Exhibit 19.4

Private Equity as % of GDP and M&A activity (in %)

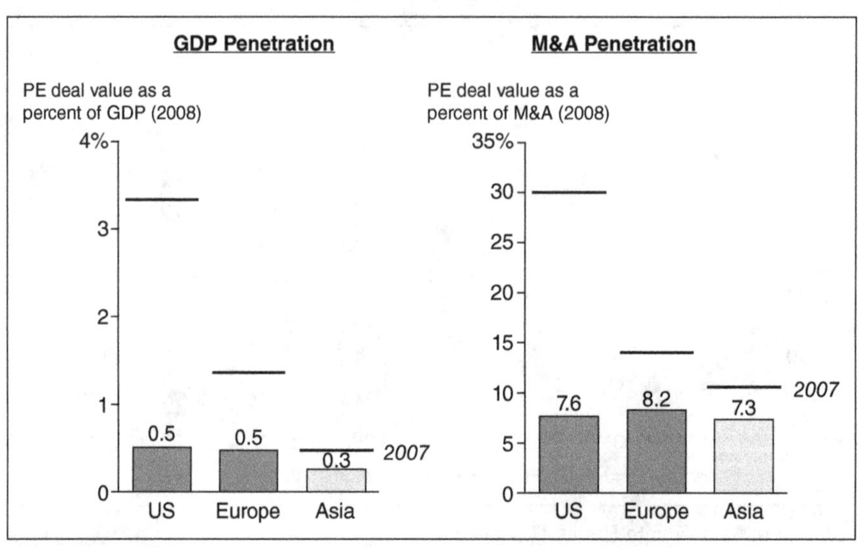

Source: Bain & Company, Asian Private Equity Overview 2008

Exhibit 19.5

Asian Private Investment Destinations (in US$ bn)

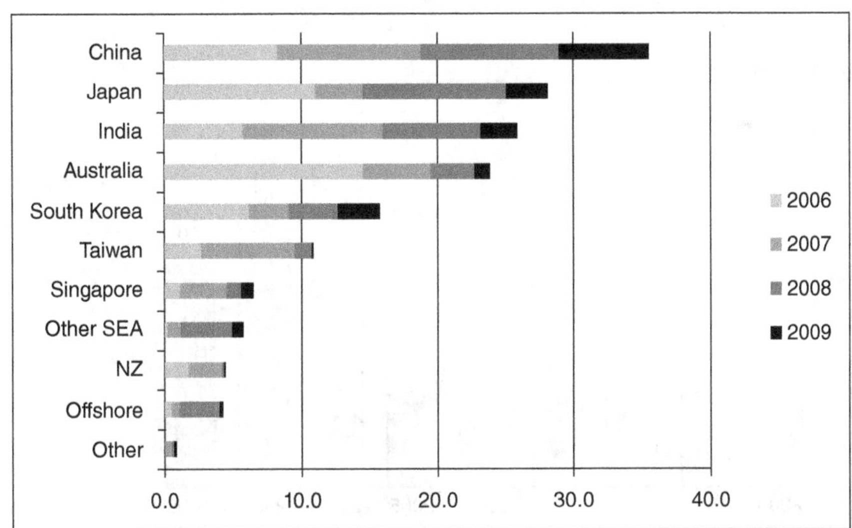

Source: Asian Private Equity Review

Exhibit 19.6

Deal Value by Funding Stage (in US$ bn)

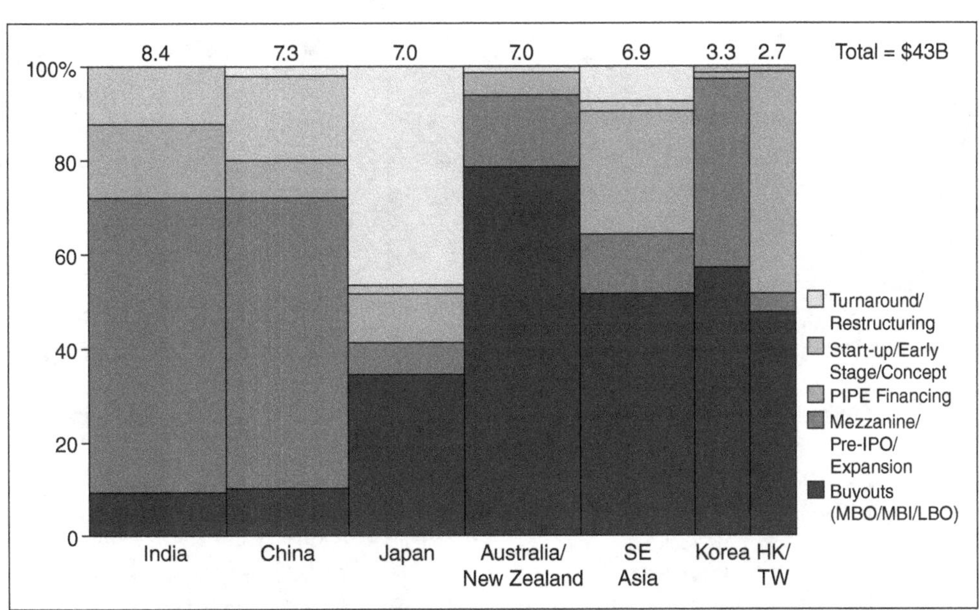

Source: Bain & Company, Asian Private Equity Overview 2008

Exhibit 19.7

Average Deal Size (in US$ m)

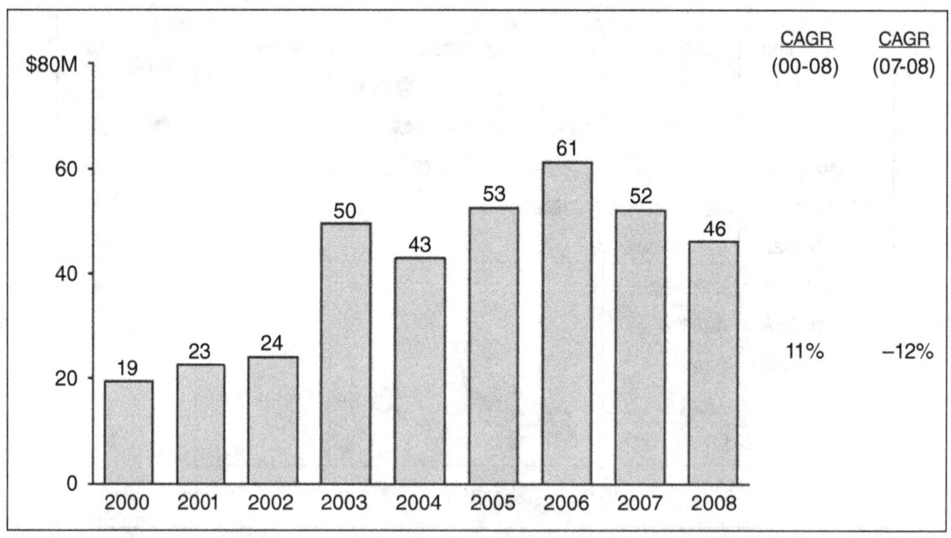

Source: Bain & Company, Asian Private Equity Overview 2008

Exhibit 19.8

Asian Private Equity Exits (in US$ bn)

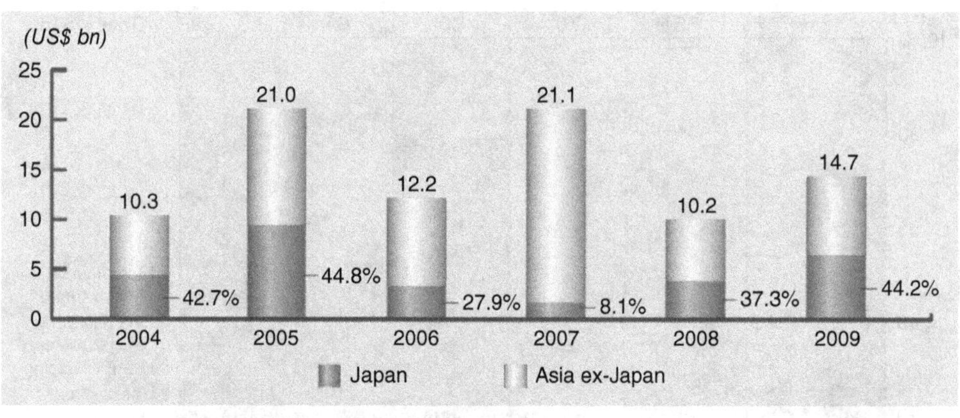

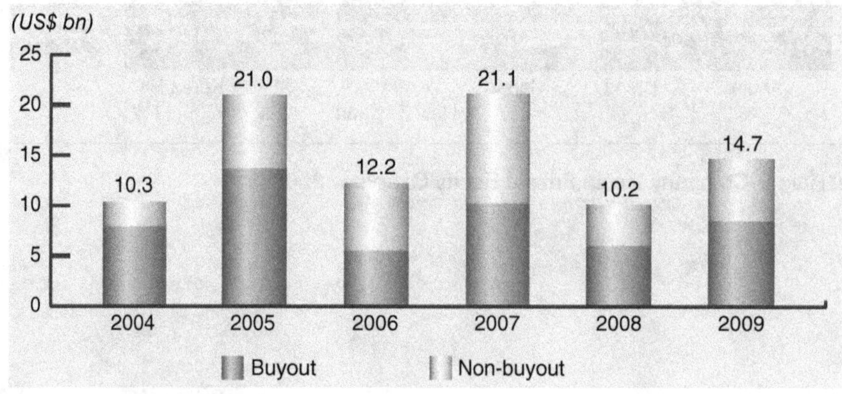

Source: Asian Private Equity Review

Exhibit 19.9

Current GDP and Expected GDP Growth for Selected Countries

Rank in 1999	Rank in 2009	Country	GDP 2009e (in USD billion)	*Growth CAGR 99-09 (in local currency)*	GDP 2014e (in USD billion)	*Growth CAGRe 2009-14 (in local currency)*	Rank in 2014
1	1	US	14,002.74	*4.2%*	16,927.84	*3.9%*	1
2	**2**	**Japan**	**4,992.85**	***-0.3%***	**5,354.41**	***2.0%***	**3**
7	**3**	**China**	**4,832.99**	***13.9%***	**8,500.10**	***11.5%***	**2**
3	4	Germany	3,060.31	*1.5%*	3,292.87	*1.4%*	4
5	5	France	2,499.15	*3.4%*	2,951.58	*3.3%*	5
4	6	UK	2,007.05	*4.3%*	2,507.61	*4.4%*	6
6	7	Italy	1,987.84	*3.0%*	2,225.27	*2.2%*	8
9	8	Spain	1,397.23	*6.3%*	1,554.15	*2.1%*	11
10	9	Brazil	1,268.51	*10.8%*	1,666.75	*8.1%*	10
8	10	Canada	1,229.37	*4.6%*	1,502.20	*4.6%*	12
13	**11**	**India**	**1,185.73**	***11.6%***	**1,739.98**	***11.1%***	**9**
23	12	Russia	1,163.65	*23.7%*	2,231.79	*13.8%*	7
15	**14**	**Australia**	**755.066**	***6.4%***	**852.705**	***4.8%***	**16**
12	**16**	**Korea**	**727.111**	***6.3%***	**934.401**	***6.7%***	**14**
21	**17**	**Turkey**	**552.18**	***24.6%***	**644.823**	***7.9%***	**18**
29	**18**	**Indonesia**	**468.389**	***16.1%***	**679.318**	***9.1%***	**17**

Source: IMF

Exhibit 19.10

The Socio-Economic Environment for Private Equity Compared with Western Europe

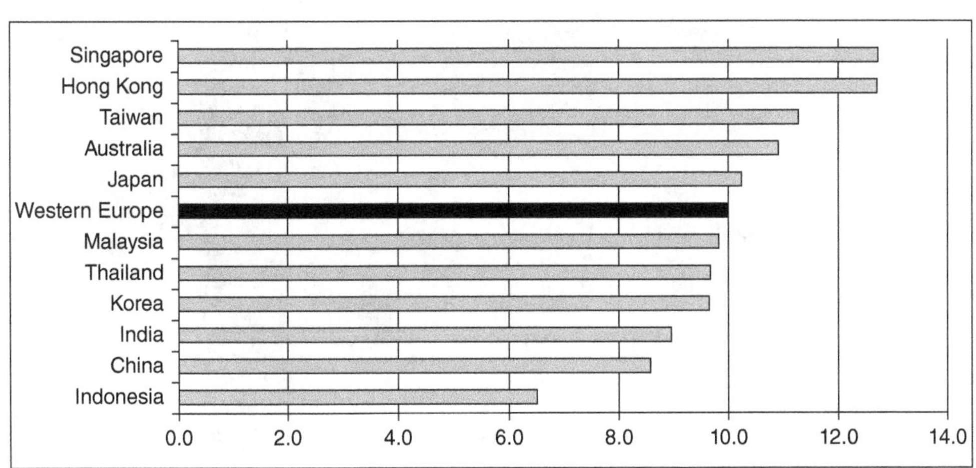

Source: INSEAD, The Climate for Venture Capital and Private Equity in Asia, 2005

Exhibit 19.11

Factors Likely to Deter LPs from Re-Investing with Some of their EM PE Managers over the Next 12 Months

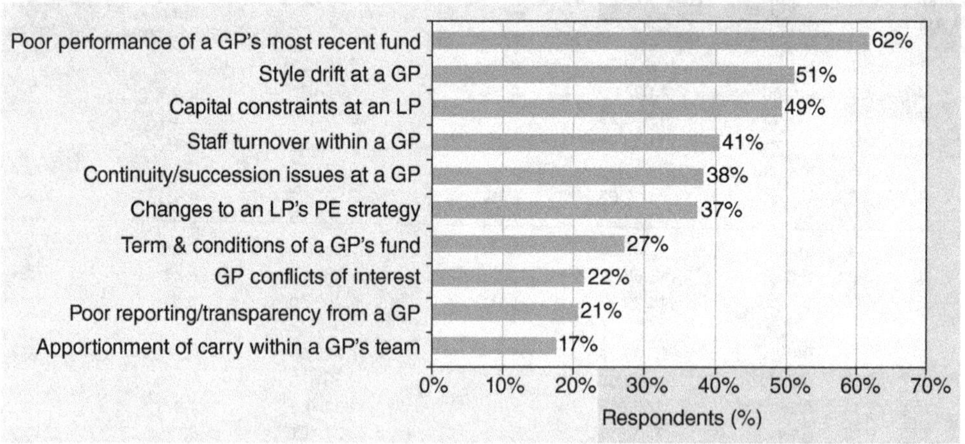

Source: EMPEA/Coller Capital, Emerging Markets Private Equity Survey, 2009

Exhibit 19.12

LPs' Perception of Risk Premiums Required for EM PE Funds Relative to Developed-Market Buyout Funds – by EM Country/Region

	2009	2008
Brazil	6.4%	6.9%
China	6.4%	6.3%
India	6.4%	6.1%
South Africa	7.0%	6.4%
Latin America (ex Brazil)	7.5%	6.7%
Middle East	7.3%	6.5%
North Africa*	8.0%	6.7%
Central & Eastern Europe (inc Turkey)	6.4%	5.0%
Russia/CIS	8.4%	6.9%
Sub-Saharan Africa (ex South Africa)*	8.4%	6.7%
Other Emerging Asia	7.3%	N/A

* "Pan Africa" in 2008 *Survey*

Source: EMPEA/Coller Capital, Emerging Markets Private Equity Survey, 2009

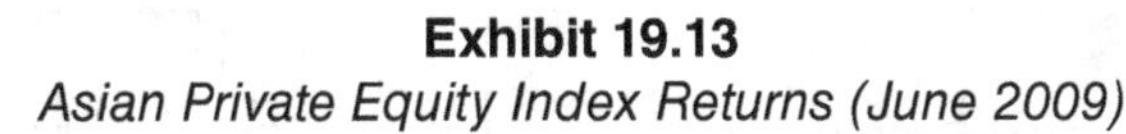

Exhibit 19.13

Asian Private Equity Index Returns (June 2009)

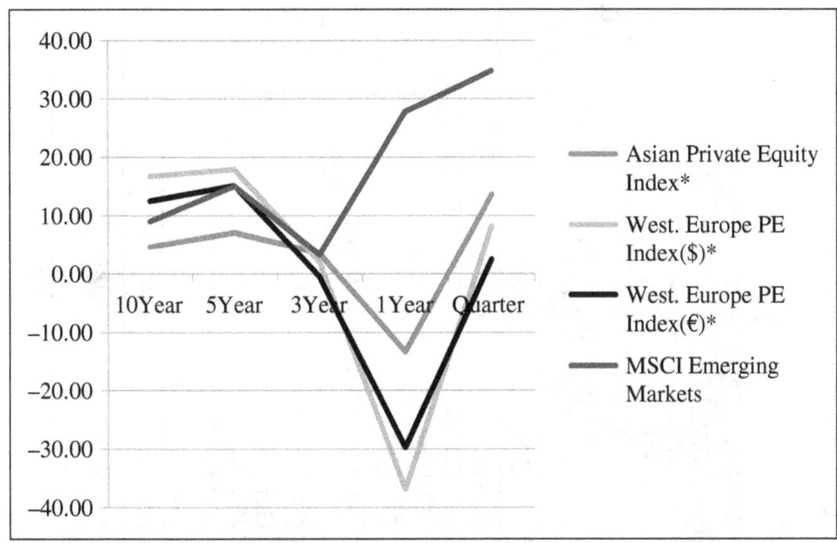

Index	10 Year	5 Year	3 Year	1 Year	Quarter
Asian Private Equity Index*	4.65	7.11	3.52	–13.27	13.62
West. Europe PE Index ($)*	16.73	17.93	2.11	–36.87	8.29
West. Europe PE Index (€)*	12.53	15.15	–0.43	–29.72	2.5
MSCI Emerging Markets	9.02	15.08	3.27	27.82	34.84

Source: Cambridge Associates, Global VC & PE index and benchmark statistics, 30 June 2009

Exhibit 19.14
Asian Private Equity Portfolio Exits

Year of Exit	Company	Country	Sector	Seller	Buyer	Transaction size	Est. Return Multiple
2009	Faceshop	South Korea	Retail & Consumer	Affinity, CLSA	LG H&H	342 EV	4-4.5x
2009	Myer	Australia	Retail & Consumer	Newbridge (TPG)	Public Market	2bn (MC at IPO)	6.0x
2009	Yingde Gases	China	Oil & Gas	Baring PE	Public Market	450m (MC at IPO)	6.5x
2008	Centurion Bank	India	Financial Services	CVC	HDFC Bank	293m	4x
2008	Shunda	China	Renewables	Actis	Suntech	99m	2.7x
2007	Tokyo Star Bank	Japan	Financial Services	Kone Star Funds	Advantage Partners	2,226m	7x
2007	Himart	South Korea	Retail & Consumer	Affinity, Temasek	Eugene Group	2,106m	3x
2006	Matrix Lab	India	Healthcare	Newbridge (TPG)	Mylan Labs	530m	3x
2006	China Yongle	China	Retail & Consumer	CDH, MS PE	Gome Electrical	677m	5-6x
2005	Bharti Televentures	India	Telecom	Warburg Pincus	Vodafone	1,500m	6x
2005	Ping An	China	Financial Services	MS PE, GS PE	HSBC	1,100m	15x
2005	TBC	Taiwan	Telecom	Carlyle	Macquarie Funds	900m	4x

Source: Various (Bain, Internet, discussions with PE professionals)

ABOUT THE AUTHORS

Claudia Zeisberger
Senior Affiliate Professor of Decision Sciences and Entrepreneurship & Family Enterprise
Academic Director, Global Private Equity Initiative (GPEI)
INSEAD

Claudia Zeisberger is a Senior Affiliate Professor of Decision Sciences and Entrepreneurship & Family Enterprise at INSEAD, and the Founder and Academic Director of the school's private equity centre (GPEI). Before joining INSEAD in 2005, she spent 16 years in investment banking in New York, London, Frankfurt, Tokyo and Singapore.

Professor Zeisberger is a founding investor of 'INSEAD Alum Ventures' (IAV), the business school's first dedicated seed fund and she actively mentors early stage companies and first-time entrepreneurs. At INSEAD, she launched Managing Corporate Turnarounds, a popular MBA elective known for its intensive computer-based simulation involving an iconic car brand and its struggle with bankruptcy. As a natural extension, she teaches INSEAD's Risk Management elective. She has frequently been nominated for the MBA Best Teaching Award in her PE elective and has been awarded the Dean's Commendation for Excellence in MBA Teaching annually since 2008.

Professor Zeisberger is known for her extensive research on PE in emerging markets, and her output is a function of her close working relationships with private equity firms and their investee companies, institutional investors, family offices and sovereign wealth funds.

Michael Prahl
Partner, Asia-IO Advisors
Adjunct Professor of Entrepreneurship & Family Enterprise,
Distinguished Fellow, Global Private Equity Initiative (GPEI)
INSEAD

Michael Prahl is the co-founder of Asia-IO Advisors, a private equity firm focused on implementing Asia and cross-border private equity investment programs for large institutional and corporate investors. Michael has spent almost 20 years in private equity, starting in venture capital during the dotcom boom. He worked for many years at a global PE firm, in Europe, the US and Asia, completing deals including regular buyouts, public to privates, PIPE's, minority investments and privatizations.

An INSEAD alumnus, Michael served as the first Executive Director of the school's PE Centre, with research interests in the areas of co-investment, family offices and market entry strategies & portfolio allocation for limited partners. Michael remains an INSEAD Distinguished Fellow attached to GPEI with a focus on LBOs and Asian private equity, and an Adjunct Professor teaching the MBA Leveraged Buyout elective.

Bowen White
Centre Director, Global Private Equity Initiative (GPEI)
INSEAD

Bowen White currently serves as the Centre Director of INSEAD's GPEI, the business school's Centre in private equity. As Centre Director, he leads its research and outreach activities and has published on topics including operational value creation, responsible investment, LP portfolio construction and minority investment in family businesses.

Bowen has spent his career working in and conducting research on the global alternative asset management industry. In the New York hedge fund industry, he researched topics from statistical arbitrage investment strategies in commodities markets to macroeconomic trends and global hedge fund performance. Having worked for both a proprietary trading firm and a fund of funds, he has seen first-hand the challenges faced by investors and allocators of capital to the hedge fund industry. An INSEAD alumnus, Bowen has also advised on a range of VC and growth equity fundraising opportunities across Southeast Asia.

ACKNOWLEDGEMENTS

To INSEAD for the opportunity to develop a PE Center, where many of the ideas that found their way into this book were proposed, tested and refined. Working with colleagues who push the boundaries of academic research and teaching provided the environment that allowed this book to come to life. INSEAD colleagues who deserve special mention include professors Balagopal Vissa, Vikas Aggarwal, and Joost de Haas whose support was invaluable to publish the respective case studies.

To our students (by now alumni): A special thank you goes to our MBA, EMBA students and the senior executives, who have over the years refined and challenged our thinking, thereby helping us to arrive at the clear and concise concepts presented here. The cases have all been rigorously tested in class and feedback from discussions was taken into account.

To the staff and researchers at INSEAD: At the PE Center, special thanks go to our research assistant Alexandra Albers, and to Tan Sze Gar who helped compile and refine our glossary. A shout-out is in order to the world class INSEAD case team in particular Isabel Assureira, Carine Dao Panam and our tireless case administrator Claire Derouin and senior editor Hazel Hamelin; their support was invaluable for the publication of *Private Equity in Action*.

To our publishing team at Wiley who worked with a team of first-time authors to bring two books to market; thanks to Thomas Hyrkiel for his steady hand and sound advice from conception to publication and to Samantha Hartley for translating our manuscript and design ideas into two well-designed books.

From Claudia a thank you to my academic mentors and colleagues at INSEAD, in particular my faculty colleagues in the Entrepreneurship department. A special thank you goes to Phil Anderson who was a fantastic sounding board after encouraging me for years to write this book. I would like to mention as well Herminia Ibarra and Erin Meyer, who shared their experience as authors and offered advice when needed.

From Michael to my business partner Denis Tse, who picked up the slack while I worked on the book, with deadlines more than once corresponding to the hot phases of a deal. Things that I've learned from him as we grew our business, I have liberally shared with the readers of this book.

From Bowen to my first mentor in New York City, David Officer, who brought me into the fold at Permal and provided the springboard that launched me to INSEAD and Asia. Many happy returns Permalinfo.

Finally, we would like to acknowledge with gratitude the support and love of our families; this book would not have been possible without their patience.

CPSIA information can be obtained
at www.ICGtesting.com
Printed in the USA
JSHW010237040322
23459JS00002B/11